WOMEN AND CITIZENSHIP IN BRITAIN AND IRELAND IN THE TWENTIETH CENTURY

Women and Citizenship in Britain and Ireland in the Twentieth Century

What Difference Did the Vote Make?

Edited by Esther Breitenbach and Pat Thane

continuum

Continuum International Publishing Group
The Tower Building, 11 York Road, London SE1 7NX
80 Maiden Lane, Suite 704, New York, NY 10038

www.continuumbooks.com

First published 2010
Paperback edition first published 2012

British Library Cataloguing-in-Publication Data
A catalogue record for this book is available from the British Library.

ISBN: 978-0-8264-3749-5 (hardcover)
ISBN: 978-1-4411-1196-8 (paperback)

Designed and typeset by Pindar NZ, Auckland, New Zealand
Printed and bound in Great Britain

Contents

List of tables and figures   vii

Acknowledgements   ix

Contributors   xi

1 Introduction   1
Esther Breitenbach and Pat Thane

2 Women and political participation in England, 1918–1970   11
Pat Thane

3 'Providing an opportunity to exercise their energies': the role of the Labour Women's Sections in shaping political identities, South Wales, 1918–1939   29
Lowri Newman

4 Count up to twenty-one: Scottish women in formal politics, 1918–1990   45
Catriona Burness

5 Scottish women's organizations and the exercise of citizenship c. 1900–c. 1970   63
Esther Breitenbach

6 The 'women element in politics': Irish women and the vote, 1918–2008   79
Mary E. Daly

7 'Aphrodite rising from the Waves'? Women's voluntary activism and the women's movement in twentieth-century Ireland   95
Lindsey Earner-Byrne

8 Conflicting rights: the struggle for female citizenship in Northern Ireland   113
Myrtle Hill and Margaret Ward

9 'Apathetic, parochial, conservative'? Women, élite and mass politics from 1979 to 2009   139
Rosie Campbell and Sarah Childs

10 Feminist politics in Scotland from the 1970s to 2000s: engaging with the changing state   153
Esther Breitenbach and Fiona Mackay

11 Women and political representation in post-devolution Scotland: high time or high tide?   171
Fiona Mackay and Meryl Kenny

12 Devolution, citizenship and women's political representation in Wales   189
Paul Chaney

13 The refuge movement and domestic violence policies in Wales   209
Nickie Charles

Selected bibliography   227
Index   235

Tables and Figures

Table 2.1 Women candidates and MPs (UK and N. Ireland)   13

Table 2.2 Municipal councils: representation of women, 1920–70   16

Table 4.1 Scotland: Women MPs, 1918–90   46

Table 8.1 Elections to the Northern Ireland Assembly, 1998   131

Table 9.1 MPs elected to the House of Commons, 1983–2005,
by sex and party   140

Figure 9.1 Sex and turnout at general elections, 1964–2005   147

Table 11.1 Scottish Parliament 2007 by party, gender and type of seat   177

Figure 11.1 Proportion of women among MSPs, by party, 1999–2007   178

Figure 11.2 Proportion of women candidates, by party, 1999–2007   179

Table 11.2 Percentage of women elected by date of election and type of
elected office   184

Table 12.1 Women candidates and elected AMs: 1999 elections to
National Assembly for Wales   193

Table 12.2 Women candidates and elected AMs: 2003 elections to
National Assembly for Wales   193

Table 12.3 Women candidates and elected AMs: 2007 elections to
National Assembly for Wales   194

Table 12.4 Gender equality: content analysis of party manifestos
in the devolved elections, 1999–2007   196

Table 12.5 The incidence of key terms featuring in political debate
recorded in the Official Record of the first term of the
National Assembly for Wales, 1999–2003   199

Table 12.6 Social policy divergence: welfare support, funding and
regulation in Wales   204

Acknowledgements

This edited collection owes it origins to an ESRC funded seminar series (Ref: RES-451–26–0042) entitled 'What difference did the vote make?', held between 2003 and 2005 in London, Edinburgh and Belfast. The series was itself partly stimulated by earlier discussions on women and constitutional change at a seminar series organized by Vivien Hart at the University of Sussex, and by conversations that we subsequently had with Vivien. This book is one outcome of the discussions which took place in the seminars. At the same time we have participated in a Leverhulme funded project, based at the Women's Library in London, which has resulted in a series of workshops on the Women's Liberation Movement being held in England, Scotland, Wales and Northern Ireland. We hope that both the book and the Women's Liberation Movement project will help to fill gaps and stimulate further research.

The book has had a long gestation period, and both happy and sad events have occurred in this time. Two of the book's contributors have given birth, while the book was being written. Sadly, we have lost both Vivien Hart, whose commitment and support was a stimulus to our work, and Ursula Masson, who contributed to the seminar series and was to have been a contributor to the book. This book is dedicated to the memory of Vivien and Ursula.

We would like to thank the ESRC for its support for the seminar series, Ben Hayes at Continuum for his support and patience, and friends and colleagues who have commented on drafts and offered encouragement.

Contributors

Esther Breitenbach
Esther Breitenbach is Research Fellow in the School of History, Classics and Archaeology, University of Edinburgh. Her current research is concerned with the impact of empire on Scottish society. Previously Research Fellow in Social Policy at the University of Edinburgh, she held secondments in the Scottish Executive Equality Unit and the Women and Equality Unit in Whitehall. She has written widely on women in Scotland and is co-editor, with Fiona Mackay, of *Women and Contemporary Scottish Politics* (2001), and, with Alice Brown, Fiona Mackay and Jan Webb, of *The Changing Politics of Gender Equality in Britain* (2002). Her most recent publication is *Empire and Scottish Society: The Impact of Foreign Missions at Home, c.1790–c.1914* (2009).

Catriona Burness
Catriona Burness has published many articles on the subject of women and Scottish politics and has worked at the universities of Dundee, Durham, Edinburgh, Glasgow and St Andrews. Her publications include *'Strange Associations': The Irish Question and the Making of Scottish Unionism, 1886–1918* (2003) and '"Kept some steps behind him": women in Scotland, 1780–1920', in Duncan Gifford and Dorothy McMillan (eds), *A History of Scottish Women's Writing* (1997).

Rosie Campbell
Rosie Campbell is Senior Lecturer in Politics at the School of Politics and Sociology, Birkbeck, University of London. She has published widely on gender and political participation, representation and voting behaviour. Her publications include *Gender and the Vote in Britain* (2007) and 'Understanding men and women's political interests: evidence from a study of gendered political attitudes', *Journal of Elections, Public Opinion and Parties (2008)*.

Paul Chaney
Paul Chaney is Senior Lecturer at Cardiff School of Social Sciences. His recent publications include *Equal Opportunities and Human Rights: The First Decade of Devolution* (2009) and *Women, Politics and Constitutional Change* (with Fiona

Mackay and Laura McAllister, 2007). He is co-editor of the academic journal *Contemporary Wales* and the *Politics and Society* book series (University of Wales Press).

Nickie Charles
Nickie Charles is Professor and Director of the Centre for the Study of Women and Gender in the Sociology Department at the University of Warwick. She has published widely on many aspects of gender including the gendered division of paid and unpaid work and the refuge movement. Her publications include *Gender in Modern Britain* (2002), *Feminism, The State and Social Policy* (2000) and (with Charlotte Aull Davies and Chris Harris) *Families in Transition* (2008).

Sarah Childs
Sarah Childs is Professor of Politics and Gender at the University of Bristol. She has written widely on gender, political representation, political parties and parliament. Her publications include *New Labour's Women MPs* (2004), *Women at the Top* (2005), and *Women and British Party Politics* (2008). She is currently writing a book on gender and the Conservative Party.

Mary E. Daly
Mary E. Daly is Professor of Irish History and Principal of the College of Arts and Celtic Studies at University College Dublin. She has written widely on Irish history, and her publications include *Commemorating the Easter Rising*, co-edited with Margaret O'Callaghan (2007), *'Slow Failure': Population Decline and Independent Ireland, c. 1920–1970* (2006) and *Women and Work in Ireland* (1997).

Lindsey Earner-Byrne
Lindsey Earner-Byrne lectures in modern Irish history in the School of History and Archives, University College Dublin. Her publications include *Mother and Child: Maternity and Child Welfare in Dublin, 1920s–1960s* (2007) and 'Managing motherhood: negotiating a maternity service for Catholic mothers in Dublin, 1930–54', in *Social History of Medicine*, 19, (2), (2006).

Myrtle Hill
Myrtle Hill is Senior Lecturer, Department of Sociology, Social Policy and Social Work, Queen's University Belfast. Her publications include 'Ulster: debates, demands and divisions: the battle for (and against) the vote', in Louise Ryan and Margaret Ward (eds), *Irish Women and the Vote* (2007), 'Gender, culture and "the Spiritual Empire": the Irish Protestant female missionary experience', in *Women's History Review*, 16, (2), (2007) and *Women in Ireland: A Century of Change* (2003).

Meryl Kenny
Meryl Kenny is ESRC Postdoctoral Fellow in Politics and International Relations at the University of Edinburgh. Recent publications include 'Gender, institutions and power: a critical review', in *Politics*, 27, (2), (2007) and, with Fiona Mackay, 'Women's representation in the 2007 Scottish Parliament: temporary setback or return to the norm?', *Scottish Affairs*, 60, (2007).

Fiona Mackay
Fiona Mackay is Senior Lecturer in Politics, University of Edinburgh. She is author of *Love and Politics: Women Politicians and the Ethics of Care* (2001) and co-editor, with Esther Breitenbach, Alice Brown and Jan Webb, of *The Changing Politics of Gender Equality in Britain* (2002), and, with Esther Breitenbach, of *Women and Contemporary Scottish Politics* (2001). Her latest book, *Women, Politics and Constitutional Change: The First Years of the National Assembly for Wales*, is co-authored with Paul Chaney and Laura McAllister (2007).

Lowri Newman
Lowri Newman is English and Study Skills tutor at the University of Glamorgan. Her publications include 'Elizabeth Andrews (1882–1960): Labour Party Women's Organiser for Wales' (with Ursula Masson), and 'Beatrice Green (1895–1927): Labour Party activist', in Keith Gildart, David Howell and Neville Kirk (eds), *Dictionary of Labour Biography*, Vol. XI (2003).

Pat Thane
Pat Thane is Professor of Contemporary British History, Institute of Historical Research, University of London. Her publications include *Women and Gender Policies: Women and the Rise of the European Welfare States, 1880s–1950s* (1990, co-edited with Gisela Bock), 'What difference did the vote make?', in Amanda Vickery (ed.) *Women, Privilege and Power: British Politics, 1850 to the Present* (2001), *Old Age in English History: Past Experiences, Present Issues* (2000), *The Long History of Old Age* (2005) and *Britain's Pensions Crisis: History and Policy* (2005, co-edited with Hugh Pemberton and Noel Whiteside).

Margaret Ward
Margaret Ward is Director of the Women's Resource and Development Agency, Belfast. Her publications include: *Unmanageable Revolutionaries: Women and Irish Nationalism* (1983), biographies of Maud Gonne and Hanna Sheehy-Skeffington, and two co-edited books (with Louise Ryan), *Irish Women and Nationalism: Soldiers, New Women and Wicked Hags* (2004) and *Irish Women and the Vote: Becoming Citizens* (2007).

1

Introduction

Esther Breitenbach and Pat Thane

The enfranchisement of women in Britain and Ireland in the early twentieth century was a defining moment in the acquisition of rights of political citizenship for women, putting them formally on an equal footing with men. But the exercise of such political rights remained differentiated by gender, since civil and social rights, acquired both before and since enfranchisement, have only slowly eroded gender inequalities in access to power. Indeed, there is a continuing asymmetry in the capacity of men and women to exercise their formal rights of political citizenship, illustrated by the under-representation of women in formal political institutions. Throughout the twentieth century the language of citizenship and rights has been articulated differently by women at different times in different contexts, but, as this book shows, from their acquisition of the vote onwards women have sought to make a reality of their rights of citizenship.

Inevitably, a collection such as this cannot provide a comprehensive account of women's political action in Britain and Ireland throughout the twentieth century, not least because both historiographical and contemporary research still have substantial gaps. We believe, however, that, as it stands, this collection serves as a useful corrective to a commonly accepted view of women's relative lack of interest in politics between the 1920s and the late 1960s and to the belief in a decline in women's activism since the 1980s. The women's suffrage movement and the Women's Liberation Movement are often described as 'first' and 'second wave' feminism respectively, a terminology criticized for implying that there were no forms of feminist action between the 1920s and the late 1960s. Since the purpose of this book is to examine women's activity in what may be broadly defined as political processes throughout the twentieth century, it is evident that we do not subscribe to a view of women's periodic political dormancy. Nonetheless, women's activism has taken place in changing constitutional, political and social contexts, which have presented both opportunities and obstacles and necessitated adaptation from women's organizations. Many women's organizations have exhibited patterns of expansion and decline over time, with discontinuities between generations of organizations. The patchwork of women's activities throughout the century shows division and fragmentation as well as the emergence of broad alliances around particular issues from time to time. The metaphor of 'waves' of feminism thus reflects the changing dynamic of women's mobilization at different times rather than describing alternating periods of activism and dormancy.

WOMEN AND FORMAL POLITICAL INSTITUTIONS

By the early twentieth century there were active campaigns for women's suffrage across Britain and Ireland. Also by this period women were acquiring the right to stand for election for local public office, such as membership of school boards, Poor Law Guardians, and some other local authorities. Women's representation in such bodies was to gain considerable impetus from enfranchisement, which was local as well as national. The forms of public institutions, criteria for eligibility for election, and the timing of women's access differed across Britain and Ireland, while reforms to local government structures, particularly in the 1920s and 1930s, tended to reduce opportunities for women to stand for office at this level. However, women became an established part of local government from the 1920s, though their representation remained low until the 1960s and 1970s. The historiography of women in local government is limited and further research is needed, particularly since local government has served as a training ground for political office at national level.

At the time of women's enfranchisement in Britain there was speculation as to how women would vote, whether as a bloc for a particular party or whether women's parties would emerge. Consequently, the major political parties made efforts to attract women voters and members, often creating special structures for women, such as women's sections. This interest in women as voters and members was not necessarily sustained, though it has re-emerged periodically. Women have not voted as a bloc, rather demonstrating allegiance to political parties on broadly similar lines to men, though at times with apparent divergences. For example, in 1950s Britain, women were more likely than men to vote Conservative, which seems to have given rise to a myth of women's innate political conservatism. More recently, in Scotland, several surveys have indicated that support for the Scottish National Party (SNP) is stronger among men than women, though the SNP shows little sign of wishing to address this gender imbalance. Only in recent decades have reliable survey data allowed a gender analysis of voting behaviour – data on UK general elections indicate no significant differences between men's and women's voting preferences since the 1980s. For earlier decades, other forms of evidence need to be investigated, such as press reports, though this is unlikely to prove conclusive.

A further question concerns the propensity of women and men to join parties. Those who join political parties, whether male or female, have only ever been a small proportion of the population, but men appear to have been more likely than women to join. The gender distribution of party membership is difficult to establish. If parties, anxious about decline, are currently wary of publishing membership figures, historical evidence indicates that women's membership of political parties rapidly became substantial after enfranchisement, and that women were sometimes the majority of members in specific localities, as for example, in some Welsh and English Labour Party branches in the inter-war years. The role of women in building party support and organization has often been reduced to the dismissive stereotype of 'making the tea'. While there was typically a gender division of labour among party activists, and women occupied a less powerful position within party hierarchies, this is a caricature that obscures the real importance of women's contribution to the development of party political cultures and solidarity. The life of the party could embrace families and generations, as observed of the Labour Party in Wales, and this was likely to be true elsewhere of the Labour Party, of the Communist Party, such as the 'Little Moscows' in the mining communities of Scotland and South Wales, and of the socializing dimension of the Conservative Party's Primrose League. In Northern Ireland, political allegiances have been deeply embedded in community and social life, with women actively maintaining loyalties in Protestant or Catholic communities.

Perhaps one reason for the focus of historians and political scientists in studies of women and politics on numbers of women in parliaments is that this provides a definite measure, while other dimensions of women's political activity cannot be systematically quantified over time, whether voting behaviour or party membership. Nor are there data systematically comparing women's representation in local government across Britain and Ireland for this period. Existing evidence on local government suggests that women's representation has tended to be higher than at parliamentary level for as long as women have been eligible for election. However, with the creation of the Welsh Assembly and Scottish Parliament the rule that the lower the level of government the higher the level of women's representation was overturned.

In recent decades, neither the UK nor Ireland has performed well in international comparisons of levels of women's representation in national parliaments. The later decades of the twentieth century did, however, witness increases in levels of women's representation in the Dáil and in the Westminster Parliament, as in many other countries. It was notably an Irish achievement to elect the first woman to the Westminster Parliament, Sinn Féin member Constance Markievicz, who refused to take her seat. The political settlement in Ireland in the 1920s saw the creation of the Irish Free State, later the Republic of Ireland, the partition of Ireland with the retention of the six counties of Ulster as part of the UK, and a devolved parliament at Stormont, which sat from 1920 to 1972. However, the political turmoil of the 1920s in Ireland caused leading women political activists to exclude themselves from high political office, because of their opposition to aspects of the constitutional settlement. This, and the dominance of a Catholic ideology firmly placing women in the home and enshrined in the 1937 constitution, led to an overwhelming male dominance within the Dáil until the 1960s. While the emergence of the Women's Liberation Movement boosted campaigning for women's representation, the work of earlier women's organizations led to the creation of the Commission on the Status of Women, which first reported in 1972. Between 1977 and 1997 the proportion of women deputies in the Dáil increased, though it seems to have reached a plateau thereafter. Family connections and the cultivation of a personal vote, significant characteristics of Irish politics, appear to obstruct women's political careers, as the time commitment needed to foster constituency support is often too great for women with caring responsibilities.

Between 1920 and 1972, 20 women stood for election to Stormont and nine were elected. In the inter-war years no women were elected to Westminster from Northern Ireland, while between 1945 and 1972 three women were elected to Westminster – two Unionists, and, most famously, nationalist candidate Bernadette Devlin in 1969. Following Bloody Sunday in 1972, the British government imposed direct rule on Northern Ireland, removing political representation within Northern Ireland and subsequently curtailing the powers of local government, effectively disenfranchising large sections of the population.

Low levels of women's representation at Westminster also characterized England, Scotland and Wales between 1918 and the end of the century. Only in 1997 did women's representation at Westminster see a marked rise to 18 per cent, still relatively low by international standards. By the late 1980s, debates about women's representation in politics were becoming widespread, especially among Labour Party activists. Women's success in getting All Women Shortlists adopted by the Labour Party was a major factor in increasing women's representation. Following the challenge to All Women Shortlists under the Sex Discrimination Act, the Labour government amended the Act in 2002 to enable political parties to take action to increase women's representation. Equality guarantees remain controversial, however, and increases in women's representation, or even maintenance of the current level, are not guaranteed at the anticipated election in 2010.

Debates about women's representation became a key part of devolution campaigns in Scotland, Wales and Northern Ireland. The political opportunities created by constitutional reform have proved favourable for increasing women's political representation, as in other countries. In Scotland and Wales, though campaigns and political cultures differed considerably, the adoption of specific measures to increase women's representation achieved this success, most notably the Labour Party practice of the twinning of seats. These were the outcome of campaigns and negotiations by women's organizations. In Northern Ireland the formation of the Women's Coalition was crucial in securing seats for women at the negotiations leading to the Good Friday Agreement of 1998, and in embedding gender and other equality commitments within this. While the devolved Assembly in Northern Ireland has had a troubled history, enduring a period of suspension, it has also seen women's representation rise, compared with the previous record in Stormont and at Westminster, though it remains lower than that in Wales and Scotland.

WOMEN'S ORGANIZATIONS AND POLITICAL CHANGE

The years following women's partial enfranchisement in 1918 saw further campaigning for full enfranchisement and the flourishing of new women's organizations. In Britain, many suffrage organizations transformed themselves into Women Citizens' Associations and Societies for Equal Citizenship, while organizations such as the Women's Institutes in England and Women's Rural Institutes in Scotland, established during the First World War, were similarly concerned with educating women in the rights of citizenship and how to use them. Working-class organizations, such as the Co-operative Women's Guild, similarly promoted active citizenship. Training women in practical skills such as public speaking; supporting women as candidates for local government or parliament; and educational activities on economic and social questions were common practices of women's sections of political parties also. A plethora of organizations emerged at national, regional and local levels, concerned with a wide range of issues, including married women's rights to property, divorce law reform, women's right to sit on juries (introduced in 1919 in England and Wales, and in 1920 in Scotland), the need for women police officers, maternal and child welfare, equal pay and women's working conditions, the marriage bar in employment, and much more. Contraception and abortion were campaigning issues, as was sexual abuse of women and children. Male-dominated institutions, whether political parties, the police or the courts, were reluctant to acknowledge women's needs or demands for action, and it was not until the 1960s that such issues became matters of wide public debate. The Women's Liberation Movement played a crucial role in making reproductive rights and sexual and physical abuse key areas of public policy.

Historical research into women's organizations in the inter-war period suggests that there was flourishing culture of associational life across Britain, among men as well as women, and that such organizations influenced legislative change and local provision, such as health facilities for women and nurseries for children. Assessing the precise impact of such organizations is unavoidably difficult and the different patterns of activity in different parts of Britain need research. Women's organizations in England are known to have lobbied for legislative change in the 1920s and 1930s, but there is as yet no systematic comparison with Scotland or Northern Ireland, for which legislation was often separately enacted. While research on women's organizations in Northern Ireland in this period remains particularly limited, groups such as the Belfast Women's Citizens' Union promoted women's participation in public life, and women appear to have continued to play an active role in philanthropic and religious organizations.

In Ireland, the Irish Women's Citizens' Association, established in 1918, emerged directly from the Irish Women's Suffrage and Local Government Association, and was eventually absorbed into the Irish Housewives' Association, founded in 1942. In the 1920s the National Women's Council was formed to promote reforms relating to women and children, while women's organizations lobbied for the right to sit on juries, which they gained in 1927. In the 1930s the

Irish Women's Social and Progressive League was established to challenge the 1937 Constitution's definition of women's primary role as being in the home. The Irish Countrywomen's Association, the largest civil organization in Ireland, aimed to improve living conditions for women in rural Ireland, though it did not challenge traditional views of gender relations. Both ICA and IHA were non-denominational, though led by Protestant women, which in Catholic Ireland meant absence of official government support. Such organizations did, nonetheless, secure improvements for women, though, in the face of religious divisions and Catholic family ideology, were less successful than women's organizations in Britain in influencing legislative change.

The Women's Liberation Movement was to emerge across Britain and Ireland within a few years from the late 1960s to the early 1970s. 'Second wave' women's movements internationally have shared a common agenda of equal rights, equal opportunities, reproductive rights, and challenging violence against women. However, political and cultural contexts varied across Britain and Ireland, shaping the emphasis, tactics and strategies, and successes of women's movements in different countries. This book provides neither a comprehensive account of 'second wave' feminism – the Women's Liberation Movement of the 1970s and feminist action in succeeding decades – across the four nations, nor a systematic assessment of its impact, both areas in need of more investigation. However, several chapters advance claims for the impact of second wave feminism, for example, in enhancing women's representation in political institutions across Britain and Ireland; in influencing policy debates in Ireland on contraception, abortion, violence against women, and divorce; in generating a flourishing network of women's groups and influencing the peace process and the 1998 Good Friday Agreement in Northern Ireland; and in shaping the policy agenda in Scotland and Wales since devolution. Contemporary analyses by sociologists and political scientists delineate the concerted and sustained action required to place 'strategic women' in positions where they can change policy, but also underline the persistent resistance to gender equality. Gains in representation may be insecure and feminist policy agendas can be co-opted and perhaps neutralized, even where implementation has been apparently successful.

CONCLUSION

This collection has aimed to explore the experience of women in politics – formal and informal – across the four nations of Ireland, England, Scotland and Wales. The respective jurisdictions within Britain and Ireland are not evenly covered, with England having the lowest profile. To some extent this reflects the still too common belief that evidence relating to England can unproblematically be thought of as evidence about 'British' society, politics and history. Ironically, this has led to scholarly neglect of specifically English experience. Though the demise of the 'British' women's movement has sometimes been lamented, as elsewhere in the UK there has been continuity of feminist action in various parts of England, whether the rejuvenated Fawcett Society based in London, black and Asian women's organizations in Leicester, Manchester, Birmingham, Brixton and elsewhere, Women's Aid groups across England, or feminist influence within the trade union movement and local government. This provides a strong argument for further comparative research, not just at 'national' level, but at regional and local levels, between areas with strong regional identities, such as Yorkshire or the North East or South West of England, and between cities.

Both the similarities and the national and regional distinctiveness that a comparative perspective reveals add to our understanding of women's changing status. Taking the long view of women's political activity, broadly defined, there are similarities in timing, forms of organization, and issues around which women have mobilized. Both the women's suffrage movement and the Women's Liberation Movement were international phenomena, in which women across Britain and Ireland took part. Women-only organizations were characteristic of these movements, though they also had male supporters. After gaining the vote, suffragists created a new generation of organizations focusing on the rights of citizenship, which was accompanied by a flourishing of women's associational culture from the 1920s, continuing even into the 1950s, a period in which women's activism has been believed to have been almost non-existent. Many such organizations encouraged active citizenship, though they were more differentiated in their objectives than were suffrage campaigns, concerned as they were with a range of policy issues and special interests. Women's entry into formal politics also took place in similar ways and at similar times, such as women's entry to local public office. After 1918 women used their votes, joined political parties, and stood for election, gaining representation at Westminster and in the Dáil, though this remained at low levels for all parts of Ireland and Britain until late in the twentieth century. 'Second wave' feminism led to increasingly vocal concern with women's representation in formal political institutions by the late 1980s. Since then, increases in representation have taken place, though unevenly across nations and parties, and the debate goes on as to how to achieve parity.

There have, however, been differences. Women in Ireland, North and South, have found it harder to increase their political representation. Periods of conflict, the nature of political party systems, and the influence of religion in shaping views of women's role, have all contributed to this situation. Changing the law on divorce, and provision of contraception and abortion, proved more achievable reforms in Britain, with Northern Ireland remaining closer to the Republic in its moral values and attitudes to gender roles. Increases in women's participation in the labour market and reductions in family size, which were general trends across industrialized countries in the later twentieth century, and which have underpinned demands for gender equality, emerged later in Ireland than in Britain. This is not to say that it is only in Ireland that religion has been influential, but its impact elsewhere is less clear. The Calvinist heritage in Scotland has been seen as creating a more patriarchal and morally authoritarian culture than in England, and there is some evidence for this view, such as the later liberalization of the law on homosexuality in Scotland. Furthermore, religious belief remained an important motive for women's involvement in public life in inter-war Britain as well as Ireland, whether in philanthropic organizations, the temperance movement, or organizations such as the National Vigilance Association. The different legislative frameworks within the UK have also meant that legal reform has not proceeded simultaneously in England and Wales, Scotland and Northern Ireland. For example, divorce law reform occurred later in Scotland than in England and Wales, women had to campaign to have the Sex Discrimination Act extended to cover Northern Ireland, and the 1967 Abortion Act does not yet apply there.

Women's actions as citizens have been conditioned by the nature of the states which govern the territories in which they live. Within the twentieth century both Irish and British states have witnessed major processes of reconfiguration: Irish independence and partition of Ireland with the six counties of Northern Ireland remaining in the United Kingdom; devolution of power to Northern Ireland between 1922 and 1972, then a period of direct rule, followed by a new devolution settlement in 1999; growing administrative devolution to Scotland over the twentieth century, followed by political devolution in 1999; devolution to Wales in 1999, with increasing powers subsequently devolved, as Wales aspires to powers similar to those of the Scottish Parliament. There have been local government reforms and reorganizations within all jurisdictions, and enhancement of the state's role in welfare provision. Membership of the European Union has also shaped economic development. In the Republic of Ireland it has led to major economic and social change, and influenced the regulation of women's employment conditions across Britain and Ireland. Such reconfigurations of the state have not always operated to create opportunities for women's access to political institutions. For example, the creation of an independent state in Ireland and partition of the North from the South reduced opportunities for women's political representation, while recent constitutional changes in the UK, the devolution of powers to Northern Ireland, Wales and Scotland, have provided opportunities for women to increase their political representation.

That women's representation in political institutions has increased very slowly is indisputable, given that full enfranchisement of women on equal terms with men was achieved in Ireland in 1922 and in the UK in 1928. Nonetheless, both the role of women in formal political institutions and the status of the positions they occupy have increased over time. Although representation in formal political institutions is a significant measure of women's exercise of the rights of citizenship, it is not the only means by which women can engage with politics and the state, nor the only means by which they can influence policy. This collection challenges the historical orthodoxy that, after gaining the vote, women had little impact upon political life until the late twentieth century. It explores the range of women's political activities across Britain and Ireland throughout the century, within the limitations of existing research, and it aims to encourage further research. Through political reforms, legislative change and public provision of welfare, women have acquired increased autonomy, greater economic independence, more control over reproduction and greater access to political power. Political parity, economic equality, and full control by women of their own bodies are yet to be achieved, but we can take encouragement from the historical record of women's collective action. Changing patterns of organization and mobilization are evident, but if fragmentation has occurred, so has regeneration and renewal. Above all, what the record shows is the continuing commitment of women to active citizenship.

2

Women and political participation in England, 1918–1970

Pat Thane

BEFORE THE VOTE

Women who were independent householders – mainly better-off widows and unmarried women – gained the municipal vote in England and Wales in 1869 and the county council vote in 1888. This also enabled them to vote for the existing separate local Poor Law Boards and for School Boards, when the latter were established in England and Wales in 1870. About one million women were eligible to vote at local level by 1900. Women voters were immediately eligible for election to Education Boards, until their abolition in 1902, when there were about 270 elected female members. Women bitterly opposed the abolition and persuaded the Conservative government to require the co-option of at least one woman to each of the local authority Education Committees that succeeded them, an unusual act of positive discrimination – in a field of activity defined as firmly within 'women's sphere' – which increased the numbers of women members to 679 by 1914–15, though 'few boards appointed more women than they had to'.[1] After a struggle, women succeeded in being, gradually, elected to Poor Law Boards, which survived until 1929. Eighty were elected in 1890, 893 in 1895, and, after a further extension of the local franchise for men and women, 1,546 by 1914–15. Women were not permitted to stand for election for town or county councils before 1907: 48 had gained election by 1914–15.[2]

This experience in local government spurred some women to demand the national vote also, though others argued that women's political role should be confined to the local, largely social service-oriented, sphere, for which they were assumed to have a special aptitude.[3] However, women played an important role in elections – national as well as local – before they had the national vote. Élite and aristocratic women had long exerted influence in elections based on a very restricted male franchise.[4] The expanded male franchise following the 1884 Reform Act spurred the political parties to canvass and organize the new, larger, more complex electorate, leading to the formation of the mass political parties that dominated much of twentieth century politics. For this purpose women were useful, and the parties organized women's associations which grew rapidly. The Women's Liberal Federation grew from 1886 to a membership of 133,215 in

1912, slipping to 115,097 by 1914, mainly due to the Liberal government's refusal to implement women's suffrage. Some Liberal suffragists shifted to campaigning for Labour in elections, since it was the only party committed to women's suffrage, though on different terms from many suffragists: Labour supported the equal franchise, an end to the property and other restrictions which excluded 40 per cent of men as well as all women, and the extension of the franchise to all men and women at age 21. Many suffragists were prepared, as a first step, to extend the restricted male franchise to the even more restricted group of women who would qualify under existing regulations.[5]

Women were members of the mixed-sex Conservative Primrose League from 1884, but it was controlled by men and decidedly anti-suffrage. By 1900 it included 74,461 (male) Knights, 64,003 Dames and 1,380,097, mainly lower-class, Associates, whose gender composition is unknown, but is unlikely to have been very different.[6] However, there were very active suffrage supporters in the Conservative Party, notably in the Conservative and Unionist Women's Franchise Association, founded 1908.[7]

The Labour Party was formed in 1900 and in 1906 the Women's Labour League (WLL) was established as a support organization. It had 5,000 members by 1914. It was led mainly by middle-class women, who had more time and resources than women struggling with poverty and paid work. The social class of most of the membership is hard to identify, but appears to have been mixed: certainly WLL membership was stronger in industrial areas of Northern England and South Wales than in Southern England.[8]

Women played an increasingly active role in elections before 1914, not only as suffrage protesters. Even some anti-suffrage male candidates thought it beneficial to include a woman supporter on their public platforms. Women had also long been active in campaigns, both single- and mixed-sex, which sought either improved rights specifically for women, e.g. in property and family law and education, or did not, such as the anti-slavery and temperance movements[9] and, in the 1900s, the Free Trade Movement.[10]

1918–45: PARTY POLITICS

In 1918 all men at last gained the vote at age 21, and some younger men as a reward for fighting, and surviving, the war. It was no longer possible to withhold the vote from the men who had risked their lives for their country. Women were enfranchised only at age 30, primarily to avert the danger of a female majority electorate, since women were a majority of the population, perhaps also due to the hope of the established political parties that older women would be less readily seduced by the rapidly growing Labour Party, especially in view of Labour's likely gains from the large numbers of newly enfranchised working-class men.[11] In 1919, parliament legislated that women might stand for parliament at age 21. This is less strange than it seems: men disqualified under previous franchise restrictions had long stood for election, some successfully, before they qualified to vote.[12] They were generally younger, upper-class men who were not yet independent householders.

There was once a conventional narrative that the outcome of this partial con-cession of the vote to women in 1918 was that the previously active and united movement became splintered, divided and less publicly effective; and that the impact of women as voters on politics and policy was slight, except possibly to reinforce conservative, and Conservative Party, values, including traditional values of domesticity; and there was a backlash against the small shift in gender relations so far achieved. After women obtained the vote on equal terms with men in 1928, the story continued, women's political involvement declined still further, reinforced by powerful and effective social pressure upon women to give primacy to their domestic roles. The Second World War brought only short-term and ambiguous gains for women, followed speedily by a reimposition of 'domestic values'. Traditional gender roles were not seriously challenged again until the late 1960s, even then with only limited and short-term effects.[13]

This narrative is not wholly mistaken, but recent research indicates that it is far from being a complete representation of a complex set of processes. The clearest evidence to support it appears to be the small number of women elected to parliament over many decades after 1918.

Table 2.1 Women candidates and MPs (UK and N. Ireland)

	Conservative		Labour		Liberal		Other		Total	
	Cands	MPs	Cands	MPs	Cands	MPs	Cands	MPs	Cands	MPs
1918	1	–	4	–	4	–	8	1	17	1
1922	5	1	10	–	16	1	2	–	33	2
1923	7	3	14	3	12	2	1	–	34	8
1924	12	3	22	1	6	–	1	–	41	4
1929	10	3	30	9	25	1	4	1	69	14
1931	16	13	36	–	6	1	4	1	62	15
1935	19	6	35	1	11	1	2	1	67	9
1945	14	1	45	21	20	1	8	1	87	24
1950	28	6	42	14	45	1	11	–	126	21
1951	29	6	39	11	11	–	–	–	74	17
1955	32	10	43	14	12	–	2	–	89	24
2959	28	12	36	13	16	–	1	–	81	25
1964	24	11	33	18	25	–	8	–	90	29
1966	21	7	30	19	20	–	9	–	80	26
1970	26	15	29	10	23	–	21	1	99	26

Source: David and Gareth Butler, *British Political Facts, 1900–1994* (London: Macmillan, 1994), p. 243.

However, these statistics should not be interpreted as meaning that, having struggled so hard for the vote, women gave up on formal politics. There were large numbers of women in the main political parties in the 1920s and 30s and all the parties sought, in different ways, to attract this large group of new voters.

Women joined the Labour Party in significant numbers immediately on gaining the vote, about 300,000 by 1927. This was about half the individual membership of the party. In some constituencies the female proportion was higher still.[14] Under the new Labour Party Constitution of 1918, WLL branches became Women's Sections of party branches. A Chief Woman Officer was appointed to preside over these, assisted by regional women's officers. Women had four reserved places on the powerful National Executive Committee of the Party, which was elected by the annual conference. Delegates of the Women's Sections met at an annual Women's Conference. However, there was no obligation on the Annual Party Conference or the National Executive Committee to take account of their decisions and, in general, the position of women in the party was weaker than the formal structures suggest. In accordance with the party constitution, the votes of individual members in the local branches were hugely outnumbered at the powerful annual conference by the male-dominated trade unions, each of which wielded votes in proportion to the size of their membership, whereas each party branch had just one vote. This remained the case until 1993.[15]

Women often felt that they had the appearance rather than the substance of power within the Labour Party and they certainly had to struggle, often unsuccessfully, to be heard. But they were not wholly ignored, and the Women's Sections and the Women's Conference provided environments in which women could develop their political ideas and skills of organization in ways which had not previously been possible.[16] Labour women could be particularly effective in local politics, especially in regions with strong traditions of women's public action, often combined with paid employment, as in parts of Lancashire.[17] They often worked together with the mainly working-class Women's Co-operative Guild (membership c. 67,000 in 1930).[18] Preston, Lancashire, was transformed from a Conservative to a Labour stronghold in the 1920s when working women formed a strong Woman's Section and persuaded an initially unsympathetic local party to adopt a programme of improvements in education, maternity and child welfare, healthcare, housing, and the provision of such public amenities as baths and wash-houses.[19] In Liverpool and elsewhere, Labour women also campaigned successfully for improved education, maternity and child welfare, baths, libraries, and recreation.[20] In other areas women met stronger resistance in local parties, and they were less successful on other issues, such as equal pay, but it can be argued that they were effective in strengthening the commitment of the party to the Welfare State it developed after World War Two.[21]

Female membership of the Liberal Party continued to fall after 1918, to 71,000 by 1924. It is difficult to judge how far this was due to its failure to enfranchise women or to the weak and divided state of the party, which also lost male support. However, by 1928, female membership had recovered, to over 100,000.[22] Many women found Liberalism attractive philosophically and in terms of its broad policy commitments, believing that the ideas of the party of John Stuart Mill continued to be consistent with support for gender equality. But the Women's National Liberal Federation had no secure position in the constitution of the Liberal Party and experienced continual frustration at the unwillingness of the party leaders to take account of its views.

There were about one million women in the Conservative Party in the 1920s.[23] In 1918 the party also reconstructed its machinery, giving women one-third representation at all levels of party organization, presided over by a Women's Advisory Committee.[24] From 1928 women had equal representation on all party bodies and all party vice-chairmen (sic) were women from 1930.[25] Nevertheless, the women in all three major political parties in the inter-war years, and for long after, expressed frustration at the unresponsiveness of their parties to their views, and at the difficulty experienced even by women with long records of party activism in achieving selection for winnable parliamentary, or even local government, seats.[26]

The women's organizations of all three political parties did, however, provide opportunities for women to develop their political ideas and organizational skills. All three aimed to educate women in the use of the vote. It is easy to caricature these organizations as subordinate to male-dominated parties, providing the tea at meetings rather than the substance of policy-making. This may underestimate the importance of sociability in political culture and the influence of women, especially in areas of social policy. They could be most effective in influencing policy at local government level, but this also did not translate into major election success, as shown in Table 2.2.

Only a minority of women, and men, joined political parties. How did the remainder vote? Voting was secret and there were no reliable opinion polls until after the Second World War. Contemporaries commented on how eager women were to vote and the percentage turnout of eligible electors was not unduly low.[27] The 1922 election was the first real test of the effects of the extension of the franchise; that of 1918 came too soon after the change. The press was very interested in the new women voters and their commentaries are the only contemporary assessments we have of women's political preferences, other than from the parties themselves. *The Times* commented in 1922:

> The greatest surprise which those in charge of the polling booths had yesterday was the number of women who appeared to vote immediately after the booths were opened . . . canvassers found themselves questioned alertly and adroitly on matters not usually considered women's questions. Foreign policy was a strong point in moving women in constituencies.[28]

Throughout the 1920s, *The Times* assessed women voters as thoughtful, independent-minded and varied in their voting patterns, choosing for whom to vote according to their assessment of political issues, i.e. that they behaved

Table 2.2 Municipal councils: representation of women, 1920–70

	1920	1930	1950	1970
GLC*	9	24	39 (26%)	16 (14%)
Bradford	2	4	8	11 (14%)
Bristol	0	4	17	18 (16%)
Brighton	2	3	8	12 (16%)
Birmingham	6	9	17	28 (18%)
Liverpool	4	12	11	10 (6%)
Manchester	4	8	13	22 (14%)
Norwich	3	7	8	9 (14%)
Leeds	0	14	17	22 (18%)
Plymouth	3	12	9	15 (17%)
Sheffield	2	12	8	20 (19%)
Newcastle	1	5	18	16 (21%)
Yarmouth	1	4	6	5 (10%)

* The area of the GLC after its formation in 1965.

Source: Patricia Hollis, *Ladies Elect: Women in English Local Government, 1865–1914* (Oxford University Press, 1987), Appendix C.

much like men.[29] The press tended to assume that women were interested in different issues from men – in food prices rather than foreign affairs – and there may have been some truth in this for many women, though it was hardly a sign either of conservatism or lack of political judgement. The press, like more recent commentators, also tended to treat 'women voters' as a single bloc, while male voters were differentiated by class, occupation, etc. But there is not much sign that in the inter-war years contemporaries assumed that women voters were particularly biased towards conservatism. Rather, commentators expressed unease and uncertainty about women's voting preferences, which they found them generally unwilling to reveal. They certainly perceived women as politically significant despite their small numbers in parliament.[30] Adrian Bingham has described Lord Rothermere's conviction that the new young women voters enfranchised in 1928 would vote Labour and the unsuccessful campaign of Rothermere's *Daily Mail* against the measure.[31] Others feared that 'there may be a great deal of indifference to political questions among the newly enfranchised women'.[32] The Labour Party greatly increased its vote in the election of the following year (the number of voters increased by 6 million over the previous election, Labour increased its vote by 3 million, the Liberals, in their best showing of the inter-war years, by over 2 million, and the Conservatives by only 600,000; the percentage turnout was unchanged, but there is no means of knowing the gender distribution of voting). Newspaper comment on inter-war elections suggests, overall, that 'women' were not wedded to a single party but, like men, shifted their allegiance according to their assessment of salient political issues. The electorate as a whole appears to have been volatile in the uncertain conditions of the 1920s and 1930s.

1918–1945: NON-PARTY POLITICS

Larger numbers of women joined non-party political organizations that were dedicated to educating women to use their civil rights and worked for highly political goals. Even before 1918, suffrage societies began to organize to raise political awareness among women, to inform them about important political issues and train them in procedures of campaigning, public speaking, committee work, and other essential skills of public life. Once women had the vote, they believed, it was important that they use it. They did not underestimate the obstacles women continued to face in the fight for a public voice. In 1917 the National Union of Women Workers (which became the National Council of Women, NCW, in 1918) formed a network of Women's Citizens Associations (WCAs) throughout the country to provide this training, on a model established in 1913 in Liverpool by Eleanor Rathbone, the feminist campaigner for family allowances and an Independent MP, 1929–46.[33] Membership of WCAs was open to all women at age 16, so that political education could begin early.[34]

The National Union of Women's Suffrage Societies (NUWSS) took on a similar role, changing its name to the National Union of Societies for Equal Citizenship (NUSEC). In 1924 it merged with the WCAs. It published pamphlets guiding women through the complexity of getting onto the voting register and of using the vote, including *The New Privilege of Citizenship* and *How Women Can Use the Vote*. These and many other women's campaigning organizations were determinedly not aligned with any political party or faith group in order to draw support as widely as possible, though party members were often also members of such organizations, and the WCAs and NUSEC were prepared to support in elections and work with party candidates, mainly female, but also male, who were active in causes favoured by the women's movement. They were anxious, in principle, to promote and support women as candidates in national and local elections and recognized that the political culture in some parts of the country was more receptive of independent candidates than in others. For example, of the 13 women elected to Cambridge City Council between 1918 and 1930, ten were independents.[35]

Beleaguered party women often needed and valued support from women who shared many of their sympathies but were outside their party. There was frequent collaboration between party and non-party women at local level despite the disapproval expressed by national party leaders. Alongside the women's organizations, which were primarily dedicated to encouraging women to use the vote and to be politically active, other organizations with a range of objectives were also committed to the political education of the new female voters. The Women's Institutes (WIs) were founded in 1915 by suffragists, some of them former militants, to give the large numbers of British countrywomen opportunities for personal and political development, partly by providing a social space which was under their own control and independent of the traditional rural hierarchy, dominated by the wives of the squire and the clergyman. The democratically elected committees of the WIs aimed to shift power relationships among rural women, while providing experience of political organizing, encouragement and training in using the vote and in campaigning for political changes of importance to them, such as improvement in the appalling state of rural housing, and much-needed access to piped water and electricity supplies. Such campaigns had some success. The WIs also encouraged women to value their work and skills, both in and outside the home, for example through selling jams, chutneys, homemade garments, and other products. They co-operated with Labour Party women in housing campaigns and in encouraging women working at home to seek a wider range of leisure activities and reduced hours of work, as men were doing in the paid workforce.[36] The view that unpaid work in the home should be valued equally with paid work was widely shared among party and non-party women.

In 1932 NUSEC established Townswomen's Guilds (TGs) as urban analogues of WIs, in acknowledgement of the success of the WIs in providing a space for women previously excluded from the political culture. The TGs had 54,000 members by 1939.[37] A similar role of encouraging political awareness and political education among women, alongside other goals, was performed by women's trade unions, professional, confessional, and single-issue groups such as the National Union of Women Teachers, the Council of Women Civil Servants, the (Roman Catholic) St Joan's Social and Political Union, the Union of Jewish Women, the Women's Sanitary Improvement and Health Visitors' Union, the working-class Women's Co-operative Guild, and many others which were founded or grew between the wars. At least 130 such organizations were active in the 1920s, almost certainly drawing into public life a larger number and a wider social range of women than ever before.[38]

Many of these organizations worked together for causes in which they felt a common interest, especially the campaign to equalize the franchise and the longer struggle against the 'marriage bar', which excluded women from work on marriage in many occupations, including teaching and the civil service. In the 1930s women showed a distinct preference for membership of more specialized women's organizations over those whose rationale was gender equality. The membership of professional, confessional, and other organizations grew as that of NUSEC (from 1932 the National Council for Equal Citizenship) declined. The number of societies affiliated to it fell from 2,220 in 1920 to 48 in the later 1930s.[39] This proliferation of women's organizations was not a splintering of the women's movement, rather it illustrates how women's organizations came to permeate public life in the decades after the vote was gained, while continuing to co-operate on key issues. These were signs that possession of the vote gave many women a feeling of legitimacy in public life, of their right to promote causes important to them.

Through these associations, and arising from this sense of legitimacy, women exerted greater influence on parliament and politics than the numbers of elected women suggests. NUSEC took on the role of providing practical support for women's campaigns for legislative change. It believed that it could 'act for the whole women's movement as a kind of Corps of Royal Engineers, engineering its Bills on already prepared territory and continually exploring and pushing forward into fresh areas.'[40] Its objectives were democratically decided at its annual conferences. It helped other organizations to draft legislation, make contact with MPs, mainly sympathetic men, and join together in public demonstrations, for example for equal pay, the equal franchise and abolition of the marriage bar. In 1919 it decided to focus upon a limited number of objectives, for 'we had learned that the field was so vast that success was jeopardised if we scattered our energies over the whole of it'.[41] It chose as its immediate objectives: equal pay for equal work; reform of the divorce law and laws dealing with prostitution and the establishment of 'an equal moral standard'; pensions for civilian widows (they had been granted to war widows for the first time during the Great War); equal rights of guardianship of children; the opening of the legal profession to women. By 1926 there had been important legislative change on all of these, with the exception of equal pay.

The years immediately after 1918 saw a strikingly rapid flow of legislation for which women's associations exerted organized pressure and which favourably affected women's lives. Some of this legislation applied to the whole of the United Kingdom and Northern Ireland, some only to England and Wales; some were applied with variants, or at different times, in Scotland and or Northern Ireland. These differences arose often from long-established legal variations across the nations in the area of family law, among others. For example, Scots law had since 1643 allowed women as well as men to sue for divorce on grounds of adultery or desertion for four years, issues on which English and Welsh women were still fighting in the twentieth century.[42] These differences and their implications for women and for gender relations have not been researched adequately, but should be, and cannot be explored further here.

Millicent Garrett Fawcett judged that between 1902 and 1914

> only two really important Acts bearing especially upon the welfare and status of women had been passed – namely the Midwives Act, 1902, and the group of Acts dating from 1907 to 1914 dealing with the qualification of women as candidates in local elections . . .

However, in the year following 'the passing of the Reform Act of 1918 at least seven important measures effecting large improvements in the status of women have rapidly gone through all their stages in both Houses of Parliament.'[43] These included the statute enabling women to be elected to parliament from age 21, and the Sex Disqualification (Removal) Act 1919 which in principle abolished disqualification by sex or marriage for entry to the professions and universities and the exercise of any public function (such as jury service or appointment to the magistracy). She regretted that this Act was less comprehensive than the Women's Emancipation Bill put forward by the Labour Party and which had passed all stages in the House of Commons, but was opposed by the government and rejected in the House of Lords, because, she believed credibly, it included an equal franchise clause.[44] In practice, after passage of the Act, considerable obstacles remained for women seeking to enter such professions as law and medicine or the higher levels of the civil service; they were the object of persistent campaigning by women through the 1920s, 1930s and 1940s.[45] Nevertheless in 1920, 200 women, including Fawcett herself, were appointed magistrates, the lowest but very important level of the system of justice, and did much to reform an institution that had been sliding into discredit.[46] And, for the first time, women served on juries. As well as admitting women to an influential area of public life, the magistracy, these changes ended the situation in which, throughout time, women involved in legal processes had faced courtrooms wholly composed of men – an experience against which organizations such as the NCW had long campaigned. There were 1,600 female magistrates in England and Wales by 1927, of a total of 25,000; in 1947, 3,700 in a total of 16,800.

Fawcett noted also as victories for women's campaigns: the Industrial Courts Act 1919 which, due to an amendment put forward by the Labour Party, allowed women to sit in these newly established courts of arbitration on such matters as pay and conditions in the workplace; the inclusion in the Charter of the newly formed League of Nations of a clause enabling women to be eligible for all League appointments. Women of many countries became active and effective within the League, especially on industrial and social questions, another important arena of political involvement for women.[47] As Fawcett put it, by 1920, 'The walls of our Jericho have not fallen at the first blast of our trumpet, but we have made great progress'.[48]

Campaigns initiated by women's groups and generally supported by NUSEC led to the Criminal Law Amendment Act 1922 which raised the age of consent from 13 to 16 and extended from six to nine months the period during which proceedings could be taken in cases of criminal assault. In 1929 the age of marriage for both sexes was raised to match the age of consent. Previously the age at which marriage was permissible was 12 for females (though consummation was prohibited until age 13) and 14 for males. This legal change owed much to the work of NUSEC, the St Joan's Social and Political Union and the YWCA.[49] In 1922 the amount of maintenance allowed to a woman and her children under a separation order was increased, giving further support to women needing to escape from intolerable marriages. Further legislation in 1925 extended the grounds on which either partner could obtain a separation, to include cruelty and habitual drunkenness, and abolished the requirement that the wife must leave the marital home before applying for a separation order. These changes were supported by a diverse set of women's associations including the Catholic Women's Suffrage Society (CWSS), the Conservative Women's Reform Association, the Labour-supporting Women's Group of the Fabian Society, the Standing Joint Committee of Industrial Women's Organizations and the Women's Co-operative Guild, the radical Women's Freedom League and the Union of Jewish Women.[50]

The Infanticide Act 1922 eliminated the charge of murder for a woman guilty of killing her child, where it was shown that she was suffering from the effects of her confinement. The long process of equalizing property rights went a step further in the Law of Property Act 1922 which enabled a husband and wife equally to inherit each other's property and granted them equal rights to the property of intestate children. The New English Law of Property, 1926, allowed both married and single women to hold and dispose of their property, real and personal, on the same terms as men. Further legislation in 1935 empowered a married woman to dispose by will of her property as though she were single; and, taking gender equality a logical step further, abolished the husband's liability for his wife's debts.

The Matrimonial Causes Act 1923 relieved wives of the necessity to prove desertion, cruelty or other faults in addition to adultery as grounds for divorce, thus bringing gender equality in the divorce courts closer.[51] Further legislation in 1937 and 1950 extended the grounds for divorce. The Bastardy Act 1923 enabled children to be recognized as legitimate on the subsequent marriage of their parents. It sought also to improve procedure to enable unmarried mothers to claim maintenance from the fathers of their children. This was promoted by the National Council for the Unmarried Mother and her Child, founded in 1918, with the Bill guided through the Commons by Neville Chamberlain, its vice-president.[52] The Adoption Act 1926 which introduced a legal procedure for adoption for the first time, sought to protect adopted children, who were often 'illegitimate'.[53]

In 1924 women acquired equal guardianship rights over infants following the break-up of a marriage. In the following year, Widows and Orphans Pensions were introduced. By 1933 these gave pensions to 725,000 women and 340,000 children, for the first time enabling these many impoverished families to escape from the Poor Law. This was an important campaigning issue for NUSEC and other groups and was seen as the first step towards family allowances, which would grant unconditional payments to mothers. Family Allowances, which had been Eleanor Rathbone's special cause, were introduced in 1945.[54]

Women's organizations played an active part in bringing about these changes. It is always difficult to be certain of the influences upon legislation, but it is difficult to believe that so may changes of this kind would have come about at this time without the efforts of newly enfranchised women. Most women's organizations agreed on a cluster of objectives, though they differed in the salience they gave to individual items. There was not the clear division historians once perceived between 'old', 'equal rights' feminists fighting for full gender equality and 'new', 'welfare' feminists concerned with more limited social improvements in women's lives. These goals could be held simultaneously and were complementary. For example, the campaign particularly promoted by WCAs for the appointment of policewomen was as much part of the fight for an 'equal moral standard' between the sexes as for wider employment opportunities for women. Victims of abuse were thought more likely to report their problems to policewomen than to men, and to receive more sympathetic support, and in a range of situations, for example when confined to police cells, vulnerable women and children were thought to need the protection of other women. Local police authorities were reluctant to respond. In 1939, 43 out of 183 police authorities employed policewomen, but they amounted to only 174 in a total force of 65,000.[55]

Women's organizations lobbied skilfully for many of the legal changes of the inter-war years. It can be argued that one reason why there were fewer flamboyant demonstrations than before the war was that women's groups had become 'political insiders rather than outsiders',[56] seeking to achieve their goals by lobbying and negotiating in the corridors of power successfully enough not to require resort to violence. Peaceful demonstrations, however, still occurred when it was judged necessary to make a public display of the united strength of women. The main focus of demonstrations in the 1920s was the extension of the franchise,[57] though they occurred also on other issues, for example against the marriage bar.[58] But at least as impressive as the public demonstrations was the quieter work behind the scenes of Whitehall.

There were limits to how much the first generation of women voters could achieve at any level. Campaigns, then as now, were most successful on issues in which the potential cost to the taxpayer was least and where they involved the public rather than the private sector. It was easier, though not very easy, to change the law on divorce than to achieve equal pay. But even in the public sector there was a gulf between legislation and implementation. It was one thing to give women the right to sue for divorce, for example, another to enable them to afford the costs of legal action and to face the social opprobrium which attached to a divorced woman in British society, at least until the 1960s. Implementation of the new legislation has not been adequately studied but statistics, e.g. of divorce, suggest that it was slow.

Gender equality in divorce law had been achieved by 1939; gender equality in the pay packet had not. Women campaigners in the inter-war years are some-times criticized for focusing too narrowly on welfare issues concerning women in the home and reinforcing conventional gender roles and neglecting the needs of women in paid work.[59] This underestimates the importance of welfare issues, given the appalling living conditions of all too many at this time. In reality there were also vigorous campaigns for equal pay and on other workplace issues, such as abolition of the marriage bar. This was abolished in most occupations during and after the Second World War, due more to the need of the economy for female labour than to women's campaigns. Campaigning was, however, effective in bringing about equal pay in much of the public sector in the mid-1950s.[60]

The social reforms for which many women campaigned were designed to reduce the burden of domesticity and increase the time available for women to spend on activities outside the home, such as better-designed housing to reduce the burden of housework, and healthcare, childcare and other services to reduce family demands on their time.[61] They also supported women who did not lead conventional domestic lives, demanding less stigmatizing support for unmarried mothers and their children, or equal divorce rights and rights over children.

Effective campaigning by women continued into the 1930s. It seems to have diminished during the later 1930s and was weak during the Second World War, though it never wholly disappeared. There were strikes and parliamentary campaigns by women for equal pay during the war, which led to the establishment of the Royal Commission on Equal Pay late in the war.[62] In the 1930s many women activists gave priority to campaigning for peace, and during the war many more put the war effort first. In wartime, gender issues were often, though not always, subordinated to the international emergency.[63]

1945–70

Women's campaigns were perhaps weaker after the war but did not disappear. The Labour government showed little obvious sympathy for gender equality and women MPs also seem to have been less supportive than their pre-war predecessors. Indeed many of them explicitly rejected the language of feminism, with exceptions such as Edith Summerskill, the Labour MP. The Conservative, and life-long feminist, Thelma Cazalet-Keir, who led the campaign for the inclusion of equal pay for teachers in the 1944 Education Act (which was lost due to Winston Churchill's opposition), lost her parliamentary seat in 1945. Thereafter she chaired the Equal Pay Campaign and was a leading supporter of the Fawcett Society.[64] The government repeatedly rejected demands for equal pay, on the grounds that redressing the inequalities which had been revealed by the Royal Commission on Equal Pay (which reported in 1946) would place excessive burdens on business which was seeking to recover from the inter-war Depression and the effects of war.[65] This was consistent with the priority this government gave to building a strong, export-led economy.

Working-class women, in particular, were compensated by the benefits they gained from Labour's welfare state measures, in particular the introduction of the National Health Service in 1948, and felt less need to campaign on many of the issues that had mattered to them before the war. The introduction of free legal aid in 1948 enabled many women on low incomes to take advantage of some of the legal gains – such as easier access to divorce – which had been achieved before the war. This may explain why working-class women remained strong supporters of Labour in the late 1940s, to a greater extent even than working men.[66] On the other hand, middle-class women, such as supporters of the Housewives League[67] who resented the constraints on consumption imposed by Labour – the continuation of rationing – tended to support the Conservatives.

A government survey in 1964 found over 100 active women's organizations, including feminist and political groups, professional associations, religious bodies and philanthropic organizations, again often working together to promote responsible and active citizenship for women and concluded that 'they exercise an undoubted influence upon the trend of domestic affairs'.[68] Large women's organizations like the Townswomen's Guilds (200,000 members in 1964) and the Women's Institutes (which reached a peak of 500,000 members in the 1950s)[69] continued to campaign and lobby government on housing issues, given the post-war shortage, while supporting the increasing numbers of married women who combined family and paid work by demanding improved childcare and equal pay.[70] They were also concerned with issues arising from the new welfare legislation, such as women's unequal pension rights, tax allowances, widows' pensions and the financial position of divorced and separated women, women's health and access to birth control information.[71] These and other issues, including wider educational and occupational opportunities for women and easier divorce, were also supported by such organizations as the National Women Citizen's Association, the British Federation of Business and Professional Women and the British Federation of University Women.[72] The Fawcett Society, another sur-vivor from the suffrage years, also kept up pressure for equal opportunities. The campaigns of the 1950s seem often to have involved older women and to have had difficulty in attracting younger women, perhaps partly because of higher marriage rates and falling ages of marriage and first childbirth after the war. But they have been little studied.

From the early 1960s, women in the Labour Party and the trade unions increasingly campaigned for equal pay.[73] Women's campaigns had some notable achievements before the emergence, from 1968, of the large 'second wave' women's movement, which was overwhelmingly a movement of younger women and tended to be hostile or indifferent to constitutional action through parlia-ment. There seems to have been little contact between the older and newer women's organizations and little awareness among the Women's Liberation Movement (WLM) of post-1918 campaigns.

Abortion was legalized in 1967, with crucial support from male MPs, and this represented the culmination of a long campaign, led mainly by women in the Abortion Law Reform Association, founded 1935.[74] The late 1960s saw a surge of legislation on liberal and gender-related issues, due partly to the return of Labour governments in 1964 and 1966. As well as abortion law reform, this included easing of the divorce law in 1969, the introduction of free birth control services in 1967, the Equal Pay Act and the Matrimonial Proceedings and Property Act 1970 which gave women an increased share of matrimonial property by recognizing the wife's non-financial contribution to the partnership. Legislation also included the legalization of male homosexual relationships in certain circumstances and abolition of capital punishment.[75] In 1975 the Sex Discrimination Act removed a number of barriers, e.g. to equal entry to the medical and legal professions and established the Equal Opportunities Commission. The Fawcett Society was espe-cially important in lobbying for this, though pressure from the European Union, of which Britain was a member from 1973, was also important. None of these pieces of legislation was perfect or achieved all that campaigners hoped, but they were a great deal better than what had gone before and their achievement owed a great deal to women's agency through a variety of campaigning organizations of the pre-WLM generation.[76]

After the war, as before, women varied in their voting preferences – among themselves and over time. From the 1950s opinion polls provide harder evidence and indicated that women voters inclined strongly to the Conservatives. At this time the Labour Party was deeply divided and losing male and female support, and the Conservative Party was delivering higher living standards appreciated by women (and men). As Harold Macmillan put it in 1957, 'Most of our people have never had it so good'.[77] Mainly middle-class, often Conservative-voting, women campaigned successfully for equal pay in the public sector, which was gained in teaching, the civil service and local government in 1955.[78] As Zweiniger-Bargielowska has shown,[79] the Conservative Party at this time was anxious to win and keep the support of women, including those in the paid workforce, evidently not simply by promoting a conservative agenda which located women only in the home. This suggests that the Conservatives did not feel that they could take women's support for granted. With good reason: 'the gender gap in party support gradually diminished after 1955' and by the 1980s 'there remained no significant gender differences'.[80]

Women have certainly used their vote since the first of them could exercise it from 1918. By the 1970s there had been real advances towards gender equality, mostly the outcome of women's organized campaigns that had real achievements, though activist women rightly felt that there was still a long way to go. This chapter has argued that voting and elected representation – hugely important though they are – do not tell us the whole story about women's – or men's – political participation. We need also to take account of extra-parliamentary campaigns and their relationship with government.

NOTES

1   Patricia Hollis, *Ladies Elect: Women in English Local Government, 1865–1914* (Oxford University Press, 1987), p. 130.

2   Hollis discusses these issues in detail.

3   Jane Lewis, *Women in England, 1870–1950* (Sussex: Wheatsheaf, 1984).

4   Elaine Chalus, '"To serve my friends"': women and political patronage in eighteenth century England', in Amanda Vickery (ed.), *Women, Privilege and Power: British Politics, 1750 to the Present* (Stanford: Stanford University Press, 2001), pp. 57–88. 57–88; Judith Lewis, '1784 and all that: aristocratic women and electoral politics', in Vickery (ed.), *Women, Privilege and Power*, pp. 89–122.

5   Sandra Holton, *Feminism and Democracy: Women's Suffrage and Reform Politics in Britain, 1900–1918* (Cambridge University Press, 1986).

6   Linda Walker, 'Party political women: a comparative study of liberal women and the Primrose League, 1890–1914', in Jane Rendall (ed.), *Equal or Different: Women's Politics, 1800–1914* (Oxford: Basil Blackwell, 1987), pp. 165–91.

7   Lori Maguire, 'The Conservative Party and women's suffrage', in Myriam Boussahba-Bravard (ed.), *Suffrage Outside Suffragism: Women's Vote in Britain, 1880–1914* (Basingstoke: Palgrave Macmillan, 2007), pp. 52–76.

8   Christine Collette, *For Labour and for Women: The Women's Labour League, 1906–1918* (Manchester: Manchester University Press, 1989), pp. 41–92.

9   Clare Midgley, *Women against Slavery* (London: Routledge, 1992).

10 Frank Trentmann, *Free Trade Nation: Consumption, Civil Society and Commerce in Modern Britain* (Oxford University Press, 2008).

11 Martin Pugh, *Women and the Women's Movement in Britain*, 2nd edn (London: Macmillan, 2000).

12 M. Takayanagi, 'Parliament and women, c. 1886–1939' (PhD thesis in progress, Institute of Historical Research, University of London, 2009).

13 Barbara Caine, *English Feminism, 1780–1980* (Oxford University Press, 1997), pp. 173–255; Harold L. Smith, 'British Feminism in the 1920s', in Harold L. Smith (ed.) *British Feminism in the Twentieth Century* (Aldershot: Edward Elgar, 1990), pp. 47–65. Pugh, *Women and the Women's Movement*, gives a more complex picture.

14 Pat Thane, 'Visions of gender in the British welfare state', in Gisela Bock and Pat Thane (eds), *Maternity and Gender Policies: Women and the Rise of the European Welfare States, 1880s–1950s* (London: Routledge, 1991), pp. 93–118.

15 See the chapter by Campbell and Childs in this volume.

16 Pat Thane, 'The women of the British Labour Party and feminism, 1906–45', in Smith (ed.), *British Feminism*, pp. 124–43; Pamela Graves, *Labour Women in British Working Class Politics, 1918–1939* (Cambridge University Press, 1994).

17 Jane Mark-Lawson, Mike Savage and Alan Warde, 'Gender and local politics: struggles over welfare policies, 1918–1939', in Linda Murgatroyd, Mike Savage, Dan Shapiro, John Urry, Sylvia Walby and Alan Warde, with Jane Mark-Lawson (eds), *Localities, Class and Gender* (London: Pion, 1985), pp. 195–215.

18 Pugh, *Women and the Women's Movement*, p. 105.

19 Michael Savage, *The Dynamics of Working Class Politics: the Labour Movement in Preston, 1880–1940* (Cambridge University Press, 1987).

20 Sam Davies, *Liverpool Labour: Social and Political Influences on the Development of the Labour Party in Liverpool, 1900–39* (Liverpool: Liverpool University Press, 1996).

21 Graves, *Labour Women*.

22 Pat Thane, 'Women, liberalism and citizenship, 1918–1930', in Eugenio Biagini (ed.), *Citizenship and Community: Liberals, Radicals and Collective Identities in the British Isles 1865–1931* (Cambridge University Press, 1996), pp. 66–92.

23 Pugh, *Women and the Women's Movement*.

24 David Jarvis, '"Behind every great party": women and Conservatism in twentieth century Britain', in Vickery (ed.), *Women, Privilege and Power*, pp. 289–316; *Pugh Women and the Women's Movement*.

25 Ina Zweiniger-Bargielowska, 'Explaining the gender gap: the Conservative Party and the women's vote, 1945–1964', in Martin Francis and Ina Zweiniger-Bargielowska (eds), *The Conservatives and British Society* (Cardiff: University of Wales Press, 1996), pp. 194–223.

26 Graves, *Labour Women*; Thane, 'Women, liberalism and citizenship'.

27 David and Gareth Butler, *British Political Facts, 1900–1994* (London: Macmillan, 1994).

28 *The Times*, 16 November 1922.

29 *The Times*, 16 November 1922; 7, 8 December 1923; 30 October 1924; 30 May 1929. Pat Thane, 'What difference did the vote make?', in Vickery (ed), *Women, Privilege and Power*, pp. 353–88.

30 Adrian Bingham, *Gender, Modernity and the Popular Press in Inter-war Britain* (Oxford University Press, 2004).

31 Adrian Bingham, "'Stop the flapper vote folly": Lord Rothermere, the *Daily Mail* and the equalization of the franchise, 1927–8', *Twentieth Century British History*, Spring, (2002), pp. 17–37.

32 *The Times*, May 30, 1929.

33 Susan Pedersen, *Eleanor Rathbone and the Politics of Conscience* (New Haven: Yale University Press, 2004).

34 Cheryl Law, *Suffrage and Power: The Women's Movement, 1918–1928* (London: I.B. Tauris, 1997).

35 Davies, *Liverpool Labour*.

36 Maggie Andrews, *The Acceptable Face of Feminism: The Women's Institute as a Social Movement* (London: Lawrence and Wishart, 1997).

37 Pugh, *Women and the Women's Movement*.

38 Law, *Suffrage and Power*.

39 Pugh, *Women and the Women's Movement*.

40 C. Moyse, 'Reform of marriage and divorce law in England and Wales, 1909–1937' (Unpublished PhD thesis, University of Cambridge, 1996), p. 111.

41 Moyse, 'Reform of marriage and divorce law', p. 161.

42 Stephen Cretney, *Family Law in the Twentieth Century* (Oxford University Press, 2003).

43 Millicent Fawcett, *The Women's Victory – and After: Personal Reminiscences, 1911–1918* (London, 1920), p. 165.

44 Takayanagi, 'Parliament and women'.

45 Law, *Suffrage and Power*; Carol Dyhouse, 'Women students and the London medical schools, 1914–39: the anatomy of a masculine culture', *Gender and History*, 10, (1), (1998), pp. 110–32.

46 Anne Logan, *Feminism and Criminal Justice: An Historical Perspective* (London: Palgrave, 2009).

47 C. Miller, 'Lobbying the League: women's international organizations and the League of Nations' (Unpublished D.Phil thesis, University of Oxford University, 1992).

48 Fawcett, *Women's Victory*, p. 165.

49 Fawcett, *Women's Victory*.

50 Fawcett, *Women's Victory*, p. 264, n. 1.

51 Fawcett, *Women's Victory*.

52 Pat Thane, 'Unmarried motherhood in twentieth century England', *Women's History Review* (2011, forthcoming).

53 Jenny Keating, *A Child for Keeps: The History of Adoption in England, 1918–1945* (London: Palgrave, 2009).

54 Susan Pedersen, *Family, Dependence and the Origins of the Welfare State: Britain and France, 1914–1945* (Cambridge University Press, 1993).

55 Louise Jackson, *Women Police: Gender, Welfare and Surveillance in the Twentieth Century* (Manchester: Manchester University Press, 2006).

56 Moyse, 'Reform of marriage and divorce law', p. 111.

57 *The Woman Teacher*, 9 July 1926, p. 305, quoted in Law, *Suffrage and Power*, p. 212–13.

58 Law, *Suffrage and Power*, p. 85.

59 Caine, *English Feminism*; Harold L. Smith, 'British feminism and the equal pay issue in the 1930s', *Women's History Review*, 5, (1), (1996), pp. 97–110.

60 Smith, 'British feminism'; Harold L. Smith, 'The problem of "equal pay for equal work" in Britain during World War 2', *Journal of Modern History*, 53 (1981), pp. 661–5; Harold

L. Smith, 'The politics of Conservative Reform: the equal pay for equal work issue, 1945–1955', *Historical Journal*, 35, (1992), pp. 401–15.

61   Thane, 'British Labour Party and feminism'.

62   Smith, 'The problem of "equal pay for equal work"'; Sonya Rose, *Which People's War? National Identity and Citizenship in Wartime Britain 1939–1945* (Oxford University Press, 2003).

63   James Hinton, *Women, Social Leadership and the Second World War: Continuities of Class* (Oxford University Press, 2002).

64   John Grigg, 'Thelma Cazalet-Keir, 1899–1989', *Oxford Dictionary of National Biography* (Oxford University Press, 2007).

65   Pat Thane, 'Towards equal opportunities? Women in Britain since 1945', in Terry Gourvish and Alan O'Day (eds), *Britain since 1945* (London: Macmillan, 1991), pp. 183–208.

66   James Hinton, 'Women and the Labour vote, 1945–50', *Labour History Review*, 57, 3, (1992), pp. 50–66.

67   James Hinton, 'Housewives in action: the Housewives' League and the Attlee Government', *History Workshop Journal*, 38, (1994), pp. 129–56.

68   Central Office of Information, *Women in Britain* (London: HMSO, 1964), quoted in Catriona Beaumont, 'Housewives, mothers and citizens: voluntary women's organizations and the campaign for women's rights in England and Wales during the post-war period', in Nick Crowson, Matthew Hilton and James MacKay (eds), *NGOs in Contemporary Britain: Non-State Actors in Society and Politics since 1945* (London: Palgrave, 2009), pp. 59–76 (p. 59).

69   Andrews, *Acceptable Face of Feminism*.

70   Andrews, *Acceptable Face of Feminism*; Beaumont, 'Housewives, mothers and citizens'; J. Freeguard, 'It's time for women of the 1950s to stand up and be counted' (Unpublished D. Phil thesis, University of Sussex, 2004).

71   Beaumont 'Housewives, mothers and citizens'.

72   Freeguard, 'Women of the 1950s'.

73   Thane, 'Towards equal opportunities?'; Elizabeth Meehan, 'British feminism from the 1960s to the 1980s', in Smith (ed.), *British Feminism*, pp. 189–204; 'Women and the Labour Party', Statement by the National Women's Advisory Committee to the National Executive Committee of the Labour Party, 1971.

74   Centre for Contemporary British History, 'The Abortion Act, 1967' (Witness seminar held at University of London, Centre for Contemporary British History, 2002). Available online at http://www.ccbh/ac/uk/witness

75   Andrew Holden, *Makers and Manners: Politics and Morality in Postwar Britain* (London: Politico's, 2005).

76   Eve Setch, 'The Women's Liberation Movement in Britain, 1969–1979: organization, creativity and debate' (Unpublished PhD thesis, Royal Holloway, University of London, 2000).

77   Speaking to a Conservative Party rally, 21 July 1957; Butler and Butler, *Political Facts*, p. 291.

78   Smith, 'The politics of Conservative Reform'; Catriona Beaumont, 'The women's movement, politics and citizenship, 1918–1950s', in Ina Zweiniger-Bargielowska (ed.), *Women in Twentieth Century Britain* (London: Longman, 2001), pp. 262–77.

79   Zweiniger-Bargielowska, 'Explaining the gender gap'.

80   Joni Lovenduski, Pippa Norris and Catriona Burness, 'The Party and women', in Anthony Seldon (ed.), *Conservative Century: The Conservative Party since 1900* (Oxford University Press, 1994), p. 616.

3

'Providing an opportunity to exercise their energies':[1] the role of the Labour Women's Sections in shaping political identities, South Wales, 1918–1939

Lowri Newman

The historiography of women and politics in Wales remains in a state of relative infancy.[2] As Jane Aaron and Ursula Masson have pointed out, this lack of representation in historical accounts underplays women's political mobilization in Wales' past.[3] This, in turn, has the effect of presenting the women currently visible in Welsh political life as dislocated from the story of their foremothers' political contributions. In fact, the roots of this modern-day political involvement were evident in the 1800s, as Aaron and Masson so effectively illustrate. By the end of the First World War, these began to flourish in new directions with the Labour Party's rapid replacement of the Liberals as the dominant party at every level in Wales, and the impact of the economic depression that hit the country for much of the inter-war period. Traditionally, it would seem that the historian's eye has been fixed very firmly in the direction of 'high' politics. That much of women's politics during the inter-war period often took place at a grassroots level, away from the pithead, and centred on issues closely connected to the home, goes some way towards explaining its lack of inclusion. This chapter focuses on the role of the women in the Labour Party Women's Sections between the wars in South Wales. The Sections provided a platform for a generation of women previously excluded by the male-dominated structure of formative years. The chapter considers some of the educational initiatives which the Sections devised in order to develop local women's sense of what it meant to be political, and examines some of the areas to which women directed their activism in local communities. Thus, it argues that the very nature of women's political contribution did much to broaden the limited nature of the established forms of Labour politics in South Wales while simultaneously making a significant contribution to the development of political identities on both an individual and collective basis.

Despite being part of the patriotic fervour that marked the 1918 'Coupon Election', Wales' support for the Liberal Party proved to be relatively short-lived going into the post-war period. A number of factors ensured that conditions were ripe for Labour to continue to increase its developing pre-war popularity in Wales: its newly organized party structure, the growing divide in the Liberal Party, the miners' reaction to the government's decision to reject nationalization of the mines, extended working-class enfranchisement, and the declining economic situation in Wales.[4] Thus, as Jim Griffiths pointed out, the 'death knell' rang for the Liberal Party which, 'just fifteen years before (in 1906) had won every seat but one in Wales'.[5] The outcome of the 1922 election saw the final nail hammered into the Liberal coffin as Labour representation reached 18 compared to the Liberals' 11. In Wales, Labour replaced the Liberal Party as the dominant party, even winning seats in rural areas like Caernarvonshire and Merioneth.[6] This newly confident political force, like its opposition, set about trying to capture the newly enfranchised female electorate. For a vast number of women in Wales, this marked the beginning of a new type of political involvement as the changed party constitution meant that Labour membership was opened to women as individuals for the first time.

LABOUR'S POST-WAR CONSTITUTION

The Labour Party created the opportunity for women to become party members as part of its 1918 constitution. The Women's Labour League (WLL) was brought into the party to form the centre of local involvement for Labour women, with the former League branches becoming known as Labour Women's Sections. In 1919, Elizabeth Andrews was appointed as the party's Chief Woman's Officer for Wales to organize women in taking up their membership. Andrews was an obvious choice for the job; already something of a stalwart in local politics, and one who wore both her support for women's rights and the Labour Party very visibly on her sleeve.[7] As women's officer, Andrews battled against the staunchly entrenched opposition to women in politics, fuelled by her commitment to the belief that, if equipped with the relevant knowledge and expertise, women could, and indeed should, become effective ambassadors for party, gender and community.[8] This was no easy feat as women's political inexperience meant that many feared ridicule for daring to enter the political scene.[9] Therefore, working with other women in the Sections was a hugely important element, as was the array of information and methods of instruction which the Sections provided.

The inter-war period, then, marked a significant period of change in women's left-wing political history in Wales. Neil Evans and Dot Jones point out that, according to official party statistics, by 1933, there were 9,160 female members in Wales; women thus formed 45 per cent of individual party membership. In 1947, the year that Andrews resigned, the number had reached 12,814.[10] In fact, in some branches, female membership far outstripped that of men. Seventy-five per cent of Cardiff's members, for instance, were women.[11] Starting with Andrews' own stamping ground, Ton Pentre, Rhondda in 1918, Women's Sections began to appear over the length and breadth of the country.[12] Although some of these were relatively short-lived, many became large organizational bodies.[13] The section at Newport, for instance, had over 2,000 members and 11 ward sections by the 1930s. In fact, female membership in Newport was the largest in all of the constituencies (with Romford, Essex coming second) in 1935.[14] The localized nature of the Women's Sections was clearly of significant appeal to working-class women who spent the majority of their time in the home.

The organization of women did not stop with the widespread formation of Women's Sections. The network was further strengthened by a series of central committees and advisory councils in various parts of Wales. The advisory councils did much work, especially in the early years of formation, to organize Sections in each constituency. Due to the extent of the growth of Sections in the various wards, it became necessary to set up central committees. These were formed in borough divisions, while federations of Women's Sections were established in county divisions; both served as acting co-ordinating bodies in their respective areas. By December 1925, there were enough advisory councils to cover the whole of Wales, including one for the North.[15] These strengthened the cohesiveness of the women's side of the movement yet further and were able to represent local interests at a national level with the capacity to 'call a "Special Conference" on any matter of particular interest to women'.[16]

EMPOWERING MOTHERS

The sustained campaign led by Andrews to make local Labour politics access-ible to women meant a deviation from traditional political subjects, which in working-class communities in South Wales tended to be centred chiefly on the workplace, to include issues that had direct appeal to the wives and mothers of those communities. Local women were introduced to the idea that politics was something that affected them and their families (particularly their children) and was an aspect of life to which they could contribute in order to bring about change.[17] As Beatrice Green told a meeting of the Abertillery Women's Section, 'No man, whatever his disposition, could know children like the women who bear them'.[18] Therefore, the focus was not on a radical upset in terms of the existing gendered roles for men and women, but instead lay on the importance of women establishing control over those aspects in which they were most closely involved. Appeals were often made to local women to actively support the party by directly referring to women's capacity to mother and the need to bring about improve-ments in this area.[19] Until this point, aspects connected to the home environment had received relatively little attention, and virtually none that stemmed from, nor reflected, women's perspectives. The overwhelming impression was that women, and the issues that most affected them, remained well outside the polit-ical spectrum. Thus, Sections equipped a number of women with the necessary knowledge and skills to enter public life so as to rectify this imbalance.

EDUCATING WOMEN MEMBERS

The Section members had access to an array of educational opportunities, chiefly orchestrated by the advisory councils with the help of local Sections and Elizabeth Andrews. Educational conferences became an increasingly popular intervention; split into three sessions, women listened to addresses on a range of subjects which combined familiar areas, connected to the domestic sphere, with less familiar issues. To women like Margaret Davis from Pontnewydd, winner of *The Labour Woman* magazine's letter-writing competition in October 1932, this was one of the strengths of the Women's Sections. Referring to the subject of trade unionism and industrial disputes, she pointed out that women often lacked 'any clear knowledge as to the causes of the trouble'. 'In an area like our own', she wrote, 'we do not always grasp the view-points of these industrial struggles quite so keenly as the women in districts like Lancashire ... [where] the women are directly engaged in the strike side by side with the men'.[20]

The formation of well-informed female members was key, with study circles devised to educate women on the development of Labour politics looking at topics such as 'The History of the Labour Movement and its Policy' and 'Labour and the New Social Order'.[21] The information-sharing objectives occupied equal space with avenues to develop skills needed to take part in the political domain. For instance, women were encouraged to develop their public speaking skills and were invited to join the speakers' classes. These were designed to introduce them to the art of public speaking, and often included mock debates and similar events.[22] Andrews herself is recorded showing the women of the West Wales Advisory Council the best way to compile and deliver a speech.[23] At the same meeting she pressed all present to put their names on to a 'speakers list'. The aim was to get all speakers to specialize in a 'particular brand of our programme'[24] to elevate women's political status and enhance their contribution to the Labour Party.

In November 1925, the East Glamorgan, Llanelly and Carmarthen, and Monmouthshire Advisory Councils decided to organize a one-day school in each of the divisions that came under the various councils' jurisdiction.[25] One or two delegates were nominated by the members of individual sections to attend these. Evidence suggests that those in attendance found them to be both enjoyable and informative, covering a wide range of topics.[26] There was general uniformity to the lectures given at the various day schools so that those in attendance (numbers averaged from 20 to 45) had access to the same information.[27] The series of schools which were held in the Rhondda Divisions, Cardiff and Barry, in the autumn of 1929, dealt with a number of subjects including 'Duties of Officers and Section Work', 'Home and the Woman's Workshop', 'Hints on Speaking and Subjects', and 'Education'.[28] These day schools sometimes combined information on topical Labour initiatives with subjects which seemed more akin to the pages of women's magazines. For example, the women who attended the Cardiff Central Division day school, in February 1928, are reported to have listened to lectures on 'Labour's Surtax Proposal' and 'Beauty and Colour in the Home'. While it was the former that *The Labour Woman* reported as 'providing an interesting discussion'; the latter reflects a move to include issues that had wider appeal and is evidence that the Sections were aware not only of the growth of women's magazines, but also of alternative women's groups organized by the Women's Institute, and, in the coalfield, the voluntary sector.[29]

By the late 1920s, weekend schools were also run under the auspices of the Labour Women's Advisory Councils. These were generally held at Easter or during the summer months until early September. Women had the option of either attending as resident or day students. The first school of this type was held on 3–5 September 1927 in Barry. The East Glamorgan, Monmouth and West Wales Advisory Councils 'joined in this new venture and sent twenty-seven students between them'.[30] The mixed agenda included an explanation of 'Labour's Land Policy', 'Constitution of British Parliament', 'World Disarmament', and 'Future Work of Sections and Advisory Councils'. The event was 'voted a great success, and the social evenings and the outing to Fonty Kerry [sic] . . . were greatly appreciated'.[31]

As the 1920s progressed, it became apparent that attendance at day and weekend schools suffered as a result of Wales' worsening economic climate.[32] In response, the various advisory councils, federations and Sections granted a number of scholarships, for which members could apply in order to attend.[33] These proved popular and accounted for a significant number of those in attendance; of the 49 women who went to the weekend school for the whole of Wales in September 1931, 26 had obtained scholarships.[34] As the Depression worsened, members came to rely more and more on these. In 1937, of the 41 resident students, 36 owed their presence to the possession of a scholarship. There is evidence, however, that despite difficult times, the weekend schools managed to make a financial profit.[35]

For many women weekend schools provided a completely new experience; of those who attended in Barry in 1937, 25 had never before been to a school of this kind.[36] The weekend schools provided women with more time to explore issues like 'Health and Education', 'Employment and Remuneration', 'Taxation' and 'Peace'. This was an important, useful aspect to some of the women in the audience who, at the Barry school in 1931 for example, 'showed an extreme keenness to understand the intricacies and vagaries of finance' in the discussion which followed the lectures.[37] The weekend schools mixed conventional political subjects with a varied social programme and went to lengths to ensure that an equal balance of the two was achieved. The September school of 1931, held in Swansea, included a range of socials, dancing and a trip to the sea.[38] Later, a weekend school held in Caerleon College during the Easter weekend of 1933 – which included a visit to the Roman Camp between lectures – was the 'first attempt in this direction for men and women together'.[39] The venture was successful as it was repeated in subsequent years.[40]

ACCESSING THE LOCAL POLITICAL SCENE

To Elizabeth Andrews, the Sections and advisory councils formed 'the working women's university'.[41] From this women were encouraged to 'graduate' into local politics. Although it may have been something of a 'rarity' for women to have 'prominent roles in politics', as Evans and Jones claim,[42] that Labour women managed to achieve representation as councillors, Justices of the Peace (JPs) and so forth during the inter-war period is surely evidence of their political development.[43] Furthermore, in view of the gendered culture in which they operated, their efforts are even more commendable. As *The Labour Woman* pointed out to its readers in 1936, 'There is much to be done to convince members inside the movement as well as voters that women can be capable and efficient councillors.'[44] This was certainly accomplished by women like Rose Davies, Eliza Williams, and Mrs Hart who all succeeded in forging successful careers in public life. These women broke the resistance of what had previously seemed to be impenetrable barriers in their local areas. In Newport, Mrs Hart was the first woman councillor, first woman JP and first female mayor; while in the Rhondda and Aberdare respectively, Eliza Williams and Rose Davies had similarly impressive lists of 'firsts' under their belts which signified their considerable reputations.[45] The contribution of women like these meant that by the 1930s, it was not unheard of for women to be chairs of their respective local councils.[46]

Despite these developments, however, in view of the established patriarchal underpinnings of the Labour Party, and the relative newness of women to politics, it would be unrealistic to expect large numbers of women to be in the position of being catapulted into the council chambers. In addition, many had to negotiate their politics around children and domestic responsibilities. That said, evidence points to a newly acquired political confidence, with some making inroads into local politics as they came to recognize the specific contribution they could make. Some, like the Treharris Women's Section, managed to forge successful working relationships with the local, male-dominated, Labour Associations and Trades Councils.[47] The Pontypridd Women's Section, too, implemented a number of measures through its local trades council. These included an all female sub-committee to look after the interests of female employees in the area, a committee for the administration of funds received by the 1926 Central Distress Committee for special distribution among women and children, and the nomination of a woman, a Mrs Withers, as the trades council's official representative to represent female claimants for unemployment benefit at the Labour Exchange.[48]

Thus women achieved a degree of influence in local communities primarily in those areas of reform directly connected to improving conditions for local women. This was particularly evident in welfare and housing reform, which lagged behind that in England. In theory, the provisions and services of the 1918 Maternity and Child Welfare Act should have brought improvements to the health of mothers and children; however, how, and indeed if, these were provided was at the discretion of the local authorities.[49] This meant that the act, the legacy of the hard work of pre-war groups like the WLL and Women's Co-operative Guild, led to the delivery of inconsistent healthcare in those areas where it was implemented.[50] Thus Labour women in South Wales resumed the fight of the pre-war period to fully implement the legislation in their respective areas. Evidence shows that this met with some success, with the agitation from the Caerwent Women's Section, for example, succeeding in getting a maternity and child welfare centre established in Caldicott in 1920.[51] Rose Davies, too, was a major figure in securing a clinic and treatment centre as well as a maternity centre in Aberdare.[52]

Despite these interventions, the maternal death rate remained a very real problem in Wales with only 13 maternity hospitals serving the whole of Wales.[53] In 1937, a Ministry of Health report revealed that the death rate related to childbirth in Wales between 1924 and 1933 was 35 per cent in excess of the rate for England. In addition, it was found that while maternal mortality rates as a whole in England and Wales fell between 1928–35, in Wales they rose from 5.79 per thousand deaths in 1928, peaking at 6.61 in 1934.[54] Many women, under the orchestration of the Labour Women's Advisory Councils, dedicated a considerable amount of time and effort sending circulars and deputations to county councils and staging large district meetings to discuss council proposals on matters specifically related to maternal mortality.[55] Following the 1935 Labour Women's Conference report on 'Maternal Mortality and Maternity Services', a number of committees were established to investigate local maternity and child welfare services in their respective areas of Swansea, the Rhondda, Merthyr, Newport, Llanelli, Monmouthshire, Barry and Cardiff.[56] According to Elizabeth Williams, Chair of the local Maternity and Welfare Committee, 'Swansea's record of progress' was due to constant agitation from women activists.[57]

Labour women maintained that an improved standard of healthcare for women would only be achieved if women were involved at a policy-forming level.[58] The introduction of County Council Maternity and Child Welfare Committees, under the 1918 Act, made this a very real prospect during the inter-war period. The committees' principal concern was to ensure that adequate services were provided in their local areas. As well as council members, the committees also included co-opted non-council members who had experience of working with matters related to health and maternity. The Act stated that every committee had to include two women. Some male council members, at least in the formative stages of the act's orchestration, viewed women's involvement on the committees less than favourably. Elizabeth Andrews discovered this when she and others campaigned, in writing, to the all-male county and borough councils in Wales suggesting that they co-opt two representatives of women's organizations onto the Maternity and Child Welfare Committees. One county councillor referred to the letters as 'wild hysterical effusions' sent by women who 'know not what they are talking about', while another county dismissed them as 'a lot of interfering busybodies'.[59]

However, despite the existence of a sexist element within the local political scene, the inter-war years witnessed a number of women occupying seats on local, decision-making, policy-implementing bodies. By November 1919 for example, Elizabeth Andrews was appointed, together with five other local women, as a co-opted member of the Maternity and Child Welfare Committee in her area of the Rhondda.[60] Indeed, it became standard practice to include a number of women on these committees and the women of the Labour Party were well represented as a result.[61] Labour women's political input at a decision-making level in health-related issues was further extended by the selection, in 1919, of both Elizabeth Andrews and Rose Davies to serve as members of the Ministry of Health Welsh Consultative Council. The council was established to survey the existing health services in Wales and to devise effective strategies aimed at improving them. Andrews and Davies made a significant contribution towards securing provisions for home-helps for nursing and expectant mothers, as well as working towards the reorganization of maternity benefits on the basis of a scheme of national endowment for mothers (although this latter scheme was unsuccessful). Both Andrews and Davies served on the council until it was disbanded in 1926.[62]

Housing reform was another aspect in which local women managed to make some improvements. Like maternal health, this was an area closely connected to women's sense of self and personal experience. The housing situation in Wales was particularly dire at this time, in terms of both quantity and quality of houses built.[63] Areas of South Wales were especially badly affected. The estimated number of houses which needed to be built in the Rhondda, for instance, was recorded as being between 1,500 and 2,000 at the beginning of the inter-war period.[64] In view of the disproportionate number of hours spent by women in the home, the housing problem brought significant implications, and occupied a key position on Labour women's agenda. It was widely held within the ranks that the housing issue needed to be addressed from a female perspective if women in the home were to achieve better working conditions. Elizabeth Andrews pointed out that 'Homes are the Women's Workshops, and we have to organise and work, and use our Political Power to see that the most important Workshops in the country have the best conditions'.[65] Most valley homes were without a separate area for the preparation and storage of food and lacked any form of separate washroom or facilities. The absence of running water too had a dramatic effect on the number 'of premature births and extreme female ailments' as women were often responsible for transporting water from community pumps.[66]

While Labour women's support for the right of every working-class family to have access to affordable accommodation echoed the party agenda, their approach to the subject reflected a very definite gendered component. Many of them voiced their concern over the layout of the houses' interiors. This was not merely because, as Elizabeth Andrews pointed out, 'men build houses but women make homes'.[67] Rather, male planners often missed aspects of design which women saw as being essential to their daily activities.[68] Indeed this perspective came to be acknowledged as worthy of inclusion in housing initiatives.[69] So, Labour women, as with maternal health, lobbied Welsh councils to ensure that the representation of working women on housing committees and sub-committees was fully implemented. Indeed, there is evidence to suggest that working women's perspective on housing design was recognized by the main political parties after the First World War.

The Women's Housing Sub-Committee to the Ministry of Reconstruction was appointed in 1918 to inspect, as part of a pilot scheme, a number of houses that were intended for working-class occupants. The sub-committee, which was strongly influenced by Labour women, advised the Ministry on the layout of the houses 'with special reference to the convenience of the housewife'.[70] The recommendations put forward were based on the wishes expressed by the numbers of working-class women consulted by the group and included arrangements for heating and hot water supply, a separate scullery for washing and cooking, the number, size and ventilation of rooms and the position of the bath, preferably in a separate bathroom.[71] The Women's Committee influenced other government-appointed committees, including the Tudor-Walters Committee, whose report was to set the standards for houses built between the wars.[72]

So, while at a national level, the extent of women's influence was debatable,[73] at a local level they were able to use the experience provided by women's sections to good effect.[74] While not everyone was in the position to achieve the same degree of success as women like Rose Davies, that they succeeded in getting some of their recommendations put into practice can be viewed as an advance for women's politics generally in South Wales at this time. However, a greater number of women still were involved in an aspect of political activity that was more closely linked to developing the cultural element of Labour Party politics.

ENHANCING A LABOUR PARTY CULTURE

Women played a key role in extending the appeal of Labour politics by way of innovative methods of public spectacle and pageantry, reminiscent of the kind of mass politics of the early nineteenth century.[75] Perhaps it is this that has led some historians, in the past, to see their role as 'supportive' and 'secondary', forming a kind of lower order politics which drew on the influence and experience of the domestic sphere.[76] This chapter, like the work of Krista Cowman in taking a cultural approach to Labour history, argues that social activities lay at the foreground of socialist developments.[77] They were central to what John Marriot terms 'a culture of labourism'.[78] Involvement in local Labour politics not only provided a means of working towards political reform, but also served to boost the morale of like-minded individuals while alleviating the pressures brought about by economic decline.

The wide range of indoor and outdoor Labour Party events was certainly well supported at this time. The Swansea Labour rally and mass demonstration, held in the summer of 1935, reportedly attracted a crowd of at least 3,000, with women from the local wards and divisions part of the occasion's 'intense activity'.[79] Participation of this type was greatly encouraged by the leaders of Women's Sections and was echoed by *The Labour Woman*. Suggesting that each Section made its own banner, the magazine maintained that

> Women members who show their belief in the party by walking in procession with it
> do a great deal to bring other women along, and to show them how well worth it is to

be part of the movement. A public demonstration like this of the solidarity of men and women workers is of special value.[80]

Thus, public evidence of women's allegiance to the party was not only a useful method of attracting more female members, but also served as a means of expressing a unified collaboration with male activists.

Labour women's distinct contribution to the formation of socialist communities in their local areas was extended yet further through the inclusion of children. In this respect, they can be seen as using their familial role for the advantage of the party. The Penderry women ensured inter-generational involvement, deciding that places on their 1935 tableaux should be reserved for the daughters of members only, and maintained that 'this rule be strictly kept'.[81] Mass canvassing was another area which saw women and children combining their efforts to aid Labour's success. Elizabeth Andrews, looking back at her time as women's organizer for Wales, recalled the part played by children in arousing enthusiasm during mass canvassing.[82] In Marriott's words, occasions like these 'became public celebrations of collective identities'.[83] He maintains that children's participation in particular derived more from a sense of fun than political consciousness although he also suggests that for many people, young and old, there was an 'instinctive, traditional identification with the party'.[84] Evidence suggests that by involving children in events of this kind women played a part in creating such identification.

Many of the Labour-run social events were arranged by the women in local organizations, either in their capacity as members of Women's Sections or as elected members of the predominately female Labour social committees.[85] These were not always purely social events, but sometimes combined the 'Educational and Social purposes' which the Newport Labour Party's paper, the *Newport Citizen*, identified in August 1938 as the key reasons for the establishment of Women's Sections.[86] The multi-faceted nature of these social arrangements is effectively illustrated by a series of reports in the May edition of the *Newport Citizen*. While the Central Women's Section is reported as holding 'a successful supper and social evening', the Alexandra Section's evening focused on international issues and was shared by a number of Basque children, while the social and supper at Maindee included a lecture from the parliamentary candidate Peter Freeman.[87] All of the socials were enjoyable solidarity-enhancing events, with the political and social dimensions evident in differing degrees. Many were intended to bring an uncomplicated pleasure to those who attended while simultaneously carrying a party political undertone. Others, like the pageant in Swansea and the meeting of Newport's Alexandra Section, combined pleasurable experiences with more serious, and overtly political, issues. In these cases, peace, anti-fascism and international solidarity were expressed in celebratory style. The *Newport Citizen*'s restricted view as expressed in August 1938 downplays the political element that was so evident in Section meetings. Furthermore, it demonstrates the tendency to separate social and educational aspects of politics from 'serious politics'.

Not all of the social evenings were women-only events; some were intended for the combined enjoyment of male and female members. Some wards held regular monthly social gatherings while others looked forward to annual events.[88] Generally the evenings included dancing, refreshments, games and music. While male activists are reported as 'presiding' over matters, the women are seen mainly as the providers of refreshments, with both providing the musical accompaniment.[89] The *Newport Searchlight* observed that 'The refreshments were in the hands of the ladies, to whom great credit is due for the excellent manner in which they carried out their duties, and the splendid work done beforehand.'[90] This suggests that the women were also involved in a lot of the preparatory work that was needed for these events to take place successfully. Therefore, women are connected to this kind of under-rated 'background' work which no doubt ensured their 'supplementary and supportive' status in local affairs, a position which writers at the time rarely questioned and to which historians have since paid insufficient attention.

Social events were also a key method of raising much-needed funds for local Labour organizations.[91] Duncan Tanner has indicated that these kinds of activities provided three-quarters of the Newport Division's income.[92] Proceeds were put into a social fund, the sole purpose of which was to provide children with a day of entertainment. These children's socials took a variety of forms. For example, in March 1925 the members of the St Julian Ward, in the Newport area, organized an occasion for 200 local children that included fancy dress, a lavish and plentiful tea, and dancing to a live jazz band. The *Newport Searchlight* pointed out that it was to the 'ladies' in particular that 'great credit is due for the admirable organisation of the Social, and also the practical work to which they devoted themselves unsparingly. It is due to their zeal and their energy that the Social passed off without a hitch from start to finish.'[93]

Charabanc outings were another frequently used method of providing an opportunity for enjoyment, as well as a chance for local people to enjoy a change of scenery. Generally these were held annually, taking place in the summer months and were for the benefit of adults and children alike. Some wards, like the one in Crindau in the Newport area, enjoyed more than one outing a year.[94] Members paid a weekly amount during the preceding months, while some of the children's outings were funded by events organized by the Women's Sections.[95] The arrangements for these outings were carried out by the women of the party who were responsible for collecting fares, and for the general 'fine tuning' of necessary preparations.[96] The range of destinations included London, Hereford, Monmouth, and trips to seaside towns like Barry, Tenby and Porthcawl.[97] Excursions of this kind proved extremely popular and often involved large numbers of people. The Newport Party's annual children's day trip in 1928, for instance, involved more than 3,200 individuals and had to be spread over three days.[98]

Evans and Jones point out that Labour women sometimes took the opportunity to combine 'recreation with spreading the word' during charabanc outings, with

the distribution of leaflets and meetings being held on their arrival.[99] Elizabeth
Andrews stressed the effectiveness of such contact with the rural constituencies
that the charabancs visited.[100] In 1927, as part of 'Women's Month', the women
of South Wales travelled in fleets of charabancs, visiting local towns and villages;
their initial appearance apparently disturbing the local constabularies.[101] The
women of East Glamorgan set off in 50 charabancs and two cars all decorated
with red and gold and carrying slogans and banners. Everybody involved wore
rosettes and many children were in fancy dress. A series of meetings was held and
leaflets given out. The day ended with a picnic, dancing and games on the beach at
Southerndown.[102] These social events can be seen as multi-purpose, often being
held for the benefit of members and their children, and for the party as a whole.

Indeed, there was a real need for children, and adults too for that matter,
in South Wales to take part in occasions of these type. The success of these
ventures, illustrated by the positive reports in the press and by the numbers in
attendance at the occasions, is all to the credit of the women concerned. Labour
women supplied the much-needed element of social life to local people, that of
pleasure and enjoyment. Particularly in some of the larger mining towns, they
also contributed towards reinvigorating a flagging community spirit.[103] Aspects
such as these, I would argue, were essential components in establishing a sense
of community identity that was distinctively Labour in nature. Belonging to such
a collective was important to both individual and ideological survival, which
depended upon 'human personalities and their well-being'.[104] Women recognized
that these needed to be nurtured from childhood and demonstrated a commitment to the well-being of the community's children, not only in their demands
for political reform, but also in their agenda of social activities. For many Labour
women, this was a reflection of what socialism was meant to be.

While Labour women from Wales did not achieve representation at
Westminster until 1950, that women were politically active at a grassroots level
in Wales before this should not be overlooked. Evidence from the inter-war
period shows that many took up Elizabeth Andrews' clarion call and became
active members of the women's network created at this time. Many women joined
in response to Andrews' call for the mobilization of mothers as they made the
connection between external forces and their domestic roles. In many respects,
women's political involvement did much to blur the distinction between private
and public, while the various educational initiatives created by the women's
network developed a dimension to women's identities which had previously
lain dormant. For the majority, their politics both stemmed from and reflected
relations to others: class, gender, community and family. Furthermore, the
combination of sobriety and gaiety was a reflection that 'Socialism has to do with
the whole of life, and in a real sense should teach us the art of living'.[105] Indeed,
women worked to establish Labour politics as a way of life rather than merely a
party political experience and developed a political form that permeated many
levels of identity. Thus, it is clear that the Labour Party Women's Sections played
a significant role in the formation of women's identities as 'Labour women',

although the extent to which this could be exercised in the public realm varied between individuals. To conclude, and in agreement with Jane Aaron and Ursula Masson, in view of women's greater presence in today's devolved Wales, 'it is all the more important to remember and to reclaim, as a significant part of our political inheritance' the little acknowledged figures of the past who made a distinctive contribution to the development of political forms and identities.[106]

NOTES

1 Adapted from 'Our women councillors', *The Labour Woman* (*LW*), December 1920, p. 137.

2 Works include: Ursula Masson, '"Political conditions in Wales are quite different": party politics and votes for women 1912–15', *Women's History Review*, 9, (2), (2000), pp. 369–88; Ursula Masson, 'Florence Rose Davies, ILP, County Councillor, c. 1875–1959', in Keith Gildart, David Howell and Neville Kirk (eds), *Dictionary of Labour Biography Volume XI* (Basingstoke: Palgrave Macmillan 2003), pp. 39–47; Neil Evans and Dot Jones, '"To help forward the great work of humanity": women in the Labour Party in Wales', in Duncan Tanner, Chris Williams and Deian Hopkins (eds), *The Labour Party in Wales 1900–2000* (Cardiff: University of Wales Press, 2000), pp. 215–40.

3 Jane Aaron and Ursula Masson, 'Foreword', in Jane Aaron and Ursula Masson (eds), *The Very Salt of Life: Welsh Women's Political Writings from Chartism to Suffrage* (Dinas Powys: Honno, 2007), pp. i–ii.

4 James Griffiths, *James Griffiths and His Times* (Ferndale, Rhondda: W.T. Maddock and Co., n.d.), pp. 21–5; Kenneth O. Morgan, *Wales in British Politics: 1868–1922* (Cardiff: Cardiff University Press, 1991), pp. 282–97; Chris Williams, *Capitalism, Community and Conflict: The South Wales Coalfield, 1898–1947* (Cardiff: University of Wales Press, 1998), pp. 49–57.

5 Griffiths, *James Griffiths*, p. 25.

6 Morgan, *Wales in British Politics*, p. 297.

7 Elizabeth Andrews, *A Woman's Work Is Never Done* (Ystrad Rhondda: Cymric Democrat Publishing Society, 1951); Elizabeth Andrews, *A Woman's Work is Never Done* (Ursula Masson, ed.), (Dinas Powys: Honno Classics, 2006); Ursula Masson and Lowri Newman, 'Elizabeth Andrews', in Keith Gildart, David Howell and Neville Kirk (eds), *Dictionary of Labour Biography: Volume XI* (Basingstoke: Palgrave MacMillan, 2003), pp. 1–11; Lowri Newman, 'A distinctive brand of politics: women in the South Wales Labour Party, 1918–1939' (Unpublished MPhil. thesis, University of Glamorgan, 2003).

8 Elizabeth Andrews, 'Wales – then and now: 1919–1947', *LW*, February 1948, p. 28; Andrews, *A Woman's Work*, p. 31; Councillor W. Harris, 'Notes on political organisation', *Colliery Worker's Magazine* (*CWM*), January 1923, p. 10; East Glamorgan Labour Women's Advisory Council Minutes 1925–1960; 'Wales Reports' *LW*, 1918–1939'.

9 Andrews, *A Woman's Work*, (Ursula Masson edn) p. 25.

10 Evans and Jones, '"To help forward the great work of humanity"', pp. 220–1.

11 National Conference of Labour Women Minutes 1930, p. 59.

12 Elizabeth Andrews, East Glamorgan Advisory Council, Spring Conference 1926, in East Glamorgan Women's' Advisory Council Minutes 1925–1960; 'Wales Report (WR)', *LW*, April 1919, p. 48; *Rhondda Leader*, 9 December 1920; 'WR', *LW*, January 1925, p. 203; 'WR', *LW*, April 1925, p. 60.

13 Chris Williams, *Democratic Rhondda: Politics and Society, 1885–1951* (Cardiff: University of Wales Press, 1996).

14 *LW*, February 1925, p. 28; 'Parties with highest women's membership in 1935', *LW*, June 1936, p. 83; 'WR', *LW*, December 1934, p. 192.

15 'WR', *LW*, December 1920, p. 192; Andrews, *A Woman's Work*; 'WR', *LW*, January 1921, p. 13; 'WR', *LW*, September 1923, p. 151; 'WR', *LW*, December 1925, p. 203.

16 West Wales Labour Women's Advisory Council Minutes, 2 September 1939.

17 Susan Lawrence, 'Women's duty', *Swansea Labour News (SLN)*, 7 January 1922.

18 'Woman in the state', *South Wales Gazette*, 7 January 1921.

19 Andrews, *A Woman's Work*; 'WR', *LW*, January 1933, p. 15.

20 Margaret Davis, 'What my Section means to me', *LW*, October 1932, p. 155.

21 'WR', *LW*, November 1923, p. 181.

22 Elizabeth Andrews, 'The Section Programme', *LW*, June 1933, p. 91; 'WR', *LW*, November 1921, p. 180; 'WR', *LW*, March 1923, p. 44.

23 West Wales Labour Women's Advisory Council Minutes, 12 October 1937.

24 Ibid.

25 'WR', *LW*, November 1925, p. 190.

26 'WR's in *LW* for this period; West Wales Labour Women's Advisory Council Minutes, 2 July 1938; Penderry Women's Section Minutes, 2 July 1935 and 6 March 1936.

27 See copies of 'WR's, *LW*, 1925–39.

28 'WR', *LW*, October 1929, p. 157.

29 'WR', *LW*, February 1928, p. 28; 'WR', *LW*, November 1935, p. 175; Newman, 'A distinctive brand'.

30 'WR', *LW*, October 1927, p. 157.

31 Ibid.

32 'WR', *LW*, November 1928, p. 172.

33 'WR', *LW*, April 1934, p. 63.

34 'WR', *LW*, October 1931, p. 159.

35 West Wales Labour Women's Advisory Council Minutes, 12 October 1937.

36 'WR', *LW*, August 1937, p. 128.

37 'WR', *LW*, October 1931, p. 159.

38 Ibid.

39 'WR', *LW*, May 1933, p. 79.

40 'WR', *LW*, May 1933, p. 79; 'WR', *LW*, June 1934, p. 95; 'WR', *LW*, February 1935, p. 31.

41 Andrews, *A Woman's Work*, p. 7.

42 Evans and Jones, '"To help forward the great work of humanity"', p. 226.

43 'WR', *LW*, May 1932, p. 71; 'WR', *LW*, April 1934, p. 63; 'WR', *LW*, March 1936, p. 40; 'WR', *LW*, October 1936, pp. 159–60; 'WR', *LW*, March, 1937, p. 48; 'WR', *LW*, April 1937, p. 63; 'WR', *LW*, December 1937, p. 192; 'WR', *LW*, May 1938, p. 80; 'WR', *LW*, June 1939, pp. 95–6.

44 'WR', *LW*, December 1936, p. 192.

45 'WR', *LW*, December 1937, p. 192; 'WR', *LW*, May 1932, p. 71; Masson, 'Florence Rose Davies', pp. 39–47; Rose Davies' papers.

46 'WR', *LW*, June 1939, pp. 95–6.

47 'WR', *LW*, October 1920, p. 161.

48 Pontypridd and Labour Trades Council Minutes (PTLC), 18 May 1931, 1 June 1931, 7 June 1926, 21 November 1926, 29 November 1926, 5 December 1926, 13 December 1926.

49 'Report of the work of the Labour Party in women's interests at home and abroad, May–April 1923–1924', *LW*, June 1924, p. 56; 'The women's page', *CWM*, March 1925, p. 68.

50 'Mothers and babies', *LW*, September 1918, pp. 42–3.

51 'WR', *LW*, July 1920, p. 97.

52 'Our women councillors', *LW*, October 1920, p. 157.
53 Deirdre Beddoe, *Out of the Shadows: A History of Women in Twentieth-Century Wales* (Cardiff: University of Wales Press, 2000).
54 Report on Maternal Mortality in Wales, 1937, cited in Beddoe, *Out of the Shadows*.
55 'WR', *LW*, January 1930, p. 16; 'Maternal Mortality campaign in Wales', *LW*, April 1930, p. 59; *Newport Labour Searchlight (NLS)*, November 1932 (Municipal Election Edition); 'WR', *LW*, December 1932, pp. 188–9; 'WR', *LW*, January 1934, p. 15; 'WR', *LW*, December 1937, p. 192.
56 'WR', *LW*, July 1935, pp. 111–12.
57 Elizabeth Williams, 'The welfare of mothers', *LW*, March 1936, pp. 40–1; Penderry Women's Section Minutes, 3 December 1935.
58 'Mothers and babies', *LW*, September 1918, p. 43.
59 Andrews, *A Woman's Work*, p. 31.
60 *RL*, 16 November 1919.
61 See various copies of *LW* and minute books for examples.
62 'Our women councillors', *LW*, October 1920, p. 157; *RL*, 30 January 1960; Rose Davies' papers.
63 Deian Hopkin, 'Social reactions to economic change', in Trevor Herbert and Gareth Elwyn Jones (eds), *Wales between the Wars* (Cardiff: University of Wales Press, 1988); Dennis Thomas, 'Economic decline', in Trevor Herbert and Gareth Elwyn Jones (eds) *Wales between the Wars*; 'Labour women in conference', *LW*, July 1919, p. 77.
64 Evidence of Elizabeth Andrews, *Reports and Minutes of Evidence on Second Stage of Coal Commission Inquiry*, Vol. II, 20 July 1919, p. 1019.
65 'The women's page', *CWM*, March 1923, p. 69.
66 Andrews, Evidence, p. 1019; Glasier, 'The Labour women's battle', *Glamorgan Free Press and Rhondda Leader*, 20 June 1924.
67 Elizabeth Andrews, 'Wallpaper and nerves', *LW*, April 1930, p. 52.
68 See Rose Davies, 'Our men's views on women's work', *LW*, November 1923, p. 175, for her reaction to Herbert Morrison's *Better Times for the Housewife*.
69 'Housing', *LW*, January 1920, p. 4.
70 Letter from Gertrude Emmott (Chair of the Women's Housing Sub-Committee) to the *Pontypridd Observer (PO)*, 22 June 1918.
71 Emmott, *PO*, 22 June 1918; Deirdre Beddoe, *Back to Home and Duty: Women between the Wars, 1919–39* (London: Pandora, 1989), p. 94.
72 Beddoe, *Back to the Home*, p. 94.
73 Martin Pugh, *Women and the Women's Movement in Britain 1914–1959* (London: Macmillan, 1992); Pamela Graves, *Labour Women: Women in British Working-Class Politics, 1918–1939* (Cambridge University Press, 1994).
74 *LW*, February 1925, p. 28; 'WR', *LW*, December 1934, p. 192.
75 Dorothy Thompson, 'Women and nineteenth-century radical politics: a lost dimension', in Juliet Mitchell and Anne Oakley (eds), *The Rights and Wrongs of Women* (London: Pelican, 1976), pp. 112–38.
76 Graves, *Labour Women*, p. 157; Williams, *Democratic Rhondda*, p. 16.
77 Krista Cowman, '"Giving them something to do": how the early ILP appealed to women', in Margaret Walsh (ed), *Working Out Gender: Perspectives from Labour History* (Aldershot: Ashgate, 1999), pp. 119–34.
78 John Marriott, *The Culture of Labourism: The East End between the Wars* (Edinburgh: Edinburgh University Press, 1991), p. 5.

79   *South Wales Evening Post (SWEP)*, 17 June 1935.
80   'Eight million women wanted', *LW*, September 1920, p. 157.
81   Penderry Women Section Minutes, 14 May 1935.
82   Elizabeth Andrews, 'Wales – then and now: 1919–1947', *LW*, February 1948, p. 28.
83   Marriott, *Culture of Labourism*, p. 180.
84   Ibid., pp. 182–3.
85   See minutes of Pontypridd Trades and Labour Council, Penderry Women's Section, etc.
86   *Newport Citizen (NC)*, August 1938.
87   *NC*, May 1938.
88   *NLS*, 20 May 1925 and 30 January 1925.
89   *NLS*, 6 March 1925 and 30 January 1925.
90   *NLS*, 6 March 1925.
91   *NLS*, 13 February 1925.
92   Duncan Tanner, 'Women and Labour, 1918–1939: the evidence from Wales', paper presented at the Institute of Contemporary British History 14th Summer Conference, London, 10 July 2000.
93   *NLS*, 3 April 1925.
94   *NLS*, 27 March 1925.
95   *NLS*, 6 February 1925; Penderry Women's Section Minutes, 23 June 1937.
96   *NLS*, 27 March 1925.
97   *NLS*, 6 February 1925; *NLS*, 27 March 1925; Penderry Women's Section Minutes, 23 June 1937.
98   Tanner, 'Women and Labour'.
99   Evans and Jones, '"To help forward the great work of humanity"', p. 223.
100 Elizabeth Andrews, 'Labour women in Wales', *LW*, November 1937, p. 163.
101 Marion Phillips, 'The Editor's monthly letter', *LW*, July 1927, p. 104; 'WR', *LW*, July 1927, p. 109.
102 'WR', *LW*, July 1927, p. 109.
103 Morgan, *Wales in British Politics*.
104 Evans and Jones, '"To help forward the great work of humanity"', p. 225.
105 Elizabeth Andrews, 'The Section Programme', *LW*, June 1933, p. 91.
106 Aaron and Masson, 'Foreword', p. iv.

4

Count up to twenty-one: Scottish women in formal politics, 1918–1990

Catriona Burness

Myths abound that Scotland is a chauvinistic country – of the male chauvinistic pig variety . . . and that Scotswomen face greater difficulties in getting to Parliament. Machismo, it is argued, is a greater trial than selection boards. Yet Scotland's record in electing women Members of Parliament is better than that of the UK as a whole. One hundred and nine women have trod the corridors of power . . . sixteen of them from Scotland. That is a proportion which far exceeds the old Goschen population percentage formula.[1]

So wrote Margaret Bain (later Ewing), then the former nationalist MP for Dunbarton East, in 1980. Historically, this was true but Mrs Thatcher's election as Britain's first female Prime Minister in 1979 coincided with the return of only one Scottish woman MP, the worst position since 1923. Scotland has since continued to return fewer women MPs than the UK average, a fact underlined by campaigners for better women's representation since the 1980s. However, the figures, whether in Scotland or the UK, are low – low enough to be considered as statistically insignificant, even if politically significant. Few women entered the political arena. The 10 per cent threshold was crossed only in 1997 and the previous highest levels of Scottish women's representation occurred in 1959, 1964 and 1992, with the return of five Scottish women MPs – 7 per cent – a level overtaken in Finland as long ago as 1906. This was scarcely the irruption of 'petticoated generals, ministers, and legislators' feared by anti-suffrage campaigners![2] Only 21 women were elected as MPs for Scottish constituencies between 1918 and 1990 – six Conservatives; 11 Labour; one Liberal Democrat; and three Scottish nationalists (see Table 4.1).

This chapter focuses on women in formal politics in Scotland up to 1990, examining how the parties responded to dealing with women as voters, members, candidates and representatives, with Scotland's first female representatives at Westminster meriting attention as firsts. Although the Conservatives provided Scotland with its first woman MP, the most consistent advocate and deliverer of female representatives was the Labour Party, while women within the Scottish National Party also became associated with 'a tradition of women' from the 1970s. Each of these aspects is considered. The 1980s campaign for Scottish

Table 4.1 Scotland: Women MPs, 1918–90

1.	1923–38	Katherine, Duchess of Atholl (Con.)	Perth & Kinross (West)
2.	1929–31	Miss Jennie Lee (Lab.)	North Lanark *
	1945–70		Staffordshire Cannock
3.	1931–45	Rt Hon Miss Florence Horsbrugh (Con.)	Dundee
4.	1931–35	Mrs Helen Shaw (Con.)	Bothwell
5.	1937–45	Mrs Agnes Hardie (Lab.)	Springburn *
6.	1945–70	Rt Hon Margaret (Peggy) Herbison (Lab.)	North Lanark
7.	1945–59	Mrs Jean Mann (Lab.)	Coatbridge
8.	1945–46	Mrs Clarice Shaw (Lab.)	Kilmarnock
9.	1946–66	Lady Grant of Monymusk (Con.) (as Lady Tweedsmuir after 1948)	Aberdeen South *
10.	1948–69	Mrs Alice Cullen (Lab.)	Gorbals *
11.	1958–59	Mrs Mary McAlistair (Lab.)	Kelvingrove *
12.	1959–79	Rt Hon Betty Harvie Anderson (Con.)	Renfrewshire East
13.	1959–87	Rt Hon Dame Judith Hart (Lab.)	Lanark (Clydesdale 1983–)
14.	1967–70	Mrs Winifred (Winnie) Ewing	Hamilton *
	1974–79	(SNP)	Moray & Nairn
15.	1973–74	Mrs Margo MacDonald (SNP)	Govan *
16.	1974–79	Mrs Margaret Bain (SNP)	Dunbartonshire East
	1987–2001	(as Mrs Ewing)	Moray
17.	1982–83	Mrs Helen McElhone (Lab.)	Queen's Park *
18.	1983–87	Mrs Anna McCurley (Con.)	Renfrew West & Inverclyde
19.	1987–2001	Mrs Maria Fyfe (Lab.)	Maryhill
20.	1987–2001	Mrs Ray Michie (Lib. Dem.)	Argyll & Bute
21.	1990–2005	Mrs Irene Adams (Lab.)	Paisley North *

Summary: Total: 21 women MPs. By party: six Conservative; 11 Labour; one Liberal Democrat; and three Scottish Nationalist.

* Indicates first elected in a by-election.

Source: Drawn from House of Commons Information Office Factsheet M4, Appendix B, and House of Commons Library, Research Paper 05/33, *General Election 2005*.

devolution and the promotion of women in politics is also introduced, although this development is explored more fully in the chapter by Esther Breitenbach and Fiona Mackay in this volume.

THE SCOTTISH CONTEXT

The Scottish political landscape is distinctive. The Liberal Party dominated Victorian and early twentieth-century Scottish politics despite the split created by the raising of the Irish Home Rule issue. The emergence of Liberal Unionism in 1886 gave the historically unpopular Conservative party an ally and an appeal that it had previously lacked in Scotland. The Liberal landslide victory in 1906 and subsequent Liberal victories in January and December 1910 seemed to signal the end of that appeal. The Unionist merger in 1912 took place at a nadir of Conservative and Liberal Unionist electoral fortunes. However, the Conservative party did not simply reappear in 1912. In Scotland the party fought elections as 'Unionists' until the 1960s, retaining the name decades after it was dropped in favour of 'Conservative' in England and Wales. This acknowledged the need for a distinctive appeal in Scotland and historic anti-Conservative feeling.[3] The First World War, however, shattered Liberal unity and introduced new alignments within the wartime coalition.

By 1924 the once mighty Scottish Liberal Party was reduced to a rump of eight seats, squeezed between the emerging Labour Party (26) and the Unionists who took a majority of the Scottish seats (36). The Labour Party first took a majority of the Scottish seats in 1929 but as partners in the coalition governments of 1918, 1931 and 1935, the Unionists were the most dominant of the Scottish inter-war parties. They also regained ground in Glasgow, and as late as the 1950s held seven of the 15 city constituencies, while taking a majority of the Scottish seats in 1955. From 1945 the rise of the Labour Party was a key theme. However, Scottish nationalist electoral successes from 1967, gradual Liberal advance on the basis of constituency focused campaigns, and party realignments in the 1980s created four-party politics by the 1980s. Conservative decline once more became a defining feature of Scottish politics, plumbing new depths in 1997 when Scotland (and Wales) became 'Tory-free zones'.

THE PARTIES AND THE 'WOMAN QUESTION'

Votes for women were a new, unknown factor in 1918 and many dreaded the emergence of a 'Woman's Party'. However, the general election took place within weeks of the passing of suffrage reform and Christabel Pankhurst's defeat as the sole candidate in Smethwick, ensured that the Woman's Party's prospects were still-born. Only one woman candidate stood (as an Independent) in Scotland in 1918 and she lost her deposit.[4] The *Scotsman* made the welcome discovery that 'there was no appearance of anything like a tendency to a block vote'[5] and that women voted on the same party lines as men did. Women were the political novelty of the 1920s but the novelty faded as the women's vote assumed manageable dimensions for the party managers. The preoccupation of the parties was winning women's votes, not in providing the electors with women to vote for, and women voters contributed to the emergence of a new political landscape.

The extension of the suffrage to women in 1918 had implications both for party structures and electoral appeals. After 1918 both the Liberal Party and the Unionist Party developed party structures within which women were initially far more visible than in the Labour Party, merging their hitherto separate male and female organizations. In the case of the Liberal Party, merger was short-lived. After the 1922 election the Scottish Liberal Federation (SLF) consulted local associations on how best to ensure that 'greater interest would be taken by the women', and later recommended that local Liberal parties should set up Women's Sections where they did not already exist.[6] By 1925 the Federation itself had formed a women's committee.[7] Although heavily preoccupied with running bazaars to rescue Liberalism from its dire cash crisis, the Women's Educational and Social Council could at least send resolutions and have representation at Annual Conference.[8] A sense of purpose behind the commitment to equality was clearest at all levels, including the parliamentary level, over 1918–22. Two of the three women candidates to stand in Scotland in 1922 were Liberal, Mrs Alderton in Edinburgh South, and Mrs Smith, better known as the novelist, Annie S. Swann, in the Maryhill division of Glasgow. The other woman candidate, Helen Fraser, 'an educationalist',[9] stood as a National Liberal in Govan.

Yet the Liberals apparently found it difficult to draw women into the party, and in particular, to involve women on equal terms with men. Despite a promising start only eight of the 33 Scottish women candidates over 1918–45 were Liberals. In Scotland, the Liberal Federation had a key role to play in placing candidates, partly due to the increasing difficulty of getting candidates as the Liberal Party faced disintegration and decline. Selection was negotiated between the Liberal Whip, the Scottish Federation Secretary, and local deputations 'in some cases ten strong'.[10] At the 1923 election the Federation rushed as many as 22 candidates into the field within eight days – none of them women – and the Scottish Secretary Webster commented that 'the candidates available were unfortunately limited . . . or another five or six could easily have been placed'.[11]

Difficulties in finding candidates worsened[12] but no Liberal women stood for Scottish seats at either the 1929 or 1931 elections. Two female candidates stood in 1935, while another was forced to stand down in the singular circumstances of the 1938 West Perthshire by-election, discussed below. In 1945 Lady Glen-Coats, the only Liberal woman candidate, suffered the humiliation of becoming the first Liberal candidate to lose their deposit in Paisley, a former Liberal stronghold. No special shame on her, however, as the Liberals lost all their Scottish seats in 1945. The Liberal Party as such never returned a Scottish woman MP, coming closest with the election of Liberal Democrat Ray Michie in 1987.

The Scottish Unionists adopted the guiding post-suffrage principle

that women should be admitted to all Associations on the same footing as men. . .
The Council was unanimous in agreeing that the fusion between men and women's
Associations should be absolute and that the organisations should on no account remain
separate.[13]

In England and Wales women joined their local Women's Unionist Association
as a matter of course – but in Scotland forming local women's branches proved
unpopular, lest this encouraged the formation of a women's grouping in politics
(in or out of the Unionist Party). Any tendency towards separate organization
aroused suspicion. Two women organizers were appointed in 1919 in the West
and East of Scotland. They were not appointed 'for the sole purpose of organising
women' in case this added to 'the danger of separate male and female organisations emerging'.[14]

Yet the Unionists were determined to draw women into the party. They began
organizing women's meetings and in January 1920 Lady Baxter stressed that 'it
was better that such meetings should be addressed by bad speakers than that
they should not be held at all.'[15] The Tories built up a large membership during
the inter-war years. In 1925 membership in Glasgow alone was over 21,000,
compared with an estimated Scottish Independent Labour Party (ILP) membership of around 8,000.[16] Although we do not have a membership breakdown
between men and women, the vital contribution of women party workers at every
subsequent election was acknowledged.

The National Party of Scotland (NPS), formed in 1928, and the fore-
runner of the Scottish National Party (SNP), issued a nationalist variation on
'down-to-earth' appeals made to women voters by all the parties, most typically
addressing women as wives and mothers.[17] In April 1929 'Aunt Jean's Advice to
Women Voters' counselled three young girls – Jeanie, Flora and Elspeth – on how
to vote: 'Why not vote for the Nation, as Nationalists? . . . Is it not time, think you,
to have done with parties; to think rather of the interests of your native land and
its people – your own kith and kin?'[18]

There are other indications that the NPS was keen to involve women. In
January 1929 the party paper, the *Scots Independent* reported from Kinghorn,
Burntisland and Kirkcaldy that a meeting held in Lady Lockhart's home had
led to a Women's Section being formed with Lady Lockhart as President.[19] The
paper listed 99 local NPS branches and secretaries in August 1932 and 15 of the
local branch secretaries were female. The branches were organized in ten areas;
of nine area secretaries named, one was a woman: Catriona Cameron, Secretary
of the West Renfrewshire Federation.[20] The branch reports also indicate women's
emergence as speakers and apparently as election agents – for instance, 'the excellent and self-sacrificing work of Miss Jean S. Fraser' during the Montrose Burghs
by-election in 1932 was commended.[21] Clearly there were several attempts to
develop organization among women. These efforts now appear to be almost
entirely forgotten, not least by present-day SNP women activists.

Elma Campbell was the only nationalist woman parliamentary candidate of the inter-war years. She stood for parliament twice in Glasgow St Rollox, first at the by-election of May 1931 and then at the general election later that year. A former Glasgow University Conservative debating champion, she rose rapidly on joining the NPS. She was described as 'one of our most brilliant speakers', having addressed audiences of 'over four thousand in St Andrew's Halls, Glasgow'.[22] Her by-election poll of 15.8 per cent and general election poll of 13.3 per cent of the votes cast were among the best nationalist results up to that point.[23] A teacher in Greenock, she was refused leave of absence during both campaigns. It was remarked that 'the amount of work put in was simply astonishing when one considers that the candidate attended on average seven meetings each night'. Her marriage to Thomas Gibson in March 1932 and his employment in London removed both from the Scottish political scene. Otherwise she might have contested other elections for the SNP during the 1930s. Her focus was very much on nationalism *per se*, and her interest in women's activities seems to have been organizational, and not in women's issues as such.

The Labour Party turned to the question of how best to organize to win women's votes as early as 1916. The Women's Labour League then successfully appealed to the second Scottish Labour Party Conference for help 'in anticipation of the competition of the organisations which will be set up by the middle classes to capture the women's vote for Reaction'.[24] They wanted the appointment of a Women's Organiser, branches of the Women's Labour League in every constituency, and other assistance. By 1919, Agnes Hardie had been appointed as Scottish Women's Organiser and the first Scottish Labour Women's Conference held. This became an annual event by 1926. Better representation of women on the party's Scottish Executive was secured by increasing the number of seats reserved for Women's Sections from one to four. In the wake of the sex-equality legislation of the 1970s Labour women dismantled their separate structures as the age of equality had dawned! By 1980 a rescue operation was mounted to resuscitate the women's organization. Historically, the key role of male-dominated trade unions, combined with a low female membership, left women less visible in the Labour Party than in the Unionist Party.

While all selection procedures became wider after 1945, from 1918 would-be Labour candidates faced a far more competitive selection procedure than either Liberal or Unionist women as 'in the Labour Party there had always been an attempt to consult the constituency party members in drawing up the shortlist and agreeing the prospective candidate'.[25] The ability to bring sponsorship was a key factor in selections, and after the break with the ILP in the early 1930s union backing became crucial. Given the important part played by male-dominated unions such as the National Union of Mineworkers, women were at a disadvantage in securing sponsorship.

Nonetheless, the ILP believed that a woman speaker always attracted crowds and tried hard but apparently found it difficult to recruit women for their speakers' panel. Jean Mann, later Labour MP for Coatbridge from 1945–59, recalled being outmanoeuvred in her objections to going onto the panel as she couldn't possibly leave her five children by the discovery that her husband had already agreed to babysit: 'I was pushed into it. No woman setting out to have six of a family is planning a parliamentary career. It just happened – pushed into it by men.'[26] Promoted particularly by Labour, outdoor meetings were a feature of inter-war political propaganda and women speakers were rare. Labour's first woman MP Jennie Lee was among the exceptions but, for all her eloquence, she thought that 'They were just as much impressed by my university degree as by my oratory. And just as important, I came out of the right stable. I was Michael Lee's grand-daughter [of the Fife and Clackmannan Miners' Union].'[27] However, the Conservatives carried off the historic 'first' of returning Scotland's first woman MP.

SYMBOLIC FIRSTS

The Duchess of Atholl became Scotland's first female MP when, in 1923, she won the seat which her husband, then Lord Tullibardine, had held from January 1910 until his succession to the peerage in 1917. She had been identified as a most suitable female candidate and was persuaded to stand by a powerful combination of leading Unionists. Apart from her aristocratic social and political connections, she had an extensive background of service on public bodies, sitting on as many as 25 committees in 1920.[28] She had also been active in Scottish Unionist circles and knew most of her party leaders personally. Taken together with her personal qualities as a conscientious and hard worker on behalf of her chosen causes she must have seemed the obvious choice as the first Scottish Unionist MP. In terms of forwarding women's representation, however, she was not the obvious choice, having spoken publicly against votes for women before 1918. In 1924 she was the only woman MP to vote against reducing the female voting age to 21, arguing that 'a great extension of this kind looks like taking advantage of the heroic sacrifices of those men [lost during the First World War]'.[29]

Sheila Hetherington, her biographer, commented on the irony of the Duchess of Atholl, of all people, becoming Scotland's first female MP. She was an 'anti-feminist . . . trail-blazing almost by accident certainly never by design'.[30] Although the Duchess continued to infuriate feminists, for example, opposing equal pay in the Civil Service in the 1930s, her own career mapped out a series of firsts. In 1924 she became the first Conservative woman minister on her appointment as Parliamentary Under-Secretary at the Board of Education over 1924–9, following Labour's earlier appointment of Margaret Bondfield as a junior minister in 1923. Katharine Atholl was preferred over Nancy Astor on account of her knowledge of education and Baldwin's feeling that she would be 'loyal and decorous'.

After 1929, however, humanitarian concern for women and children contributed to her adopting causes that set her at odds with her party. The first of these was opposition to the practice of female circumcision in Kenya, a campaign which met with blank incomprehension in the House of Commons. 'Die-hard' opposition to Indian Home Rule followed, linked to concern over the position of women and children in India without, as she saw it, the restraining influence of the British Raj. Growing criticism in her own constituency did not prevent her from resigning the Unionist Whip over the India Bill. Yet, as the *Scotsman* reported, the West Perthshire Conservatives could live with the Duchess on India.[31] Opposition to the fascist rebels in Spain, concern for Spanish women and children, vocal opposition to appeasement, and a spate of publications such as the best-selling *Searchlight on Spain*, were another matter. She became an increasing embarrassment to the Unionist Party and apparently more marginalized than other anti-appeasers:

> Firstly, she was a woman; for most of the men, the trade of politics was still exclusively a male domain. Secondly, she was viewed as being old and dowdy. This too was unfair, since many MPs were themselves much older and dowdier than she was . . . Thirdly, Kitty – and to an extent Churchill too – were seen to have abandoned their fellow aristocrats at a time of crisis.[32]

In May 1938 the West Perthshire Unionists decided to look for another candidate for the general election. The attitude of her local and national party, combined with a worsening international situation, led her to resign and fight a by-election in December 1938 as an Independent. Now dubbed the 'Red Duchess' by angry Unionists, she still expected to win. The Liberal candidate, Mrs Coll MacDonald, reluctantly stepped down to give her a clear run against the official Unionist candidate but with the full weight of the Unionist machine flung into the constituency, she lost by 1,333 votes. It was one of the last victories of appeasement and the closing of a parliamentary career of British and Scottish importance. The Duchess had made a major contribution in parliamentary debate, ranking third in Brian Harrison's measurement of gross debating contributions of the inter-war women MPs, and in opposing the India Bill in 1935 she contributed 42 per cent of all that was said by women MPs that year.[33]

The North Lanark by-election of March 1929 returned Jennie Lee to become Scotland's first Labour woman MP at the age of only 24. Apart from the help poured in by Labour Party members, she had the unexpected support of British bookies. Furious at the introduction of a bookmakers' levy by then Chancellor Winston Churchill, bookies turned up from all over the country to help make sure that the Unionists lost the seat. The *Scotsman* commented that the 6,578 majority won by Jennie Lee exceeded 'even her own expectations', and went on:

> During the campaign . . . it was stated that the Roman Catholics had been advised to vote for the Liberals because of the uncertainty of Miss Lee's attitude on the question of birth control, but it is now apparent that the advice was not accepted.[34]

At the 1929 general election Jennie Lee held the seat but with a reduced majority. In 1931, however, she lost, confronted by a tide of support for a National government, the emerging hostility of right wing miners' union leaders, and above all, the fury of the Catholic Church. Fellow ILP members, Maxton, McGovern and Campbell Steven, failed to persuade her of the need to support the Scurr amendment for increased provision for Catholic schools: 'I was livid with contempt . . . All they cared about was saving their seats. They succeeded. I went under.'[35] Despite being furious with Maxton, and critical of his leadership of the ILP, Jennie Lee could not bear to leave the ILP on the break with Labour – an attitude which led her future husband, Nye Bevan, to call her 'my Salvation Army lassie'.[36] She fought North Lanark again in 1935 but as an ILP candidate against a Unionist and an official Labour candidate. The official Labour intervention ensured Unionist victory. Jennie Lee did not stand again in Scotland, although she was elected as Labour MP for Cannock in Staffordshire in 1945 and served as a minister during the Wilson governments. Scotland thus lost one of its most charismatic if controversial female representatives.

SCOTLAND'S WOMEN MPS

Apart from her charisma, youth was Jennie Lee's marked characteristic as a Scottish woman MP. Her election at the age of 24 remains exceptional. Jo Swinson's election as Scotland's second Liberal Democrat woman MP in 2005 at the age of 25 comes closest. Of the 21 women representing Scottish seats up to 1990, only seven were under the age of 40; Anna McCurley was 40, and the rest over 40 when they first entered parliament. Those under 40 at their first election were Jennie Lee (24); Peggy Herbison (38); Lady Grant of Monymusk, later Lady Tweedsmuir (31); Dame Judith Hart (35); Winnie Ewing (38); Margo MacDonald (30); and Margaret Bain, later Ewing (29). The Duchess of Atholl was 49 when she first entered parliament. The oldest when elected was Agnes Hardie, who became MP for Glasgow Springburn at the age of 63 following the death of her husband, the sitting MP, in 1937; she served until her retirement in 1945.

By the 1960s the number of Scottish women MPs stood at a record 7 per cent. The selection and election of women MPs, however, brought no guarantees of establishing a tradition of a seat as 'a woman's seat'. Retiring women MPs tended to be replaced by male candidates. The lack of women at Westminster does not seem to have been a burning issue over the period but a few did swim against the tide. For example, the organization Women for Westminster drew hundreds of women to a public meeting in Glasgow in 1944 on the need for more women in politics. Women for Westminster, founded in 1942 and merged with the National Women's Citizens' Association in 1949, 'had as its main aim, increasing the number of women MPs'.[37] In 1945 George Bernard Shaw wrote to every Labour woman candidate asking for her views on his proposal of the 'Coupled Vote'. This was the suggestion that every constituency should have two representatives, a man and a woman. Jean Mann, although concerned about the lack of women at Westminster, was sceptical:

Is a housing, or rent question concerning children, peculiar to one sex? Would conflict not arise as to who should handle which? And would there be a dominant partner? As to the House of Commons, much overcrowded with 630 members, what would it be like with 1260? . . . think of the voters at a general election. The issue might be man or woman. Spoiled papers enormous . . .[38]

Jennie Lee described her friend, Rebecca Sieff, Chair of Women for Westminster, as 'born before her time, with every fibre of her being, she resented the restrictions imposed upon her because of her sex', but Lee refused to join, saying, 'No, Becky, I shall always vote on policy issues, not on the sex of the candidate.'[39] None of the early women MPs were likely to disagree with her. In this sense, pressure to increase the number of women representatives was muted and also constrained by party loyalty.

Obviously relatively few women stood for parliament or were elected as MPs over the period from 1918 to 1990. The women who became MPs tended to share advantages of family connections with politics and a higher than average level of education, and were mainly married and childless. As Jean Mann observed, Lady Tweedsmuir

probably created a precedent by attending and taking part in debates right up to a few weeks of the birth of her child and fooled everyone about her pregnancy. . .. Moreover, she would sit waiting to catch the Speaker's eye for hours, even in the seventh month – No, it couldn't be true, could it?[40]

Jean Mann herself was exceptional in entering into political activity during the inter-war years while her five children were young. Maxton teased her that she was 'known all over Scotland as "haud the wean" Jean, and that all over . . . the comrades had to decide who would take the chair, who would lift the collection, and who would "hold her bairn".'[41] However, she was 56 years old when finally elected MP for Coatbridge in 1945.

The Scottish Labour women MPs typically had long involvement in the party behind them. Clarice McNab Shaw and Agnes Hardie were striking examples. Although Agnes Hardie followed her husband as MP for Springburn, she personally pioneered paths for women. A former shop worker, she was a founder member of the Shop Assistants' Union and its first female organizer. She also became the first Women's Organiser of the Labour Party in Scotland, and Glasgow's first woman MP. She became known as the 'Housewife's MP' on account of her voluble attacks on the price of meat or shortage of potatoes.[42] These attacks certainly aroused anxiety among Unionist women, prompting them to react with leaflets setting out the 'true facts'.[43] After 1945 Jean Mann took on the mantle of the 'Housewife MP', although neither she nor Hardie were typical housewives, while there was also a reaction against this 'housewife's focus' among younger women. Yet of the earlier Scottish women MPs, Agnes Hardie and Jean Mann showed the greatest inclination to identify themselves with women's issues, and were later to be followed by Maria Fyfe who specifically addressed herself to women's under-representation in politics. However, although from 1923 to 1990 Labour returned the highest number of women MPs, the success of charismatic female nationalists in the 1970s began the association in the public mind of the SNP and women.

HAMILTON AND SCOTLAND'S 'HOME RULE HOUSEWIFE'

The 1960s brought several indications that the SNP was becoming a more serious political force. As Webb noted, 'for the first time, they found themselves to be both the standard-bearers of nationalism and a united party'.[44] The growth of the party membership during the 1960s was 'almost legendary', rising from less than 2,000 in 1962 to 50,000 in March 1967, and to 100,000 in April 1968. The number of local branches rose from 21 in 1962 to 472 by 1968,[45] while the number of SNP candidates increased at each election: five in 1959; 15 in 1964; and 23 in 1966.[46] This went alongside Unionist decline – Unionist seats fell from 36 in 1955 to 20 by 1966 – and an erosion of the Labour vote. As Hanham put it:

> All over Britain there was a flight from Labour, which in Scotland assumed surprising proportions and culminated in the loss of one of the safest Labour seats in the House of Commons at Hamilton in 1967 and in an unprecedented clear-out of Labour town councillors in 1968.[47]

The impact of the Hamilton by-election was electrifying. As the victor, Winnie Ewing, put it: 'The advice I was given was "try to come a good second" . . . The *Hamilton Advertiser* had to change its front page for the result. The headline was "Winnie Wins by a Mile!".'[48] Margaret Ewing recalled this time as 'very heady . . . It projected the SNP as a credible political party . . . Nationalism was a new dynamic movement with repercussions for the whole political system.'[49] Winnie Ewing carried the heavy weight of nationalist aspirations. She found being the only Scottish nationalist at Westminster between 1967 and 1970 'a hideous experience . . . Westminster is very cruel. Being in a minority of one is an acid test of the system.'[50] Outside Westminster she spoke at innumerable public meetings throughout Scotland, reflecting the rise of the SNP from the status of a minor party to that of a third party.[51] It all made for a steep learning curve for a woman who had spoken at few political meetings before being persuaded to stand as the Hamilton by-election candidate. She described it as 'fearsome. I had no researcher, no helper, and hundreds of people hanging on my every word.'[52] Although she was a court lawyer, much was made of the fact that she was a married woman of 38 with three young children; Terence was then aged four, Annabelle, seven, and Fergus, ten.[53]

Her influence as a role model was immense, not simply because she won the Hamilton by-election but because it marked the beginning of a lengthy political career. She served as MP for Moray and Nairn from February 1974 until

1979, and snatched victory from the jaws of defeat to become Member of the European Parliament for the Highlands and Islands from 1979–99. She ended her representative career as a Highland member of the newly created Scottish Parliament from 1999–2003, while she held party posts, including that of party president until 2005. Known in Europe as 'Madame Ecosse', her hold on the Highlands Euro-seat was widely reckoned to be based on a personal rather than a party vote. Keith Webb identified her as 'probably the first nationalist leader to attain individual prominence'.[54] Ewing herself said, 'My becoming an MP certainly influenced my party in giving encouragement to other women. I was able to become an MP as a mother of three young children.'[55]

She urged several other women to become parliamentary candidates and the rapid procession of nationalist women MPs in the 1970s did a great deal to associate the SNP with women. The SNP put up more women candidates than all the other parties combined in 1970 and the highest number of women at the 1974 elections. Dubbed the 'Blonde Bombshell' and much photographed with her two young daughters, Margo MacDonald was briefly MP for Glasgow Govan after a sensational by-election victory in November 1973. Margaret Bain became MP for Dunbarton East in October 1974 by the narrowest of margins – 22 votes. One elector told Bain in 1974, 'Between you, and Janette Jones and Phyllis Watt, if you all get elected, you'll nag the House of Commons into giving Scotland independence!'[56]

The nationalist women MPs undoubtedly encountered sexist attitudes, partly illustrated by Winnie Ewing's 'daily crucifixions' at Westminster from 1967–70. First elected as relatively young women of 29, both Margaret Bain and Margo MacDonald had to fight against being stereotyped as 'dolly birds'. Both also separated from their then husbands during the 1970s. Barbed comment pursued Margo MacDonald during her unsuccessful Hamilton by-election campaign in 1978: '"Where's Mr MacDonald, then?" shrieked a venomous woman, weeding her garden as Margo passed'.[57] Comment on Margo MacDonald sometimes appears particularly sexist: 'this hard-hitting, tough talking, oil-grabbing, splendidly constructed woman who detests being summed up by the size of her bra (37).'[58] She later commented, 'I was very conscious at that time (1973) that other politicians regarded me as "a clever wee lassie", rather than their equal. But I'd had to get over that hurdle with my colleagues in Scotland and I did it by knowing just as much if not more than they did about the goals we were striving for.'[59] Her success in establishing herself as a propagandist was clear at the Hamilton by-election; the posters just called her 'Margo.'[60] She wrote that she thought of 'women in politics as politicians', but reluctantly had 'to concede that the majority of people regard them as a rather different group of politicians', and found it 'so UNFAIR that, even in 1975, the standards applied to women should be so much more exacting.'[61]

This experience, however, is not unique to nationalist women MPs, and although as Margaret Ewing said, 'It has been encouraging for other women in the party to be able to look at Winnie, Margaret and Margo',[62] the SNP tradition of women was inevitably limited up to 1990.

MRS THATCHER'S ACCIDENTAL LEGACY: CONSTITUTIONAL CHANGE AND WOMEN'S POLITICAL REPRESENTATION IN SCOTLAND

Scottish women MPs were in short supply at Westminster in 1979, the one and only representative being Labour's Judith Hart. The ensuing debate on women's representation in Scotland unfolded as Thatcherism came to dominate British politics. Reactions to Mrs Thatcher's controversial leadership spanned political realignment and the emergence of new parties, and the revival of the campaign for Scottish devolution after its prematurely announced death in March 1979.

Women's representation became entwined with these developments. New political parties such as the Social Democratic Party (SDP) and the Greens adopted measures intended to encourage women candidates. Formed in 1981 as a breakaway from Labour, the SDP candidate selection rules sought a minimum of two women on every shortlist where possible. In 1987 the Alliance put up the highest number of women candidates of all the parties – 105 in the UK and 16 in Scotland.[63] On eventual merger with the Liberals, the Liberal Democrat rules stated that there must be at least one woman on a shortlist if a woman is nominated. During the 1980s the Greens also explored options, such as setting targets for women candidates. From 1987 the Labour party played a key role in increasing women's political representation, sharpening the focus on women in politics in the revived devolution debates over 1988–91.

In 1987 the so-called 'Doomsday Scenario' arrived. Although Mrs Thatcher won a parliamentary majority of 102, in Scotland her party suffered its worst election defeat since 1910, shrinking from 21 to ten seats. Against this background, the cross-party organization, the Campaign for a Scottish Assembly (CSA), invited a committee of prominent Scots to draw up a report on the state of the current government of Scotland, and to suggest what should be done about it. Its report, *A Claim of Right for Scotland*, was launched in July 1988 and recommended setting up a Constitutional Convention to press the claim for a Scottish Assembly. The governing Conservative party refused to take part but by late 1988 all the opposition parties had agreed to participate in the Convention and strong support came from the trade union movement, from the churches, and from local authorities. The SNP, however, withdrew in early 1989. The Green party later withdrew in early 1991 but rejoined in 1995.

In response to the *Claim of Right* and the setting up of the Constitutional Convention, a cross-party and non-party grouping, 'A Scottish Women's Claim of Right', was launched in April 1989, because 52 per cent of the population provided only 4 per cent of its MPs.[64] The campaign mounted a series of conferences in 1989, won a certain amount of publicity, made a submission to the Scottish Constitutional Convention, and contributed articles on women's representation to the Scottish press.[65] The organization faded within a year perhaps because the Convention apparently acted on their concerns.

However, the first meeting of the Constitutional Convention on 30 March 1989 was dubbed 'mainly manly'. Only 23 women attended the first meeting of around 140 delegates from political parties, local authorities, trade unions, churches, business and industry, ethnic minorities and the Campaign for a Scottish Assembly.[66] The Convention unanimously acknowledged the sovereign right of the Scottish people to determine their own form of government and undertook to prepare a scheme for a Scottish Assembly or Parliament. Detailed work was carried out in a series of working groups. Criticism of the low numbers of women involved in the Convention led Labour women members to push for the creation of a Women's Issues working group to consider the question of making a Scottish Parliament truly representative. This ensured that the group chaired by Labour MP for Glasgow Maryhill, Maria Fyfe, focused in particular on the under-representation of women.

Several barriers to women taking an equal part in the process were identified in submissions to the group, in particular, domestic responsibility. Discrimination against women in party selection procedures was not cited as a barrier, however; the underlying assumption was that women were ruled out of consideration well before any selection meetings.[67] The interim report listed several proposals intended to boost women's representation. Submissions were unanimous in favouring office hours for parliament business and taking recesses in line with Scottish school holidays. There was a consensus that MSPs should hold their seat as a full-time salaried post, and that there should be office expenses along with a flexible system of child and carer allowances and crèche facilities. Fixed-term parliaments and the development of a committee structure to deal with the main business of a Scottish Parliament were recommended. Westminster was cited throughout as a powerful negative model.[68] Predictably, by far the most difficult area was that of electoral arrangements since the political parties had clear vested interests.

The Convention debate on women's political representation raised the question of quotas within the Labour party via the 50:50 option. Originally proposed by the Women's Committee of the Scottish Trades Union Congress (STUC), 50:50 simply held that half of the elected representatives should be men and half should be women. It was argued that the principle could apply under either a First-Past-the-Post (FPTP) or Proportional Representation (PR) electoral system as 'two categories of voting would still be applicable'.[69] At its 1990 Scottish conference, Labour ruled out FPTP for elections to a Scottish Parliament and decided that men and women should be equally represented in the chamber. Maria Fyfe said on her retirement in 2005 that her 'proudest political achievement' as an MP was involvement in 'the 50:50 campaign to ensure that the Scottish Parliament started life with an almost equal representation of women, up there with the Scandinavian countries.'[70] Meanwhile parallel developments within the Labour party aimed at boosting women's representation at Westminster. The 1994 party conference endorsed the policy of having 'women-only' shortlists in the next round of parliamentary selections in half of the non-Labour seats, a move now recognized as a key factor in the eventual return of an historic 120 women MPs, 101 of whom were Labour deputies, in 1997.[71]

CONCLUSION

This account of women in Scottish politics is necessarily brief and highly selective. Scotland had a marginally better record than the UK as a whole in returning women to the Commons and the lead extended into ministerial positions. Five of the 21 Scottish women MPs elected up to 1990 became government ministers, a high level given that only 36 women served as British ministers over the period. These included the Duchess of Atholl, the first Conservative female minister; Florence Horsbrugh; Margaret (Peggy) Herbison; Lady Tweedsmuir; and Judith Hart, whose ministerial career spanned nine years, including the cabinet appointment of Paymaster-General from 1968–9. However, the position deteriorated from 1979 and record numbers of Scottish women politicians seemed far away in 1990. In 1991, when there were only three Scottish women MPs, Isobel Lindsay summed it up tersely:

> The most striking feature of the position of women in Scottish politics is the significant lack of progress in the past fifty years. The evolutionary approach, based on the assumption that change would take place gradually and inevitably, was a plausible position in the early period after gaining formal electoral equality in 1928. By the 1980s . . . the supposed "march of progress" had been left somewhere near the starting line.[72]

Yet deterioration produced a determination to ensure that the uneven and highly fragile pattern of women's political representation at Westminster was not reproduced in a new Scottish Parliament. As recently as 2005, the Fawcett Society calculated that 'at the current rate of change it will take the Conservatives 400 years to achieve equal representation [in the House of Commons] . . . the Liberal Democrats . . . 40 years . . . [and] . . . the Labour party around 20 years.'[73] In this context, recent developments within the Scottish Parliament and Welsh Assembly are literally years ahead of predictions in relation to Westminster, and it should be acknowledged that over 1918–90, Scottish women endured a long, slow march.

NOTES

1   Margaret Bain, 'Scottish women in politics', *Chapman*, 27–8, (1980), p. 8. In 1888 as Chancellor, Goschen introduced a population percentage formula upon which government expenditure in Scotland was based, known since as the Goschen Formula.

2   See Catriona Burness, '"Kept some steps behind him": women in Scotland, 1780–1920', in Douglas Gifford and Dorothy McMillan (eds), *Scottish Women's Writing, Volume 1, 1780–1920* (Edinburgh: Edinburgh University Press, 1997), pp. 103–18; and Catriona Burness, 'The long slow march: Scottish women MPs', in Esther Breitenbach and Eleanor Gordon (eds), *Out of Bounds: Women in Scottish Society, 1800–1945* (Edinburgh: Edinburgh University Press, 1992), pp. 151–73.

3   See Catriona Burness, 'Strange Associations': The Irish Question and the Making of Scottish Unionism, 1886–1918 (East Linton: Tuckwell Press, 2003).
4   Scotsman, 9 and 30 December 1918.
5   Scotsman, 10 December 1918.
6   Scottish Liberal Federation (SLF), Vol. 2, 13 July 1923.
7   SLF, Executive Committee, 25 March and 24 April 1925.
8   SLF, Executive Committee, 31 March 1926.
9   Scotsman, 11 November 1922.
10 SLF, Vol. 2, Report for the Executive by Mr Webster on 1923 election, 19 December 1923.
11 Ibid.
12 SLF, Vol. 2, Central Organising Committee, 7 December 1928.
13 Scottish Unionist Association (SUA), Minute Book 1, 15 February 1918.
14 SUA Eastern Office, 26 July 1920.
15 SUA Eastern Office, 21 January 1920.
16 Gordon Brown, 'The Labour Party and political change in Scotland, 1918–29: the politics of five elections' (Unpublished PhD thesis, University of Edinburgh, 1982).
17 See Catriona Burness, 'Drunk women don't look at thistles: women and the SNP, 1934–94', in Scotlands, 1, (2), (1995), pp. 131–54, for a fuller discussion of the NPS and SNP early women's organization and activity.
18 The Scots Independent, April 1929, p. 72.
19 The Scots Independent, January 1929, p. 26.
20 The Scots Independent, October 1928, pp. 174–5.
21 The Scots Independent, August 1932, p. 152.
22 The Scots Independent, January 1930, p. 28.
23 Fred W. S. Craig, Minor Parties at British Parliamentary Elections, 1885–1974 (London: Macmillan, 1975).
24 Scottish Advisory Council of the Labour Party, Report of Second Annual Conference, 23 September 1916, pp. 6–7.
25 Elizabeth Vallance, Women in the House (London: Athlone, 1979), p. 27.
26 Jean Mann, Woman in Parliament (London: Odham, 1962), p. 10.
27 Jennie Lee, My Life with Nye (Harmondsworth: Penguin, 1981), p. 71.
28 Sheila Hetherington, Katharine Atholl, 1874–1960: Against the Tide (Aberdeen: Aberdeen University Press, 1989).
29 Ibid., p. 65.
30 Ibid., pp. 120–1.
31 Scotsman, 11 November 1935.
32 Sheila Hetherington, Katharine Atholl, p. 182.
33 Brian Harrison, 'Women in a men's house: the women MPs, 1919–45', in Historical Journal, 29, (3), (1986), pp. 623–54.
34 Scotsman, 23 November 1929.
35 Jennie Lee, My Life with Nye, p. 94.
36 Gordon Brown, Maxton (Glasgow: Fontana, 1988), p. 310.
37 The Women's Library, London Metropolitan University, 5 Campaigning Organizations, Appendix 5.1 (5BWW), essay on women's organizations, 'Central Women's Electoral Committee'.
38 Jean Mann, Woman in Parliament, p. 42.
39 Jennie Lee, My Life with Nye, p. 168.
40 Jean Mann, Woman in Parliament, pp. 17–18.

41　Ibid., p. 120.

42　Elizabeth Vallance, *Women in the House.*

43　SUA, Western Office, Minute Book 5, Women's Cmmt, 4 May 1938.

44　Keith Webb, *The Growth of Nationalism in Scotland* (Glasgow: Pelican, 1977), p. 99.

45　Harry Hanham, *Scottish Nationalism* (London: Faber, 1969), p. 204.

46　Ibid., p. 184.

47　Ibid., p. 182.

48　Interview with Winnie Ewing, 4 August 1993.

49　Interview with Margaret Ewing, 30 June 1993.

50　Interview with Winnie Ewing, 4 August 1993.

51　Roger Levy, *Scottish Nationalism at the Crossroads* (Edinburgh: Scottish Academic Press, 1990), discusses 'minor' and 'third' party status and the rise of the SNP to 'third' party status in the 1970s.

52　Interview with Winnie Ewing, 4 August 1993.

53　*Daily Telegraph*, 6 November 1967.

54　Keith Webb, *Nationalism in Scotland*, p. 101.

55　Interview with Winnie Ewing, 4 August 1993.

56　Interview with Margaret Ewing, 30 June 1993.

57　*Scotsman*, 5 June 1978.

58　*Daily Express*, 14 January 1976.

59　*Glasgow Herald*, 3 April 1978.

60　*Scotsman*, 5 June 1978.

61　*Scottish Daily News*, 14 May 1975.

62　Interview with Margaret Ewing, 30 June 1993.

63　Elizabeth Vallance, 'Two cheers for equality: women candidates in the 1987 general elections', in *Parliamentary Affairs*, 41, (1988), pp. 86–91.

64　Leaflet issued by 'A Scottish Women's Claim of Right', April 1989.

65　See Jackie Roddick, 'Women and voting systems', *Radical Scotland*, December 1989–January 1990.

66　Emma Simpson, "Mainly manly": the Scottish Constitutional Convention and the implications for women's representation' (Edinburgh University Politics Honours dissertation 1990).

67　See 'Women and a Scottish Parliament', in *Towards Scotland's Parliament, Consultation Document and Report to the Scottish People, Oct 1989* (Edinburgh: Scottish Constitutional Convention, 1989), pp. 85–103.

68　'Women and a Scottish Parliament'.

69　Ibid., p. 102.

70　See http://en.wikipedia.org/wiki/Maria_Fyfe (accessed 4 December 2009).

71　See Joni Lovenduski, 'Gender politics: a breakthrough for women?', in *Parliamentary Affairs*, 4, (1997), pp. 200–12.

72　Isobel Lindsay, 'Constitutional change and the gender deficit', in *A Woman's Claim of Right in Scotland: Women, Representation and Politics* (Edinburgh: Polygon, 1991), pp. 7–13 (p. 7).

73　See http://www.fawcettsociety.org.uk for documents on 'Women and the general election 2005', 'Women's representation in British politics', and a press release on the record number of women MPs.

5

Scottish women's organizations and the exercise of citizenship c. 1900–c. 1970[1]

Esther Breitenbach

By the late nineteenth century Scottish women had become increasingly active in charitable and philanthropic work, and had begun to gain access to public bodies at local level. They were becoming more active in the trade union movement and in labour movement organizations such as the Co-operative Women's Guild.[2] Women also played a leading role in the Scottish temperance movement, lobbying for restrictions on the availability of alcohol.[3] Women's role in the Presbyterian churches was afforded greater recognition through new forms of organization such as the Church of Scotland Woman's Guild, and through their contribution as missionaries, albeit within male-dominated structures of governance.[4] Thus by the time of partial enfranchisement in 1918, Scottish women were making their presence felt in public life in various ways. Because of women's low level of representation in formal political institutions, particularly as MPs, much previous historiography of twentieth-century Scottish politics has tended to ignore or underestimate women as political actors. Recent research, asking questions about the types of organization which women formed, their activities and objectives, has begun to fill this gap. A picture is emerging of continuing organization and action after enfranchisement, with new forms of organization arising to meet new circumstances, often with continuity of personnel from older organizations. Evidence remains somewhat fragmentary, however, with some notable gaps such as the period between the outbreak of the Second World War and the rise of the Women's Liberation Movement (WLM) in the early 1970s. This chapter focuses primarily on women's action and engagement in voluntary organizations before the rise of 'second wave' feminism, but also discusses briefly the women's suffrage movement and the growth of women's representation in local government. Women were more likely to be active at local level than in parliamentary politics, and it is also clear that there were links between women's organizations, political parties and political representatives.

THE WOMEN'S SUFFRAGE MOVEMENT

The women's suffrage movement in Scotland was initiated in 1867, when the Edinburgh National Society for Women's Suffrage was founded.[5] By the turn of

the century there were many locally based suffrage societies across Scotland affiliated to the National Union of Women's Suffrage Societies, and also a proliferation
of suffrage organizations with different support bases and positions. For example,
in 1902 the Glasgow and West of Scotland Association for Women's Suffrage was
formed, representing the movement's constitutionalist wing, while in subsequent
years militant organizations were also established in Scotland. The Pankhursts'
Women's Social and Political Union (WSPU), founded in 1903, established a
Glasgow branch in 1906, which had left-wing affiliations.[6] The WSPU in Scotland
had its own Scottish council, regarding itself as having some autonomy from
the parent organization, which provoked tensions with the Pankhursts.[7] The
creation of the Women's Freedom League (WFL) in 1907, by WSPU seceder
Theresa Billington-Greig and her supporters, led to WFL branches in Scotland,
with Glasgow and Edinburgh becoming prominent centres by 1909.[8] In 1912, the
WFL, following its summer campaign in Scotland, organized an Edinburgh to
London march culminating in a deputation to the Prime Minister.[9] The Scottish
Churches League for Woman Suffrage was founded the same year,[10] while the
following year the Northern Men's Federation for Women's Suffrage was set up.[11]
The year 1912 also ushered in the period of increasing WSPU militancy, and
Scotland as a Liberal stronghold became a particular focus for action.

This rising militancy ended with the outbreak of war in 1914. As elsewhere
in Britain, war divided opinion among suffrage supporters in Scotland. Some
suffrage organizations devoted themselves to the war effort, while others called
for peace, promoting peace organizations and demonstrations. Supporters of the
war effort often demonstrated an awareness of how support could further their
cause. Most notably Elsie Inglis' work in creating the Scottish Women's Hospitals
was explicitly aimed at strengthening the cause of votes for women as well as
fulfilling humanitarian aims.[12] There is evidence of continued campaigning for
the vote in Scotland during the war, for example by the WFL and Northern Men's
Federation, while local societies sent in resolutions and held demonstrations.[13]
With the enactment of the Representation of the People Act in February 1918,
many suffrage societies dissolved, while some transformed themselves into
organizations such as Women Citizens' Associations. Some organizations, such
as the WFL, continued to exist, campaigning in the 1920s for further extension
of the franchise.[14] Suffragettes had been concerned not only with the vote, but
also with issues such as low pay and working conditions, domestic violence and
prostitution, women's entry to higher education and medicine, among others,
and the pursuit of such objectives provided a basis for continuing organization.

By 1918 the women's suffrage movement in Scotland had existed continuously
since 1867, and had been articulated through a variety of organizational forms,
changing over time as women's demands became stronger and the wider political
context changed, most importantly the rise of organized labour and left-wing
parties. The mushrooming of new organizations and alliances in the 1890s
and 1900s indicates the growing support for women's enfranchisement, and is
also suggestive of the input of new generations of campaigners. In this context,

Elspeth King's comment that the Glasgow and West of Scotland Association for Women's Suffrage appeared to have little knowledge of the efforts of campaigners in the 1870s and 1880s is instructive, since it suggests that there was not a direct continuity in the membership of such organizations either through individuals or through inter-generational links.[15] It is also clear, that while the demand for the vote united many women, and attracted male supporters, divisions remained over tactics. Furthermore, while the movement gained widespread support, it also provoked organized opposition, such as the Scottish National Anti-Suffrage League which was established in 1910 and had its women supporters.[16] Indeed, it is an irony of history that the Duchess of Atholl, prominent in anti-suffrage circles, was to become Scotland's first woman MP.

LOCAL GOVERNMENT[17]

Opportunities for women to seek public office had arisen with the creation of school boards by the 1872 Education (Scotland) Act,[18] and were extended in the 1880s and 1890s at local government level. Women ratepayers were granted burgh enfranchisement in 1881, were allowed to vote but not stand for county councils in 1889, and in 1894 received the right both to vote and stand for parish councils.[19] By 1896 there were 76 women school board members across Scotland. Those who stood often had backgrounds in philanthropic or women's movement organizations, and were sometimes backed by the latter, for example, Edinburgh and Glasgow Associations for Promoting Lady Candidates at School Board and Parochial Elections. In 1918 school boards were replaced by education authorities, on which women continued to serve.[20] In 1929 local government reorganization led to education authorities' functions being transferred to local authorities. Some women from education authorities were co-opted onto education commit-tees of local councils,[21] many of which stipulated that education committees must have some women members, while others stood for election as councillors in succeeding years.[22] In some cases a school board background formed the basis for a longstanding political career, for example that of Labour Party activist, Clarice McNab (later Clarice McNab Shaw), who served successively on school board, town and county councils, before being elected MP for Kilmarnock in 1945 (unfortunately she was prevented by illness from taking up her seat).[23] Similarly, Minna Cowan was elected in 1914 to the Edinburgh School Board, served on the succeeding education authority and was co-opted as a member of the Education Committee after the 1929 reforms. An active Conservative Party member, she stood as a Unionist candidate in 1929 and 1935,[24] and though not elected, was highly regarded by the Scottish Unionist Association as a speaker and well-known political figure. The Duchess of Atholl, too, prior to her election as MP, had served on the education authority in Perthshire.

    Research on the history of local government in Scotland is very limited in gen-eral, with women's role in particular being neglected. Recent research by Kenneth Baxter on the period between 1918 and 1955 has made an important contribution and indicates that women became established in municipal politics after 1918, particularly in the cities.[25] Before 1918, while there are no comprehensive data, there are examples of women councillors on parish and town councils. Edinburgh Parish Council had three women members by 1888,[26] Mary Lily Walker and Agnes Husband were the first women elected to Dundee Parish Council in 1902, and Lavinia Malcolm of Dollar was the first woman elected to a town council in Scotland in 1907. Malcolm became Scotland's first woman provost in 1913.[27] Clarice McNab was elected to Leith Town Council in 1913, the first Labour town council member in Scotland.[28] There were, however, few other women burgh councillors before 1918.

After 1918 the number of women councillors on burgh and county councils increased, and after 1919 women began to be elected to the four major city councils of Edinburgh, Glasgow, Aberdeen and Dundee, most notably the first two.[29] In 1919 Ella Morison Millar became the first woman city councillor in Scotland following her election to the Morningside ward of Edinburgh, subsequently serving on the council until 1949. By 1937 Edinburgh city council had 11 women councillors. Glasgow acquired its first women councillors in 1920 when five women were elected. By 1945 Glasgow had 11 women councillors, 12.3 per cent of elected councillors. In Aberdeen no woman was elected until 1930, when Isabella Burgess succeeded, though there had been women candidates in most previous elections. In Dundee the first woman councillor, Lily Miller, was elected in 1935, though women had stood in previous years, including Miller. Women councillors thus became an established part of the municipal scene, though numbers were relatively small.[30] Co-options during the Second World War, when no elections were held, increased the number of women councillors. However, women's increasing involvement in city councils seems to have halted by the mid-1950s. As with the cities, levels of women's representation on burgh and county councils varied greatly. Women councillors began appearing on councils in towns like Greenock, Clydebank and Perth around 1919, while other small town councils had no women councillors until well after the Second World War. There were very few women county councillors before the 1930s, though by the 1940s most counties had one or two.

Local party politics were complex, and did not directly reflect strategies at parliamentary constituency level. For example, the Liberal Party and the Unionist Party did not officially field local candidates, but operated through centre-right alliances of 'Moderates' or 'Progressives'. These alliances came to be dominated by the Unionist Party, as Liberal Party fortunes declined. At the same time, Labour Party support increased, particularly in Glasgow and the West of Scotland. The Labour Party fielded the most women candidates in each of the four cities in the period between 1918 and the mid-1950s, though not always in winnable seats. Depending on the local political scene, however, other parties could fare better – in Edinburgh, for example, the majority of women councillors were Moderates/ Progressives. A feature of local politics in both Edinburgh and Glasgow in the 1930s was the brief rise and fall of Protestant parties: Protestant Action in

Edinburgh and the Scottish Protestant League in Glasgow.[31] These parties were militantly anti-Catholic, fielded high proportions of women candidates and also drew much of their support from women.

Before 1914 many women who stood for public office were connected to the women's suffrage movement and other women's organizations, some of which were specifically established to support women candidates. After 1918 women's organizations also continued to support women candidates, but party affiliation became more significant. Baxter argues that 1918 signalled a significant increase in women's participation in local government. One contributory factor was the impact of enfranchisement, which energized women to exercise their new rights of citizenship, whether through feminist organizations or political parties. However, previous experience of women's movement organizations and/or public service continued to characterize women candidates for local councils. Even in the 1940s women with previous service on parish councils and education authorities (where women's levels of representation were higher than on city, burgh, or county councils) continued to come forward as candidates. The generation of the 1950s, however, had not had a comparable training ground available to them, which Baxter suggests may help to explain the relative decline in numbers of women councillors by the mid-1950s.[32] Typically, women candidates and councillors had experience in education, social welfare and maternal and child health, and existing evidence, though limited, suggests that these continued to be major concerns of women as elected representatives. In the inter-war years these concerns tallied closely with the dominant concerns of Scottish politics – housing, unemployment, welfare and health.

WOMEN'S ORGANIZATIONS AND PROMOTION OF CITIZENSHIP

A new type of organization established by middle-class women was the Women Citizens' Association (WCA). Inaugurated in 1918, WCAs arose directly from the women's suffrage movement.[33] The Edinburgh Women Citizens' Association (EWCA), for example, had as its formal objects citizenship education, women's representation, and reforms necessary to secure 'a real equality of liberties, status and opportunities between men and women'.[34] The EWCA pressed for enfranchisement of women on the same basis as men, lobbied on legislation, and supported local actions. They followed the methods of the constitutional suffrage societies – petitions, letters to the press, deputations, and public meetings – and worked with sympathetic MPs to put forward Parliamentary Questions and Private Members' Bills. Membership was dominated by middle-class professional women and the wives of businessmen, professors, senior journalists, and so on, although the EWCA made attempts to attract working-class members. Overlapping memberships created a network of organizational links between, for example, local women's and children's welfare bodies, the National Union of Societies for Equal Citizenship, the WFL, the Women's Peace Crusade, Scottish

Co-operative Women's Guild (SCWG), and the International Council of Women, among others. A Scottish network, the Scottish Council of Women Citizens' Associations, was formed in 1919 (existing until 1990).[35] Key issues on which they focused were education, social work, public health and local government. WCAs throughout Scotland supported members who stood as councillors.

Browne argues that there was a flourishing women's associational culture in the inter-war years, including the above organizations and others such as the Scottish Women's Rural Institute (founded in 1917) and the Business and Professional Women's Federation (founded in 1938).[36] Welfare issues, such as maternal and child health were prominent concerns, though issues such as leisure and crime also attracted attention. The Arbroath WCA contributed to a case study for the 'Women's Health Enquiry', which resulted in Margery Spring Rice's book, *Working Class Wives* (1939).[37] Wright similarly describes an active network of women's organizations functioning across urban Scotland in the post-1918 period, with the EWCA and Glasgow Society for Equal Citizenship (GSEC) as influential members.[38] Through non-party organizations, the middle-class EWCA had links to the Unionist Party and the Liberal Party, while a split between middle-class Moderates and socialists within the GSEC developed in the 1920s.[39] Housing policy, views on the position of married women, and state support through family endowments and nursery provision seemed in particular to cause differences of opinion, though this did not preclude contact with organizations such as the SCWG. The Dundee Women Citizens' Association (DWCA), active in the inter-war years, actively supported the election of women candidates to education authorities and the town council.[40] As temperance supporters, the DWCA no doubt contributed to Prohibitionist Edwin Scrymgeour's by-election victory of 1922. While membership declined in the 1930s, the war seems to have led to a revival, with the DWCA actively supporting the war effort and investigating social conditions in the city. Indeed a Standing Conference of Dundee Women's Associations was established in 1944, although the post-war years were to witness decline in DWCA membership.

Another women's organization whose formation was influenced by the suffrage movement was the Scottish Women's Rural Institute (SWRI). Catherine Blair, an active supporter of women's suffrage, began urging the creation of women's institutes in 1916, based on the Canadian model of Women's Institutes (WIs), founded in 1897.[41] The creation of WIs was promoted as a means of harnessing the energies of women in agricultural communities to support the war effort, and to address anxieties about food supplies that arose from war-time conditions. The first local institute was established in 1917, and thereafter many were established across Scotland, subsequently forming themselves into regional federations. The WIs aimed to fulfil both educational and social functions, as well as being concerned with domestic economy, and their activities reflected this mix of aims. Blair's account emphasized that education in citizenship was an essential aim of the organization, and she called on WIs to lobby the government with other women's organizations, Townswomen's Guilds and Women Citizens'

Unions. Her vision of the role of the SWRI was not universally shared, however, and it is not clear to what extent her account presents an accurate picture of the WIs and their ethos.[42]

RELIGIOUS AND PHILANTHROPIC ORGANIZATIONS

Women were also motivated by religious and moral beliefs to actively participate in organizations and campaigns. The temperance movement, which by the late nineteenth century had become a popular movement in Scotland, represents a prominent example. A well-established women's organization, the British Women's Temperance Association Scottish Christian Union (SCU), functioned as part of both a British and an international movement. As Smitley has demonstrated, the SCU had overlapping membership with suffrage organizations and supported women's suffrage.[43] It actively encouraged women to vote in local polls on licensing, following the Temperance (Scotland) Act 1913 and the Temperance Poll Act 1920.[44] Though the success of campaigns was limited, the temperance movement notably helped secure the election in Dundee of Prohibition Party MP, Edwin Scrymgeour, with women's votes being deemed influential.[45] In this period temperance organizations, such as the Band of Hope, continued to flourish, as much for the social and leisure opportunities they provided as for any commitment to the principle of temperance.[46] Women's involvement in temperance campaigns was premised on a view of their qualities as guardians of morality and purity, which, while facilitating active citizenship, did not challenge the prevailing domestic ideology.

Women's concerns about the regulation of morality were also evident in other organizations and campaigns. Some of these were mixed-sex organizations, in which women, including feminists, played a prominent role. For example, the National Vigilance Association established a Glasgow branch in 1910 and an Edinburgh-based East of Scotland branch in 1911.[47] The latter, supported by prominent feminists, Frances Balfour and Elsie Inglis, was concerned with the promotion of 'social hygiene'. This included campaigns around the regulation of prostitution, vigilance work in patrolling streets, parks, stations and docks, campaigns to restrict the sale of 'rubber goods', and for the appointment of women police. Child sexual abuse was an issue that also began to emerge in the inter-war years. 'Lady child-savers', working in Magdalene Institutions, the Scottish National Society for the Prevention of Cruelty to Children and the Young Women's Christian Association (YWCA), brought to light cases of incest and sexual abuse.[48] Evidence of such abuse was brought to the Committee on Sexual Offences against Children and Young Persons in Scotland in 1924–5,[49] and there was a campaign to amend the law. Feminist organizations, including the EWCA and the GSEC, were active in this campaign. Such organizations also pressed for the appointment of policewomen to investigate child sexual assault cases. By the mid-1920s female officers were sometimes involved in such cases,[50] though campaigns for women police continued until the 1940s.[51] That many victims of abuse were infected with venereal disease (VD) was a cause for concern, while the spread of VD linked to prostitution prompted attempts at regulation, resulting from time to time in vigorous campaigns.[52] Professional women in medicine and philanthropic work played an important part in alerting courts and policy-makers to such problems. These examples suggest that women found many ways to exercise their rights of citizenship in the inter-war years, but also that middle-class feminism could be wedded to ideologies of social control and moral regulation, which were tinged with eugenicist beliefs.

Women continued to play an active role in churches and church organizations throughout the twentieth century. Mass membership organizations such as the Church of Scotland Woman's Guild suffered a declining membership with growing secularization, but also witnessed a transformation as the impact of feminist ideas made itself felt. Until the 1950s, however, women's attendance at church and membership of church organizations remained substantial.[53] Such organizations provided social and leisure activities for women, as well as vehicles for charitable and philanthropic work and for the expression of interest in social issues. This included support for welfare provision such as the work of health visitors attached to the Church of Scotland Deaconess Hospital, involvement in university settlement and home mission schemes, and support for issues such as temperance, maternal and child welfare services, and encouragement of women's contribution to the war effort in both world wars.[54] It remains unclear, however, to what extent the concerns of women churchgoers or Guild members translated into representations to government bodies. Women's role within the Church of Scotland was enhanced with their admission to eldership in 1966 and with the ordination of the first woman minister, Catherine McConnachie, in 1969.[55] In 1970 the President of the Woman's Guild, Elizabeth Anderson, was invited to join the Women's National Commission, established in 1969 by the Wilson government.[56] The presidency of Maidie Hart from 1972–5 saw the development of a Christian feminist perspective and in 1977 Hart was a founder of the Scottish Convention of Women,[57] which was to play an active role in the women's movement in Scotland until the 1990s.[58]

THE SCOTTISH CO-OPERATIVE WOMEN'S GUILD

The Scottish Co-operative Women's Guild (SCWG), established in 1892, had as its primary objectives the promotion of the principles and ideals of co-operation among women and the training of women 'to take their place in the home, in the social circle and in the Co-operative Society'.[59] In the early twentieth century it extended its activities, affiliated to the Labour Party, and campaigned vigorously in the 1910 election. This politicization was accompanied by a commitment to Sabbatarianism, and a belief that crime and poverty were the result of intemperance. 'Guildswomen were encouraged to "acquaint themselves with social questions such as housing of the poor and the drink question".[60] Additionally, the SCWG campaigned on issues such as the medical inspection of schoolchildren, school meals, and minimum wages for Co-operative employees. As well as supporting the extension of the franchise, the SCWG developed its members' organizational skills, for example, through public speaking classes. The impact of this was felt in the 1915 rent strike, which apparently began when members of the Kinning Park Co-operative Society decided to withhold demanded rent increases.[61]

The noticeable shift of emphasis in the SCWG toward wider political and social questions suggests a growing divergence between middle-class and working-class organizations, with housing becoming a major source of division. Housing conditions were a particularly significant issue in Dundee and Glasgow, and in Glasgow had become the major political issue by 1915. This period witnessed greater involvement by women in agitation over housing, with the most celebrated instance being the 1915 Glasgow Rent Strike, in which the Glasgow Women's Housing Association became the organizing force.[62] In response to the Rent Strike, the Rent Restriction Act 1915 was passed, ushering in successive Acts controlling rents which were to effectively remain in place until the 1970s. Further, less spectacular, rent strike action occurred in Clydebank in the 1920s, with women again playing a crucial role.[63] Further evidence of the SCWG's radicalism was its raising of the issue of birth control, to the displeasure of the leading men in the Labour Party.[64] It is not clear to what extent the SCWG sustained a radical perspective, though its close relationship to the Labour Party was to produce tensions with some of the SCWG's most active members, when, following the Second World War, Communist Party members were proscribed from holding office in the SCWG.[65]

The SCWG was a mass-membership organization, which grew from around 1,500 members in the early 1890s to over 10,000 by 1910. While there were some fluctuations over time, in particular with the two wars causing a temporary dip in membership, this was approaching 30,000 in the inter-war years, reaching a peak of just over 43,000 in 1947–8.[66] War-time rationing strengthened the movement temporarily, but thereafter numbers continued to decline. The SCWG maintained a continuing interest in citizenship and representation,[67] though few women were elected to senior positions in the co-operative movement itself.

TRADE UNIONS

Trade union organization among women increased in the late nineteenth century, manifested through their membership of organizations such as the Women's Protective and Provident League (WPPL), the Scottish Council for Women's Trades (SCWT), trades councils and the Scottish Trades Union Congress (STUC).[68] At this time, the WPPL and SCWT drew together voluntary and philanthropic groups concerned with the working conditions of women, particularly in the 'sweated' trades, and members included representatives from academic institutions, church and voluntary organizations.[69] However, in the years before the First World War, the National Federation of Women Workers (NFWW), closely allied to the Labour Party, became the focus of women's unionism in Scotland. The early 1920s saw a shift away from separate women's trade union organization. The NFWW (which operated throughout Britain) by 1921 was amalgamated with the General and Municipal Workers' Union, and there is evidence that subsequently trade unions were urged to accept women members on equal terms, for example, as put forward in a resolution by Glasgow Trades Council in 1925.[70] The 1920s depression reduced women's trade union membership, due to unemployment. The STUC responded to the decline of women's membership by inaugurating a Women's Conference, first held in 1926, and the following year an Organization of Women Committee was set up, initially chaired by a man appointed by the STUC, though after 1933 both positions of chair and secretary to the Committee were taken up by women.

The STUC conducted a number of surveys of female trade union membership in this period, and made efforts to organize and educate women. In 1924 the trade union density of women workers was 12 per cent, and women constituted 24.2 per cent of STUC membership. By 1931 this had declined to a density of 7.2 per cent, with women constituting 19.7 per cent of STUC membership. In 1939, 8.5 per cent of women workers were unionized, making up only 14.2 per cent of STUC members.[71] The STUC Organization of Women Committee attempted to build a stronger relationship with a range of organizations, such as the Labour Party and the SCWG, and also made contact with organizations such as the YWCA, British Temperance Association and Church Guilds. It also attempted to set up local Trade Union Women's Groups, with some success.[72] As well as educating women about current social and political issues, such groups encouraged women to improve public speaking and communication skills. Numbers, however, were small and groups had difficulty maintaining themselves. Furthermore, despite its efforts to build links, the STUC Women's Committee did not always get support from trade unions, trades councils, or local Co-op Women's Guilds branches. However, the Women's Committee's practice of working jointly with other women's organizations, 'this shrewdly nurtured talent for making common cause', has been judged a major contribution to the STUC.[73] This capacity to facilitate alliances was again in evidence in the campaign for the Scottish Parliament and for equal representation.[74]

The Second World War had an impact on women's unionization, unlikely to have been sustained in the post-war years as men returned home and many women left paid employment. The war also witnessed action on equal pay. According to Arnot, in the inter-war years there was little support for equal pay for working-class women and much sympathy for male demands for a family wage, with women's work often regarded as only a temporary phase preceding marriage.[75] Nonetheless, women sometimes advanced this demand and were involved in many strikes, though not always union members and not always supported by unions or male colleagues. Women's war-time entry into work such as engineering facilitated organization around equal pay and other demands. For example, Agnes McLean, trade union and political activist, led a brief equal pay strike in 1941 at the Hillington Rolls Royce plant near Glasgow, and led a further strike in 1943.[76] As early as 1952 McLean succeeded in negotiating an agreement on equal pay at Rolls Royce.[77] McLean continued to actively promote equal pay, as a member of a women's committee on this issue in Hillington factories in 1968, at a series of trade council meetings held across Scotland in the same year,[78] and in supporting equal pay resolutions at the STUC.[79] Whether there was wider action across Scotland over equal pay remains a matter for research.

CONCLUSION

Evidence of women's activity in organizations in Scotland and of their attempts to influence policy-making from local to national level during the twentieth century remains fragmentary. Recent research has made an important contribution to filling some gaps, particularly in the inter-war years. But the war years, 1914–18 and 1939–45, and the post-war years between 1945 and the late 1960s remain much in need of investigation. It has become a cliché within British historiography that the world wars witnessed shifts in women's role and status in society, due largely to paid employment in non-traditional jobs during the wars. This contributed to changing expectations, as well as facilitating the organization of women workers and the articulation of demands as workers. But it is only part of the story. Suffragists did not stop lobbying for the right to vote during the First World War, while new organizations emerged both before and after the war. Central to these organizations' ethos was the aim of extending women's role as citizens, whether within the SWRI or WCAs, and the claim to citizenship was itself validated by participation in the war effort, which in turn gave women confidence to make claims for greater equality. This experience was multi-faceted and affected different groups of women in different ways, which merit more in-depth investigation. Similarly, in the Second World War, women's lives changed not only through participation in paid work, but through their greater involvement in representative bodies such as councils, and on the various committees created to control and oversee administration during the war.

Less clear are the continuities between war-time and peace-time experience after the Second World War, with only hints of change in 1950s and 1960s Scotland. There was an apparent stasis by the mid-1950s with regard to women's representation on local councils, and decline in memberships of what had previously been mass women's organizations, such as the Church of Scotland Woman's Guild and the SCWG. K. M. Callen's slim history of the SCWG, published in 1952, noted that 'There are a large number of rival women's organisations which have been formed in recent years', but does not indicate what these were.[80] Rafeek notes that women members of the Communist Party were active in various organizations and campaigns in the 1950s and 1960s, including 'the women's assembly – a broad-based national body'.[81] However, no indication is given as to the membership of this body. Similarly, he notes Communist Party women's involvement in campaigns on health, childcare and nursery schools in the 1950s, and in the mid-1960s in campaigns for cervical screening. The latter seems to have been genuinely broad-based, and was UK-wide, involving Women's Co-operative Guilds, the WLF, the Labour Party and the TUC, while groups such as the Dundee Business and Professional Women's Association also actively supported the campaign.[82]

The emphasis of some women's organizations on the domestic role of married women and on women as mothers appears to have become less appealing in this period, when more women participated in the labour market, including married women. It also coincided with the increasing participation of women in higher education, though women remained a small proportion of the student body at this time, and with a reorientation of women in terms of aspirations for work and careers. Also, reproductive rights emerged publicly and controversially as a major issue for women. To what extent older women's organizations adapted to this changing context requires further investigation, but there seems to have been a significant disjuncture between their activities and the new WLM groups, started spontaneously by a largely younger generation of women. It took some time for organizational links and alliances to develop between these different generations of organizations.

While evidence of women's organizations' activities, their engagement with the state, and influence on policies at local and national level remains fragmentary, some tentative conclusions may be advanced. The relationship between women's organizations and political parties appears to have been crucial in determining their scope for action and their effectiveness. Relationships between women's organizations have also been a crucial factor in the capacity for mobilization around issues relevant to gender equality and women's welfare. Mass mobilizations, such as that around women's suffrage, have been rare, and indeed women's organizations have often been divided and fragmented according to class differences, differences in moral values, differences of marital status, and differences between urban and rural interests. Women's organizations have had a continuing commitment to actively exercising their rights as citizens and to increasing their representation in public and political life, though these objectives have been pursued more energetically at some times than at others. There has been much more diversity of opinion, however, about the purposes for which such rights should be exercised, and disagreement about how women's role in society should be defined.

NOTES

1   I am grateful to Kenneth Baxter, Sarah Browne and Valerie Wright for their comments on an earlier draft of this chapter.

2   Eleanor Gordon, *Women and the Labour Movement in Scotland 1850–1914* (Oxford: Clarendon, 1991).

3   Megan Smitley, '"Woman's mission": the temperance and women's suffrage movements in Scotland, c. 1870–1914' (Unpublished PhD thesis, University of Glasgow, 2005).

4   Lesley Orr Macdonald, *A Unique and Glorious Mission: Women and Presbyterianism in Scotland 1830–1930* (Edinburgh: John Donald, 2000).

5   Leah Leneman, *A Guid Cause: The Women's Suffrage Movement in Scotland* (Aberdeen: Aberdeen University Press, 1991).

6   J. J. Smyth, *Labour in Glasgow 1896–1936: Socialism, Suffrage and Sectarianism* (East Linton: Tuckwell, 2000).

7   See Elspeth King, 'The Scottish Women's Suffrage Movement', in Esther Breitenbach and Eleanor Gordon (eds), *Out of Bounds: Women in Scottish Society* (Edinburgh: Edinburgh University Press, 1992), pp. 121–50.

8   King, 'The Scottish Women's Suffrage Movement'.

9   King, 'The Scottish Women's Suffrage Movement'.

10 Macdonald, *A Unique and Glorious Mission*.

11 Leneman, *Guid Cause*.

12 Leneman, *Guid Cause*.

13 Leneman, *Guid Cause*.

14 Leneman, *Guid Cause*.

15 King, 'The Scottish Women's Suffrage Movement'.

16 Leneman, *Guid Cause*.

17 The section which follows draws extensively on recent doctoral research by Kenneth Baxter, to whom I am very grateful for giving me access to his thesis. Kenneth Baxter, 'Estimable and gifted'?: women in party politics in Scotland c. 1918–1955' (Unpublished PhD thesis, University of Dundee, 2008).

18 Jane McDermid, 'School board women and active citizenship in Scotland, 1873–1919', in *History of Education*, 38, (3), (2009), pp. 333–48.

19 Sue Innes and Jane Rendall, 'Women, gender and politics', in Lynn Abrams, Eleanor Gordon, Deborah Simonton and Eileen Janes Yeo (eds), *Gender in Scottish History since 1700* (Edinburgh: Edinburgh University Press, 2006), pp. 43–83.

20 Kenneth Baxter, 'Women in party politics in Scotland'.

21 McDermid, 'School board women'.

22 Baxter, 'Women in party politics in Scotland'.

23 Ewan, Elizabeth, Sue Innes, Sian Reynolds and Rose Pipes (eds), *The Biographical Dictionary of Scottish Women* (Edinburgh: Edinburgh University Press, 2006). Hereafter cited as 'Ewan *et al.*, *BDSW*'.

24 Entry by Sue Innes in *Oxford Dictionary of National Biography Online* (http://www.oxforddnb.com), accessed 9 June 2009.

25 Baxter, 'Women in party politics in Scotland'.

26 Baxter, 'Women in party politics in Scotland'.

27 Innes and Rendall, 'Women, gender and politics'; Ewan *et al.*, *BDSW*.

28 Ewan *et al.*, *BDSW*.

29 Baxter, 'Women in party politics in Scotland'.

30 Baxter, 'Women in party politics in Scotland'.

31 Baxter, 'Women in party politics in Scotland'.

32 Baxter, 'Women in party politics in Scotland'.

33 For accounts of Women Citizens' Associations, see Sue Innes, 'Love and work: feminism, family and ideas of equality and citizenship, Britain 1900–1939' (Unpublished PhD thesis, University of Edinburgh, 1998); Sue Innes, 'Constructing women's citizenship in the inter-war period: the Edinburgh Women Citizens' Association', in *Women's History Review*, 13,

(4), (2004), pp. 621–47; and Sarah Browne, *Making the Vote Count: The Arbroath Women Citizens' Association 1931–1945* (Dundee: Abertay Historical Society, 2007).

34 Innes, 'Love and work', p. 161.
35 Innes, 'Love and work'; Browne, *Making the Vote Count*.
36 Browne, *Making the Vote Count*.
37 Margery Spring Rice, *Working Class Wives: Their Health and Conditions* (Harmondsworth: Penguin, 1939).
38 Valerie Wright, 'Education for active citizenship: women's organisations in interwar Scotland', in *History of Education*, 38, (3), (2009), pp. 419–36.
39 Annmarie Hughes, 'Fragmented feminists? The influence of class and political identity in relations between the Glasgow and West of Scotland Suffrage Society and the Independent Labour Party in the west of Scotland, c. 1919–1932', in *Women's History Review*, 14, (1), 2005, pp. 7–31.
40 Sarah Browne and Jim Tomlinson, 'Dundee: a "Women's Town"?', unpublished conference paper.
41 Catherine Blair, *Rural Journey: A History of the SWRI from Cradle to Majority* (London and Edinburgh: Thomas Nelson and Sons, 1940).
42 Recent, but as yet unpublished, research should shed light on this question. See Valerie Wright, 'Women's organisations and feminism in interwar Scotland' (Unpublished PhD thesis, University of Glasgow, 2008).
43 Smitley, '"Woman's Mission"'.
44 Macdonald, *A Unique and Glorious Mission*.
45 Graham Smith, 'The making of a woman's town: household and gender in Dundee 1890–1940' (Unpublished PhD thesis, University of Stirling, 1996).
46 Callum Brown and Jayne Stephenson, '"Sprouting Wings?" Women and religion in Scotland c. 1850–1950', in Breitenbach and Gordon (eds), *Out of Bounds*, pp. 95–120.
47 Vivienne Cree, *From Public Streets to Private Lives: The Changing Task of Social Work* (Aldershot: Avebury, 1995).
48 Linda Mahood and Barbara Littlewood, 'The "vicious" girl and the "street-corner" boy: sexuality and the gendered delinquent in the Scottish child-saving movement, 1850–1940', in *Journal of the History of Sexuality*, 4, (4), (1994), pp. 549–78.
49 See Roger Davidson, '"This pernicious delusion": law, medicine, and child sexual abuse in early-twentieth-century Scotland', in *Journal of the History of Sexuality*, 10, (1), (2001), pp. 62–77.
50 Davidson, 'Law, medicine and child sexual abuse'.
51 Cree, *From Public Streets to Private Lives*.
52 Roger Davidson, *Dangerous Liaisons: A Social History of Venereal Disease in Twentieth-century Scotland* (Amsterdam: Rodopi, 2000).
53 See Callum Brown, *Religion and Society in Scotland since 1707* (Edinburgh: Edinburgh University Press, 1997).
54 Mamie Magnusson, *Out of Silence: Church of Scotland Woman's Guild, 1887–1987* (Edinburgh: The Saint Andrew Press, 1987).
55 Magnusson, *Out of Silence*.
56 Magnusson, *Out of Silence*.
57 Magnusson, *Out of Silence*.
58 See the chapter by Breitenbach and Mackay in this volume.
59 Gordon, *Women and the Labour Movement*, p. 266.
60 Ibid., p. 267.

61 Gordon, *Women and the Labour Movement*.
62 James J. Smyth, 'Rents, peace, votes: working-class women and political activity in the First World War', in Breitenbach and Gordon (eds), *Out of Bounds*, pp. 174–96.
63 See Sean Damer, *Rent Strike!: The Clydebank Rent Strike of the 1920s* (Clydebank, 1982).
64 See J. J. Smyth, *Labour in Glasgow*; Elspeth King, *The Thenew Factor: The Hidden History of Glasgow's Women* (Edinburgh and London: Mainstream, 1993); Annmarie Hughes, '"The politics of the kitchen" and the dissenting domestics: the ILP, labour women, and the female "citizens" of inter-war Clydeside', in *Scottish Labour History Society Journal*, 34, (2002), pp. 34–51.
65 Neil Rafeek, *Communist Women in Scotland* (London: Tauris, 2008).
66 K. M. Callen, *History of the Scottish Co-operative Women's Guild: Diamond Jubilee, 1892–1952* (Scottish Co-operative Wholesale Society, 1952).
67 Callen, *Scottish Co-operative Women's Guild*.
68 See Sheila Lewenhak, *Women and Trade Unions* (London and Tonbridge: Ernest Benn, 1977); Esther Breitenbach, *Women Workers in Scotland* (Glasgow: Pressgang, 1982); Gordon, *Women and the Labour Movement*.
69 See Gordon, *Women and the Labour Movement*.
70 See Lewenhak, *Women and Trade Unions*.
71 For the STUC's work on organization of women in this period, see Julie Arnot, 'Women workers and trade union participation in Scotland 1919–1939' (Unpublished PhD thesis, University of Glasgow, 1999).
72 Arnot, 'Women workers and trade union participation', p. 153.
73 Keith Aitken, *The Bairns O' Adam* (Edinburgh: Polygon, 1997), pp. 132–3.
74 See the chapter by Breitenbach and Mackay in this volume.
75 Arnot, 'Women workers and trade union participation'.
76 McLean was an active trade unionist for many years, and a member of the Communist Party from the 1940s to the 1960s. She joined the Labour Party in 1969, and served as a councillor on Glasgow District and Strathclyde Regional Councils. See entry on Agnes McLean by Neil Rafeek in Ewan *et al.*, *BDSW*, p. 236.
77 Neil Rafeek, *Communist Women*.
78 Entry on Agnes McLean by Neil Rafeek in Ewan *et al.*, *BDSW*, p. 236; Rafeek, *Communist Women*.
79 Angela Tuckett, *The STUC: The First Eighty Years, 1897–1977* (Edinburgh: Mainstream, 1986).
80 Callen, *Scottish Co-operative Women's Guild*, p. 20.
81 Rafeek, *Communist Women*, p. 95.
82 Browne and Tomlinson, 'Dundee: a "women's town"?'.

6

The 'women element in politics': Irish women and the vote, 1918–2008

Mary E. Daly

In recent decades Ireland[1] has been transformed from a social and economic backwater into one of the most rapidly changing countries in Europe, and women have benefited enormously from this transformation. In 2007 just under 50 per cent of women were in paid work, compared with 21 per cent in 1988. The majority of recent medical and law graduates are women and women have made significant inroads in the professions, business, public service and academia, though they continue to be under-represented in senior positions. Three of the 15-member Cabinet appointed in 2008 were women, one as Tanaiste (Deputy Prime Minister), the second woman to hold that position.[2] Since 1990 Ireland has elected two women as President (head of state). A woman has served as leader of a political party, albeit a small one. Other indicators are less favourable: only two of the 20 junior ministers at the time of writing in 2009 – a pointer to the next generation of cabinet ministers – were women. Irish women have made little progress in parliamentary elections since the early 1990s, despite dramatic economic and social change. The 2007 general election returned 20 women (12 per cent of deputies) to Dáil Éireann (the parliamentary lower house), the same number as in 1992 and 1997, and two fewer than 2002.[3] In 1999 Galligan and Wilford concluded that 'having made modest progress during the 1980s', women's representation had plateaued by 1997.[4] This verdict would appear to have been confirmed by two subsequent general elections.

Ireland has been declining in global rankings for female parliamentary representation for several years: in 2000 Ireland ranked forty-third;[5] in 2006 Ireland was seventy-eighth of 188 countries,[6] and eighty-fifth out of 187 countries in 2009.[7] A study of changing gender political representation classified Ireland among the countries where women have made 'small gains'.[8] The 1997 UK general election saw a near doubling in the proportion of women MPs – from 9.5 to 17.2 per cent. In Spain the proportion of women elected to parliament rose from 21.6 per cent in 1999 to 36 per cent in 2004.[9] A majority of the 2008 Spanish Cabinet were women. The comparison with Spain is interesting in that Ireland and Spain were traditionally regarded as conservative, Catholic states. Catholicism no longer holds sway in contemporary Ireland: church attendance has fallen significantly, so religion does not account for the low rate of female representation. We must look for other explanations.

This chapter is divided into four sections. The first three are historical, taking the story from the nineteenth century until the present. The closing section reflects on the nature of Irish political parties and the electoral system, and their impact on women candidates.

BEFORE THE VOTE

Ireland was a pioneer in mass politics, despite being poor, agrarian, Catholic and governed by another country. Daniel O'Connell's campaigns for Catholic emancipation (successful) and repeal of the union (unsuccessful) bear comparison with Andrew Jackson's US Democratic Party in their mass appeal. The Home Rule party of the 1880s, with its party pledge, payment of MPs, and network of local branches was another precocious development that served to further politicize the Irish public. At a time when the electorate was restricted by gender and property requirements, Irish elections saw significant participation by non-voters. Hoppen has identified several women who achieved significant local political influence, including a Miss Forrest of the Gort Hotel – the 'right-hand man' of local MP Sir William Gregory, though the most consistent role for women in nineteenth-century elections was as rioters.[10] The riot is an interesting pointer, because the Ladies Land League – one of the first instances of women's political activism, favoured tactics regarded as too extreme by their male colleagues.[11] Excluded from the mainstream positions of voter, election candidate or party officer, women were relegated to the margins. This began to change in the closing years of the century. Propertied women became eligible to stand for election as Poor Law Guardians in 1896; the 1898 Irish Local Government Act gave women who met the property qualifications the right to vote in all local elections; and women could stand for election to urban and rural district councils. In 1899, 85 women were elected as Poor Law Guardians, 31 served as Rural District Councillors and four as Urban District Councillors, but women were disqualified from serving on borough and county councils until 1911.[12]

The Irish women's suffrage movement can be traced back to 1876 and the foundation of the Dublin Women's Suffrage Association (DWSA). The campaign gained momentum in the years immediately before the Great War, with the founding of the Irish Women's Franchise League, a more militant body than the long-established Irish Local Government and Women's Suffrage Association (successor to the DWSA), and groups representing regional, political and religious affiliations.[13] The emergence of an Irish suffrage movement well ahead of most rural Catholic countries reflects Ireland's mass politicization, membership of the United Kingdom, and the relatively advanced level of women's education. On the eve of the First World War the suffrage campaign in Ireland and Britain became inextricably entwined with the Home Rule question. From 1911 the survival of Asquith's government was dependent on the support of the Irish Party in

Westminster; the party came under pressure to exact a commitment for women's suffrage in return for their votes, but declined to do so. This decision encouraged Irish suffragists with nationalist sympathies to gravitate towards more militant nationalist groups. But as tensions rose over Home Rule and Ulster unionism many active suffragists chose to concentrate their energies on nationalist or unionist campaigns.[14] Women played a substantial, though subordinate role in the Ulster Covenant campaign, expressing mass opposition to Home Rule,[15] and likewise in the 1916 Rising and Anglo-Irish War. In 1917 four women were appointed to the 24-person Sinn Féin executive, and Sinn Féin committed itself to female suffrage on identical terms to men. When Britain granted the vote to women over 30 in 1918, Constance Markievicz, veteran of many nationalist and labour movements, was the first woman elected to Westminster, though in keeping with the Sinn Féin policy of abstention she sat not in Westminster but in Dáil Éireann, the illegal assembly that first met in January 1919, where she was appointed Minister for Labour.

Six women were returned to the Second Dáil in 1920, all unopposed. Four were relatives of dead republican heroes. They included Margaret Pearse, mother of 1916 leader Patrick Pearse, and Mary MacSwiney, sister of the Sinn Féin TD [Teachta Dála – deputy to the Dáil] and Lord Mayor of Cork, Terence MacSwiney, who died on hunger strike – a former suffragist and a significant political force in her own right.[16] When the Dáil voted to accept the Anglo-Irish Treaty giving Dominion status to 26 counties – a compromise on the demands for a 32-county republic, all six women deputies voted against the Treaty. Cumann na mBan, the women's wing of the Irish Volunteers (later IRA), voted by a wide margin to oppose the Treaty. Women were proportionately more prominent among republican opponents of the Treaty than among the activists in the 1919–21 Anglo-Irish War. Fifty women were imprisoned for republican activities during 1919–21; almost 400 were imprisoned in the years 1922–4.[17] The prominent role taken by women in opposing the Anglo-Irish Treaty was a defining moment in the construction of the Irish female politician not least because it was the first occasion that women legislators voted on a major issue. Women deputies refused to compromise on the commitment to a republic. Supporters of the Treaty accused them of 'rattling the bones' of dead heroes.[18] In 1924 a pro-Treaty account of the Irish Revolution described republican women as 'the implacable and irrational upholders of death and destruction . . . We know that with women in political power there would be no more peace.'[19] This implied that women were unfit for normal political life. However in March 1922, in the bitter after-math of the Treaty split, Dáil Éireann passed a decree, proposed by Kathleen O'Callaghan (widow of the murdered Lord Mayor of Limerick), providing for votes for women on identical terms to men.[20] The provision was included in Article 14 of the 1922 Constitution: a Constitution rejected by the majority of women activists.

INDEPENDENT IRELAND: 1922–72

Irish politics since the 1920s have been dominated by two major parties, whose origins lie in the divisions over the Treaty and Civil War: the pro-Treaty party, Fine Gael (originally Cumann na nGaedheal) and Fianna Fáil – representing the overwhelming majority of those who opposed the Treaty. Labour, a longstanding third party, had strong links with the trade union movement. Until the 1980s Sinn Féin refused to recognize the state by entering the legislature. Politically active women, like men, were divided on the national question, though a higher proportion of women than men refused to recognize the new state, remaining outside the parliamentary system. Did this weaken women's political role in the new state? Some historians believe that the conservatism of post-independence Ireland left no place for women in politics – a thesis generally supported by references to the Catholic church, the cultural values affirming the role of women in the home, the climate of censorship and intolerance of deviance from conventional norms.[21] What is striking is the implicit assumption that the only possible roles for women were as a feminist, radical republican or a socialist. If so, there is little to be explained about women's minimal role in politics in the newly independent Ireland because radical or left-wing movements attracted very few votes in this rural peasant property-owning Catholic state.

Women could be found in all parties, but with the possible exception of Sinn Féin they were a marginal force. In 1922 women who supported the Treaty founded Cumann na Saoirse (the League of Freedom); the group was represented on the committee that established Cumann na nGaedheal, and three members, Eileen Costello, Jenny Wyse-Power and historian Alice Stopford Green, served in the first Senate.[22] Wyse-Power was a founding vice-president of Cumann na nGaedheal but was replaced by Margaret Collins O'Driscoll, TD, sister of the late Michael Collins, apparently because of her opposition to legislation banning the employment of married women in the civil service.[23] In 1926 a majority of anti-Treaty republicans broke away to form Fianna Fáil. Although Mary MacSwiney and a number of prominent republican women remained with Sinn Féin, six members of the first Fianna Fáil executive were women. They included former suffrage activist Hanna Sheehy-Skeffington, Constance Marckievicz, Dorothy Macardle and Kathleen Clarke, widow of 1916 leader Tom Clarke. None of the women held key officer positions and they were not part of the close circle that determined policy, however the strong female representation suggests that women were regarded as important in securing support for the new party. Fianna Fáil was initially committed to abstention from Dáil Éireann because members refused to take the oath of allegiance (which included a reference to the British monarch). In August 1927 the party abandoned this position because the recently enacted Public Safety Act would have resulted in their seats being reassigned to other candidates. Constance Markievicz died shortly before Fianna Fáil entered Dáil Éireann, leaving Kathleen Clarke as the sole Fianna Fáil woman deputy. Although Clarke took her seat with misgivings, Macardle and Sheehy-Skeffington left the party in protest at the decision.[24] Their departure was not caused by disagreement over gender issues, but by a refusal to compromise on the oath of allegiance.

The self-exclusion from the parliamentary system of talented women with impeccable republican credentials – like Hanna Sheehy-Skeffington and Mary MacSwiney – may have closed the door to women holding cabinet office for many decades. Until the 1960s Irish politics was dominated by men who had played an active role in the struggle for independence. Given the conservative nature of Irish society, it was difficult for a woman to achieve a public profile that would ensure a Dáil seat, let alone a cabinet position, without personal or family connections to the Irish revolution. Fine Gael recruited candidates from pre-independence Irish political dynasties and the legal profession, in addition to veterans of independence movement. Labour representatives tended to be drawn from trade unions; until the 1960s most Labour deputies represented rural constituencies, where they relied on the votes of agricultural labourers. Many were also veterans of the War of Independence. Sporting success was another route into politics for those without family connections. These alternative pathways offered little scope for women candidates.

Political opportunities for women were further constrained by administrative and political reforms. The abolition of smaller units of local government such as Boards of Guardians of Poor Law unions, rural district councils and tuberculosis committees closed many of the elected political offices which women held prior to 1920. Thirty-six local authorities were dissolved between 1923 and 1931, including Dublin and Cork corporations. Local elections were postponed on four occasions between 1923 and 1943. Many independent councillors were elected during the 1920s, including a number of women, but by the 1940s local authorities were increasingly dominated by the major parties.[25]

The most common route for women into the legislature was as the widow or close relative of a TD, often first elected in a by-election following his death. Of the 119 seats filled in by-elections from 1922 to 2000, women were returned in 12 – a success rate of 10 per cent, more than twice the percentage of women returned in general elections. Not all successful women elected in by-elections were related to dead TDs, though the majority were.[26] The selection of widows as electoral candidates has been widely criticized, however it reflects the strong familial succession that is characteristic of Irish politics. Many prominent male politicians succeeded a close relative in a by-election or general election. The election of widows reflects a wider social pattern. For much of the twentieth century Irish society was relentlessly opposed to women (even single women) taking paid employment that might be attractive to men, but it was widely accepted that a widow should run the family farm, family business or return to work in the civil service following the death of a husband, if there was no suitable male relative to assume the breadwinner role. In recent times daughters are more likely to succeed to a family seat than widows,[27] a change which probably reflects improved longevity and the introduction of pensions for widows of TDs in 1968.

In 1979 Maurice Manning asked whether the 24 women who sat in Dáil Éireann from 1922–77 'made any significant contribution to our laws or to the national debate on important matters? Is there any body of laws which bear their imprint? The answer must be a resounding no'.[28] This is rather unfair: women deputies were at least as vocal as the average male backbencher. Like other backbenchers they were more likely to contribute through Parliamentary Questions than debates. Bridget Rice, widow of a Fianna Fáil TD, served from 1938 to 1954 and spoke on adoption, including the adoption of Irish babies in the USA, the ban on married women teachers, conscription of Irish citizens into the US armed forces and other topics, including agricultural policy.[29] Long-term electoral success in Dáil Éireann is generally associated with active constituency work rather than contributions to debates; the priorities of women deputies were identical to those of male backbenchers.

The only woman politician to articulate a form of maternalist feminism was Helena Concannon, who served as a National University of Ireland representative in Dáil Éireann (1933–7), and in the Senate (1938–52).[30] An historian and author of many books on Irish women, all with a strong Catholic, nationalist theme,[31] she spoke in favour of the controversial Article 41 in the 1937 Constitution which recognized the place of women in the home.[32] Senators Jennie Wyse-Power (1922–36) and Kathleen Clarke opposed the 1935 Conditions of Employment Bill which included clauses giving the Minister for Industry and Commerce authority to regulate the numbers of women working in specific occupations,[33] and Wyse-Power spoke in favour of protecting the citizenship rights of Irish women in foreign marriages,[34] but the main feminist campaigns on the Conditions of Employment Act and the 1937 Constitution were fought outside the legislature and the party system.[35] Divisions over the national question – particularly between those who remained committed to extra-parliamentary movements, and the rest – undoubtedly weakened the feminist case, especially when republican women used international feminist gatherings as a platform to promote militant republicanism.[36]

Irish electoral politics was reinvigorated in the late 1940s with the emergence of Clann na Poblachta, a new party that attracted many former republicans who had not entered parliamentary politics, and campaigners for a range of social programmes such as improved healthcare and housing.[37] The party recruited a number of high-profile women, such as: Mrs. B. Berthon Waters, described as 'something of an economics guru'; trade union leader and veteran republican Helena Moloney; Margaret Skinnider, 1916 veteran and president of the Irish National Teachers' Organisation; and the writer Maura Laverty. Laverty stood for election in 1948, as did the former Fianna Fáil TD Kathleen Clarke but neither was successful. Kathleen McDowell, a leader of the Irish Housewives' Association (IHA) – an organization founded during the war to campaign against high prices and food and fuel shortages – was an unsuccessful Labour candidate. In 1954 however, Maureen O'Carroll, IHA member and secretary of the Lower Prices Council, an umbrella organization formed by the Dublin Trades Union Council, was elected on the Labour ticket. The fact that her father had been a republican prisoner was not a disadvantage.[38] The profile of these women suggests a gradual transition towards female candidates with a track record of activism on social issues. But the liberal campaigns in Dáil and Senate throughout the 1950s and 1960s were articulated by Noel Browne and Senator Eoin Sheehy-Skeffington – son of Hanna Sheehy-Skeffington. No woman played even a minor role until 1969 when Mary Bourke – better known as Mary Robinson – was elected to the Senate.

Women were more significant in backroom politics. Mary (Molly) Davison worked for the Labour Party from 1922, serving as party secretary from 1950 to 1967; she was a member of the Seanad in 1950–1 and from 1954–69. The Labour newspaper, the *Irish People*, was edited by women, initially in 1945–6 by Mrs Berthon Waters, who subsequently joined Clann na Poblachta, and later by Sheila Greene. The most important woman in Irish politics throughout the 1960s was Catherine McGuinness, speechwriter and confidante of Labour leader Brendan Corish from 1961–7 and co-author of the 1963 Labour manifesto. She resigned in 1967 when her husband was expelled from the party;[39] in later years she served as a senator and a member of the Supreme Court.

'SECOND WAVE' FEMINISM AND BEYOND

The political representation of Irish women was broadly in line with other Western democracies until the 1970s. At that time Sweden was the only European country where women secured more than 10 per cent of parliamentary seats.[40] The Commission on the Status of Women, which reported in December 1972, devoted a chapter to the topic of 'Women in Politics and Public Life'. Politics was not the Commission's primary concern; much greater attention was given to the ban on married women in the public service and equal pay. Few submissions concerned women's participation in politics;[41] however the Commission met representatives from Fianna Fáil, Fine Gael and Labour[42] to discuss this topic. Their report presented a gloomy picture of women in national electoral politics. In the four elections between 1957 and 1969, 8 to 11 per cent of candidates for Dáil seats were women, and women accounted for 2 to 4 per cent of those elected. Women were much more successful in by-elections, but all the successful women by-election candidates between 1957 and 1969 were widows, as were eight of the nine women returned in general elections.[43] Half of the women who sat in Seanad Eireann (eight out of 16) during this period were Taoiseach's nominees. The low success rate of women in general elections might suggest systemic bias against female candidates, but it is probably explained by the fact that a significant number stood as independents. Women fared better in local elections: 54 of 118 women candidates in the 1967 local elections (total 3,142 candidates) were successful and women standing for county council seats had a success rate of 69 per cent against 49 per cent for men.[44] The Commission suggested that any woman wishing to become a national political representative should first stand for election to a local authority. They cited the findings of a

Gallup Poll, published in April 1970 and based on surveys carried out over the previous year, which showed a marked difference in attitudes towards politics on the part of men and women. Forty-seven per cent of women described themselves as 'only a little interested', or 'not interested' in politics, compared with 35 per cent of men; 25 per cent of women described themselves as 'very interested' in politics, compared with 33 per cent of men. Only 11 per cent of women surveyed would join a political party, against 18 per cent of men, and only 3 per cent of women surveyed were members of political parties, compared with 9 per cent of men. On the basis of this poll the Commission estimated that women accounted for approximately one-quarter of party members. But according to information supplied by the three main parties, only 6 per cent of party office-holders were women, the majority serving as secretary or treasurer of a local branch. Only 8 per cent of women office-holders were chair or vice-chair of a party branch. The 123 members of the national executives of the three major parties included only three women.[45]

The Commission held women partly to blame for their low representation in politics. They highlighted the need to make women aware that 'politics is not meant to be a male preserve'. If women were to have an effective say in formulating the policies that affected their lives, they must get involved in politics; this change in mindset would require an effective programme of civic and public education. Political parties should make greater efforts to attract women, and women members should be given posts of responsibility on merit.[46] But in a report containing 49 recommendations (17 relating to equal pay and employment), it is noteworthy that no specific actions were recommended to increase women's representation in politics.

The publication of the report of the Commission on the Status of Women prompted women's groups to establish a permanent Council for the Status of Women to monitor the implementation of the Commission's recommendations. The Council's activities included educational and development programmes designed to give women the opportunity to participate fully in political, social and economic life.[47] One of the groups affiliated to the Council for the Status of Women was the Women's Progressive Association. This Association, later renamed the Women's Political Association (WPA), was founded in 1970 by Margaret Waugh, wife of a Dublin doctor, to assist and encourage women to become involved in politics, irrespective of party affiliation. Waugh founded the WPA because she was outraged at the 1970 Arms Trial, when two former cabinet ministers, Charles Haughey and Niall Blaney, were acquitted on charges of supplying guns to the IRA. She contacted TCD senator Mary Robinson to discuss the possibility of establishing a women's party, but they agreed instead to create a non-party association to encourage women to enter politics. Robinson was the first president of the WPA. Its mission was to increase women's representation in parliamentary and local government so that women would play an equal role in key decisions regarding Irish society. The WPA sent teams of canvassers to work on local and national election campaigns of women candidates; it also brought together women across the political parties to campaign on a variety of issues of common interest. In 1974 the WPA worked with the Business and Professional Women's Clubs to establish the Women's Talent Bank – a database of women with the expertise to serve on government boards.[48]

The WPA campaign slogan for the 1977 general election was 'Why Not a Woman?'. First preference votes for women doubled from 42,268 in 1973 to 81,967 votes. Six women were elected, compared with four in 1973, and three of the Taoiseach's 11 Seanad nominees were women. For the first time in the history of the state more than 5 per cent of Dáil and Seanad members were women.[49] From 1977 the proportion of women elected rose in successive general elections to a peak of 13.7 per cent in 1997. 'Second wave' feminism, the publication of the report of the Commission on the Status of Women, and the formation of the WPA contributed to the increase. Connolly notes, 'The WPA has provided a constant supply of women candidates (successful and unsuccessful) to the established political parties since the mid-1970s, including several women who held ministerial and cabinet office.'[50] Connolly lists eight women ministers who were members of the WPA. Although the WPA remained neutral with respect to party politics, no woman elected to Dáil Éireann on the Fianna Fáil ticket was a member.

In October 1975 the Fianna Fáil national executive received a letter from the WPA urging them to promote women candidates. In their reply the national executive pointed out that the party had recommended that 'a representative number of lady candidates' should be selected at the last local government elections and had issued a discussion document on the role of women in Irish society.[51] While there is no direct evidence that Fianna Fáil acted in response to the WPA's request, party leader Jack Lynch added six women to the list of candidates selected by party conventions for the 1977 general election. They included 24-year-old Mary Harney, the first woman auditor of Trinity College Dublin's élite debating society, the Hist.[52] When Harney was not elected, Lynch nominated her to the Seanad, one of three women in his list of 11 nominees. Fianna Fáil won the 1977 election by a landslide and the association of electoral success with modernity and female candidates undoubtedly prompted Garret FitzGerald to target women candidates. FitzGerald, who became leader of Fine Gael following the 1977 general election, embarked on a major modernization drive. In his memoirs FitzGerald expressed the opinion that 'we should try to unleash the political potential of women, whose consciousness of their own worth and rights had been aroused by the non-political – even at times anti-political – feminist movement of the early 1970s.'[53] FitzGerald's description of the feminist movement as 'non-political – even at times anti-political' suggests a limited understanding of the movement, as does his offer to establish a Fine Gael women's organization – an offer rejected by Fine Gael women. Despite these limitations, FitzGerald's drive to reform the party proved beneficial for women: the 1979 local elections saw a 60 per cent increase in the number of Fine Gael women councillors,[54] and more veterans of the WPA were elected on the Fine Gael ticket than for any other political party. In 1981, Nuala Fennell, journalist, founder member of the Irish Women's Liberation Movement and activist in organizations campaigning for reform of family law and support for deserted wives, became 'the first avowed feminist from the second wave of feminism to be elected to the Dail'.[55] She was followed in 1982 by Monica Barnes and Gemma Hussey, women with similar feminist credentials. Lynch and FitzGerald were not feminists; by the late 1970s promoting more women candidates was pragmatic politics.[56]

Youth wings of the major parties, and university branches – initiatives of the mid- and late 1960s – proved almost as effective at recruiting women into politics as feminist organizations.[57] Successful women politicians are still drawn in significant numbers from political families, though they do not necessarily succeed directly to a 'family' seat; many begin their political careers as active members of local branches.[58] Many of the women elected to Dáil Éireann since the 1970s grew up in political households; some were daughters of failed Dáil candidates or county councillors.[59] This suggests that the impact of 'second wave' feminism should not be measured solely by the number of women politicians who were involved in feminist groups such as the Council for the Status of Women or the WPA. 'Second wave' feminism encouraged women from political families to play a more prominent public role; it also prompted political leaders to promote women candidates.

In 1977 Maire Geoghegan-Quinn (FF) was appointed as Parliamentary Secretary to the Department of Industry and Commerce, the first woman to hold this junior ministerial rank; in 1979, as Minister for the Gaeltacht (the Irish-speaking communities), she became the first woman to hold cabinet rank since Constance Markievicz in 1919–21. Geoghegan-Quinn entered politics by the traditional family route: elected at a by-election following the death of her father. Although never formally identified with feminist issues, as Minister for Justice she was responsible for the enactment of the 1993 Criminal Justice (Sexual Offences) Act which decriminalized homosexual acts and enacted an identical age of consent for homosexual and heterosexual relations. Every Cabinet since 1979 has had at least one woman member; 1992 was the first occasion that two women were appointed to cabinet posts. In 1993 Mary Harney, who resigned from Fianna Fáil in 1985 to join the new Progressive Democrat Party, became the first woman to lead a national party. Harney has served as Minister for Enterprise and Employment and Minister for Health; in 1997 she became the first woman Tanaiste. During the 1990s the two largest parties, Fianna Fáil and Fine Gael, elected women as deputy leaders. Women have held most of the key ministerial offices including Justice, Enterprise and Employment, Agriculture and Health – the major outstanding posts not yet held by women are Foreign Affairs, Finance and Taoiseach.

Has the appointment of women ministers advanced gender agendas? In 1982 Garret FitzGerald appointed Nuala Fennell as Minister for State with responsibility for women's affairs. Fennell's role was to co-ordinate policy across the various departments on matters relating to women, but her mission proved difficult.[60]

The 1980s were marked by increasingly bitter arguments and referendums over the right to life of the foetus and divorce. Women deputies were divided on these issues; several who adopted a more liberal position than their party came under pressure to toe the party line.[61] There is no firm evidence that women deputies had a significant impact on the positions adopted by the political parties on these issues. Women have proved much more effective on family law reform, equality in education and social welfare entitlements – topics that attracted cross-party support. By the 1990s Frances Gardiner noted 'a new willingness to gender-proof policy, be it labour affairs, justice or education'.[62]

In 1990 Mary Robinson was elected as President of Ireland; when she stepped down in 1997 she was succeeded by Mary McAleese. The success of Mary Robinson, Senator for Dublin University (1969–89), is noteworthy, not least because she had been an unsuccessful Dáil candidate for the Labour Party in the 1977 and 1981 general elections. Mary McAleese, Robinson's successor as President, was an unsuccessful Fianna Fáil Dáil candidate in 1987.[63] The Robinson presidency may have been responsible for the record number of women elected in 1997, but the long-term effect appears limited. Many women who entered politics through 'second wave' feminism have retired from active politics; the new generation of women candidates is more likely to emerge from conventional party politics. The election of two women Presidents, the waning of 'second wave' feminism, and the broadening of equality issues to embrace immigrants, ethnic minorities, and people with disabilities, have reduced the political imperative to promote gender equality in politics. There is a sense that Irish women have been relegated to the less powerful elected roles – President, or Member of the European Parliament. In 1997 four of the five candidates for the presidency were women – including nominees of the three major parties. In 1999 women secured five of the 15 Irish seats in the European Parliament, and in 2004 women again won five seats, despite a reduction in Irish representation to 13. Do Irish parties and voters see the presidency and Europe as the woman's sphere – a way to satisfy pressures for women's representation without significantly intruding into the critical areas of Dáil Éireann and government ministries?

ACCOUNTING FOR THE UNDER-REPRESENTATION OF WOMEN IN IRISH POLITICS

As the number of women deputies increases so too does the level of consciousness about how difficult it still is for women to be elected . . . The difficulty stems not from the electorate who have shown they will vote for good women candidates, but rather from the obstacles encountered by women as they battle through what are still male-dominated political parties.[64]

In 1992 Irish women TDs formed a loose association called Group 84 – the number of women deputies needed if women were to form a majority in Dáil Éireann.[65] Yet in 2002 the National Council of Women of Ireland[66] noted only a marginal rise (1 per cent) in women's presence in Dáil Éireann over the past ten years.[67] Part of the explanation for women's low rate of electoral success relates to the Irish political system and what Irish voters expect from elected representatives. The Second Commission on the Status of Women identified 'compelling structural and attitudinal reasons why women were not involved full-time in political life' – these included limiting cultural and social values; difficulties in combining family life, work and politics; 'and the ongoing reluctance of political parties to select women candidates'. They described the structures of parties and practices as 'not friendly towards women'.[68]

Irish politics continues to be dominated by parties that are not distinguished by major ideological differences. A 2008 study of voting behaviour concluded that the absence of strong ideology, combined with an electoral system based on proportional representation and multi-seat constituencies, puts considerable pressure on candidates to develop a 'personal vote'.[69] Constituency service is a key factor in voters' decisions.[70] Paul Sacks described the TD as 'the country-man's personal emissary to an anonymous state'. Sacks shows how the increasing involvement of the state in providing welfare supports and financial supplements for economic and other purposes has served to enhance the role of party organizations as 'intermediaries between man and state' – both local and national.[71] The perception of the TD as the intermediary with county managers, senior civil servants and other organizations of state – offices traditionally dominated by men – may have damaged the standing and authority of women politicians. Sacks also highlighted the role of local networks – often originally built on the basis of old IRA organizations; these networks drew heavily on kinship, and they fed off traditional Irish sociability based around pubs, evening visits to private houses, and participation in key organizations such as the Gaelic Athletic Association. Local networks and traditional Irish sociability were heavily gendered. Thus the grassroots strength of Irish electoral politics, and the manner in which it reflected Irish society, reinforced male dominance. All accounts of the life of an Irish TD or would-be TD emphasize what a time-consuming activity this is, and the import-ance of attending funerals and social functions to ensure and sustain electoral success. The Second Commission on the Status of Women suggested that Irish politics was predicated on 'the serviced male' – a male politician supported by a wife who ran the home, family and acted as unpaid political aide.[72] In 2006 Independent TD Mildred Fox announced that she was retiring from politics. Fox was elected to Dáil Éireann in 1995 in a by-election following the death of her father; by 2006, as the mother of three young children, she was not prepared 'to commit to another five years of being absent in the evening time'.[73] The pressures of the politician's lifestyle and the primacy of constituency business may help to explain why women have a lower rate of incumbency; many successful women politicians have retired from active politics at a much earlier age than male counterparts. Incumbents are believed to have a significant electoral advantage, and women's lower rate of incumbency may help to explain why successful Irish women TDs get fewer votes on average than men. Only one woman ranked among the top 50 vote-getters in the period 1918–2000,[74] and she (Labour TD Eithne Fitzgerald) lost her vote in the general election in 1997.

The Second Commission on the Status of Women recommended a number of strategies to improve women's participation in national politics, including abolition of the dual mandate (where TDs also served as local councillors) and positive action by parties to increase female representation – quotas were described as 'a key strategy'. The Commission also recommended quotas of women on the National Executive and other party committees, and Exchequer funding for women's officers for political parties, in line with the existing practice of funding youth officers.[75] The 2002 report by the National Council of Women in Ireland (NCWI) added to this list, recommending that 50 per cent of government funding for political parties should be tied to a requirement that women constitute at least 40 per cent of candidates in local and national elections and 40 per cent of the party executive. The NCWI also recommended reforming the Dáil calendar to make it more female-friendly and providing support for women's community groups in order to promote greater female participation in national and local politics.[76] Comparative data from other European countries indicates that the most effective means of increasing the proportion of women in parliament is to insist on a quota of female candidates. In 1997 the British Labour Party quota for female candidates, coupled with a Labour landslide, resulted in a doubling of women MPs in Westminster. Comparative studies also suggest that women fare better under Proportional Representation (PR) than under the direct vote, but the PR systems in question tend to be a list system, or a partial list system. Women also appear to fare better when national parties impose candidates – this may explain the better success of Irish women in by-elections, where the national executive or party leader might exercise disproportionate influence on the selection. Successive governments have expressed at least token support for the goal that women should account for 40 per cent of nominees on state boards, but there is no comparable commitment to a quota for women electoral candidates. The personal and the local are dominant features of Irish politics, and there is little evidence of political willingness to address these issues.

'Second wave' feminism played a key role in raising women's involvement in electoral politics: its impact can be seen not just in the candidates, TDs and women ministers who were politicized through their involvement in feminist causes but in the growing number of successful women politicians recruited from traditional political backgrounds. But with waning momentum in the feminist movement, the advance of women in Irish politics appears to have stalled – or been diverted into areas such as the presidency and the European Parliament. The barriers to further advancement of women today remain much as they were in the early years of the state: the persistence of an electoral system that favours personal candidates, family political connections and a high level of constituency activity. While the Second Commission on the Status of Women has described the current electoral system as not friendly to women, the profile of women candidates for the presidency or the European Parliament suggests that women have managed to establish strong personal campaigns in these elections, as in the case of successful MEPs such as: Kathy Sinnott, campaigner for children with intellectual disabilities; former Eurovision song contest winner Dana Rosemary-Scallon, now identified with conservative Christian 'family values'; Marion Harkin, campaigner for the west of Ireland; presidential candidate Adi Roche, a campaigner for Chernobyl children; and two successive Presidents, Mary Robinson and Mary McAleese. These success stories might suggest that Irish women have learned how to build personal campaigns that take advantage of the Irish political landscape – but primarily in political contests other than Dáil Éireann.

NOTES

1   In regard to the period after 1922, 'Ireland' refers to the Republic of Ireland.
2   Mary Harney, then leader of the Progressive Democrats was Tanaiste from 1997 to 2006. The woman appointed Tanaiste in 2008 was Fianna Fáil deputy, Mary Coughlan.
3   *The Irish Times*, 28 May 2007.
4   Yvonne Galligan and Rick Wilford, 'Women's political representation in Ireland', in Yvonne Galligan, Eilis Ward and Rick Wilford (eds), *Contesting Politics* (Boulder, CO/Oxford: Westview/Political Studies Association of Ireland, 1999), p. 131.
5   Frances Gardiner, 'The women's movement and women politicians in the Republic of Ireland, 1980–2000', in Angela Bourke, Siobhan Kilfeather, Maria Luddy, Margaret MacCurtain, Gerardine Meaney, Mairin Ni Dhonnchadha, Mary O'Dowd and Clair Wills (eds), *The Field Day Anthology of Irish Writing, Vol. 5: Irish Women's Writing and Traditions* (Cork: Cork University Press, 2002).
6   *The Irish Times*, 28 May 2007.
7   Data compiled for the Inter-Parliamentary Union from information provided by 31 October 2009. See http://www.ipu.org/wmn-e/classif.htm (accessed 27 November 2009)
8   Pamela Marie Paxton and Melanie M. Hughes, *Women, Politics and Power: A Global Perspective* (London/Los Angeles: Pine Forge Press, 2007), pp. 17–18.
9   Ibid., p. 76.
10 K. Theodore Hoppen, *Elections, Politics and Society in Ireland 1832–1885* (Oxford: Clarendon Press, 1984).
11 On the Ladies Land League see Margaret Ward, *Unmanageable Revolutionaries: Women and Irish Nationalism* (London: Pluto Press, 1983).
12 Rosemary Cullen Owens, *A Social History of Women in Ireland 1870–1970* (Dublin: Gill & Macmillan, 2005).
13 Owens, *Social History of Women in Ireland*.
14 Cliona Murphy, *The Women's Suffrage Movement and Irish Society in the Early Twentieth Century* (London and New York: Harvester Wheatsheaf, 1989); Jason Knirck, *Women of the Dáil: Gender, Republicanism and the Anglo-Irish Treaty* (Dublin/ Portland: Irish Academic Press, 2006).
15 The Covenant was signed by over 218,000 men; women were precluded from signing but over 234,000 women signed a supplementary declaration of support. Myrtle Hill, *Women in Ireland: A Century of Change* (Belfast: Blackstaff, 2003).
16 Charlotte Fallon, *Soul of Fire: A Biography of Mary MacSwiney* (Cork: Mercier, 1986).

17 Hill, *Women in Ireland*.
18 Dáil Debates (DD), vol. 3, 20 December 1921–6 January 1922. The accusation was widely used.
19 P. S. O'Hegarty, *The Victory of Sinn Féin* (Dublin: Talbot Press, 1924), pp. 104–5.
20 DD, vol. 2, cols 197–214, 2 March 1922. The extended electoral register came into effect in 1923.
21 Margaret O'Callaghan, 'Women and politics in independent Ireland, 1921–68', in Bourke *et al.* (eds), *Field Day Anthology*, pp. 120–34.
22 Ibid., p. 122. Ward, *Unmanageable Revolutionaries*, claims that most members of Cumann na Saoirse were wives of government members (p. 173).
23 O'Callagan, 'Women and politics in independent Ireland'.
24 Margaret Ward, *Hanna Sheehy-Skeffington: A Life* (Cork: Attic Press, 1997). Clarke resigned from Fianna Fáil in 1943.
25 Paul Sacks, *The Donegal Mafia* (New Haven and London: Yale University Press, 1976).
26 Maedbh McNamara and Paschal Mooney, *Women in Parliament: Ireland: 1918–2000* (Dublin: Wolfhound, 2000).
27 Yvonne Galligan, Kathleen Knight and Úna Nic Giolla Choille, 'Pathways to power: women in the Oireachtas 1919–2000', in McNamara and Mooney, *Women in Parliament*.
28 Maurice Manning, 'Women in Irish national and local politics 1922–77', in Margaret MacCurtain and Donncha Ó Corráin (eds), *Women in Irish Society: The Historical Dimension* (Dublin: Arlen House, 1979), p. 95.
29 McNamara and Mooney, *Women in Parliament*.
30 In 1938 University Dáil seats were replaced with Senate seats.
31 Mary O'Dowd, 'From Morgan to MacCurtain: women historians in Ireland from the 1790s to the 1990s', in Mary O'Dowd and Maryann Valiulis (eds), *Women and Irish History* (Dublin: Wolfhound, 1997).
32 DD, vol. 67, cols 241–8, 12 May 1937.
33 Seanad Debates (SD), vol. 20, cols 1247–50 (Wyse-Power), cols 1256–69 (Clarke), 27 November 1935. Mary E. Daly, *Industrial Development and Irish National Identity, 1922–1939* (Syracuse, NY and Dublin: Syracuse University Press/Gill & Macmillan, 1992).
34 SD, vol. 19, col. 1576, 3 April 1935.
35 Ward, *Unmanageable Revolutionaries*.
36 This happened most notably at the 1926 congress in Dublin of the Women's International League for Peace and Freedom. Ward, *Hanna Sheehy-Skeffington*; Rosemary Cullen Owens, 'Louie Bennett', in Mary Cullen and Maria Luddy (eds), *Female Activists. Irish Women and Change 1900–1960* (Dublin: Woodfield, 2001).
37 Niamh Purséil, *The Irish Labour Party 1922–73* (Dublin: UCD Press, 2007); Eithne McDermott, *Clann na Poblachta* (Cork: Cork University Press, 1998). On the IHA see the chapter by Earner-Byrne in this volume.
38 Purséil, *The Irish Labour Party*.
39 Purséil, *The Irish Labour Party*.
40 Data in Appendix 1. Galligan *et al.*, 'Pathways to power', p. 61.
41 Commission on the Status of Women (Dublin, 1972), Prl. 2760, para. 481.188.
42 Ibid., Appendix A, p. 254.
43 Commission on the Status of Women, 1972, Table 20, p. 190.
44 Ibid., Tables 22, 23, pp. 193–4.
45 Ibid., para. 485, p. 189.
46 Ibid., paras 496, 497, pp. 194–5.

47 Linda Connolly, *The Irish Women's Liberation Movement: From Revolution to Devolution* (Cork: Cork University Press, 2002).
48 'Political legacy of Margaret Waugh', letter by Gemma Hussey to *The Irish Times*, 16 May 2008; 'Pioneer of advancement of women in public and political life', Margaret Waugh Obituary, *The Irish Times*, 24 May 2008. June Levine, 'The women's movement in the Republic of Ireland, 1968–80', in Bourke *et al.* (eds), *Field Day Anthology*, pp. 177–87.
49 Women accounted for 5.3 per cent of Dáil and Seanad, compared with 3.9 per cent in 1973 and 4.3 per cent in 1957 – the previous historic high.
50 Connolly, *Irish Women's Movement*, pp. 104–5.
51 University College Dublin Archives, Fianna Fáil Organisation Committee, P 176/370, 6 October 1975.
52 Levine, 'The women's movement', p. 183.
53 Garret FitzGerald, *All in a Life* (Dublin: Gill & Macmillan, 1991), p. 327.
54 FitzGerald, *All in a Life*.
55 McNamara and Mooney, *Women in Parliament*, pp. 116–17.
56 William Murphy, 'Between change and tradition: the politics and writings of Garret FitzGerald', *Éire-Ireland*, 43, (1&2), (2008), pp. 154–78.
57 Una Claffey, *The Women Who Won* (Dublin: Attic Press, 1993).
58 Galligan *et al.*, 'Pathways to power'.
59 Claffey, *Women Who Won*.
60 Murphy, 'Between change and tradition'.
61 Gardiner, 'The women's movement and women politicians', p. 232.
62 Ibid., p. 236.
63 McNamara and Mooney, *Women in Parliament*.
64 Claffey, *Women Who Won*, p. 8.
65 Ibid.
66 The Council is funded by the Irish government.
67 National Council of Women of Ireland (NCWI), *Irish Politics: Jobs for the Boys* (Dublin 2002), Foreword by Yvonne Galligan.
68 Second Commission on the Status of Women (Dublin, 1991), PL 9557, p. 213.
69 Michael Marsh, Richard Sinnott, John Garry and Fiachra Kennedy, *The Irish Voter: The Nature of Electoral Competition in the Republic of Ireland* (Manchester: Manchester University Press, 2008), p. 217.
70 Marsh *et al.*, *The Irish Voter*.
71 Sacks, *The Donegal Mafia*.
72 Second Commission, p. 215.
73 Stephen Collins, 'Fox puts children ahead of politics', *The Irish Times*, 27 November 2006.
74 McNamara and Mooney, *Women in Parliament*.
75 Second Commission.
76 NCWI, *Irish Politics: Jobs for the Boys*.

7

'Aphrodite rising from the Waves'?[1]
Women's voluntary activism and the women's movement in twentieth-century Ireland

Lindsey Earner-Byrne

Once enfranchised – and leaving the 'national question' to one side . . .
– there should be only one strongly marked line of cleavage between the
reorganised suffrage societies. Some will devote themselves without break to
further agitation for a complete measure of enfranchisement, whilst others
will prefer to turn their attention to social reform and educative work,
making the demand for full enfranchisement subsidiary to the opportunities
afforded by what they have already gained.[2]

In March 1918 Lucy Kingston,[3] an Irish suffragist, ventured to predict what the Representation of the People Act 1918 would mean for Irishwomen. Her concerns included: the moral threat party politics posed to the women's movement; that women would not form a different voting block from men; that political feminism would be subsumed by social feminism. She hoped that women would unite across religious lines to change the moral environment of their social and political cultures. Many of her observations were prescient: the national question in the short term did lure women from the women's movement; party politics proved a stronger pull than gender issues for many politically active women; women failed to form a different voting block, and social activism provided the principal vehicle for female expression for much of the century.

The crude biography of the Irish women's movement regards the period 1916 to 1922 as a heyday, followed by a period of political retrenchment between 1922 and 1968 when women lost many democratic rights and failed to launch, much less win, a sustained campaign based on feminist principles.[4] Facilitating the notion that women in Ireland 'disappeared' post-independence (1922) is the view of Ireland as an intrinsically backward, overwhelmingly Roman Catholic, rural and agricultural society. However, it was tradition that often provided the context for change: it was, after all, to protect family life that many women claimed a right to a public life. The relationship between tradition, change and modernization is complex and multi-faceted and women's organizations have always played a role, albeit not a unified one, in defining, limiting and extending the boundaries of that relationship.

This chapter will examine the role played by the most active voluntary women's organizations between 1922 and 1968. If Irish society presented specific constraints to a women's movement, what opportunities were there for female activism? Was religion relevant in the formation of women's organizations? Can all women's organizations be viewed as examples of social feminism? How effective a lobby group did Irish women form? This chapter will also analyse the relationship between the older women's groups and the more radical women's movement that emerged in the late 1960s. Were the tensions merely generational or did they expose deeper divisions? Was the establishment of 'state feminism'[5] a greater testament to women's influence on social policy than the fractured legacy of the Women's Liberation Movement?

IRELAND IN CONTEXT

The Irish women's emancipation movement emerged in the second half of the nineteenth century and charted a similar route to that in Britain.[6] Experts in Irish women's history regard the Irish movement as 'part of a wider phenomenon in western society'.[7] The reminiscences of a leading Irish suffragist acknowledged the influence of the British movement:

> The Votes for Women movement in England some years later stirred a responsive chord in some Irish feminist breasts, but for some years we did nothing to start a fire on our own. Then, in the late summer of 1908, stimulated by the English revolt, a group of us got together and planned an Irish 'Suff' group which was to have the same aims . . .[8]

The Irish women's movement in the nineteenth and early twentieth centuries encompassed a wide range of issues associated with the British movement: married women's property rights, education, health and morality, poverty, class, and trade unionism.[9] Complicated and shaped by the emerging nationalist and unionist movements, the women's movement continued to share links and develop tensions with the English movement prior to 1918.[10] However, as the wider political narrative intensified and the issue of women's suffrage was dragged into the issue of Home Rule, Irish women found it increasingly difficult to find space or support in the chaotic political scene. As with the British movement, the Irish movement experienced tensions between 'constitutional feminists' and the emerging militant feminist groups. Coupled with these tensions were those between unionism and nationalism: the Irish Women's Suffrage and Local Government Association (IWSLGA), for example, although non-political, had an overtly loyalist ethos which eventually led to the resignation of nationalist feminists like Hanna Sheehy-Skeffington.[11] Likewise, the Irish Women's Federation League (IWFL) was also avowedly non-political, but exuded a nationalist ethos from its inception.[12] This situation was further complicated by those women, mostly also self-professed suffragists, for example Inghinidhe na hÉireann and later Cumann na mBan, who believed the 'national question' should come first.[13] This process was not dissimilar to the one women underwent in the face of the

Great War, and in the Irish case the international war merely compounded that process, particularly for unionist women.[14] Thus the Irish women's movement was doubly taxed: challenged by nationalism, and jingoism.

The Representation of the People Act 1918 was extended to Ireland, but in a country already in the grips of its revolutionary period it had all sorts of political resonances. In the wake of the Act republican and suffrage women's organizations came together to support the campaign of two female Sinn Féin candidates. Only one, Constance Markievicz, was returned, making her the first woman to be elected to the Westminster Parliament.[15] Militant suffragists regarded this not as a triumph, but as a testament to the fact that women's equality was a long way off, as the newspaper *The Irish Citizen* (the voice of Irish feminism) declared: 'Under the new dispensation the majority sex in Ireland has secured one representative. This is the measure of our boasted sex equality.' The lesson the election teaches is that reaction has not died out with the Irish party.'[16] Markievicz's election was symbolic of more than just 'continued reaction' in Irish society: as a Sinn Féin candidate she abstained.[17] Her empty seat was an augur of a political culture that would elect few other women in the unfolding century to sit at the table of national politics.[18]

Political activism must be gauged in more imaginative ways than the acquisition of government seats. Lobbying is a major method of political expression and power. Linda Connolly identified two strands of the women's movement which maintained a women's agenda throughout what she has convincingly dubbed the 'abeyance' period of 1922–70. Connolly divides these groups into the 'élite-sustained movement base' and 'a parallel network of women's groups'.[19] The élite group sought to continue feminist activities following the foundation of the Irish Free State, providing a consistent critique of the new state's treatment of women.[20] The second group concentrated on support-oriented activities and social services, acting as lobby groups for women's needs within the conservative framework of independent Ireland.[21] In fact, the division is far from clear, the support-oriented societies often lent their weight to the campaigns against state discrimination throughout the twentieth century.

Similarly, in most cases both these groupings were drawn directly from pre-1922 organizations. For example, the Irish Women's Citizen's Association (IWCA) (1918) began life in 1876 as the Dublin Women's Suffrage Association and following the Local Government [Ireland] Act 1898 became the Irish Women's Suffrage and Local Government Association. The IWCA was eventually absorbed into the Irish Housewives' Association (IHA), founded in 1942.[22] The IHA, dominated from its inception by Protestant women, remained throughout its life a non-denominational, non-party organization with an urban bias. It laid direct claim to the heritage of the first wave movement. Thus analysis of the trajectory of the IWCA provides an indication of how interlinked these women's organizations were and how continuity rather than discontinuity characterized the Irish women's movement. It began as an élite feminist organization fighting specifically for the right to the vote and mutated over time into a vehicle for the support and articulation of female citizenship in a broader sense. By the mid-twentieth century it was an organization that played a leading role in the emergence of what Alibhe Smyth called 'state feminism' in the late 1970s.[23]

Following the foundation of the Irish Free State and the introduction of universal suffrage in 1922, a series of Acts, such as the Juries Act 1927,[24] the Conditions of Employment Act 1936,[25] and the 1937 Constitution were all interpreted by various women's groups as attacks on the integrity of female citizenship. In 1924, Lucy Kingston founded the National Women's Council to 'promote joint action among women's organisations in Ireland . . . and reforms with special reference to women and children.'[26] Hanna Sheehy-Skeffington formed the Irish Women's Social and Progressive League to focus a women's campaign against the 1937 Constitution and, finally, an amalgam of existing women's organizations (many pre-1922) formed the Joint Committee of Women's Societies and Social Workers against the 1937 Constitution.[27] The Joint Committee, with 28,000 affiliated members, represented a wide range of women's groups of all religions including the IWCA and the Irish Countrywomen's Association.[28] Women's groups were moderately successful in obtaining alterations to some of this legislation.[29] In principle, however, they remained intact markers of a society that would fortify the male-breadwinner ideal at the expense of any equal rights agenda and, often, irrespective of the reality of family life.[30] For example, the concept that women should not have the same automatic rights/duties of citizenship remained in the Juries Act 1927, which made women's jury service an opt-in duty. Article 41.3 of the 1937 Constitution, which defined women's primary role as in the home, remained a hollow gesture of patriarchy, though Children's Allowance (introduced in 1944) was payable to the father until 1973.[31]

This reality marked a crucial difference with the British movement which, when viewed from a feminist perspective, proved a much more effective organ of change. Once British women gained equal suffrage their influence on legal and social policy increased and various pieces of legislation ensued. Martin Pugh was able to point to a series of 'women's legislation' in the 1920s which marked a change in 'politicians' attitudes towards women', ranging from the Married Women (Maintenance) Act 1922[32] and the Matrimonial Causes Act 1923[33] to the Guardianship of Infants Act 1925.[34] Equivalent legislation in Ireland came decades later.[35] In fact, legislation appeared to move in the opposite direction in Ireland during 1920s and 30s when divorce (1925 and 1937) and contraception (1929 and 1935) were prohibited.[36] Likewise, women's groups failed to win the introduction of women police,[37] the exact increase in the age of sexual consent sought,[38] and the full restoration of jury service obligations. In Ireland the issues such as divorce, contraception and abortion that were to become hallmarks of the radical feminist movement of the 1970s were rarely conceptualized as women's issues prior to that period. In fact, in the early 1970s when the issue of contraception was raised consistently in the Dáil it was still cast primarily as a civil rights issue for Protestants rather than a women's issue.[39] However, for much of the twentieth century the illegality of all three reflected a national consensus (across religions) on morality only consistently questioned from the 1960s onwards. The fact that the Irish women's movement did not make systematic feminist demands on the state has led some to conclude that the women's movement was moribund. Possibly because the largest and most successful women's organizations (in terms of influence and outreach) did not regard themselves as feminist, radical or antagonistic to the status quo, they have been overlooked by an historical agenda that defined female activism as exclusively feminist and political success as the sole indicator of activity and social influence.

In fact, an examination of the largest women's civil organizations paints a more vivid picture of women's activism post-independence and makes sense of the ebb and flow of the women's movement from the 1870s to the 1980s within a framework that is both uniquely Irish and highly influenced by international debates and movements. By accepting and analysing the Irish women's movement on its own terms it is possible to examine and understand the opportunities and constraints posed by Irish society and reveal how the women's movement evolved. The most popular vehicle for female activism in twentieth-century Ireland was either religious or lay support organizations rather than feminist political bodies. In general, women responded to the constraints of Irish society by organizing social women's movements, that focused on improving women's day-to-day lives in an impoverished and rigid society. These women's organizations approved of the ideals espoused by Irish culture that the family was the organic unit of society headed by a father with a mother as its heart and children its purpose.

RELIGION AND THE IRISH WOMEN'S MOVEMENT

Religion in Ireland provided a potential theatre of operation for women. Margaret O'Callaghan has pointed out that there is ample evidence of 'Catholicism as enabling and deeply powerful in the personal lives of many women.'[40] Furthermore, the vast majority of Catholic women who pursued social activism in Ireland were nuns. As Maria Luddy points out, by 1901 nuns made up 'more than a quarter of the professional adult women workers enumerated in the census returns.'[41] The large numbers of Roman Catholic religious sisters who ran hospitals, orphanages and schools throughout Ireland represented the most significant body of Irish women involved in voluntary activism.[42] This is one of the possible reasons for the relative dearth of Catholic laywomen involved in voluntary activism in Ireland, for which they were betimes rebuked by Catholic theologians.[43] Catriona Clear has described nuns as 'islands of female self-determination', but she has also raised the crucial question of their representativeness: were they typical of women of their time?[44] These women were not feminist, nor were they revolutionaries (quite the contrary, they generally upheld the social and class values of Irish society). However, they did educate generations of Irish women, prop up the health and welfare system for much of the twentieth century, and present many young women with their only image of working women. In the very serious confines of the Roman Catholic Church, Irish nuns were a continuous and visible presence.

Did the nunnery absorb potentially active Catholic women into an institutionalized and conservative force in Irish society? Had there been no convents would more Irish women have been involved in social activism that challenged women's role in society? Luddy has argued that because 'Catholicism, unlike the various Protestant denominations, fostered no sense of solidarity among lay Catholic women to pursue change for women in society', it can be regarded as a neutralizing influence on 'women's instinct for social criticism and social change.'[45] There is certainly no evidence that had Catholic women organized in greater numbers outside convent walls they would have been any more critical of the status of women in society. Organizations with large numbers of Catholic women, such as the Catholic Social Service Conference and the Legion of Mary, had a profoundly conservative view of women. However, the Mothers' Union,[46] a Protestant organization of mothers, was also highly conservative and non-critical regarding women's role.[47] As long as women in general organized around religion rather than gender their critical instincts tended to be 'neutralized'. That said, the largest civil organization in Ireland, the Irish Countrywomen's Association, which had large numbers of Catholic members but had predominately Protestant leadership, was notable for its uncritical attitude regarding the cultural assumptions about women's role in society. These women, similar to women in most of the civil organizations in Ireland, irrespective of religious persuasion, were critical of how Irish society failed to support the ideals it espoused. Women's critical instincts were perhaps less neutralized than deflected: in general Irish women, for much of the twentieth century, reserved their criticism not for the gender presumptions of society but for the apparent insincerity of those convictions. They regarded it as their chief purpose to call upon the Irish state to match its vision with policy initiatives and tangible support.

Nineteenth- and twentieth-century debates regarding the role of religion in Irish society were ferocious. Therefore, the profile of the main women's organization is noteworthy: in spite of the political and cultural pressures of the early twentieth century, multi-denominationalism remained the hallmark of the main women's organizations in the country. For organizations like the ICA to insist on a 'non-sectarian' ethos was a considerable feat in early twentieth-century Ireland. There were religious nuances and tensions embedded in these organizations, but the struggle to remain non-denominational is an essential part of their history nonetheless. It was largely the Protestant aristocracy that held leadership positions in voluntary organizations as they had the time, money and connections. From the outset the United Irishwomen (UI), later the ICA, was under Protestant management, which reflected the hierarchy of rural Ireland, and the privileges of class.[48] However, from its earliest days the ICA had a large Catholic membership.

The non-denominational stance of the main women's organizations was an implicit challenge to the Irish Free State where 'non-denominationalism' was highly suspect. The ICA did come under pressure for having in its early days, according to the Minister for Agriculture, 'a distinct aroma of ascendancy about it':[49] social code for being too British/Protestant – or somehow not *really* Irish.

This was perhaps part of the reason why the organization could not secure funding from the Irish government despite supporting the ideals espoused by every administration in government throughout the period. In 1937, it informed the government that 'of 80 similar rural associations . . . New Zealand and Ireland alone receive no government grant'.[50]

The ICA was also denied the approval and open support of the Roman Catholic hierarchy because of its 'non-sectarian' constitution. In practical terms, the organization's non-denominational stance provided it with categorization problems; neither religious group could openly identify with the organization, thereby reducing its funding opportunities. A combination of financial and official isolation made it increasingly difficult for organizations like the ICA to maintain their non-denominational stance. Essentially what unsettled the Roman Catholic hierarchy was the ICA's focus on materialism rather than spirituality – a heresy in poverty-stricken Catholic Ireland, which, making a virtue of necessity, almost glorified poverty and damned materialism.

Diarmaid Ferriter has unearthed evidence of the ICA's internal struggle and determination to maintain non-denominationalism. In 1952, an ICA member was photographed by press attending a conference of the World Union of Catholic Societies in Rome and the newspaper caption read: 'ICA member attends Catholic conference'.[51] The ICA executive informed the member that she had not been representing the society and should not have identified herself as a member for the photograph. However, internally there were power struggles in the organization that emerged as religious tensions. For example, at the society's Golden Jubilee in 1960 there was a heated debate over the fact that four 'non-Catholic' officers were elected to head the committee that would lead the Jubilee celebration. One member declared the election to be 'the quintessence of tolerance in our predominantly Catholic state'. Another retorted: 'this is not proof of tolerance but of apathy and reluctance on the part of our Catholic members who feel they are inferior to our non-Catholic sisters who are ever anxious to seek and accept office and leadership'.[52]

Democracy prevailed and the ICA held fast to the principles of its non-sectarian constitution; the members remained on the committee, but the tensions this debate revealed are interesting. Were they social or religious in origin? Was there a sense that the ICA's coming of age should have meant that Catholics were represented in positions of leadership commensurate with their membership numbers? It is likely that these disputes, masquerading as religious friction, were equally about in-house politics and localized social tension – the solidifying, for example, of the Catholic middle class? The ICA was the sum of its parts and this dispute reflected a sense that some members did not feel its parts were equally represented at management level.

In 2004 Kathleen Delap,[53] a dedicated ICA activist, died. Her obituary in *The Irish Times* outlined her social background as 'prosperous Protestant'. Embedded in the obituary were the social codes of religious division that the author, despite Delap's lifelong commitment to a non-sectarian organization, felt it necessary to explain: 'She had intended to study law but opted for architecture. Because TCD did not have a course she attended UCD . . .'[54] Trinity College Dublin (TCD) was traditionally the Protestant university and University College Dublin (UCD) the Catholic university. In view of how deep the religious anchors were in Irish society, the ICA emerges as a remarkable organization for its insistence, largely upheld, that: 'There shall not be any discussion of a party political or sectarian nature, nor shall any resolution which can be construed to be party political or sectarian be proposed or discussed at any meeting of the Association.'[55]

Non-sectarianism in women's voluntary groups was largely a Protestant pre-1922 legacy. There were indications that these organizations paid a price for their non-sectarian credentials, not just with regard to official acceptance and funding, but also in the degree to which they felt able to engage with certain issues. In the 1960s and 70s, when the moral climate in Ireland was changing and issues such as contraception, divorce and abortion were emerging as open for debate, the IHA and ICA were remarkably constrained. The reason both organizations gave was a general feeling that such issues were potentially 'religion sensitive'.[56] The price of consensus was not confronting so-called 'moral issues', despite the fact that they were rapidly being conceptualized as 'women's issues'. In 1974, the Council for the Status of Women (CSW) was unable to issue a press release in support of the Commission on the Status of Women in Irish Society's (established 1970) recommendations on family planning, due to the inability of its affiliates (including the ICA and IHA) to arrive at an agreed position.[57] In 1978, the ICA sent a family planning survey to its 30,000 plus membership. Only a minority responded (1,200) and quite a few claimed the issue was 'sectarian and unconstitutional'.[58] It proved virtually impossible to canvass members for their opinion on birth control.

Connolly argues that the Irish women's movement 'both reflects and subverts Anglo-American white feminism in unusual ways'.[59] What is remarkable, in view of the myriad of factors that served to divide and separate Ireland from wider international trends in women's activism, is the degree of similarity. This was due in large part to the leadership role played by Protestant Irish women and the inclusive and non-denominational nature of the most prominent organizations. These factors combined provided both the basis for similarity and difference: Protestant leadership ensured certain Anglo-American characteristics in the Irish movement, while the large Catholic membership contributed some of its crucial differences.

IRISH WOMEN'S MOVEMENT: AGENTS OF CHANGE OR IMPROVEMENT?

The ICA was inspired by the co-operative movement and the desire to make rural Ireland a better place for women. It sought change in order to bolster a traditional way of life, thus intrinsically changing that way of life and the perception of it.[60] Though not a self-declared feminist organization, the ICA explicitly sought social change. Its rally call, 'A woman's place is where she can best help her home', was reminiscent of its nineteenth-century predecessors.[61] The domestic arena was thus extended into the public realm. The ICA, while traditional and innovative, was not unique.

The ICA was such a potent source of support for women precisely because it was embedded in Irish society, because it valued the basic social and cultural tenets of that society, and wished to protect a living rural community with women at the centre of its future.[62] Female emigration was a big issue for rural Ireland throughout the century and the ICA argued that until life in rural Ireland was improved for women the tide would never be stemmed.[63] To that end the ICA established a campaign to encourage brides-to-be to refuse to marry unless their home had running water.[64] The organization produced witty posters that read 'Who said "Love, Honour and Carry Water"?',[65] which were essentially about getting Irish women to use their domestic lobbying power to improve their own living standards. The Irish government eventually acknowledged that the ICA had been 'prime movers in the demand for such amenities as electricity, piped water, better housing and better transport'.[66]

There is also evidence that the ICA sought to have the notion of women's work re-evaluated. In 1937 the ICA ran a series of articles on 'Visiting Our Neighbours', which stressed the different experiences of rural women throughout the world. One article, featuring women in Finland, seemed envious of the attitude to women's work: 'The wife works in the fields with her husband, or, if wealthier, she may take an outside post and pay a maid to look after the house, but the point is: she works. Marriage does not interfere with careers.'[67] The ICA was aware that similar women's organizations fared better across the water. In 1951 Mrs Alexander of the Seal Women's Institute, Kent, England, visited ICA guilds throughout the country. She informed one guild that the Women's Institutes (WI):

> have always been greatly encouraged by their Government and have been given grants to carry out their work, which by her description is very much like the work and interests of the ICA. They have direct contact with Government bodies, such as the Ministry of Education and the Ministry of Agriculture. This has been a tremendous help to the WI and has also meant that they have influence which they have been able to use to good effect. Mrs Alexander greatly admired the courage and initiative of the ICA in carrying on for so many years supported only by the subscriptions and money-making efforts of its own members. She considered we had had a tough time . . .[68]

In 1950 the organization, at the request of the Department of Agriculture, assisted Margaret Hockin of the Food and Agricultural Organisation in her study of women's work in rural Ireland.[69] This exercise, the organization believed, helped them to 'become visible to the male establishment'.[70] This theme of visibility was crucially important to how women's role in Irish society was perceived by contemporaries and consequently how it has been recorded by historians. As the ICA was not a self-professed feminist organization its achievements in 'consciousness-raising', confidence-building and self-improvement tended to be overlooked or seen as part of a traditional framework that 'kept women oppressed', rather than an organization for women about women.

The IHA was also primarily interested in improving the living conditions of women. The organization championed the rights of the poor, advocated social citizenship, and operated as the state's first consumer watchdog. It was one of the first women's organizations (post-1922) to take to the streets in protest about the failure of the government to introduce a free mother-and-child scheme in 1951.[71] It was its membership of the International Alliance of Women which led to the formation of the Ad Hoc Committee on the Status of Women in Ireland in 1968 with other women's groups (including the ICA) to lobby for a national commission to investigate the status of women in Ireland.[72] In this it was successful and the Commission, established in late 1969 by the government, had as its remit: 'the making of recommendations on the steps necessary to ensure the participation of women on equal terms with men in the political, social, cultural and economic life of the country'.[73] The report of the Commission on the Status of Women, published in 1972, formed the blueprint for the re-evaluation of women's position in Irish society.[74]

A SISTERHOOD?

The ICA and the IHA were not apart from Irish society; they did not reject it: their power came from relevance rather than revolution. As Ferriter argues, 'to provide can often encompass as great a degree of radicalism, innovation and energy as to agitate'.[75] During the 1960s and 70s, as feminism began to emerge as a political issue in modern Ireland, the ICA clearly identified itself as a 'women's organisation not a feminist one'.[76] In 1985, Mamo MacDonald, the president of the ICA, claimed that while radical feminists may demand contraception it was poultry, not the pill, that interested most of the women she represented.[77] She wrote: 'for all the publicity which our more militant sisters can generate, the ICA has a more revolutionary and direct bearing on the vast majority of Irish women'.[78] However, there was an acknowledgement of a sisterhood.

The radical feminist movement that emerged in the early 70s in Ireland may have resisted their lineage but more things bound than separated them from the women's movement. As Nell McCafferty, the epitome of this new radical feminism, noted:

> I used to in my callous youth condemn the ICA for being reactionary and square with their emphasis on running water and electricity. I remember in the seventies attacking them because they weren't looking for the Pill. And then I retired to Crosshaven later that decade and joined them . . .[79]

Tweedy, the founder of the IHA, makes explicit the continuity in the women's movement:

So many people believe that the women's movement was born on some mystical date in 1970, like Aphrodite rising from the waves. It has been a long continuous battle in which many women have struggled to gain equality, each generation adding something to the achievements of the past.[80]

They were 'links in the chain' that stretched from the mid-nineteenth century through to the late twentieth century, one that can be clearly mapped by personnel, organizations merging and joining forces, and a deep sense of a female legacy of activism. This was a fraught sisterhood, but it was a sisterhood. Not all the many histories of the women's movement are contained within a feminist conceptual framework. They were all agents, nonetheless, in developing a critique of women's status in Ireland throughout the twentieth century.[81]

There is little doubt that the so-called 'second wave feminist movement' appeared to break like a wave upon Irish shores.[82] The Irish Women's Liberation Movement (WLM) emerged in the summer of 1970 from a small Dublin café where many different groups of intellectuals and artists gathered.[83] Its founding members, being predominately journalists, were aware of the importance of public exposure[84] and were convinced that 'You had to shock in order to make things better.'[85] Nonetheless, a measure of the particular social environment in Ireland is the fact that these radical young women did not include divisive issues such as divorce and abortion within their framework for change. These issues were, it appears, initially ignored through ignorance.[86] Though it drew on the American movement and the experience of the civil rights movement in Northern Ireland, its focus had a uniquely Irish flavour. As McCafferty observed: 'We were more interested in avoiding pregnancy than achieving orgasm.'[87] For so long the nightmare fate of any Irish girl was lone motherhood.[88] The radical 'mould breaking' feminists were instinctively shaped by the Catholic ethos from which they emerged.

The Irish WLM is best remembered for its launch appearance on the popular talk show programme on Irish television, *The Late Late Show*, in 1971 and the Contraceptive Train staged on 22 May 1971.[89] However, as McCafferty notes, after the Contraceptive Train outing the organization was unsure of 'what to do for an encore'.[90] Structural problems and tensions between socialist members and other sections of the group who wished to have a more stringently feminist focus eventually led to its implosion.[91] The energies aroused were not entirely dissipated, with many women investing their new found awareness in other organizations and women's liberation remained on the public agenda for the following decades. However, by the early 1980s there was a sense of pessimism among many of the founders, which was captured by Ailbhe Smyth:

We know that the encounters of the 1970s over contraception, rape, equal pay – were mere skirmishes, a phoney war, prior to the battles of the 1980s against the serried ranks of church and state, staunch defenders of the Faith of our Fathers and the myth of motherhood . . .[92]

There was also evidence that some Irish women felt alienated by the radical feminist movement, feeling that: 'They're holding on to this image too long. I mean that's gone and done with. This bra burning.'[93] Others felt pressurized or judged by the movement: 'They make housewives feel they're inadequate compared to the ones that are out doing something, contributing something to society besides staying home.'[94]

The legacy of this radical wave of feminism is yet to be properly assessed, but its immediate results were fractured though significant: the formation of single-issue organizations, for example, Action, Information, Motivation (AIM) (1972), Contraceptive Action Campaign (1976), and the Rape Crisis Centre (1977).[95] It certainly succeeded in altering the parameters of the debate on the status and rights of women in Ireland. However, this altered public discourse would not have been as readily achieved without such immediate access to the media or the groundwork done by longstanding women's organizations which had chipped away for decades at the edifice of state exclusion. In many ways the radical women could only consider operating outside 'the system' because other women's groups served the function of system engagement.

CONCLUSION

The impact of the Irish women's movement was as varied as the movement's composition. Many social service organizations provided a social outlet, a support network and an education. Others acted as lobby groups to improve the position of women. This lobbying could be directed at voters, policy-makers, husbands, the legal system or religious leaders. Indeed, many women's organizations did a bit of all of the above and, however divergent their make-up, emphasis or core-ideals, there was a strong sense of female co-operation and connection between them all and very little evidence of friction and resistance.

Historians are increasingly questioning the interpretation of Irish women as passive agents prior to their awakening in the late 1960s. This is partly as a result of a growing tendency to place Ireland in an international context, but ironically also because historians are increasingly analysing Irish society on its own terms. There is little doubt that in analysing Irish women's civil organizations in light of the particular social environment that Ireland presented one can appreciate the opportunities and constraints they faced while acknowledging the international context and its considerable influence. An examination of the Irish women's movement in its totality allows for a fuller understanding of its complexity and diversity, and a broader interpretation of the politics of agitation as demonstrated by women for women.

NOTES

1   Hilda Tweedy, *A Link in the Chain: The Story of the Irish Housewives Association 1942–1992* (Dublin: Attic Press, 1992), p. 111.

2   Lucy Kingston, 'The Irishwoman's outlook', in *The Englishwoman*, 37, January–March 1918, reprinted in Maria Luddy (ed.), *Women in Ireland, 1800–1918: A Documentary History* (Cork: Cork University Press, 1995), p. 185.

3   Lucy Kingston epitomizes the continuity and complexity of the Irish women's movement. She was involved in the IHA, Irish Women's Suffrage Federation, the Irish Women's Reform League, the Irish Women's International League and the National Council for Women.

4   Mary O'Dowd, 'Church, state and women: the aftermath of partition', in Chris Curtain, Pauline Jackson and Barbara O'Connor (eds), *Gender in Irish Society* (Galway: University College Galway, 1987), pp. 3–33; Rosemary Cullen Owens, *Smashing Times: A History of the Irish Women's Suffrage Movement 1889–1922* (Dublin: Attic Press, 1995); Carol Coulter, *The Hidden Tradition: Feminism, Women and Nationalism in Ireland* (Cork: Mercier Press, 1993). Both Valiulis and Beaumont have questioned this. From the 1990s historical research began to broaden both the conceptualization of women's activism and the notion of the women's movement. Maryann Valiulis, 'Engendering citizenship: women's relationship to the state in Ireland and the United States in the post-suffrage period', in Mary O'Dowd and Maryann Valiulis (eds), *Women and Irish History* (Dublin: Wolfhound, 1997), pp. 159–72; Catriona Beaumont, 'Women and the politics of equality: the Irish women's movement, 1930–1943', in O'Dowd and Valiulis (eds), *Women and Irish History*, pp. 185–205.

5   Ailbhe Smyth, 'The contemporary women's movement', *Women's Studies International Forum*, Special Issue on Feminism in Ireland, 11, (4), pp. 331–41 (p. 341). By 1982 a new 'state feminism' was adopted by government with the appointment of a Minister of State for Women's Affairs and Family Law Reform.

6   From the outset the Irish women's movement was nourished by contact with an international network of women. Carmel Quinlan, *Genteel Revolutionaries: Anna and Thomas Haslam and the Irish Women's Movement* (Cork: Cork University Press, 2002); Mary E. Daly, '"Oh, Kathleen Ni Houlihan, your way's a thorny way!": the condition of women in twentieth-century Ireland', in Anthony Bradley and Maryann Valiulis (eds), *Gender and Sexuality in Modern Ireland* (Massachusetts, 1997), pp. 102–26.

7   Mary Cullen, 'Women, emancipation and politics, 1860–1984', in J. R. Hill (ed.), *A New History of Ireland, Vol. 7, Ireland, 1921–1984* (Oxford: Clarendon Press, 2003), pp. 836–82 (p. 836).

8   Hanna Sheehy-Skeffington, 'Reminiscences of an Irish suffragette' (1941), published as part of the pamphlet, *Votes for Women: Irish Women's Struggle for the Vote* (1975) and cited in Angela Bourke *et al.* (eds), *The Field Day Anthology of Irish Writing, Vol. 5: Irish Women's Writing and Traditions* (Cork: Cork University Press, 2002), p. 91.

9   Cliona Murphy, *The Women's Suffrage Movement and Irish Society in the Early Twentieth Century* (Philadelphia: Temple University Press, 1989); Rosemary Cullen Owens, *Louie Bennett* (Cork: Cork University Press, 2001); Maria Luddy, 'Women and politics in nineteenth-century Ireland', in O'Dowd and Valiulis (eds), *Women and Irish History*, pp. 89–108 (p. 91).

10 Cullen Owens, *Smashing Times.*

11 Quinlan, *Genteel Revolutionaries*; Margaret Ward, 'From marginality and militancy: Cumann na mBan, 1914–1936', in Austin Morgan and Bob Purdie (eds), *Ireland: Divided Nation, Divided Class* (London, 1980), pp. 96–110.

12 Quinlan, *Genteel Revolutionaries.*

13 Margaret Ward, *Unmanageable Revolutionaries: Women and Irish Nationalism* (London: Pluto Press, 1983); Cullen Owens, *Smashing Times*; Murphy, *The Women's Suffrage*

Movement. Shannon Byrne argues that historians have overstated the conflict between suffragists and nationalists and failed to examine the large degree of consensus that existed. Shannon A. Byrne, 'Conflict in consensus: Irish suffragists and nationalists, 1908–1918', (Unpublished MA thesis, University College Dublin, 2006).

14 Diane Urquhart, *Women in Ulster Politics 1890–1940: A History Not Yet Told* (Dublin: Irish Academic Press, 2000).

15 Cullen, 'Women, emancipation and politics'.

16 *The Irish Citizen*, April 1919, p. 656. The death of the Irish party is a reference to the demise of the Irish Parliamentary Party and the Home Rule movement in the face of the emergence of Sinn Féin and separatism nationalism post-1916.

17 Sinn Féin was a radical nationalist party founded in 1905. In 1918 successful Sinn Féin election candidates refused to take up their seats in Westminster; this was known as abstentionism.

18 Daly, '"Oh, Kathleen Ni Houlihan'; Catherine Shannon, 'The changing face of Cathleen ní Houlihan: women and politics in Ireland, 1960–1996', in Bradley and Valiulis (eds), *Gender and Sexuality*, pp. 257–74.

19 Linda Connolly, *The Irish Women's Movement: From Revolution to Devolution* (Dublin: Lilliput, 2003), p. 58; Beaumont in O'Dowd and Valiulis (eds) *Women and Irish History*, pp. 185–205; Catriona Beaumont, 'Gender, citizenship and the state in Ireland, 1922–1990', in Scott Brewster, Virginia Crossman, Fiona Becket and David Alderson (eds), *Ireland in Proximity: History, Gender, Space* (London and New York: Routledge, 1999), pp. 94–108.

20 Valiulis, 'Engendering citizenship'.

21 Diarmaid Ferriter, *Mothers, Maidens and Myths: A History of the Irish Countrywomen's Association* (Dublin: ICA, 1994); Aileen Heverin, *ICA: The Irish Countrywomen's Association: A History, 1910–2000* (Wolfhound Press, Dublin, 2001); Tweedy, *A Link in the Chain*.

22 Tweedy, *A Link in the Chain*.

23 Smyth, 'The contemporary women's movement'.

24 The Juries Act, 1927, allowed women to sit on juries only if they specifically applied. This was a concession to the women's movement as the original bill had excluded women altogether. Beaumont, 'Gender, citizenship and the state'.

25 Section 16 of the Conditions of Employment Act, 1936, allowed the Minister for Industry and Commerce to limit the number of women working in any given industry. Daly noted this section was never enforced. Beaumont, 'Gender, citizenship and the state'; Mary E. Daly, 'Women in the Irish Free State, 1922–1939: the interaction between economics and ideology', in Joan Hoff and Maureen Coulter (eds), *Irish Women's Voices Past and Present* (Indiana: Indiana University Press, 1995), pp. 99–116.

26 For details of the Council's affiliates see the memorandum submitted to the Commission on Vocational Organisation by the Joint Committee on Vocationalism', 15 November 1940 (Document 200, Ms. 941, Vol., 20, p. 1), National Library of Ireland. I am grateful to M. ÓhÓgartaigh for a copy of this document.

27 See letter to the Executive Council from the Joint Committee of Women's Societies and Social Workers, 24 May 1937, regarding the 1937 Constitution and the rights of women: 'Women, position under Constitution 1937', Dept. Taoiseach, S9880.

28 Dept. Taoiseach, S9278.

29 Beaumont, 'Gender, citizenship and the state'.

30 Lindsey Earner-Byrne, 'Reinforcing the family: the role of gender, morality, and sexuality in Irish welfare policy, 1922–1944', *The History of the Family*, 13, (4), (2008), pp. 360–9.

31   Finola Kennedy, *Cottage to Crèche: Family Change in Ireland* (Dublin: Institute of Public Administration, 2001).

32   This allowed a woman a maximum of 40 shillings for herself and 10 shillings for each child on separation. Martin Pugh, *Women and the Women's Movement in Britain 1914–1959* (London: Macmillan, 1992), p. 108.

33   This provided women with equal grounds for divorce. Pugh, *The Women's Movement in Britain*.

34   This provided for equal rights between the sexes with respect to guardianship of infants. Pugh, *The Women's Movement in Britain*.

35   Divorce was legalized in 1995, equal guardianship rights were secured in 1964.

36   Kennedy, *Cottage to Crèche*.

37   Despite a sustained campaign, women police were not introduced in Ireland until 1959. The women were officially stonewalled by politicians that considered the agitation for women police as 'an artificial business without any real roots in the country'. Minute to M. O. Muimhneachain, Secretary, Department of Taoiseach, from S. A. Roche, Dept. of Justice, 23 November 1939, Dept. Taoiseach, S16210. See Beaumont, 'Women and the politics of equality'.

38   The Committee of Inquiry into the 1885 Criminal Law Amendment Acts (Carrigan Committee) established in 1930 was largely as a result of pressure by women's groups and 18 of the 29 witnesses called were women. This committee resulted in the raising of the age of sexual consent to 17 years. Maria Luddy, *Prostitution and Irish Society, 1800–1940* (Cambridge University Press, 2007).

39   Dr Browne, *Dáil Eireann Debates*, col. 1437, vol. 258, 9 February 1972.

40   Margaret O' Callaghan, 'Women in politics in independent Ireland, 1921–1968', in Bourke *et al.* (eds), *Field Day Anthology*, pp. 120–34.

41   Maria Luddy and Mary Cullen (eds), *Women, Power and Consciousness in Nineteenth-Century Ireland* (Dublin, 1995), p. 23.

42   Connolly suggests that Catholic women in Ireland deliberately engaged with organized Catholicism to find personal fulfilment denied them elsewhere. Connolly, *The Irish Women's Movement*, p. 61.

43   For example, Revd L. McKenna, *An Irish Catholic Women's League* (Dublin, 1917).

44   Caitriona Clear, *Nuns in Nineteenth-Century Ireland* (Dublin: Gill and Macmillan, 1987), p. 34.

45   Luddy, 'Women and politics in nineteenth-century Ireland', p. 71.

46   The Mother's Union claimed 11,907 members in 1940. Memo submitted to the Commission on Vocational Organisation, p. 6.

47   E. Davidson, *The Mother's Union, Its Vision, Our Failure* (Dublin: Church of Ireland Printing Co., 1936).

48   Sarah McNamara, *Those Intrepid United Irishwomen: Pioneers of the Irish Countrywomen's Association* (Limerick: Parteen, 1995).

49   Ferriter, *Mothers, Maidens and Myths*, p. 11.

50   Ibid., p. 15. The ICA finally received government funding in 1951.

51   Ibid., p. 51.

52   Ibid., p. 53.

53   Kathleen Delap was one of the three ICA members who sat on the Commission for the Status of Women in Ireland established in 1970.

54   'Kathleen Delap: Irish countrywomen's activist who worked locally, thought globally', in *The Irish Times*, 13 November 2004.

55 Ferriter, *Mothers, Maidens and Myths*, p. 53.
56 *Commission on the Status of Women Report* (Dublin, 1972), paras 568–74. Cited in Tweedy, *A Link in the Chain*, p. 47.
57 Tweedy, *A Link in the Chain*.
58 Ferriter, *Mothers, Maidens and Myths*, p. 54.
59 Connolly, *The Irish Women's Movement*, p. 35.
60 *Farmer's Gazette*, 2 January 1937.
61 Ferriter, *Mothers, Maidens and Myths*, p. 17.
62 The ICA details its own history and its emphasis on improving rural life. See 'Memo of the Irish Country Women's Association to the Commission on Vocational Organisation, July, 1940' (Doc. 196, Ms. 941/vol. 20).
63 Mary E. Daly, *The Slow Failure: Population Decline and Independent Ireland, 1920–1973* (Madison Wisconsin: University of Wisconsin Press, 2006).
64 Daly, *The Slow Failure*.
65 Ferriter, *Mothers, Maidens and Myths*, p. 46.
66 Editorial, *The Irish Times*, 14 April 1961.
67 *Farmer's Gazette*, 18 September 1937, p. 961.
68 *Farmer's Gazette*, 23 June 1951, p. 750.
69 Heverin, *ICA*; Ferriter, *Mothers, Maidens and Myths*.
70 Heverin, *ICA*, p. 107.
71 The mother-and-child scheme was to provide a free maternity service for all mothers and medical care for all children under 16 years. Lindsey Earner-Byrne, 'Managing motherhood: negotiating a maternity service for Catholic mothers in Dublin, 1930–1954, *Social History of Medicine*, 19, (2), (2006), pp. 261–77 (p. 274).
72 The report on the Ad Committee's meeting with the Taoiseach outlines the role of the committee in lobbying for the establishment of a commission on the status of women, 13 November 1969. Dept. Taoiseach, Cabinet, 96/6/184.
73 The Department of Finance was anxious that the terms of reference of the commission be broader than 'equal pay'. Cabinet 96/6/184.
74 *Report of the Commission on the Status of Women* (Dublin: Stationery Office, 1972).
75 Ferriter, *Mothers, Maidens and Myths*, p. 61.
76 Ibid., p. 60.
77 Daly questions the relevance of the women's movement to many women's lives. Daly, 'Women in the Irish Free State'.
78 Ferriter, *Mothers, Maidens and Myths*, p. 60.
79 Ibid., p. 60.
80 Tweedy, *A Link in the Chain*, p. 111.
81 Connolly's main thesis is to challenge the assumption that women were 'passive or tangential subjects in socio-historical change.' Connolly, *The Irish Women's Movement*, p. 6.
82 June Levine, 'The women's movement in the Republic of Ireland, 1968–80', in Bourke *et al.* (eds), *Field Day Anthology*, pp. 177–87.
83 Anne Stopper, *Mondays at Gaj's: The Story of the Irish Women's Liberation Movement* (Dublin: The Liffey Press, 2006).
84 McCafferty noted that within a month of its foundation they had turned the women's pages in the national newspapers to the cause of liberation. Nell McCafferty, *Nell* (Dublin: Penguin Ireland, 2004).
85 Máirín Johnston cited in Stopper, *Monday at Gaj's*, p. 47.
86 McCafferty, *Nell*.

87 Ibid., p. 202.
88 Lindsey Earner-Byrne, *Mother and Child: Maternity and Child Welfare in Dublin, 1922–60* (Manchester: Manchester University Press, 2007).
89 McCafferty, *Nell.*
90 Ibid., p. 230.
91 Pat Brennan, 'Women in revolt', in *Magill*, April 1979 cited in Levine, 'The women's movement in the Republic of Ireland'.
92 Smyth, 'The contemporary women's movement', p. 341.
93 Cited in *The Irish Housewife: A Portrait* (Dublin: Irish Consumer Research, 1986), p. 78.
94 Ibid., p. 79.
95 Connolly, *The Irish Women's Movement.*

8

Conflicting rights: the struggle for female citizenship in Northern Ireland

Myrtle Hill and Margaret Ward

INTRODUCTORY: THE FORMATION OF THE NORTHERN IRISH STATE

While the experiences of women in civil and political life in the six north-eastern counties of Ireland in many ways paralleled those of their contemporaries in both the rest of Ireland and in Britain, the constitutional conflict which dominated its history over the course of the twentieth century inevitably influenced events and helped determine both the nature and extent of women's participation in the public arena. From its establishment in 1920 the newly constituted state of Northern Ireland was dominated – politically, socially and economically – by the pro-British unionism which had led to rejection of the independence claimed by the remaining 26 counties of the island.[1] Vulnerable to hostility from Irish republican ambitions both within and outside its borders, the new unionist-dominated parliament – for whom Catholicism was associated with Republicanism and Protestantism with Unionism – presided over a regime characterized by sectarian division, discrimination and violent disruption.[2] With this unionist power-base remaining firmly in place until the late 1960s it is perhaps not surprising that, when demands were made for reform in the area of political representation, they focused almost exclusively on the religious/political divide. Other equality discourses, around gender, sexuality, disability or race, began to emerge only in the final decades of the century and even then it proved difficult to transcend the boundaries of the over-simplistic 'two communities' binary.[3] Moreover, though our focus is on the struggle for full female citizenship, the determination of women themselves either to support nationalist aspirations or strengthen the link with Britain should not be underestimated as valid political goals.

Nonetheless, and although the movement was fractured by competing nationalist identities, women from the North of Ireland had been well represented in the suffrage campaigns of the late nineteenth, early twentieth centuries,[4] and there is at least some evidence to suggest that, while the story of the subsequent pursuit of the rights of female citizenship has been considerably undermined by the violent dynamics and recurring crises of mainstream politics, there is a story to be told. In telling that story, by pulling together, assessing and analysing published work on the topic, this chapter also identifies significant gaps in the research and suggests an agenda for the way forward.

STORMONT RULE 1922–72

In pre-partition Ireland, as in Britain, women over the age of 30 had been granted the vote in February 1918 and, while politicized women in the six counties had previously engaged in a range of activities reflecting their particular national or party allegiances, their newly won rights provided them with a more effective platform and a greater degree of influence. The extent of that influence was, however, significantly affected by the wider political context, with those on the nationalist side isolated by unionist domination of political and economic life and further disadvantaged by the abstentionist policy adopted by most parties representing their interests.[5] Those women who identified with and supported unionism, on the other hand, were likely to have enjoyed greater access to those in power and to be in a position to influence their decisions.

The most active of these could be found in the Ulster Women's Unionist Association (UWUA), formed in 1911 and described by Diane Urquhart as 'the largest female political group Ireland had ever seen'.[6] Enjoying middle-class leadership and a wide and popular following, UWUA members had fully participated in the struggle against Home Rule, and their wide communications network, embracing both the local aristocracy and the populist Orange Lodges, played an important role in strengthening unionist solidarity. The organization's significance in influencing newly enfranchised women was acknowledged in the decision of the powerful all-male Ulster Unionist Council to grant them 12 seats in 1920.[7]

Though the 1920 Government of Ireland Act was viewed by the unionist camp as an unhappy compromise, in the immediate aftermath of its passage the main priority of the pro-British majority was the consolidation and maintenance of unionist power in the newly created province. For women as well as men, Northern Ireland's first elections, held in 1921, provided an opportunity for a focused and targeted campaign. The Duchess of Abercorn's rallying cry to unionist women stressed that though UWUA members had not been among those who had

> clamoured for the vote, . . . now it had been given to them, she was confident they intended to use it to the safety, honour and welfare of their Church, their country, their homes, and their children by helping to put a strong local government in power.[8]

The vulnerability of the new state was cited as a key reason for the organization's preference for male candidates, with its members concentrating on ensuring that all potential women voters were officially registered and that they understood the system of proportional representation that was to be used to contest the 52 seats.[9]

Women on the nationalist side were also involved in supporting their political representatives, though the abstentionist policy of many nationalist parties put them at a severe disadvantage because the decision not to recognize or participate in the new state resulted in a lack of structures and organization at both local and national levels. The Ladies' Auxiliary of the Ancient Order of Hibernians was probably the most popular nationalist organization for women in the North, carrying out similar work to that of the UWUA. Established in 1910, the Hibernians underwent something of a revival in Ulster in the 1920s, with 42 branches established by 1923. Largely working-class in composition, and relying heavily on family networks, this organization provided visible and enthusiastic support to constitutional nationalist Joseph Devlin.[10] On the republican side, Cumann na mBan, first formed in 1914 to facilitate women's engagement in that earlier period of the struggle against British rule, carried out propaganda and electioneering work for Sinn Féin. However, given the immediate background to this election, and with national rather than gender identity the major priority, it is perhaps hardly surprising that, as Urquhart notes, 'no female parliamentary [or municipal] candidates were forwarded by nationalist parties in Ulster from 1921 to 1940'.[11]

The geographical boundaries of the new state ensured that unionist electoral success was virtually inevitable, and the return of 40 of their number, to the nationalists' 12, together with the latter's absence from parliament ensured their domination of the political arena. The two women who took their seats in the new parliament buildings at Stormont opened by King George on 22 June, Julia McMordie and Dehra Chichester, also had sound unionist credentials; each was the widow of a former unionist MP and both were active members of the UWUA. McMordie, Vice-President of the UWUA, had been the first woman member of Belfast City Council and an Alderman and served at Stormont for four years.[12] Dehra Chichester (becoming Parker in 1928), was able, during her 25 years in parliament, to make an impact as one of the staunchest supporters of unionist policy. Her party loyalty and her articulate defence of unionism was rewarded – serving as parliamentary secretary to the Ministry for Education from 1937 to 1944 and as Minister for Health and Local Government from 1949 to 1957, she was the only woman cabinet minister during the entire life of the Northern Ireland Parliament. In her support of controversial legislation which ensured the maintenance of Protestant/unionist power both locally and regionally, Parker claimed to be 'representing thousands of women in the Six Counties . . .'. In 1935, however, she made it clear that that representation had little to do with gender equality; that she was 'not an advocate . . . that women in every case should have equal duties and equal rights with men'.[13] Arguing that the unionist government had always 'shown the greatest sympathy in that direction', she maintained that any additional intervention was unnecessary.

The gender imbalance reflected in the discourse around and in the make-up of this first parliament set the pattern for decades to come. Although women made up an electoral majority of 52 per cent after the passage of the Representation of the People Act in 1928, and both unionist and nationalist political leaders courted their support by granting access to various committees and increasing links between male and female organizations, the need for more female representation at the forefront of politics was not advocated by either party leaders or their followers. Moreover, from the 1929 election the dropping of proportional representation in favour of a simple majority vote reinforced the domination of the unionist/nationalist question and effectively sidelined other interest groups.

Between 1920 and the imposition of Direct Rule from Westminster in 1972, only 20 women were put forward as candidates to Stormont (they shared a total of 43 candidacies including by-elections).[14] Nine of these were successfully elected; six were unionist – (including the two discussed above) and staunchly loyalist: Margaret Waring (1929–33), Dinah McNabb (1949–65), Elizabeth Maconachie (1953–69) and Anne Letitia Dickson (1969–72). Like their predecessors in Northern Ireland's first parliament, these women were regarded by the electorate as defenders of the majority unionist position and, similarly interpreting their role, they neither individually nor collectively presented any challenge to the patriarchal conservative nature of the region's political culture. The remaining three women MPs represented the University constituency in Belfast; however, as Independents, they neither fitted so easily into the conventional mould nor were able to make an effective impact. For example, Lilian Calvert resigned in 1953 because she believed that Northern Ireland could not improve its 'tragic unemployment circumstances' while partition continued, while Sheila Murnaghan, Northern Ireland's first woman barrister and the only Liberal ever to serve in the Stormont Parliament (1961–9), devoted much time to producing a Human Rights Bill to make discrimination illegal on the basis of race, creed, colour or political belief. She also wanted to set up a human rights commission to investigate allegations of discrimination, but her proposals were firmly rejected by the Stormont government.[15]

During this period, in addition to its regional parliament, Northern Ireland also elected 12 representatives to Westminster. The record of women's participation in this body was even more dismal, with no female candidates standing for election in the inter-war period and only three elected prior to 1972. Patricia Ford, a unionist, who succeeded her father in North Down, served only two years before her retirement in 1955. Florence McLaughlin, a member of the Executive Committee of the UWUA, sat at Westminster between 1955 and 1964. Despite the higher profile of women at Westminster more generally, the only other woman to represent Northern Ireland during the twentieth century was Bernadette Devlin, a 22-year-old nationalist, whose story is inextricably linked with the civil disturbances of the late 1960s, and will therefore be discussed below.

It is usually agreed that, in the formal world of politics, participation at local level was more accessible and amenable for women. Granted admission to all areas of Irish municipal administration by 1911, it is perhaps in this area that we would expect to see their main contribution to public life. However, with sectarian divisions minimizing Catholic input, levels of female participation were also not so high as might have been expected and, moreover, those women who were elected were placed in the least powerful positions. Thus, for example between 1896 and 1940, although a total of 260 women served as Poor Law Guardians and local government councillors in Ulster, the majority of these – 67 per cent – were in the least powerful position of Poor Law Guardians. The gendered nature of the hierarchy is all too evident through all components of municipal government during this period. At the topmost level only 4 per cent of women in local government served as county borough councillors, 3 per cent as county councillors and 2 per cent as borough councillors. More worryingly, with women contesting these positions relatively late, only minimal progress occurred between the beginning and end of the period.[16] Despite female elect-oral majorities in Antrim, Armagh, Down and Derry, and the urging of UWUA for women candidates to come forward, the winning of the female vote in this area did not result in any dramatic rise in their representation. Diane Urquhart identifies the key reasons for this – the practical considerations of time, money and the apathy of the nationalist community for whom unionist dominated local government held little attraction and offered few rewards.[17]

Nonetheless, while the support of husbands and families eased the way for some women, philanthropic endeavours provided other public-spirited individuals with the motivation, experience and confidence to enter public life at local level. As Maria Luddy points out, charitable activities in pursuit of temperance, child protection or better educational opportunities, while most frequently inspired by religious faith, brought upper and middle-class women into close contact with the poor and outcast and often had a politicizing effect.[18] A minority of women were therefore able to exercise their civic responsibilities, usually in areas deemed appropriate to their gender – public health, education and housing. The concerns of Julia McMordie, the first woman appointed to Belfast Corporation in 1918, were typical:

> When I first joined the Corporation I chose Committees where I thought I could be of service, such as The Public Health, The Maternity and Child Welfare, The Children's Act, The Tuberculosis . . . I am also a Member of the Belfast Education Committee, and Chairman of the School Medical Services Sub-Committee . . . I am very much interested in the Health and well being of the Citizens, more especially of the children . . .[19]

Over the course of the past decade, feminist historians have turned their attention to women's engagement in 'informal politics' in the years between the end of the suffrage movement and the rise of 'second wave' feminism. In the Republic this has produced convincing evidence that what was previously seen as a barren period in terms of the campaign for female citizenship was in fact one in which a strong thread of continuity in female activism can be traced. Such a detailed re-examination has not yet occurred in the North. There is some evidence of an alternative, though muted, female discourse during Northern Ireland's first election campaign, with the Belfast Women's Advisory Council and Belfast Women's Citizens' Union calling for the selection of women candidates to deal with issues such as Poor Law reform, education, moral reform, child welfare and other areas where women's input was felt to be particularly appropriate.[20] Although little has survived in the historical records, the existence of these pressure groups suggests that female concern with political inequalities continued to be articulated. This is consistent with the small number of records relating to individual suffragist activists who went on to challenge gendered limitations to citizenship through engagement with co-operative, trade union or other religious or welfare-based organizations.[21]

It is difficult, however, to argue for the existence of sustained female political activism in the North between the 1920s and the 1960s, particularly through the kind of networks which have now been recognized as of significance in the Republic.[22] Recent research suggests, for example, that the Irish Housewives Association and the Irish Countrywomen's Association either did not have direct parallels in the six counties or, where some presence is indicated, sufficient sources have not survived (or, as for example for the Northern Ireland Federation of Women's Institutes, are not accessible) to enable us to draw firm conclusions. Christopher Shepard concludes that, outside the home, women in Northern Ireland mainly engaged in traditional activities and were much more likely than their UK counterparts to be members of religious, rather than secular political organizations.[23] The significance of both Protestant and Catholic Churches in helping to shape the lives of Irish men and women has been clearly recognized and, as Shepard points out, organizations such as the Legion of Mary and the Women's Missionary Association of the Presbyterian Church in Ireland provided opportunities both for informal training in public life and the exercise of civic duty. While the latter organization engaged women in extensive (and successful) fundraising enterprises, opened up a range of administrative positions within the church, and facilitated overseas work in education and medicine, one interesting example of the work of the Legion of Mary was its provision of faith-based welfare services for unwed mothers in Belfast.[24]

CHALLENGING THE STATUS QUO

Though unionist domination of political life appeared impregnable and its conservatism invulnerable to challenge, it can be seen in retrospect that, from mid-century, pressures were building beneath the surface which would threaten and eventually break the status quo. Especially significant was the impact of welfare legislation introduced by the post-war Labour government in Britain which had particular consequences and nuances when applied to Northern Ireland.[25] For example, the widening of the gap in social provision and the social infrastructure between Northern Ireland and the Republic, especially in the field of health and social services, 'rendered the enthusiasm of the minority for joining the South more muted',[26] and encouraged the growing Catholic middle class to seek reform rather than abolition of the state in which they resided. Consequently, it was the first cohort of young Catholic professionals produced by the welfare state's free grammar and university education system that formed the backbone of the civil rights movement.

During the 1960s a range of pressure groups emerged to protest about the sectarian social and economic policies which had characterized successive unionist regimes; however, women's role in this important period is often overlooked. West of the Bann, for example, where it was council strategy to control local voting strength through the allocation of public housing, it was women who took the initiative in demanding change in local housing policy. Given the impact on their daily lives, this is not surprising; as one County Tyrone woman put it, of all the problems facing Catholics, discrimination in housing 'was the sorest, because it was always with you'.[27] In Dungannon, for example, a market town whose inhabitants were 50 per cent Catholic/Protestant, no Catholic had been allocated a permanent council house for 34 years when a group of local women led by Angela McCrystal, frustrated by the council's negative reaction to a petition outlining their grievances, formed the Homeless Citizens League in 1963. The parades and squats they organized attracted some media interest and the following year the Campaign on Social Justice (CSJ) was formed to collect data on the housing situation and further increase public awareness. Patricia McCluskey, a social worker and wife of a local Catholic doctor, played a leading role in these organizations, and was one of three women on the 12-person committee which succeeded in having four CSJ members elected to local government in that year, of whom she was one. Catherine Shannon believes that Patricia McCluskey 'Played a significant role in heightening the Catholic sense of grievance and in preparing large segments of the northern Catholic community to move beyond personal and local grievances to embrace the broader political ideology of civil rights',[28] while Bernadette McAliskey agrees that 'the contribution of Patricia McCluskey in laying the foundations for the civil rights movement has never been properly acknowledged'.[29]

The most significant of the new organizations was the Northern Ireland Civil Rights Association (NICRA), formed on 1 February 1967. Chaired by left-wing veteran trade unionist Betty Sinclair and composed of CSJ members, trade unionists, republicans, Communist Party members and liberal Protestants, the NICRA's target was the lack of democracy and the repressive nature of the state and it called, among other things, for one man, one vote, one family, one house and the repeal of the Special Powers Act. This latter, draconian, piece of legislation, first introduced in 1922 and made permanent in 1933, allowed for the setting up of special courts which could detain suspects without trial for unspecified periods. The issue of voting was perhaps more critical to the quality of everyday life for Catholic women; with property-based plural voting, the manipulation of local government boundaries and discriminatory allocation of housing used to ensure unionist majorities even in areas where there was a Catholic majority, voting rights directly impacted on individual living standards. However, the gendered nature of the call never seemed problematic, with the leadership of NICRA focusing primarily on the need to unite the working classes across the religious divide. Following the example of American civil rights activists, their main tactic was to organize marches that would take in both sections of the community. Recognizing the threat to their monopoly on power, the unionist government declared such marches illegal, and the resulting violent confrontations between police, marchers and loyalists led to the breakdown of law and order and the introduction of the British army, that marked the beginning of over 30 years of the euphemistically named 'Troubles'.[30]

While a few younger women took limited leadership roles in NICRA and provided the bulk of backroom support, and many more joined its ranks, nothing happened to change gender roles in what was an extremely traditional society. The contested constitution and large disaffected minority ensured that the significance of interlocking religious and political identities – and the links between them – were apparent in all aspects of life. Religion impacted particularly on moral, social and sexual behaviour, over which both Catholic and Protestant Churches retained a tight hold, and religious values were influential in 'defining the appropriate position of women in the home and in the family'.[31] Married women were barred from working in the Northern Ireland Civil Service until as late as 1972, compared with 1946 in Britain. Such attitudes impacted on all activities. Nell McCafferty, speaking of her involvement in the Citizens Action Committee established in Derry in the wake of the infamous attack on the civil rights march of 5 October 1968, remembered that when she and a friend wanted to go into the City Hotel, they were intimidated by the presence of 'knots of men . . . our nerve failed us . . . I railed at our sense of exclusion all the way back'.[32] While the situation changed in some respects (for example, her mother and her mother's friends became involved in political changes – which meant being out of doors late at night, something that generation had never done and which in itself partly challenged the traditional gender order), McCafferty also says that when the Citizens Action Committee altered in July 1969, becoming the Citizens Defence Association, it was another all-male group. Despite her friendship with its leading figures and her personal involvement in Derry political life, she was not invited to its inaugural meeting.

Devlin, in *Mother Ireland*, also testified that women were not so free on the other side of the barricades: 'women in Derry were still preparing three meals a day and men in Derry were still eating them'.[33] During periods of extreme local tension, however, women were more likely to be visibly engaged in public activities within their communities. Catherine Shannon writes of the ingenuity of the women in Derry's Bogside area in August 1969, as they devised nappies soaked in lemon juice or vinegar as gas masks to protect those being bombarded by police with CS gas during several days of violent rioting which followed a clash between loyalists and nationalists. But, while Shannon inadvertently perpetuates an image of the subordinate role played by women at this period,[34] Nell McCafferty's biography, on the contrary, describes the work of her mother, friends and sisters in the preparing of petrol bombs, tearing up material taken from the cotton factories to act as fuses.

More recently, there has been greater recognition of women's engagement in and varied responses to the violence and disruption which marked this period. Feminist historians and commentators in particular have drawn attention to the 'accidental activists' who, in defence of their children, their menfolk and their communities, challenged or supported military and paramilitary groups, and sustained family life in the absence of husbands, fathers, sons and brothers interned or on the run.[35] The situation of male republican prisoners was kept high on the agenda by women who, through organizations such as the Relatives Action Committee (RAC), mounted a high-profile campaign in support of their demand to be granted political status. The revitalization of Cumann na mBan facilitated the more direct participation of republican women and there were also women members of the Irish Republican Army (IRA). By 1971 Armagh's women's prison held 236 female political prisoners. On the other side of the political divide, a small number of women were, more briefly, members of the Ulster Defence Association (UDA), with female supporters of loyalism also active on the streets during periods of crisis. Women were also involved in a Loyalist Prisoners Committee, though their concerns focused on the welfare of men, who viewed their actions as upholding, not breaking, British rule in Ireland. Unsurprisingly, women's engagement with peace movements was considered much more acceptable by the authorities,[36] with 'cross-community' initiatives most likely to receive government funding. And of course, women were among those who died as a direct result of the conflict, albeit in much smaller numbers than men – 322 as opposed to 3,279 between 1969 and 1994.[37]

Despite such grassroots involvement, however, women were not acknowledged as serious players in the field of politics. As is the case in other areas of conflict, the militaristic nature of daily life strengthened and reinforced existing gender divisions. Cathy Harkin, later a founder member of Derry Woman's Aid, memorably described Derry society during the 1970s as an 'armed patriarchy', such was the plethora of armed groups, republican, loyalist, police and army, and, as Harkin said, both Orange and Green nationalism retained their 'ultra conservative view of women as both the property of, and the inferior of, men'.[38]

However, while Northern Ireland's male politicians were locked in a battle of mutual recrimination, one young Catholic woman mounted a challenge to the status quo by accessing and directly confronting the formal world of national politics. Bernadette Devlin's election to Westminster in April 1969 as the nationalist 'unity' candidate was remarkable in many ways, not least in a young woman being the acceptable candidate in an extremely conservative rural constituency. Devlin, originally from County Tyrone, was a student at Queen's University Belfast, where in 1968 she had been one of the founder members of People's Democracy, a student-based organization which argued that the civil rights sought by Northern Ireland's Catholics could only be obtained through the establishment of a socialist republic. Her defeat of the widow of the former unionist MP in the mid-Ulster by-election was undoubtedly due to anti-British sentiment. But it did not just mark a victory for republican socialism; as only the third female to represent Northern Ireland at Westminster since the formation of the state, she was the first who was not unionist and at 21 was also the youngest woman MP in the parliament's history. Predictably, it was on her youth and gender rather than her political beliefs that the media focused its attention.

> Almost the entire British Press refused to take her seriously, ignoring her views or representing them as something of a joke. Fleet Street treated her like some kind of clockwork doll, an amusing diversion from the mainstream of parliamentary life: the general coverage of her early days as an MP combined sexism with patronizing trivialization and a refusal to see her in any other terms than 'swinging youth' and the then fashionable mini-skirt.[39]

One Ulster Unionist MP, touring Canada and America in an attempt to undermine Devlin's fundraising efforts, referred to her as 'this wild irresponsible child who is a danger to any civilized society and who has left behind her a trail of human misery and suffering.'[40] The *Observer* on the other hand recognized her potential. When she began appearing regularly in Westminster, it was remarked that she used her position there 'with a confidence and wit which is making members of both sides of the house sit up and take notice.'[41] Devlin by no means confined herself to conventional political activities, however, and was to serve four months in Armagh women's prison for her activities during the 'Battle of the Bogside' in August 1969. Her time at Westminster was turbulent and she was regarded by many as a disruptive element, but, despite losing her Westminster seat in 1974, failing to win a seat in the 1979 European elections, and surviving an assassination attempt in 1981, Devlin continues to work for those most marginalized within society. Today she campaigns for new migrant communities in the South Tyrone area.[42]

The formal political arena was transformed by the level of civil disruption unleashed by local events. In the wake of Bloody Sunday, January 1972, one-third of the community – including church and respectable middle-class figures – withdrew all allegiance to the state, rendering the region virtually ungovernable. The British government response was the abolition of the Stormont Parliament and the imposition of Direct Rule. Power over the most contentious areas of local government, such as housing, health, social services and education, passed from elected officials to a range of newly established organizations under the control of the Northern Ireland Office. While the removal of power from local government can be viewed as an assault on democracy, the failure of Northern Ireland's local political institutions to operate within democratic principles proved no longer acceptable. Moreover, in the longer term, as Patrick Buckland points out, the imposition of Direct Rule had profound implications for politics in the North. It meant that 'the affairs of Northern Ireland ceased to be the sole prerogative of Northern Irishmen' and that 'the longer the conflict continued the more it had international ramifications'.[43] It would take many years of crisis management before political power was returned to Stormont.

FEMINISMS IN THE NORTH

International influences were also evident in the emergence of a Women's Liberation Movement in the north of Ireland in the mid-1970s, although local developments were also significant. As Monica McWilliams points out,

> the civil rights movement, campaigns against government cutbacks and locally based community development initiatives all helped to develop a degree of political acumen amongst women activists in the early seventies in Northern Ireland which was later to become useful in their struggles around women's rights.[44]

It is also possible to trace earlier instances of activism by individuals and groups on behalf of women themselves, whether through challenging Thatcherite policies or focusing attention on the issue of domestic violence.[45] It was a weekend of films organized by a group of women meeting at Queen's University in 1975, however, which led directly to the formation of the Northern Ireland Women's Rights Movement (NIWRM) and the first concerted collective attempts to challenge the deeply entrenched gendered divisions in public and private life.[46]

The intention of NIWRM was to act as an umbrella organization that would bring together and provide a stronger focus for those already working to draw attention to gender discrimination, and the movement attracted activists from a wide range of backgrounds. The trade union movement was well represented, as were civil rights and communism and, though feminism came to be associated much more closely with nationalist ideology, so too were women from across the wide republican–unionist spectrum. Early campaigns focused on the claiming of employment rights already granted to women in Britain, and the first victory, in 1976, was winning the extension of the Sex Discrimination Act to Northern Ireland and the establishment of the Equal Opportunities Commission.

However, political allegiance is to more than one ideal, and for those who disputed the right of Westminster to legislate for any part of the island, this strategy was problematic. Questions of rights and equalities touched on different aspects of identity and individual women – shaped by background and experience – prioritized them differently. During the decade that followed, those who engaged with feminist issues responded in a variety of ways to the situations in which they found themselves. New groups formed and disbanded, representing particular interest groups or focusing on specific issues. Those who aimed to combine their prior commitment to socialism with feminist and nationalist concerns, for example, formed the Socialist Women's Group in 1975, dissolving two years later with many members reuniting in the more explicitly feminist Belfast Women's Collective. Women Against Imperialism (WAI) and the RAC provided forums for campaigns more closely linked with the rights of political prisoners. Women's Aid began the difficult process of providing places of safety for women abused by men while, reflecting its broadly liberal approach, the NIWRM continued to highlight inequalities in employment and public life and to lobby for further reforms in areas particularly impacting on women – for example in demanding the extension of the UK's 1967 Abortion Act to Northern Ireland – a campaign which has not yet been won.[47]

While, over the course of the following decade, alliances were made to challenge some of the more blatant examples of female oppression,[48] lasting unity under the umbrella of gender was never a reality. The most publicized example of feminist division in the North was over the issue of female republican prisoners – with some in the women's movement anxious to distance themselves from the prisoners' political stance while others regarded the strip-searching to which they were subjected as a straightforward matter of abuse against women, the tensions generated by the ongoing conflict inevitably came to the surface.[49] The high profile of the female prisoners' campaign, which was widely supported by feminists outside Ireland, reinforced the perception that feminism went hand in hand with an anti-government stance and made it more difficult for women from unionist backgrounds to associate with the movement. Those who were vehemently opposed to the existing political establishment, on the other hand, were likely to have found a more coherent political agenda in radical feminist activism. Looking back on this difficult time, one woman acknowledged that, in a context of violence and fear, 'we failed to talk about our divisions in a manner which made us face them and not deny them'.[50]

As has been argued elsewhere, it is important to ensure that the disagreements among feminists – a trait familiar to all left-wing groupings – do not divert attention from the very real legacies of their influence and activism.[51] Though the wider social context was also, of course, important, perhaps one of the most significant of these was the development of women's role in civil society. Much of this originated in local community organizations where women came together to provide support, resources and leadership in response to the 'democratic deficit' of political stalemate.[52] In Craigavon, for example, a new town planned to draw people from the crowded streets of Belfast to rural County Armagh, the first Advice Centre formed by local women proved an essential source of information and support to residents of the large incomplete estates lacking either infrastructure or representation. The NIWRM established a Women's Advice Centre in the centre of Belfast in 1979 and other groups emerged in west Belfast following internment (members of Women Against Imperialism played a role in the setting up of Falls Road Women's Centre), with women suddenly finding it necessary to engage in dialogue with local politicians and to educate themselves in legal and welfare rights. Although some co-operated across traditional sectarian boundaries, most groups worked within their own locality, running classes on health, politics, local environmental issues, history and creative writing. The political origins and loyalties of the women involved often differed widely, but by focusing on common experiences of poverty and marginalization they worked to ensure that issues affecting working-class women were heard at government level. By the mid-1990s it was estimated that there were around 400 women's groups in the North, in nationalist, unionist, urban and rural areas. A host of other networks evolved at county level, to bring together rural women or older women, or to facilitate research and developmental activities.

Clearly, these groups cannot simply be labelled 'feminist', though leadership from the broad women's movement was often evident, and their greatest impact was probably on the personal lives of women who were offered support and education. Though individual consciousness-raising and a means to community solidarity also frequently resulted from their activities, as a 1996 report from Democratic Dialogue suggested, 'non-institutional or even anti-institutional activities are empowering to the individual, but the ability to exert influence and assert change, over and for others, is limited'.[53] Nonetheless, Kate Fearon points out that 'although their numbers reflected local women activists' fragmentation, their existence nevertheless suggests that many women felt an identity as women, and wanted to organise together with other women'.[54] Moreover, the Opsahl Commission, which consulted individuals and groups throughout Northern Ireland on the region's political future during 1992 and 1993, also considered this issue and commented that

> while there is no simple relationship between women's political participation and the resolution of the conflict, the experience of women's involvement in local community groups suggests that they could have an important contribution to make in the search for a political and constitutional settlement.[55]

And, in retrospect, it is difficult not to conclude that this type of network did indeed serve as an important conduit, offering at least the potential for women's engagement in later political developments.

POLITICS UNDER DIRECT RULE

Given that the operation of local government was accepted as one of the major causes of the outbreak of civil unrest in the late 1960s, it is perhaps not surprising that under Direct Rule the system underwent a process of total reorganization, with significant consequences for its exercise of authority. The transfer of major services to centralized bodies limited the activities of the 26 new councils to what has been disparagingly described as 'bins, bogs and burials'. But while a 1967 report on local councils had suggested that 'a general streamlining of the local government system would attract plenty of good candidates, including more women',[56] many men with political ambition were reluctant to run for office in this difficult period and levels of female representation were disappointing. Only 4 per cent of councillors were women in 1972, with the number of female candidates subsequently increasing at a slow but steady rate, from 9.5 per cent to 14 per cent in the five elections held between 1972 and the early 1990s, and a rise in the numbers elected from 7 per cent to 12 per cent in the same period.[57] On the other hand, as Derek Birrell points out, despite their limited functions, after 1972 these new bodies represented 'the only elected forum of local politicians in Northern Ireland'.[58] As such, they were much more dominated by political parties than previously and also played a significant role in the community. So it could be argued that female representation in this area, while continuing to be limited, nonetheless provided women with practical experience in the public arena and a more visible presence in party politics.

Women were represented in the various bodies appointed by government to take responsibility for services previously carried out by councils. As Miller *et al.* observe, responsibility for the fair and efficient administration of public housing, education and the health and personal social services, the oversight of the police service, and the monitoring of equality legislation in a bitterly divided society has invested these appointed agencies in Northern Ireland with 'immense symbolic and practical significance'.[59] With the proportion of female membership reaching 32 per cent by the mid-1990s, they are surely correct in their conclusion that 'over the last twenty years . . . patronage rather than election has proved a surer route to more equitable representation by women'.[60]

The confrontational nature of the local political arena, in which competing nationalist/republican/unionist/loyalist parties distrusted not only each other but both the British and Irish governments, ensured that, following the imposition of Direct Rule, gender was not a real issue in elections to the various regional institutions which came and went during the following decade. Only four women took their seats among 78 men in each: the Northern Ireland Assembly elected in 1973, the Constitutional Convention of 1975–6 and the 1982–6 Assembly. Making little progress in terms of political stability, nor did these bodies do much to advance the cause of female citizenship. Those women elected to the first two bodies were unionists and, while it is important not to dismiss this aspect of women's participation, the hostility of this political philosophy to feminist aspirations is already clear. Rhonda Paisley, daughter of the leader of the Democratic Unionist Party (DUP), stated that, within its ranks,

> During my time (short though it may be) of involvement in unionist politics, I have witnessed no inclination to take on board feminist issues. If anything, the longer I am involved the more distasteful I find attitudes and the more superficial I believe the majority of male elected representatives are in their interests in feminist concerns.[61]

Despite the strength of female membership within the major unionist parties (60 per cent of the DUP and 42 per cent of the Ulster Unionist Party (UUP) in 1995)[62] – both men and women retained a strong attachment to traditional family values, and especially to an essentialist understanding of motherhood, which militated against their advancing women's participation in public life. Though women were represented on decision-making bodies, steadfast opposition to any affirmative action ensured their exclusion from key leadership roles throughout much of this period.[63]

On the nationalist side where, by the 1980s, representatives were beginning to take their seats in regional political institutions, both Sinn Féin and the Social Democratic and Labour Party (SDLP) were more proactive in their engagement with female members, who made up 47 per cent and 33 per cent of their respective party memberships in 1995. Women were also better represented on their national executives (Sinn Féin, nine out of 24; SDLP, six out of 15), and it is generally agreed that the growing importance of the women's sector within Sinn Féin and the republican movement more generally can be traced to pressures from groups such as WAI and the RAC, and the high profile given to republican women prisoners. Nonetheless, and although Sinn Féin was the first local party to operate a policy of positive discrimination, frustration with their progress within mainstream republicanism led to the formation of Clar na mBan (Women's Agenda) by women concerned with their exclusion from the developing 'peace process' in 1995. Republican feminists made it very clear that they expected Sinn Féin to give greater consideration to women's issues as the party continued its move into the political arena.[64] The Alliance Party, with a 50 per cent female membership, also has a strong record of female involvement and in 1995 women, one of whom was also the party's vice-chair, made up one-third of the 12-member executive.[65] Although all the major parties had policy statements on women's issues by this stage, levels of both commitment and effectiveness varied significantly.

At community level, women began to organize to build the capacity of women to engage in political debate. Women into Politics was set up in 1993 following a conference ('Breaking the Silence – Women Speak Out') which highlighted women's fears surrounding the political stalemate in Northern Ireland. Its intention was to encourage grassroots women to talk about politics while at the same time organizing events at which women had the opportunity to question politicians.[66] American money funded DemocraShe, which offered training and development courses to women from all political parties. Many of its graduates are now elected politicians. While funding is more difficult in today's climate, such strategies offer some hope for the longer term.

While mainstream public discourse remained focused on breaking the constitutional stalemate between unionism and nationalism, during this decade an alternative – female – discourse that gradually increased linkages between formal and informal politics resulted in a greater visibility of women and their participation in a range of extra-parliamentary forums. The new momentum of this period, building on the groundwork of women in the voluntary and community sectors discussed above, was encouraged by the paramilitary ceasefires and by the discourse generated by a range of national and international initiatives, such as the Women into Politics project, the Northern Ireland Women's European Platform, and the 1995 UN World Conference on Women in Beijing.[67] The Northern Ireland Women's European Platform (NIWEP) was established in 1988 as the Northern Ireland response to the formation of the European Women's Lobby (EWL). Through its membership of the EWL it provides women in Northern Ireland with a voice in Europe and, through its consultative status at the United Nations (UN), with the ability to participate in key UN mechanisms promoting gender equality. NIWEP was a significant figure in the early years of the peace process, in 1995 making a joint response with the National Women's Council of Ireland to the Forum for Peace and Reconciliation, held in Dublin and sponsored by the Irish government, and also attempting to engage the British government and political parties in the issue of parity of representation for women in forthcoming elections.[68]

Women's engagement was further energized by the input of individual politicians from Britain, Ireland and further afield. The Equal Opportunities Commission, the Council for the Status of Women in the Republic, and Clar na mBan, for example, were vocal in their demands for greater female participation in politics, while President Mary Robinson and Baroness Jean Denton (a Tory minister at the Northern Ireland Office from 1994 to 1997 with responsibility for the economy) were also important advocates of the women's sector. In America, the Clinton administration was keen to facilitate the fledgling peace process; the 'Vital Voices' seminars, an initiative of Hilary Clinton's to promote the participation of women in leadership roles within political systems, were an important aspect of this. Held on either side of the Atlantic, these high-profile seminars highlighted the importance of women's contribution to the political process and ensured that their views were at least being articulated.

In June 1995 Monica McWilliams, at the time a senior lecturer at the University of Ulster and a prominent supporter of the women's movement, organized a conference in Draperstown supported by Baroness Jean Denton and Lady Jean Mayhew, wife of the then Secretary of State.[69] This event, 'The Way Forward', provided a forum for progressing the aspirations of these individuals and groups and, as Elisabeth Porter argues, 'articulated widespread urgency to instil feminist voices not only in the peace process, but in actual political decision-making'.[70] The conclusion was that a specific strategy to develop women's participation was required. The real difficulty, of course, lay in translating this energy and ambition into practical and effective political activity and an opportunity to do so was presented when elections to an all-party Forum for Political Dialogue were announced in February 1996. Given the critical nature of this body, which would conduct the negotiations for a constitutional settlement, women's participation was considered essential and, following a process of consultation and discussion, the decision was taken to form a gender-specific party which would provide an alternative platform, both to air issues of concern to women, and to ensure their involvement in making the decisions that would determine the future of the six counties.

Monica McWilliams and Avila Kilmurray, Director of the Northern Ireland Voluntary Trust, were at the forefront of developments, but inclusivity was a central aim of the Northern Ireland Women's Coalition (NIWC), which was formally launched on 17 April 1996. Cross-community support was a difficult but core principle; as community worker and Shankill Road activist May Blood put it, 'we will have our differences but we will agree to differ. We are committed to keep working until we reach an accommodation'.[71] Building and debating policies around the principles of inclusion, equality and human rights, the party embarked on six weeks of hectic activity which included navigating a steep learning curve in political technicalities, public speaking and dealing with the media. The detailed story of those weeks provides fascinating insight into not only the range of attitudes towards, and *of*, women, but also the personal and political implications and often overlooked practical details of electoral campaigning. It was felt that the electoral list system would require a threshold of 10,000 votes to guarantee NIWC two seats. Their goal was therefore to put forward 100 women and for them to gain 100 votes each, which made the project realizable. Although not quite reaching this target, it was a measure of the group's efficiency and determination that, at the end of this period, they were able to put forward 68 candidates for constituencies from across the religious and political divide, with a further two on the regional list.[72]

The complex electoral system put in place for this election, designed to ensure the inclusion of smaller, usually marginalized, political parties (particularly loyalist organizations that the government wanted to entice into the political sphere), undoubtedly favoured the NIWC and also provided opportunities for those representing other interest groups, resulting in an unprecedented number of candidates. Of the 846 candidates put forward on constituency lists to contest 90 seats, 262 (31 per cent) were women while the remaining 20 places were contested by 180 candidates on the regional list; 36 per cent of the latter were female. However, a much lower percentage put female candidates at the top of their party lists – ranging from the SDLP's 13 per cent to UUP's 1 per cent.[73] With the main focus of the election remaining firmly fixed on the constitutional question, the success of the NIWC on polling day took everyone by surprise and introduced a new and liberalizing force into Northern Ireland politics.

In addition to the two seats won by the NIWC, Sinn Féin returned four women, the SDLP three, as did the DUP, with Alliance and the UUP each returning one, making a total of 15 in the 110-strong forum. Only the top two or three from every party were invited to the negotiating table when talks began, and the only women involved at this level were from the NIWC: Monica McWilliams and Pearl Sagar, a community worker from a unionist background. The Northern Ireland Forum was only in existence for two years, but during its lifetime women were closely involved in the frequently controversial negotiations which led to the signing of an historic agreement on Good Friday 1998.

The NIWC has been the subject of considerable analysis and a summary does not do justice to the amount of debate it generated, but it sheds light on the range of responses to the new initiative. For many women 'on the ground', it was refreshing to have a different party to vote for, which was not vociferously sectarian and which claimed to represent their particular concerns. Others viewed the party as a catalyst for change. Support was given by Senator Mary Henry in the Republic and Kathleen Stephens, then US Consul-General in Belfast and, importantly, at the highest political level of Tony Blair's New Labour government, by Mo Mowlam, Secretary of State for Northern Ireland from 1997 to 1999, the first and to date the only woman to have held the post. Acknowledged as playing a central role in negotiating the difficult road to peace, Mowlam's inclusivity – she was often criticized for talking with both republican and loyalist activists – went beyond the male power structures which dominated the headlines, and embraced those who had long been excluded from the decision-making process.

There was unease from women inside and outside the political arena in the North. Having won only 1.03 per cent of the overall vote, it was felt by some that the election of two 'women's party' representatives was undemocratic. Others, including many in the broader women's movement, were uncertain of the validity of the novel approach of sidestepping the constitutional question, concerned that it weakened rather than increased women's influence in the realm of politics. Some female politicians were resentful of the prominence given to the Coalition. Rachel Ward quotes one SDLP woman who expressed her anger 'that suddenly the whole media discovered women in politics, as if women did not exist before Monica McWilliams and Pearl Sagar came forward'.[74] Reaction from male politicians varied, ranging from acceptance to disdain, to the undiluted hostility of mainstream unionists. While the misogyny of the latter group's personal attacks were – at the very least – frustrating, McWilliams, in commenting on their 'bully-boy' tactics, observed that it was 'evidence that the NIWC was beginning to get its message across'.[75]

The Agreement reached on 10 April 1998 was comprehensive, containing provisions relating to police reform, judicial reform, equality legislation, human rights protection, a civic forum, and measures relating to prisoners', victims' and language rights. The NIWC was central to the process of formulating clauses on equality, human rights, decommissioning of weapons, and the civic forum. In addition, they proposed wording to affirm 'the right of women to full and equal political participation' that was included in the final Agreement. Later, their two Members of the Legislative Assembly (MLAs) would be particularly vocal in their advocacy of family-friendly policies for the Assembly, for example challenging occasions when Standing Orders were suspended so that debates could continue after the agreed time of 6 p.m.[76]

DEVOLVING POWER

On 25 June 1998, 296 candidates stood for the elections to the new Northern Ireland Assembly. Voting was by proportional representation, but without the list system. Sixteen-and-a-half per cent of the candidates were women and only 13 per cent, or 14 of the 108 members elected to the new Assembly, were women. As the Table 8.1 indicates, the general pattern was the by now familiar one of lower representation of women within unionism and a relatively high presence

Table 8.1 Elections to the Northern Ireland Assembly, 1998

Party	Candidates			Elected	
	Total	Female	%	Total	Female
Sinn Féin	37	8	21.6	18	5
SDLP	38	6	16.2	24	3
UUP	48	4	8.3	28	2
DUP	34	4	11.8	18	1
Alliance	22	6	27.3	6	1
UK Unionists	13	1			
PUP	12	1			
NIWC		8	100	2	2

Note: Eleven women were selected by a variety of smaller and minor parties.

Source: Galligan *et al.*, *Contesting Politics* (Boulder, CO/Oxford: Westview/Political Studies Association of Ireland, 1999), pp. 134–5.

of nationalist women. The NIWC, which had fielded eight candidates, returned two, McWilliams and Jane Morrice.

Although two women were appointed to ministerial posts – Brid Rogers of the SDLP to Agriculture, and Bairbre de Brun, Sinn Féin, to Health, Social Services and Public Safety, Rogers was not impressed, claiming that, 'the two women were given the two that nobody else wanted'.[77] With only 17 of 110 committee places allocated to women, it is hard not to agree that commitment to gender equality has largely been a matter of rhetoric rather than reality.

It is perhaps obvious in retrospect that the transition to peaceful co-operation between Northern Ireland's divided communities would not be smooth, and there have been numerous crises and several stops and starts to the process in the decade since the signing of the Agreement. Moreover, although this document referred to 'the right of women to full and equal political participation', and a report by the Northern Ireland Committee of the Irish Congress of Trade Unions and the Equality Commission for Northern Ireland argued that the Assembly, as a key player in shaping the equality agenda, 'has the potential to transform the situation of women', there is so far very little evidence of this. In 2003, the number of women elected to the Assembly increased to 18 and this was repeated four years later: at 16.7 per cent this represents a small increase on past performance, and is closer to the 20 per cent female membership of the UK House of Commons, though lagging far behind the other devolved assemblies in the UK. Moreover, in the elections of 2003, held against a backdrop of significantly heightened tension, a polarization along traditional sectarian lines meant the loss of electoral support for smaller, newer parties, including the NIWC, who lost both their seats. The continuing focus on traditional constitutional and military matters, which also makes it difficult for women politicians to work as a group across party lines, has had a negative impact on women's ability to participate fully in public life.

One noteworthy change in the pattern of party representation is the increase in the number of successful female DUP candidates – three in 2007. However, at present, there are no female Ulster Unionist MLAs in the Assembly, a situation of considerable embarrassment to the party. The passage of legislation enabling parties to use all-woman shortlists has not been used by any of the parties, although the SDLP and Sinn Féin continue to reserve places for women on their executive bodies (40 and 50 per cent respectively), as does the smaller Progressive Unionist Party (PUP), which emanated originally from the Ulster Volunteer Force. Despite its paramilitary ties, it is the only party in the Assembly led by a woman, as Dawn Purvis was appointed leader in January 2007 following the untimely death of David Ervine. However, as Irene Murphy, party member, feminist and community activist, points out, the gender balance in the party generally is not strong: 'the party grew out of a very macho environment, and showing men their issues are not the only issues is hard.'[78]

There has been a significant increase in the election of women from Northern Ireland to both Westminster and Europe. From having had no female representation in Westminster in 1997, three women (out of a total of 18 seats) were elected to Westminster in 2001 and were returned in 2005 – one each from the DUP, UUP and Sinn Féin. In Europe, Sinn Féin's Bairbre de Brun was elected to the European Parliament in 2004 and re-elected in 2009, together with Diane Dodds of the DUP. Less positively, while the percentage of women councillors has continued to rise, reaching 21 per cent in 2008, the ongoing review of Public Administration, which will reduce the number of councils from 26 to 11, threatens to impede that progress.

CONCLUSIONS

As Hinds and Gray point out, 'In Northern Ireland no party has developed a sound strategy to redress gender imbalance among their representatives,'[79] and unless positive action measures are taken, it is unlikely that women will be the beneficiaries of the peace process. While there is an opportunity to ensure the mainstreaming of equality within a reformed system of public administration, including public appointments and political representation, this is dependent upon the implementation of positive action measures, including quotas for gender-balanced representation, and many political parties remain resistant to any such suggestion.

Women activists have argued that, as a society still emerging from conflict, UN Security Council Resolution (UNSCR) 1325, 'Women, Peace and Security', should be fully implemented within Northern Ireland, thereby mandating gender parity in all institutions arising from the conflict, including the Northern Ireland Assembly. The argument has been heard at the highest level, but British resistance is partly linked to reluctance to have Northern Ireland viewed internationally as more than a British 'domestic' issue, as responsibility for the promotion of UNSCR 1325 within Britain is located within the Foreign and Commonwealth Office.

There has been considerable activity concerning the development of a Bill of Rights for Northern Ireland, another issue written into the Agreement. It was agreed that any Bill should address the 'particular circumstances' of Northern Ireland. These have been defined in narrow terms by the unionist parties, who argue for issues to be limited to security, the Irish language and the competing rights of Ulster Scots, rights for victims of the Troubles, employment discrimination, etc. Women's specific needs, particularly with regard to political and public under-representation, lack of reproductive rights and gender-based violence, are not regarded as 'particular' to Northern Ireland and therefore, it has been argued, should be excluded. Further progress on this contentious topic is now (in 2009) dependent on political goodwill at Westminster and the uncertain future of the Labour government.

Katherine Side explains the failure of the Northern Ireland Assembly to implement the equality agenda contained in the Good Friday Agreement, particularly women's political rights, as due to 'the slow pace of equality and gender mainstreaming, reluctance on the part of political parties to take up available (United Kingdom) legislation to advance women's candidature for political office and the limits of a rights based discourse in Northern Ireland'. She argues that 'the potential for expanding these rights must involve a wider range of approaches and actions, including expanded conceptualisations of equality and citizenship rights', and concludes that 'The Agreement can only serve as a vital tool to secure equality rights when its aspirations and promises are accompanied by political will and positive action and when the benefits of advancing women's civil and political citizenship rights in Northern Ireland in the post-Agreement period are recognised as beneficial for all citizens'.[80] In similar vein, Brown et al., in a comparative study of Northern Ireland and Scotland, argue that the process towards devolution opened up new opportunities for women in both countries to mobilize around the issues of political representation in its broadest sense. But while political activists in Scotland have made significant gains in representation, their counterparts in Northern Ireland have experienced much more difficulty and achieved significantly less. Brown et al. conclude, however, that devolution is 'a process not an event', and that 'gender has been and will continue to be an important dimension of that process of constitutional change as it evolves throughout the UK'.[81] For women in Northern Ireland, despite decades of unremitting effort, such a conclusion might appear unduly optimistic. Political divisions continue to hinder progress and gender-based concerns, far from assuming their rightful importance, remain largely invisible within the body politic.

NOTES

1   Thomas Hennessey, *A History of Northern Ireland 1920–1996* (Dublin: Gill and MacMillan, 1997); Theodore W. Moody, *The Ulster Question 1603–1973* (Cork and Dublin: Mercier Press, 1974).

2   John Darby, *Northern Ireland: The Background to the Conflict* (Belfast: Appletree Press, 1983).

3   Myrtle Hill, Fran Porter, Caroline McAuley and Eithne McLaughlin, *Eighty Years of Talking about Equality in Northern Ireland: A History of Equality Discourses and Practices* (Belfast: Equality & Social Inclusion in Ireland Project, 2006), Working Paper 5.

4   Myrtle Hill, 'Ulster: debates, demands and divisions: the battle for (and against) the vote', in Louise Ryan and Margaret Ward (eds), *Irish Women and the Vote: Becoming Citizens* (Dublin: Irish Academic Press, 2007), pp. 209–30; Margaret Ward, '"Ulster was different?" Women, feminism and nationalism in the North of Ireland', in Yvonne Galligan, Eilis Ward and Rick Wilford (eds), *Contesting Politics: Women in Ireland, North and South* (Colorado and Oxford: Westview Press, 1999), pp. 219–39.

5   Ward, '"Ulster was different?"'.

6   Diane Urquhart (ed.), *The Minutes of the Ulster Women's Unionist Council and Executive Committee 1911–40* (Dublin: The Women's History Project in association with Irish Manuscripts Commission, 2001), p. xi.

7   Nancy Kinghan, *United We Stood: The Official History of the Ulster Women's Unionist Council 1911–1974* (Belfast: Appletree Press, 1975).

8   Diane Urquhart, *Women in Ulster Politics 1890–1940* (Dublin: Irish Academic Press, 2000), p. 72.

9   Kinghan, *United We Stood*.

10 Urquhart, *Women in Ulster Politics*.

11 Urquhart, *Women in Ulster Politics*, p. 116.

12 Maedhbh McNamara and Paschal Mooney, *Women in Parliament: Ireland 1918–2000* (Dublin: Wolfhound Press, 2000).

13 Diane Urquhart, 'The political role of women in North East Ulster, 1880–1940' (Unpublished MA thesis, Queens University Belfast, 1996), p. 261.

14 Robert Lee Miller, Rick Wilford and Freda Donoghue, *Women and Political Participation in Northern Ireland* (Aldershot: Avebury, 1996).

15 McNamara and Mooney, *Women in Parliament: Ireland 1918–2000*.

16 Urquhart, *Women in Ulster Politics*.

17 Urquhart, *Women in Ulster Politics*.

18 Maria Luddy, *Women and Philanthropy in Nineteenth-Century Ireland* (Cambridge University Press, 1995).

19 Quoted in Urquhart, *Women in Ulster Politics*, pp. 167–68.

20 Minutes of the Executive Committee of the UWUA, PRONI, letters, February 1921 and April 1921.

21 Hill, 'Ulster: debates, demands and divisions'.

22 Linda Connolly, *The Irish Women's Movement from Revolution to Devolution* (Hampshire and New York: Palgrave, 2002).

23 Christopher Shepard, 'Women activists and women's associations in Ireland, 1945–68' (Unpublished PhD thesis, Queens University Belfast, 2007).

24 Ibid.

25 John McGarry and Brendan O'Leary, *The Politics of Antagonism: Understanding Northern Ireland* (London and Atlantic Highlands, NJ: The Atlantic Press, 1996).

26 Michael Cox, Adrian Guelke and Fiona Stephen (eds), *A Farewell to Arms? From 'Long War' to 'Long Peace' in Northern Ireland* (Manchester and New York: Manchester University Press, 2000), p. 26.

27   Fionnuala O'Connor, *In Search of a State: Catholics in Northern Ireland* (Belfast: Blackstaff Press, 1993), p. 182.

28   Catherine Shannon, 'Women in Northern Ireland', in Mary O'Dowd and Sabine Wichert (eds), *Chattel, Servant or Citizen: Women's Status in Church, State and Society* (Belfast: Institute of Irish Studies, 1995), pp. 238–53 (p. 241).

29   Bernadette (Devlin) McAliskey, 'A peasant in the halls of the great', in Michael Farrell (ed.), *Twenty Years On* (Dingle: Brandon, 1998), pp. 75–88 (p. 77).

30   Bob Purdie, *Politics in the Streets: The Origins of the Civil Rights Movement in Northern Ireland* (Belfast: Blackstaff Press, 1990).

31   Valerie Morgan and Grace Fraser, 'Women and the Northern Ireland conflict: experiences and responses', in Seamus Dunn (ed.) *Facets of the Conflict in Northern Ireland* (London, 1995), pp. 81–96 (p. 83).

32   Nell McCafferty, *Nell* (London: Penguin, 2004), p. 125.

33   Anne Crilley, *Mother Ireland* (Derry: Derry Films and Video Collective, 1998).

34   Shannon, 'Women in Northern Ireland'.

35   Monica McWilliams, 'Struggling for peace and justice: reflections on women's activism in Northern Ireland', *Journal of Women's History*, 6, (4), (1995), pp. 13–39.

36   Marie Hammond Callaghan, 'Surveying politics of peace, gender, conflict and identity in Northern Ireland: the case of the Derry Peace Women in 1972', *Women's Studies International Forum*, 25, (2002), pp. 33–49.

37   Marie-Therese Fay, Mike Morrisey and Marie Smyth, *Northern Ireland's Troubles: The Human Costs* (London: Pluto Press, 1999).

38   Cathy Harkin and Avila Kilmurray, 'Working with women in Derry', in Bourke *et al.* (eds), *The Field Day Anthology of Irish Writing, Volume 5: Irish Women's Writing and Traditions* (Cork: Cork University Press, 2002), pp. 384–87 (p. 386).

39   Bronwen Walter, *Outsiders Inside: Whiteness, Place and Irish Women* (London: Routledge, 2001), p. 85.

40   *Belfast Telegraph*, 2 September 1969.

41   *Observer*, 30 September 1969.

42   In 1982, she twice failed in an attempt to be elected to the Dublin North Central constituency of Dáil Éireann and in 2003 she was barred from entering the United States.

43   Patrick Buckland, *The Factory of Grievances: Devolved Government in Northern Ireland 1921–1939* (Dublin and New York, 1981), p. 132.

44   Monica McWilliams, 'Women and political activism in Northern Ireland 1960–93', in Bourke *et al.* (eds), *Field Day Anthology*, pp. 374–77 (p. 375).

45   Lynda Edgerton, 'Public protest, domestic acquiescence: women in Northern Ireland', in Rosemary Ridd and Helen Callaway (eds), *Caught up in Conflict: Women's Responses to Political Strife* (London: Palgrave MacMillan, 1986), pp. 61–79.

46   Eileen Evason, *Against the Grain: The Contemporary Women's Movement in Northern Ireland* (Dublin: Attic Press, 1991).

47   See Margaret Ward, *A Difficult, Dangerous Honesty: 10 Years of Feminism in Northern Ireland* (Belfast: Women's News, 1987).

48   Perhaps the best-known example was in 1976 when feminists came together to protest against the sentencing of Noreen Winchester for the murder of her father who had sexually abused her since childhood; she was freed by royal pardon in 1977.

49   Begoña Aretxaga, *Shattering Silence: Women, Nationalism and Political Subjectivity in Northern Ireland* (Princeton: Princeton University Press, 1997).

50   Quoted in Miller *et al.*, *Women and Political Participation*, p. 18.

51 Myrtle Hill, 'Lessons and legacies': feminist activism in the North c. 1970–2000', *Women's Studies Review*, 9, (2004), pp. 135–50.

52 Carmel Roulston, 'Gender, nation, class: the politics of difference in Northern Ireland', *Scottish Affairs*, 18, (1997), pp. 54–67.

53 Democratic Dialogue, *Power, Politics, Positionings: Women in Northern Ireland*, Report No. 4 (Belfast, 1996).

54 Kate Fearon, *Women's Work: The Story of the Northern Ireland Women's Coalition* (Belfast: Blackstaff Press, 1999), p. 3.

55 Quoted in Rachel Ward, 'The Northern Ireland Peace Process: a gender issue?', in Chris Gilligan and Jon Tonge (eds), *Peace or War? Understanding the Peace Process in Northern Ireland* (Aldershot: Ashgate, 1997), pp. 150–62 (p. 152).

56 Derek Birrell, *Local Government Councillors in Northern Ireland* (Glasgow: Centre for the Study of Public Policy 83, 1981), pp. 5–6.

57 Miller *et al.*, *Women and Political Participation*.

58 Birrell, *Local Government Councillors*, p. 7.

59 Miller *et al.*, *Women and Political Participation*, p. 11.

60 Ibid.

61 Quoted in Myrtle Hill, *Women in Ireland: A Century of Change* (Belfast: Blackstaff Press, 2003), p. 231.

62 Yvonne Galligan and Rick Wilford, 'Gender and party politics in Northern Ireland', in Galligan *et al.* (eds), *Contesting Politics*, pp. 169–84.

63 A rare exception here is Anne Dickson, who succeeded Brian Faulkner as leader of the short-lived Unionist Party of Northern Ireland (1976–81).

64 Clar na mBan, *A Women's Agenda for Peace* (Derry, 1994), Conference Report.

65 Galligan and Wilford, 'Gender and party politics'.

66 See http://www.womenintopolitics.org (accessed 27 November 2009)

67 Monica McWilliams and Avila Kilmurray, 'Athene on the loose: the origins of the Northern Ireland Women's Coalition', *Irish Journal of Feminist Studies*, 2, (1), (1997), pp. 1–21.

68 Bronagh Hinds, 'Women working for peace in Northern Ireland', in Galligan *et al.*, *Contesting Politics*, pp. 109–29.

69 Fearon, *Women's Work*.

70 Elisabeth Porter, 'Northern Ireland Women's Coalition', *Australian Feminist Studies*, 11, (24), (1996), pp. 317–20 (p. 317).

71 McWilliams and Kilmurray, 'Athene on the loose', p. 19.

72 Fearon, *Women's Work*.

73 McWilliams and Kilmurray, 'Athene on the loose'.

74 Ward, 'The Northern Ireland Peace Process: a gender issue?', p. 159.

75 Fearon, *Women's Work*, p. 58.

76 Margaret Ward, *The N.I. Assembly and Women: Assessing the Gender Deficit* (Belfast: Democratic Dialogue, 2000).

77 Ward, *The N. I. Assembly and Women*.

78 Quoted in Rosemary Sales, *Women Divided: Gender, Religion and Politics in Northern Ireland* (London: Routledge, 1997), p. 176.

79 Bronagh Hinds and Anne Marie Gray, *Women and the Review of Public Administration* (Belfast: The Review of Public Administration in Northern Ireland, 2005), p. 12.

80 Katherine Side, *Women's Civil and Political Citizenship in the Post-Good Friday Agreement Period in Northern Ireland* (Belfast: Centre for Advancement of Women in Politics, 2007), Occasional Paper 14.

81 Alice Brown, Tahnya Barnett Donaghy, Fiona Mackay and Elizabeth Meehan, 'Women and constitutional change in Scotland and Northern Ireland', *Parliamentary Affairs*, 55, (2002), pp. 71–84 (pp. 82–3).

9

'Apathetic, parochial, conservative'? Women, élite and mass politics from 1979 to 2009

Rosie Campbell and Sarah Childs[1]

This chapter traces women's participation in UK politics from 1979 to 2009, at the élite and mass levels. The focus is upon women in the party political élite (as party members, party activists and as parliamentary representatives) and women in the electorate (as voters). First, we examine women's struggle for political participation within the three main UK parties, Labour, Conservative and Liberal Democrats, and show that women have largely been the drivers of a gradual, yet still incomplete, feminization of party politics.[2] Party membership may be broadly equal among women and men, but at Westminster women remain significantly under-represented – at still, in 2009, less than 20 per cent of MPs. Inter-party differences are evident: at the 2005 general election Labour women MPs numbered 98, Conservative women MPs 17 and Liberal Democrats ten. This asymmetry reflects the use of 'equality guarantees' – All Women Shortlists (AWS) – by the Labour Party in 1997 and 2005. This suggests that all political parties have a long way to go – and will have to make some hard decisions about equality strategies before parity of representation is achieved. The second part of the chapter turns its attention to women's mass participation in the UK. It finds that women remain less interested and involved in partisan politics than men but that they are more involved in civic activities and more interested in social welfare. Nonetheless, male and female voting levels are equal. These observations together challenge old clichés about women's apathetic and apolitical nature even while there exist important, if subtle, differences in the way men and women at the mass level engage with the political process.

WOMEN AND PARTY POLITICS: MEMBERS, ACTIVISTS AND PARLIAMENTARY REPRESENTATIVES

We know very little about the current make up of the membership of the major British political parties, since the parties are cautious about publishing membership data and do not release the proportion of men and women members. The data that is available indicates that the era of mass membership of political parties is over. The Labour Party had a surge in membership of 40 per cent before the 1997 election, but since then membership has declined from just over 400,000 members in 1997 to around 200,000 in 2005. The Conservatives have similarly seen a decline, from 400,000 in 1997 to just over 250,000 at present, while the Liberal Democrats had nearly 83,000 members in 1999 but have a current membership of roughly 75,000.

The number of women members of the House of Commons has increased markedly in recent years, as Table 9.1 demonstrates: in 1983 there were just 23 women MPs; by 2005 this figure had risen to 128. Careful scrutiny of the table reveals that the improvement in the level of representation of women at Westminster is largely accounted for by the increase in the number of Labour women MPs. Later in this section we will examine the recruitment processes employed by the political parties and show that the Labour Party's use of AWS accounts for their success in getting women selected for winnable seats. Although women were better represented in the House of Commons in 2005 than they were in 1983, the proportion of women legislators is still low, both internationally (the House of Commons was ranked fifty-sixth in the Inter-Parliamentary Union's league table of women's representation in 2009)[3] and within the UK (women constituted 47 per cent of members of the National Assembly for Wales, 33 per cent of members of the Scottish Parliament and 32 per cent of members of the Greater London Assembly at the time of writing in 2009). Furthermore, women are better represented in local government in England than

Table 9.1 MPs elected to the House of Commons, 1983–2005, by sex and party

Party	1983	1987	1992	1997	2001	2005
Labour	209	229	271	418	412	354
Women	10	21	37	101	95	98
% of total	**4.8**	**9.2**	**13.7**	**24.2**	**23.1**	**27.7**
Conservative	397	376	336	165	166	198
Women	13	17	20	13	14	17
% of total	**3.3**	**4.5**	**6**	**7.9**	**8.4**	**8.6**
Liberal Democrat	23	22	20	46	53	62
Women	0	1	2	3	6	10
% of total	**0**	**4.5**	**10**	**6.5**	**11.3**	**16.1**
Other	21	23	24	30	25	31
Women	0	2	3	3	4	3
% of total	**0**	**8.7**	**12.5**	**10**	**16**	**9.7**
All MPs	650	650	651	659	659	645
Women	23	41	60	120	118	128
% of total	**3.5**	**6.3**	**9.2**	**18.2**	**17.9**	**19.8**

Source: Sarah Childs, Joni Lovenduski and Rosie Campbell, *Women at the Top* (London: Hansard, 2005).

they are at Westminster (women made up 29.3 per cent of English councillors in 2007).[4]

THE LIBERALS, SDP AND THE LIBERAL DEMOCRATS

The contemporary Liberal Democrats derive from an alliance, then merger, in the mid-late 1980s, of the old and successful Liberal Party of the nineteenth and early twentieth century (and its less successful rump of the middle twentieth century) with the Social Democratic Party (SDP), established in 1981.[5] The alliance with the SDP and the subsequent merger of the Liberal Party and the SDP in 1988 had important consequences for the role of women within the party. The SDP had been formed by moderate members of the Labour Party alienated by the party's swing to the political left in the 1980s. These individuals were used to working within a party that was more explicitly pro-feminist than the Liberal Party and provided an impetus for change. Indeed, as Elizabeth Evans argues, 'typically the SDP were more engaged and pro-active than Liberals in their approach to women's representation and women's interests'.[6] For example, the SDP were committed to including women's issues within their policy platforms and the issue of women's parliamentary representation was high on the agenda. In contrast, women's issues and the Women's Liberal Federation were at the Liberal Party's margins. As the Alliance, two joint policy papers on women's issues were produced: in the language of the papers, women's representation would be on the basis of fairness rather than equality. The choice of the word 'fairness' reveals tensions within the Alliance regarding how to combine a commitment to the greater representation of women alongside a belief in individualism and meritocracy.[7] However, a new approach to women's representation was a feature of the merger between the two parties and 'quotas at the point of short-listing became a part of the new constitution'.[8] Thus, the newly formed Liberal Democrats were the first British party to apply a quota rule to selection procedures for general elections. Despite this historic first, there was a rather different outcome when the party considered AWS, following Labour's use of them in 1997. In 2001 a motion to introduce AWS was put to the party conference: supported by the older women feminists within the party, it was defeated by a cohort of younger women who saw the proposal as demeaning. The tension dividing women Liberal Democrats remains, hindering attempts to improve the parliamentary representation of women overall. Eschewing AWS, the party relies on equality rhetoric, encouraging women to seek selection, and equality promotion measures such as training, equal opportunities selection procedures and financial support.[9]

THE CONSERVATIVE PARTY

The Conservatives had a history of mobilizing women, starting with the Primrose League in the nineteenth century. As indicated by Pat Thane in her chapter in this volume, while many Conservative Party members were anti-suffrage, the party also contained active suffrage supporters. Reorganization of party structures after 1918 ensured women's representation within these. After the Second World War the separate women's branches were abolished and the Women's Sections became 'women's constituency advisory committees' whose main function was to provide catering at events and carry out the bulk of work at election time. A parliamentary sub-committee of the Women's National Advisory Committee (WNAC) was established in 1946. It was not until Edward Heath became leader of the party in 1965 that the demands of the WNAC for the incorporation of women's concerns into party policy were successful. Under Heath's leadership a committee on women's rights was established. In terms of wider party membership, in the 1950s the Conservative Party had approximately 2.8 million members, about half of whom were women.[10] The party's ambivalence towards its women members – as evidenced by its policy towards the Conservative Women's Organization (CWO) – in the late 1990s and early 2000s was clear. The CWO's very existence was questioned and the relationship between it and the wider party deteriorated. This ambivalence also appeared to play out in apparent differences between two types of woman member of the Conservative Party:[11] the traditional woman party members, fewer in number than before, as working women found themselves with little time for hosting Conservative tea parties; and the 'career' women seeking political office, and parliamentary representation, but who did not, or rarely, at least publicly, see themselves as gendered political actors.

Since 1979 women's participation in the parliamentary Conservative Party élite has been a strange mix of individual success and downright failure. The party was the first, and only, significant British party to have a woman leader and then Prime Minister. However, Margaret Thatcher was not what most people would describe as feminist.[12] In fact, she espoused a very traditional politics towards women and the home that was in direct contradiction to her own experience.[13] She failed to promote women in politics – in 1979 women made up just 2 per cent of the parliamentary Conservative Party and they constituted less than 10 per cent in 2005. Only one other woman – Lady Young – was in any of Mrs Thatcher's Cabinets, and Young's presence was brief, as Minister of State for the Department of Education, from 1979 to 1981. In some senses Mrs Thatcher's leadership of the party served to entrench long-held Conservative views about equal opportunities. Her success was said to prove that merit alone was the criterion for selection, and it undermined demands for more interventionist measures to improve the parliamentary representation of women.

After more than eight years in opposition and several failed attempts at 'modernization', the Conservative Party elected David Cameron as party leader in December 2005. Before Cameron's election the Conservative Party was suffering from a serious image problem. Theresa May summed this up during her 2002 party conference speech, when she said that the Conservatives were perceived as the 'nasty party'. This image problem was compounded by the fact that, compared with the Labour Party, the parliamentary Conservative Party looked rather 'male, pale and stale'. Furthermore, there was evidence that the Conservatives had lost their advantage among women voters.[14] Thus, there were good reasons for Cameron to believe that a greater emphasis on issues of gender equality might pay him electoral dividends. He drew attention to the under-representation of women in the party in his acceptance speech: 'We will change the way we look. Nine out of ten Conservative MPs are white men. We need to change the scandalous under-representation of women in the Conservative party and we will do that.'[15] In a subsequent speech to the Equal Opportunities Commission in 2006, Cameron declared that it was the Conservatives' goal to make 'gender inequality history' by increasing the number of Conservative women MPs, tackling the gender pay gap and addressing childcare issues.[16]

Cameron inherited a parliamentary party that, as stated above, lagged behind the other parties: women MPs constituted nearly 28 per cent of the parliamentary Labour Party, 16 per cent of the Liberal Democrats and only 9 per cent of the Conservatives. The ability to select parliamentary candidates is the only area where local constituency associations are able to exercise any real power and they tend to guard it jealously. Research has demonstrated that the local party members who make up selection panels have favoured men over women candidates. This discrimination has been based on a false belief that voters will penalize a party for putting forward a woman candidate (no British research has found this to be the case) or a belief that women cannot, or should not, attempt to combine elected office and family life.[17] In order to bypass local prejudices, increasing the representation of women requires the reform of selection processes. The logic of equality guarantees passed the party by however as Conservative Party members are hostile to such measures.[18]

Among the initiatives undertaken by the Conservatives under Cameron was the reinstatement of the Vice-Chairman for Women, abolished during the Hague reforms.[19] This voluntary post serves two purposes: to help more women to be selected as candidates and to promote women's issues within policy debates. The immediate reforms put in place by Cameron included: suspension of selection, creation of a priority list made up of 50 per cent women candidates, and the top 100 target seats to be chosen from that list. These initiatives looked radical since they amounted to equality guarantees that were not substantively much weaker than Labour's AWS. However, the policy proved highly controversial within the party and the requirement that associations select from the priority list did not last beyond the 'progress review' that took place in the months after Cameron's announcement that action would be taken to increase women's representation. The policy moved then even further from an equality guarantee than when it was first posited.

This is not to say that the reforms were only initiated from the top down. Women within the Tory establishment had been demanding change for some time, albeit rather quietly and privately. The Conservative Party's Women's Organization was critical of the failure to integrate women's concerns and perspectives into the Conservative Party manifesto at the 2005 general election and women MPs, albeit most often off the record, challenged the 'meritocratic' basis of Conservative Party selection procedures.[20] The 2005 general election changed that. A Conservative ginger group, women2win, was formed, recognizing that the Conservative failure in the election had opened a window of opportunity for change. For the party leadership, improved representation of women within the parliamentary party became part of an attempt to reinvent the party, seeking to eliminate its reputation as 'the nasty party'. The door was open to reform for two main reasons. First, the Labour Party had been gradually eating into the Conservatives' presumed electoral advantage with women voters. Secondly, the election of 120 women Labour MPs in 1997 had the effect of making the other parties look old-fashioned. It seemed that a modern Conservative Party would simply have to include more women MPs.

Despite Cameron's reforms, it will not be possible to draw any firm conclusions about whether the party has taken seriously the challenge of the under-representation of women until after the 2010 general election. A number of additional caveats are in order: the Conservative Party élite's attitudes to women remain the most traditional among the parties. [21] Furthermore, the grass roots of the party are still rather more traditional than feminist in their attitudes to women's roles.[22] Women within the party élite are on average more feminist in their attitudes than men, but Labour men favour gender equality far more than Conservative women.

THE LABOUR PARTY

In the early years of the Labour Party, much as in the Conservative Party, women were largely organized separately from the ordinary membership, in the Women's Labour League, which later became Women's Sections. The party's 1918 constitution, however, provided for women's representation within the formal structures of the party. As Pat Thane indicates in her chapter in this volume, women were able to make some impact on education, health and welfare policies in the interwar years, although their position in the party remained relatively weak.

A process of feminization of the Labour Party began in the late 1970s. The post-1968 women's movement was suspicious of formal politics and preferred to operate in a non-hierarchical co-operative mode. But by the late 1970s the Women's Liberation Movement was more fractured and some of its supporters began to turn their attention to political parties, especially, in England, the Labour Party. Many saw the Labour Party as an inherently masculine institution and they sought to change it from the inside. The changing economic and political context in Britain also gave them the opportunity to change the party. The decline in manufacturing industry and the rise of the service sector feminized the unions, giving feminists a voice within the Labour Party at the same time as the decline of the traditional working class forced the Labour Party to seek to attract different groups of voters – with women the obvious target. Labour women demanded internal party quotas which gave them a larger presence within party structures: quotas for women were set across the party at 40 per cent, including, in 1992, 40 per cent membership of policy forums.[23] Women also demanded parliamentary sex quotas, first for all vacant seats held by Labour and winnable seats, then for half of all such seats: the 1986 Annual Conference accepted the principle, and, in 1987, the constitutional requirement was made that at least one woman should be included on any shortlist of any constituency in which a woman is nominated. At the 1989 Conference, Composite Resolution 54 accepted the principle of quotas, and in 1990 the Conference agreed the introduction of quotas for candidate selections. After the 1992 election the party elected a new leader, John Smith, who favoured quotas. He cleverly linked AWS to a party conference vote on 'one-member-one-vote' (OMOV).[24] Hence, when OMOV passed, AWS slipped through as well, and were agreed at the 1993 national conference. There would be AWS in 50 per cent of all key seats and 50 per cent of all vacant Labour-held seats. The presumed Conservative advantage among women voters was used to argue for greater parliamentary representation. The linking of the issues was largely the result of the activities of the Labour Women's National Executive Committee. AWS was to be used for the 1997 general election. However, a legal ruling in 1996, following a challenge by two male potential candidates, found that AWS contravened Sex Discrimination legislation– a decision the party leadership did not contest. Even so, there were 35 endorsed AWS candidates at the 1997 general election. Having failed to introduce legislation permitting the use of AWS for the 2001 general election, and recognizing that the party was likely to see the numbers of its women MPs decline in 2001,[25] the Sex Discrimination (Election Candidates) Act, which allows for AWS, was passed in 2002. Used again in 2005, the Labour Party's AWS delivered record percentages of women MPs. The Equality Bill going through parliament in 2009 aims to extend this legislation's 'sunset clause' (setting a date at which parliament must revisit it, inserted to appease opponents of the legislation) from 2015 to 2030.

As well as being the only major British political party to employ measures to guarantee an improvement in the representation of women, the Labour Party, when in government, has often been the leader on gender equality legislation. It was a Conservative government that introduced the first equal pay regulations in the 1950s, but Labour governments introduced the Equal Pay Act of 1970 and the Sex Discrimination Act of 1975, which set up the Equal Opportunities Commission (EOC).[26] This legislation outlawed direct discrimination on the grounds of sex in the workplace and in education. The legislation was supplemented in 2007 by a new positive duty to consider gender equality in the provision of public services pre-emptively, rather than after a case of discrimination has been made. Thus, Labour governments have been at the forefront of providing a legal framework for the promotion of gender equality.

THE IMPACT OF WOMEN MPS

We have seen that the political parties have very gradually, and at different rates, selected more women to stand as MPs in winnable seats. A question that is often raised about the necessity of increasing women's representation in the House of

Commons is whether the women will 'make a difference' once they get there. We agree with Anne Phillips, who argues that the disproportionate number of men in the House of Commons is evidence enough of discrimination (when women make up more than 50 per cent of the population), and measures to increase the number of women MPs are justified simply on the basis of fairness.[27] However, there is some evidence – in Lovenduski's phrase, 'a substantial amount of circumstantial evidence' - that women in Westminster 'act for women'.[28] Not only is it the case that under Labour since 1997 women's concerns such as domestic violence, the minimum wage, and more family-friendly employment policies (such as flexible working and working families tax credits) have been introduced, but also these have been associated with individual women ministers such as Harriet Harman and Patricia Hewitt. Moreover, empirical research has demonstrated, *inter alia*, that some women MPs are more likely to ask gendered questions in the House; disproportionately to support gendered and feminist Early Day Motions in the House of Commons; support legislation such as that permitting the use of sex quotas in UK politics and that reducing VAT on sanitary products; to use gendered arguments in arguing for reform of the hours of the House of Commons; and, more recently, to employ feminist arguments in respect of abortion legislation.[29]

WOMEN'S MASS POLITICAL PARTICIPATION

Women respond to political parties and their policies in two main ways: first in terms of the kind of political activities they are involved in, and secondly in terms of which parties they vote for. We discuss each of these in turn. Some notable early studies of political participation were scathing about women's political inclinations: 'it would appear that women differ from men in their political behaviour only in being somewhat more frequently apathetic, parochial, conservative, and sensitive to personality, emotional, and aesthetic aspects of political life and electoral campaigns'.[30] This perception was challenged by feminist researchers[31] but, certainly, early studies of political participation found that women were less active than men.

Voting in elections is the most obvious form of political participation undertaken by the mass public. Since the 1960s at least, women were slightly less likely to vote in British general elections than men.[32] This trend has now reversed and women have recently been marginally more likely to vote than men. However, the greater turnout of women is probably due to their longevity at least as much to their political commitment. The sex gap in voting in recent elections is not statistically significant and disappears entirely when age is controlled for. Older people are more likely to vote and there are more older women than older men. Figure 9.1 demonstrates that the sex gap is extremely small and that the overall decline in turnout over time is far more significant than any sex difference. We see, therefore, that there is very little difference in the political participation of men and women when it comes to voting in general elections.

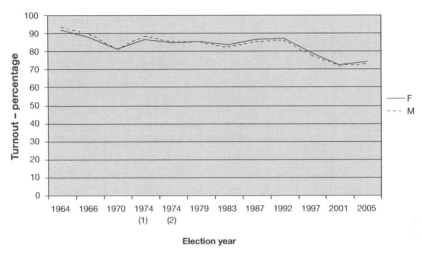

Figure 9.1 Sex and turnout at general elections, 1964–2005

Note: These figures are self-reported turnout and tend to be higher than actual election turnout.

Source: British Election Study Series.

Turnout is the lowest-cost form of mass political behaviour. Other forms of participation, such as joining or campaigning for a political party, are more time-consuming and are undertaken by smaller numbers of people. Historically women have been less likely than men to engage in these more formal political activities. The most recent research on this topic covering England is the Electoral Commission report on gender and political participation of 2004:[33] the Commission has been concerned with trying to engage groups of citizens who are politically disaffected and has also commissioned reports on participation and youth. The report builds on earlier studies and demonstrates that the gender gap in political participation has narrowed over time: women remain less likely to join, donate to or campaign for political parties, but the differences between the sexes are minimal. For example, according to the 2002 European Social Survey, 2 per cent of women and 4 per cent of men reported belonging to a political party and 10 per cent of men and 11 per cent of women reported wearing a campaign badge – gender gaps of 2 and 1 per cent respectively. Thus, according to a narrow definition of political activity, women are still slightly less involved in politics than men. Broader definitions of political participation encompass the activities of a 'good citizen', such as volunteering for charities, signing petitions and boycotting goods: this approach tends to capture more of women's activities.

According to the 2004 Electoral Commission report, women are more likely than men to engage in 'cause'-oriented activities, such as signing petitions and boycotting or buying products for political reasons, while men are more likely to be involved in 'campaign'-oriented activities, such as being members of political parties, donating to and campaigning for parties. For example, 42 per cent of women and 36 per cent of men reported signing a petition, and 36 per cent of women and 29 per cent of men reported buying a product for a political reason. The report found that the overall gender gap in formal political participation was small, but it also noted some sub-groups of women who were particularly removed from the political process. The gender gap in participation is larger among respondents with young children and married women were found to be less active than married men, while black and minority ethnic women were also found to be less active than other women. The report noted that the data was insufficiently nuanced to garner any detailed evidence about which minority groups of women were most disengaged.[34]

VOTING

Since the first large-scale opinion polls in the 1960s, a greater proportion of women in Britain have voted for the Conservatives than men. The Conservative Party was successful in attracting women's support after the Second World War, as Pat Thane discusses in her chapter in this volume, though by the 1980s there were no significant gender differences in voter support for parties. From the 1960s Labour women gained confidence and pushed for change, focusing on targeting women voters. But it was not until the 1980s that women in the party mobilized extensively. Then, in the 1990s, with the election of John Smith as party leader, those demanding change gained a real voice. The party leadership was persuaded by women activists that the Tory advantage among women voters was one reason for the Labour Party's decade of defeats. It has been argued that had women voted for the Labour Party in equal numbers to men there would have been successive Labour governments since 1945. The party's strategy of AWS, as outlined above, symbolized to women voters that it was receptive to their needs and interests. The party's policy programme also was intended to appeal to women, with plans for a Women's Ministry and a focus upon health and education, issues that women were more likely to prioritize at election time than men.

Pippa Norris described the 1997 British general election as potentially a critical turning point for the way men and women vote in Britain:[35] she identified a gender generation gap, where younger women were increasingly likely to vote Labour. A number of previous studies had noticed that, as women had entered education and the workplace in greater numbers, the old alignment, where women were more likely to vote Conservative than men, had all but disappeared. Norris suggests that this relationship may be reversing, with women moving to the left, a trend which, she argues, is evident across Western industrialized nations.[36] In the British case, analysis of the 1997, 2001 and 2005 general elections has demonstrated that younger women are now more likely to vote Labour than younger men, but the traditional gap still holds among people born before the Second World War.[37] Thus, at the aggregate level, there may appear to be no difference between the way men and women vote in Britain, but this tends to mask sex differences within sub-groups. The most significant difference between women when it comes to voting appears to be that of generation. More educated women with higher incomes tend to be to the left of less educated women with lower incomes but the generational difference, where older women are more Conservative than younger women, is the most powerful.

Explaining the gender generation gap is not straightforward – there are a number of overlapping causes that cannot easily be unpacked. Women's movement into the public worlds of work and education may have led them to shift their concerns from protecting the family from state interference to looking to the state to provide more support, thus pushing them to the left of the political spectrum. Alternatively, women's greater levels of employment in the public sphere might shift them leftwards, as might the fact that women tend to be less financially well-off than men. The problem with these explanations is that they all predict the same outcome – women voting to the left of men – and it is therefore difficult to use survey evidence to establish which has the most pronounced effect. However, although there has been a small gender generation gap in recent British general elections, the gap is not large enough to suggest that these changes in women's lives are more important than the more general factors that lead both men and women to vote for a particular party. Although the size of the gap may not be sufficient to tell us the strength of the effects, it is possible that men and women might vote for the same parties for different reasons.

A detailed analysis of who votes for which party may give us more insight into how gender affects vote choice. In particular, since 1997, the Labour Party has been highly successful at attracting the votes of middle- and high-income women who are mothers.[38] Since 1997, middle- and high-income fathers stand out from the rest of the population as being the least likely to vote for the Labour Party. Overall, women are more likely than men to say that health and education are the most important issues facing Britain today, while men are more likely to state that the economy or taxation are most important. We would argue that this suggests that New Labour's focus on health and education helped to deliver them the votes of middle-class mothers. However, we doubt that this is the only reason why the Labour Party has managed to deliver the votes of younger women. Bernadette Hayes has shown that individuals with a feminist orientation tend to vote for the Labour Party,[39] and younger feminist women are the most likely to vote Labour.[40] Thus, the Labour Party's AWS policy and its other feminist initiatives are likely to have contributed to the party's popularity with younger women. The Labour Party's focus on health and education in the 1997 and subsequent elections may have helped them to win younger women's votes, but sex differences in issue preference vary by age, with younger women more concerned about education and older women most concerned about the state of the NHS. There is not therefore a simple pattern of all women being drawn towards the Labour Party for the same reasons. Although the Labour Party has been successful in targeting particular groups of women voters, a simple relationship between sex and party of vote has not been established in Britain. Unlike in the United States, patterns of sex and voting in Britain are by no means firmly entrenched, and the shifts in priorities brought about by the economic downturn since 2008 may provide an opportunity for the Conservative Party to win back women voters.

CONCLUSION

Where does this survey of women's involvement in politics in Britain lead us? We can conclude that women have always been actively involved in Britain's political parties and their campaigning and fundraising have been crucial for elections and for the effective functioning of the party system. Over time, the nature of women's participation has changed from largely behind-the-scenes grassroots activities to membership of the political élite and reshaping the parties' election platforms. Women remain slightly less likely to be involved in formal politics than men, though the gap is very small. But parity of parliamentary representation is a long way off. The 2010 general election may see a decline in the numbers and percentages of elected women, as Labour women are ejected from parliament and the Conservative party fails to replace them with women. Consequently, campaigns for parity of representation continue. A rare 'Speaker's Conference' – a committee of the House first used in 1916–17 to consider the enfranchisement of women and all adult men – was established in 2008 to consider the under-representation of women, black and minority ethnic and disabled candidates/MPs. Debates about equality strategies will continue. No British party can depend upon women's votes at election time and all have tried different strategies to target women and groups of women. Since 1997 the Labour Party has been able to undermine the Conservatives' advantage among women but any gender gap in vote choice remains small and potentially transient.

NOTES

1   The first part of this chapter draws heavily on Sarah Childs, *Women and British Party Politics: Descriptive, Substantive and Symbolic Representation* (London: Routledge, 2008), chapter 3.

2   Studies of women and politics, like more mainstream research, rarely use England as the unit of analysis. This is despite differences between the component parts of the UK. For example, selection processes may be devolved to Scottish parties. Here we focus on selection processes for England and Wales but overall figures for parliamentary representation relate to the UK Parliament. Moreover, Northern Ireland falls outside of mainstream political party activity, having its own party system.

3   Data compiled from information provided by 31 July 2009. See http://www.ipu.org/wmn-e/classif.htm (accessed 29 November 2009)

4   *Representing the Future: The Report of the Councillors Commission* (Councillors Commission, 2007).

5   For discussion of the position of women in the earlier part of the twentieth century, see the chapter by Pat Thane in this volume.
6   Elizabeth Evans, *Women's Representation and the Liberal Democrats* (London: University of London, 2009), p. 78.
7   Evans, *Women's Representation and the Liberal Democrats.*
8   Ibid., p. 82.
9   Childs, *Women and British Party Politics.*
10 Zweiniger-Bargielowska, Ina, 'Explaining the gender gap: the Conservative Party and the women's vote 1945–1964', in Martin Francis and Ina Zweiniger-Bargielowska (eds), *The Conservatives and British Society 1880–1990* (Cardiff: University of Wales Press, 1996), pp. 194–223. This compares well to the Labour Party, where women made up at least half of the individual membership between the wars.
11 G. E. Maguire, *Conservative Women: A History of Women and the Conservative Party, 1874–1997* (London: Palgrave Macmillan, 1998).
12 Martin Pugh does cite an early article published by Mrs Margaret Thatcher that argues for mothers of young children to spend some time away from the home, suggesting that she had at least a 'feminist phase'. Martin Pugh, *Women and the Women's Movement in Britain*, 2nd edn (London: Macmillan, 2002), p. 306.
13 Beatrix Campbell, *The Iron Ladies: Why Do Women Vote Tory?* (London: Virago Press, 1987).
14 Rosie Campbell, *Gender and the Vote in Britain* (Colchester, Essex: ECPR Press, 2006).
15 6 December 2005.
16 See http://www.epolitix.com/latestnews/article-detail/newsarticle/cameronnbsppledges-action-on-gendernbspequality/?no_cache=1 (accessed 3 February 2010)
17 Laura Shepherd-Robinson and Joni Lovenduski, *Women and Candidate Selection in British Political Parties* (London: Fawcett, 2002).
18 Rosie Campbell, Sarah Childs and Joni Lovenduski, 'Women's equality guarantees and the Conservative Party', *Political Quarterly*, 77, (1), (2006), pp. 18–27.
19 William Hague was elected as leader of the Conservative Party after the 1997 electoral defeat with a mandate to reform the party.
20 Childs, *Women and British Party Politics.*
21 Rosie Campbell, Sarah Childs and Joni Lovenduski, 'Do women need women MPs?', *British Journal of Political Science* (forthcoming).
22 Campbell *et al.*, 'Do women need women MPs?'.
23 Childs, *Women and British Party Politics.*
24 The introduction of OMOV abolished the block vote which had given the (historically male-dominated) trade unions enormous power at the party conference.
25 The Labour Party returned 101 women MPs in 1997. This number fell to 95 in 2001.
26 The EOC was a government-sponsored non-departmental public body charged with promoting gender equality through research and providing support for individuals in discrimination cases. The EOC has now been amalgamated into a single equalities body – the Equality and Human Rights Commission (EHRC), which has combined the former EOC, Racial Equality, and Disability Rights Commissions, and extended its scope to cover age, religion, and sexual orientation. The gender, race and disability equality duties are likely to be repackaged together as a single equalities duty in the Equalities Act in the autumn of 2009.
27 Anne Phillips, *The Politics of Presence* (Oxford University Press, 1995).
28 Joni Lovenduski, *Feminizing Politics* (Cambridge: Polity Press, 2005).

29   Childs, *Women and British Party Politics*.
30   Gabriel Almond and Sidney Verba, *The Civic Culture: Political Attitudes and Democracy in Five Nations* (Princeton: Princeton University Press, 1963), p. 325.
31   Murray Goot and Elizabeth Reid, 'Women and voting studies: mindless matrons or sexist scientism?', in Richard Rose (ed.), *Professional Papers in Contemporary Political Sociology* (London: Sage, 1975).
32   Reliable election data are available only from 1964 onwards and although there was much speculation that women had voted Conservative in greater numbers than men before this date, there is no robust evidence available.
33   Pippa Norris, Joni Lovenduski and Rosie Campbell, *Gender and Political Participation* (The Electoral Commission, 2004).
34   The under-representation of black and minority ethnic women in British politics has been taken up by the Fawcett Society in its 'Seeing Double' and 'Femocracy' campaigns. See http://www.fawcettsociety.org.uk/index.asp?PageID=375, (accessed 29 November 2009) and by the Speaker's Conference, see http://www.parliament.uk/about/how/principal/speaker/speakers_conference.cfm (accessed 29 November 2009)
35   Pippa Norris, 'Gender: a gender-generation gap?', in Geoffrey Evans and Pippa Norris (eds), *Critical Elections: British Parties and Voters in Long-Term Perspective* (London: Sage, 1999), pp. 146–63.
36   In the United States women have been more likely than men likely to vote for Democratic presidential candidates at every election since 1980. In the 1990s Inglehart and Norris found evidence of the modern gender gap (where women are to the left of men) in several other advanced industrialized nations: Japan, Ireland, Denmark, Austria, the Netherlands, Norway, Sweden, Switzerland and Canada. Ronald Inglehart and Pippa Norris, 'The developmental theory of the gender gap: women and men's voting behaviour in global perspective', *International Political Science Review*, 21, (4), (2000), pp. 441–62.
37   Campbell, *Gender and the Vote in Britain*.
38   Campbell, *Gender and the Vote in Britain*.
39   Bernadette Hayes, 'Gender, feminism and electoral behaviour in Britain', *Electoral Studies*, 16, (2), (1997), pp. 203–16.
40   Campbell, *Gender and the Vote in Britain*.

10

Feminist politics in Scotland from the 1970s to 2000s: engaging with the changing state

Esther Breitenbach and Fiona Mackay

This chapter outlines some of the key features of 'second wave' feminism in Scotland from the 1970s to the present, taking as its major focus changing attitudes of the women's movement to formal politics and to engagement with the state, in particular local and devolved government. This does not mean that the relationship with political institutions and political parties has become the exclusive focus of feminist politics in Scotland. The movement has since its inception been heterogeneous and diverse – concerned with cultural and expressive activities as well as state-centred politics – and remains so. The 'second wave' women's movement in Scotland has not yet been systematically researched, though several accounts of feminist campaigns and groups exist, primarily by activists, but including some academic research.[1] More recently there has been a growing interest in recording the history of the movement and in analysing its characteristics.[2] Evidence drawn on here therefore has limitations, and at times we have been reliant on knowledge acquired through practical experience of our involvement in campaigns, policy debates and so on. We recognize that this is only one among several possible perspectives.

It is notoriously difficult to demonstrate the independent effect of collective action on social change. However, if we are asking about impacts of feminism, political, legislative and policy changes must be an important focus of discussion. In Scotland, as elsewhere in industrialized democracies, the 'second wave' women's movement has shared the common agenda of issues of abortion, equal rights, rape, domestic violence, and equal opportunities, and the movement has often followed a path similar to women's movements elsewhere in the UK. Over time it has made the transition from a movement strongly influenced by revolutionary left-wing, libertarian and anarchist politics hostile to parliamentary politics and to the state, to one which has embraced engagement with the state to further the aim of gender equality and which, in recent years, has particularly focused on the issue of women's representation in political institutions and on strategies for influencing gender equality policies at various levels of governance. Within the Scottish context, state reconfiguration in the form of devolution has occupied a position of primary political importance in recent decades and provided a structure of opportunities, political, institutional and discursive, for organized women to press for improvements in women's substantive citizenship.

In describing the changing relationship between feminist organizations and the state, we take a broadly decade-by-decade approach. The 1970s saw the flourishing of the Women's Liberation Movement (WLM) in Scotland, as elsewhere in the UK and in many other countries. Following an initial phase in which groups often concentrated on consciousness-raising and on one-off protests and demonstrations highlighting sexist and discriminatory practices, a number of campaigning groups emerged focusing on issues such as abortion rights or domestic violence. The 1980s witnessed the transition of feminist ideas to other organizations such as trade unions and the Labour Party as feminist activists entered them in increasing numbers in response to the rise of Thatcherism. Municipal feminism emerged in Scotland in the mid-1980s, while the renewed debate on devolution began to attract more active engagement from feminists. As the devolution campaign took off in the 1990s, an alliance of women activists and organizations demanding equal representation and women-friendly political institutions made their presence felt. At the same time, high-profile local authority campaigns against violence against women became a salient feature of the Scottish political scene following the launch of the Zero Tolerance campaign by Edinburgh District Council in 1992. By 1999 the Scottish Parliament had been created and had seen women's share of representation in the new institution reach Scandinavian-style levels. The 2000s have seen the institutionalization of gender and other equalities within the new political machinery created by devolution, while feminist organizations have negotiated a new relationship with this reconfigured state.

THE 1970s: WOMEN'S LIBERATION – FROM CONSCIOUSNESS-RAISING TO CAMPAIGNS

The WLM in Scotland emerged more or less simultaneously to the movement elsewhere in the UK and in other Western industrialized societies, and took similar forms. Browne has established that several Scottish WLM groups were in existence by 1970,[3] and in 1972 the first Scottish Women's Liberation Conference was held. By the mid-1970s women's liberation groups had come into being across Scotland, and consisted of a loosely networked and diverse range of interest groups, such as consciousness-raising groups, study and education activities, campaigning groups, writers and performers groups and networks.[4] The geographical location of groups ranged from Shetland in the far north to Galloway in the south, though most women's liberation activities were concentrated in the four main cities of Glasgow, Edinburgh, Aberdeen and Dundee, and on university campuses such as St Andrews and Stirling.

It remains a major challenge for historians of 'second wave' feminism to provide an estimate of numbers of women involved in the WLM, since lack of formal membership and of records means that for many groups such evidence simply does not exist. At any one time the numbers of women in the movement (in the sense of being regular attenders of group meetings) in Scotland in the 1970s were likely to have been in the hundreds rather than thousands. On the other hand, there was considerable turnover, feminist ideas were actively disseminated by a growing literature with a readership far beyond women's groups themselves, and feminist ideas were being taken into other organizations such as political parties and trade unions. Feminist ideas also informed women's practice in their personal lives and their working lives, whether in education, social work, community work, local government, the legal profession, journalism, and so on.

As elsewhere in the UK, the extent of mobilization around the WLM's seven demands[5] varied considerably. Most notably abortion and domestic violence became the focus of organized campaigning across Scotland, and there were also active groups in Glasgow and Edinburgh campaigning for legal and financial independence for women. Abortion was a highly politicized issue in the West of Scotland in particular, due to the presence of a substantial Catholic population, and in response to the perceived need to organize effectively in defence of the 1967 Abortion Act in Scotland a Scottish Abortion Campaign had been established by the mid-1970s.

A network of groups campaigning for refuges for 'battered women' had also come into existence by the early 1970s, and had begun to function informally as a Scottish network, while also participating in the 'national' network of Women's Aid groups from England, Scotland and Wales.[6] The Scottish Women's Aid Federation (SWAF) was formally constituted in 1976 when it received funding from the Scottish Office.[7] SWAF's aims were to lobby local councils to make housing available for refuges and to rehouse women leaving violent partners. SWAF also campaigned for changes to tenancy laws, laws on division of matrimonial property on separation or divorce, and laws giving protection to women who were victims of violence by their partners, all areas subject to separate Scottish legislation.

The demand for legal and financial independence for women aimed at ending the definition of women as men's dependants and entailed campaigns on social security benefits and pensions, independent taxation, tenancy rights, rights to mortgages and other financial products, simplification of divorce laws, laws on custody of children, and so on. Again, given that some of these laws were part of the Scottish civil justice system (though not all, with social security, pensions and taxation being key exceptions) campaigning on these issues necessitated specifically Scottish forms of organization and lobbying.

In common with Wales, a distinctive dimension of the women's movement in Scotland has been the interplay between feminism and national identity (cultural and political, although language has been less salient in Scotland). An interest in Scottish identity began to emerge in the mid-1970s, indicated, for example, by the launch of the *Scottish Women's Liberation Journal* in 1977. There were two factors influencing this. First, some approaches and analyses offered by North American feminists or by feminists based in the South of England did not fully resonate with Scottish experience, and this stimulated a desire to understand better the nature of Scottish society and history, and women's place within these. Secondly, there was a shared perception that Scotland was more culturally backward than the US and than England, and that it was more male-chauvinist and sexually repressive. Also commonly accepted was a view of the Scottish Calvinist heritage as patriarchal, authoritarian and oppressive. Again this fuelled the notion that understanding this specific historical, social and cultural configuration was necessary if feminists were to find a way of effectively challenging it.

The issue of sexual orientation also had a high profile in the movement in Scotland, as elsewhere in the UK. On the one hand, this was productive of some tension between some groups of heterosexual and lesbian women over the extent to which separatism was a desirable strategy. On the other hand, lesbian feminism provided a means of support for many women to form different kinds of sexual relationships than they had been brought up to believe were possible or appropriate. Lesbian feminists were actively involved in campaigns to change the law in Scotland, as well as establishing support organizations such as Lesbian Line.[8] While the law on homosexual acts had been liberalized in England and Wales in 1967, this was not to occur in Scotland till 1980, with Robin Cook's amendment to the Criminal Justice Bill. Feminists participated in Scotland's first gay rights organization, the Scottish Minorities Group, founded in 1969, though from the mid-1970s many lesbian feminists preferred to organize in women-only groups. Over time lesbian feminists were to become an integral part of the LGBT movement in Scotland, participating in Lesbian and Gay Pride marches and in campaigns for further legal change, such as the campaign for the repeal of Section 2A by the Scottish Parliament, which was achieved in 2000.[9]

By the end of the 1970s the WLM in Scotland may have directly involved only relatively small numbers of women, but feminist ideas had a wider audience. The late 1970s was, however, to witness a shifting of the ground for feminism. First, in so far as there was a 'national' UK women's movement, it fragmented following the last UK Women's Liberation Conference, held in Birmingham in 1978. Second, the political climate – and structure of political opportunities for feminists – changed significantly in 1979. In March of that year the referendum on a Scottish Assembly was defeated, a contributory factor to Labour's defeat in the general election of May 1979. The election ushered in a Conservative government, headed by Margaret Thatcher, a neo-liberal conviction politician.

In the run up to the 1979 referendum, the WLM in Scotland was not particularly engaged by the prospect of devolution, although individual women were supportive of devolution and some organizations, such as the Edinburgh and Glasgow Legal and Financial Independence Campaign groups, believed that it was necessary to prepare for the advent of an Assembly, whether or not this was seen as desirable in itself.[10] This indifference or, at best, ambivalence reflected the relative lack of interest in parliamentary politics then characteristic of the WLM. The perception of Scotland as a more male-dominated and sexist society gave rise to anxiety about the consequences of devolution of power to what was anticipated would be a male-dominated institution.

In the 1970s the WLM co-existed with other women's organizations, some having links to earlier generations of feminist organizations, and some which actively supported gender equality. However, there is little evidence of links between different generations of organizations at the time of the WLM's emergence,[11] and WLM groups tended to keep their distance from organizations which they perceived as liberal and middle-class. It was not until the 1980s that interconnections and working relationships began to develop between these different strands of feminist organization. One such organization, the Scottish Convention of Women (SCOW) (founded in 1977, with members from trade unions, church groups, women's organizations such as Soroptimists and Townswomen's Guilds, and local women's groups), attempted to raise the issue of women's representation within a Scottish Assembly with political parties, but this was not 'productive',[12] and in general the issue of women's representation was not raised in public debates.[13] SCOW's interest in devolution and in mechanisms for women's input into discussions on constitutional change was, however, maintained and, on raising the issue of women's representation with the Scottish Constitutional Convention in 1989, they were invited to join it.[14]

By the end of the 1970s, then, most WLM activists had not evinced much interest in women's participation in representative politics, whether at local, UK level or within a possible devolved assembly. Despite such hostility towards a state which was regarded as patriarchal and to political parties which were regarded as male-dominated and as reformist at best, by the second half of the 1970s feminists had nonetheless developed campaigns and forms of organization that engaged with the state. Networking on a specifically Scottish basis was integral to this practice, which aimed on the one hand to counter elements specific to Scottish political culture, and on the other to address Scottish institutional and legislative machinery.

THE 1980s: ANTI-THATCHERITE OPPOSITION, AND THE DEVELOPMENT OF MUNICIPAL FEMINISM

In the 1980s, the women's movement in Scotland continued to manifest itself through a wide variety of groups and activities, from community groups to women's centres, local and Scottish networks, much of it at the level of the practical feminism of everyday life.[15] This period also witnessed the emergence of black and minority ethnic women's groups such as Shakti and Hemat Gryffe Women's Aid, in Edinburgh and Glasgow respectively, with the numbers of organizations addressing information and support needs of minority ethnic women growing over time, and being more widely distributed across Scotland.[16]

The movement also became more distinctively Scottish in the 1980s and beyond, with the resurgence of devolution campaigns after the failed referendum, and with growing Scottish opposition to Thatcherite welfare state retrenchment and neo-liberal economic and industrial reforms which were seen to have a disproportionate impact on Scotland. Many feminists entered political and public institutions, such as political parties, trade unions and local government, in response to Thatcherism and to a growing acceptance of the need to engage with the state.[17] By the late 1980s feminists had become actively engaged in the devolution campaign and women's formal political representation had emerged as a key issue.

Three major factors underpinning this shift were the feminist response to Thatcherism and analysis of its impact upon women, the development of a feminist agenda in local government and in Europe, and the influence of campaigns for women's representation in political parties (particularly the Labour Party) and trade unions. Following the example of the Greater London Council and left-wing London boroughs, women activists in the Labour Party campaigned for local authority women's committees, with the first in Scotland being established in Stirling in 1984.[18] While in England the abolition of the Greater London Council and other large metropolitan authorities and attacks by central government on left-wing councils and on the power of local government in general effectively halted the development of women's committees, race equality committees and so on, this was not the case in Scotland. 'Municipal feminism' came to occupy a significant place within the Scottish political scene – as part of a wider oppositional political culture – and was important in keeping gender equality on the political agenda. Local government women's committees (and later equal opportunities committees) addressed the employment policies of local authorities themselves, aiming to eliminate sex discrimination in recruitment, promotion and pay, and also addressed the impacts of service provision on women, for example, housing, childcare provision, education, and leisure services. In addition, the equal opportunities units and staff of local authorities provided support for women's organizations through grant funding, and they created fora for consultation with local women's groups.

At the same time as these developments were taking place in the 1980s, many feminist groups continued to function in ways similar to those of the 1970s – autonomous, informal, non-hierarchical, often struggling to sustain themselves over time. Also in the 1980s, links developed between some feminists and pro-devolution groups, such as the collective which ran the journal *Radical Scotland*. The journal played a significant role in the 1980s as a platform for debate on devolution and about what sort of institutions should be created. In the mid-1980s a women's group was attached to the journal which contributed articles and encouraged other women to do so, though such contributions were not necessarily focused on devolution or independence *per se*, but often on issues equally relevant north or south of the border, such as welfare policies and women's poverty.

Overall, the 1980s represented a period in which feminists acquired greater political experience within formal arenas, as well as often creating – or reviving – women's sections within male-dominated organizations such as political parties and trade unions. They acquired political and organizational skills, and built up networks among women activists and with male allies. By the late 1980s this shift in political orientation among feminists was having an impact on the wider political debates surrounding devolution. Reacting to the formation of the Scottish Constitutional Convention in 1989, a group of cross-party and non-party women activists, Green Party members prominent among them, launched 'A Woman's Claim of Right', which, among other things, demanded that constitutional reform should guarantee equal representation for women.[19] The Constitutional Convention responded by creating a Women's Issues Group with the remit of seeking women's views on how to ensure their involvement in a Scottish Parliament.[20] These events inaugurated a period of sustained campaigning on women's political representation and on the need to ensure that any new political institution would be accessible to women.

THE 1990s: SHIFTING THE BALANCE OF POWER – DEMANDING EQUAL REPRESENTATION AND CHALLENGING VIOLENCE AGAINST WOMEN

Two issues stand out as particularly salient in the 1990s: the campaign for equal representation in a Scottish Parliament and for a woman-friendly institution; and the widespread campaigns against violence against women, undertaken by feminist organizations and local authorities in conjunction with other public sector bodies. Once the demand for equal representation had emerged, it became clear that this was an issue around which a broad based 50:50 campaign could be built, enjoying support from an alliance of self-defined feminists and other women in political parties, trade unions, feminist organizations (a leading organization among which was the newly formed Scottish feminist campaigning organization, Engender), and other women's organizations including church groups, and individual activists. This involved a complex process of networking, cross-party dialogue on strategies to ensure equal representation, and regular events co-ordinated by the Women's Co-ordination Group, a loose alliance of feminist and other women's organizations and individual activists, given administrative support by the Scottish Trade Union Congress (STUC).

A major impetus behind the devolution campaign was the perception of a 'democratic deficit' in Scotland, with Scotland being governed by a Conservative Party for which the majority of Scots had not voted. This claim of a 'democratic deficit' included a critique of Westminster politics, debates about representation and new institutional forms which would be more democratic. Women activists claimed that they suffered a 'double democratic deficit' since in addition to being governed by a party they did not support, they were largely excluded from decision-making and political office. This debate on democracy engendered a call for a 'new politics', which would entail new institutions and a new political culture. A system of proportional representation would deliver greater diversity of representatives and parties, which would govern through power-sharing, multi-party bargaining and coalition. More participation from civil society was also promoted, which would function through greater involvement in debate in the pre-legislative process, and through dialogue and consultation with government.

Though the key focus of feminist campaigning in the run-up to devolution was the demand for equal representation in the Scottish Parliament, this should be understood in the context of a wider range of demands and expectations about the nature of democracy and the potential for a different type of politics to be engendered through devolution. For example, one argument for equal representation was that it was simply a matter of social justice that political bodies should reflect the population they represent. However, a further argument was that the presence of equal numbers of women (or significantly larger numbers of women) would make a difference to policy-making and the way in which politics was conducted. There was also a widely held belief among feminist activists that women's interests were more likely to be promoted by female elected representatives. Some activists also took the view that women had a different political style, being more likely to act co-operatively and less likely to engage in confrontational politics, a style designated as typically male.

This feminist emphasis on doing politics differently, in a less confrontational and more inclusive style, resonated with broader themes of participatory democracy and helped to shape certain aspects of the new Scottish Parliament. For example, the design of the parliament chamber was to be a horseshoe shape, rather than opposing rows of benches, 'two swords' lengths' apart, as at Westminster. It was also stipulated that working hours and timing of parliamentary sessions should be 'family-friendly'. The role of cross-party committees in scrutinizing legislation was also deemed to be important in facilitating cross-party dialogue and co-operation, and the creation of a Standing Equal Opportunities Committee was regarded as ensuring that gender and other equality interests would be addressed systematically in the legislative process. For the Parliament to be inclusive and adequately reflect the needs of different groups within Scottish society, access to the Parliament and Executive were also seen as important, and this was reflected in innovations such as the Petitions Committee to which petitions could be brought from the public to initiate legislation, and in the creation of consultative mechanisms, such as the Civic Forum and Women in Scotland Consultative Forum.

As a further dimension of feminist engagement with the state, local government became increasingly important in the 1980s and 1990s as an arena in which feminist politics made an impact. Women's and equal opportunities committees in local councils had grown since 1984 to form part of local government institutional arrangements covering the majority of Scotland's population by the mid-1990s.[21] In general, equal opportunities committees, staff and units survived the 1996 reorganization of local government in Scotland. While women's and equal opportunities committees had been concerned with both the position of women as employees and with the impacts of service provision on women from the early days, in their initial phase more emphasis was often placed on employment practices and on tackling discrimination and sexual harassment. However, by the mid-1990s there was increasing emphasis on the need to provide services sensitive to women's needs and which recognized and compensated for gender inequalities. Nonetheless, changes in practice remained patchy. Areas of service provision with which such committees were concerned included education, social services, anti-poverty initiatives, housing and childcare. It was with respect to challenging violence against women, however, that feminist influence on local government was to become most apparent.

As noted previously, Women's Aid groups were first formed in Scotland in the early 1970s. Provision of refuges and campaigns against violence against women had become part of the political scene in Scotland in the 1980s and the creation of local authority women's committees had facilitated joint working between women's groups and local government and other public sector bodies, such as police forces and health authorities. In the 1990s this entered a new phase, with the launch of Edinburgh District Council's Zero Tolerance campaign in 1992. This was 'a ground-breaking public awareness initiative which challenges social attitudes and myths surrounding violence against women and children'.[22] By the mid-1990s this campaign had been taken up by several other local authorities in Scotland, covering between them the majority of the Scottish population. The campaign was explicitly feminist in its analysis of male abuse of power, used research effectively in publicizing the extent of violence against women, and was innovative in its use of imagery which refused, unlike many previous campaigns, to depict women as victims, and which also made clear that domestic abuse was not a class-specific phenomenon. Zero Tolerance succeeded, according to evaluations, in becoming a popular campaign with widespread support. Zero Tolerance campaigns invariably involved alliances between feminist organizations, councillors and council officials, as well as representatives from other public sector bodies, with multi-agency approaches being typical. Its success also depended on the degree of local community involvement generated. Furthermore the campaign was sensitive to the different circumstances and experiences of different groups of women, with initiatives being developed to research and publicize the experience of black and minority ethnic women, disabled women and rural women.

Zero Tolerance emerged from the women's movement, and presented an 'intrinsically feminist view of power relations in society'.[23] There were a number of factors which enabled this to happen – the existence of women's and equal opportunities committees in local government, networking between women's organizations and women's committees especially facilitated by the campaigns around the Scottish Parliament, the securing of cross-party support, and the support of women councillors which gave legitimacy to the campaign.[24] It also indicated a convergence between feminists inside and outside the state at municipal level, and represented the emergence of a broad-based 'women's politics', which was also manifested in the campaign for equal representation in the Scottish Parliament. The Zero Tolerance campaign provided a powerful example of the local state working to pursue feminist goals and, as such, fuelled optimism that devolution might deliver new women-friendly political institutions.

The role of local government in keeping gender issues on the agenda was thus of crucial importance in the 1980s and 1990s. It did much to facilitate networking between women's organizations and local government and to foster the development of a gender equality policy community along with the Equal Opportunities Commission (EOC), feminist academics, and new organizations such as Engender. It also provided a training ground for women politicians, with several who entered the Scottish Parliament as MSPs having a background in local government.

THE 2000s: NEW INSTITUTIONS – NEW POLITICS?

It can justifiably be claimed that feminist politics and activism made a significant contribution to the new political institutions created in Scotland at the end of the 1990s. Consequently, there was an expectation that feminist organizations would have an impact on the new Parliament's policies and mode of operation. This section provides a provisional assessment of the extent to which such expectations have been borne out.

Equal opportunities is one of the four key principles underpinning the Scottish Parliament. In institutional terms this has been played out through the creation of a Standing Equal Opportunities Committee in the Scottish Parliament, an Equality Unit in the Scottish Executive (now the Scottish Government), and commitment to equal opportunities by the Scottish Parliament corporate body (i.e. the body employing parliamentary staff). These arrangements have transformed the political landscape and provided accessibility to both the Parliament and government, and have formalized mechanisms for consultation and contact. Key questions to be addressed here are those of the adaptation of feminist organizations to the new devolved political institutions, the issues and policy approaches that feminist organizations have been most concerned with, and evidence of feminist influence in Scottish government policies.

Devolution has created new institutionalized opportunities for women's organizations to engage with the political process. The Women in Scotland Consultative Forum (WISCF) was created in 1998, prior to devolution, as a result of recommendations by the Women's Advisory Group to Scottish Office minister, Henry McLeish. It continued to exist under the devolved administration, but was reviewed in an attempt to give new momentum to development of a gender equality agenda, alongside the convening of a short-life group, the Strategic Group on Women. As a consequence of this review, a new consultative body, the Scottish Women's Convention (SWC), was set up in 2003. Unlike the WISCF, which was convened by the Scottish Executive Equality Unit, the new Convention was established as an independent body, though dependent on funding from the Scottish Executive. The Convention, open to both individuals and organizations, is a broad umbrella organization for women's organizations of a 'traditional' type and for feminist organizations. In 2005, it had around 300 members (organizations and individuals), and a steering group of 18 members, representing organizations ranging from the Church of Scotland Guild, Scottish Women's Rural Institute, STUC Women's Committee, to black and minority ethnic women's organizations and feminist organizations such as Scottish Women's Aid, Rape Crisis Scotland, and Engender. Currently it has a network of over 300,000 women throughout Scotland.[25] The SWC consults with members, responds to government consultations, and convenes groups to discuss specific areas of policy (at the time of writing, women and poverty, violence against women and children, and young women).

The creation of a consultative body for women was widely supported by women's organizations, and was also an early commitment of the Scottish Executive Equality Unit. Arguably, however, the process of creating such a body has been a slow and halting process. The Equality Unit was pressured into taking this process forward through criticism from women's organizations frustrated at lack of progress and their perception that other equality issues were pushing gender equality further down the political agenda. Similarly, the convening of the Strategic Group on Women, by the then minister responsible for equalities, Margaret Curran, was a response to criticism from women's organizations.[26] Much time has then been taken up with the process of establishing a consultative body for women's organizations. Although the SWC has now functioned for some years, in the absence of research to evaluate its impact, it is unclear to what extent its deliberations have informed policy-making.[27]

Women's organizations have also demonstrated an active interest in policy approaches and policy change, supporting at a general level a gender mainstreaming approach. This had emerged as the favoured approach among gender equality advocates such as the EOC, feminist networks and academics internationally by the late 1990s, and was endorsed by the Scottish Executive in its *Equality Strategy*, published in 2000, where it was defined thus: 'Mainstreaming equality is the systematic integration of an equality perspective into the everyday work of government, involving policy makers across all government departments, as well as equality specialists and external partners'.[28] Indeed, feminist activists within organizations such as the EOC, in local government and in academia put much effort into shaping this strategy informally through policy networks and formally through the provision of advice to government, both through working within the civil service and through research reports.[29] An offshoot of the gender mainstreaming approach has been the Scottish Women's Budget Group, which, since 2000, has campaigned for the adoption of gender budget analysis and provided analysis of Scottish government budgets.[30] Other consequences of a mainstreaming approach have been training programmes on equality issues within the civil service, improvements in provision of gender-disaggregated statistics published by Scottish Government statistical services, the introduction of equality clauses in some legislation, and an increase in government commissioned research on equality issues, including gender. The recent introduction of a gender duty (through UK legislation) reinforces this mainstreaming approach and extends it across a range of public sector bodies. This has meant the publication of gender equality plans and the institutionalization of reporting procedures on these.

While equality mainstreaming (including gender mainstreaming) is regarded as having a higher political profile in Scotland (and also Northern Ireland and Wales) than in England, it remains a moot point whether mainstreaming has delivered policy changes that materially improve women's lives. Arguably it has diverted attention and energy away from consideration of specific policy areas in favour of attending to general processes – a finding that also emerges from international research.[31] Several Scottish government policies have had positive impacts for women: increased childcare provision, the introduction of free personal care, more support to carers, for example. However, these have not arisen from organized feminist campaigns, have not necessarily been informed by a gender analysis, and nor have they resulted from a gender mainstreaming approach.

Existing evidence, albeit impressionistic, suggests that it is in fact where feminist organizations have followed a more traditional lobbying strategy or taken advantage of involvement in governance-type arrangements, such as working parties, that they have been most successful. The case of domestic violence policy provides the most striking example to date of feminist influence on the policy agenda. A *National Strategy on Domestic Abuse* was launched by the Scottish Executive in 2000, making a commitment to actions which included preventive measures, education and awareness-raising campaigns, service provision and protection of victims of violence.[32] Scottish Women's Aid played a key role in shaping this strategy, which developed at a Scottish level much of the multi-agency work already in existence at local authority level. Women's Aid and other anti-violence women's organizations exerted a significant influence over the shape and content of the final National Strategy, including the feminist definition of domestic abuse, its links with other forms of violence against women, the insistence on detailed work-plans and reporting mechanisms, and the commitment of significant resources to supporting specialist services such as refuge provision. The agenda has been driven forward as a result of sustained campaigning of organizations such as Scottish Women's Aid, strong political leadership provided by women ministers and female parliamentarians together with some key male allies, and the secondment of an expert on domestic abuse from Scottish Women's Aid into the Scottish Executive to develop policy and oversee implementation.[33] A recent UK-wide survey of specialist violence against women's support services found that service provision in Scotland was distributed more equally than elsewhere.[34]

We have argued that on the one hand gender mainstreaming has been supported by activists, but that it is not clear what this has delivered, and on the other that the most successful feminist interventions have been undertaken by organizations experienced in formulating legislative and policy demands and in working with government at different levels. At the same time, there has been a gradual definition of the key areas of policy seen as priorities for action at a general level. The Strategic Group on Women report focused on employment and pay, childcare and other forms of caring, poverty and exclusion, violence, influence and decision-making – areas which have long been understood as the most important for the advancement of gender equality.[35] The Scottish Government's *Gender Equality Scheme*, published in 2008, identified the following as priority areas for improvement: tackling violence against women, the gender pay gap, poverty, occupational segregation, childcare, improving networks with men, and transgender equality. Actions reported under these headings were, however, often small-scale initiatives rather than any significant legislative or policy change.[36] Where feminist organizations have focused on specific policy areas, the issues that most consistently feature are the gender pay gap, poverty, violence against women, and participation in decision-making.

Work on equality issues in local government has continued into the 2000s, though neither this nor the impact of the far-reaching local government reorganization in 2007 has yet been researched. It seems likely, however, that political and administrative change within councils will have had negative impacts, in terms of loss of expertise and continuity, notwithstanding the new gender duty with which councils must comply.

CONCLUSION

This chapter has charted the changing relationship of feminist political action to the state since the WLM's emergence in the 1970s. Our account does not encompass the full range of feminist activity, practice or ideas. However, we see this aspect of feminist politics as of major importance, and argue that feminists have demonstrably influenced the political landscape in Scotland – through shifting the gender balance of political representation and through policy change and influence in areas relevant to gender equality. The sustained commitment of the generation of women activists politicized through their engagement with the WLM in the 1970s, the renewal of feminist organization and recruitment of further generations of activists in subsequent decades, and the development of alliances between a wide range of feminist and other women's organizations have been crucial to these changes. However, our account also suggests that broad alliances, such as that coalescing around the demand for equal representation, are unlikely to prove sustainable in the longer term, while more focused policy demands appear to have difficulty in generating active campaigns. Feminism has demonstrated a capacity to renew itself, but has also often proved fluid and difficult to define. Further research and analysis of different feminist positions, organizational forms, strategies and tactics is needed if we are to understand more fully how change is achieved and how it is impeded – for example, the mapping of organizations and their interconnections, the formation of policy networks, and case studies of policy change and of campaigns.

Nothwithstanding our argument that feminism has made a perceptible difference to Scottish politics, further gains and progress remain in question. We have suggested that feminist organizations in the post-devolution period have so far demonstrated only a limited capacity to articulate well-developed policy demands or strategically frame demands which resonate with other political trends. We suggest that the following factors may have played a part. First, devolution has intensified the system of multi-level governance, in which all levels have a role in either promoting gender equality or acting as barriers to it.[37] Despite the enhanced powers that devolution has delivered to Scotland, key powers governing areas such as pay and poverty remain reserved to Westminster, while EU directives also have a major influence on equal pay provisions and conditions of employment and other areas of policy. Thus, if it is understandable that the Scottish Parliament has become the major focus of attention for feminist organizations, there are limits to what it can achieve on its own. Secondly, it inevitably takes time for a new institutional framework to take shape and for policy actors to adapt to this, as illustrated, for example, by the time taken to elaborate a gender mainstreaming strategy and consultation mechanisms. Thirdly, expertise in political lobbying in Scotland has been relatively underdeveloped, and is still in need of further capacity-building, not just for feminist organizations but in other sectors as well. Fourthly, it may be that the broad-based women's politics that has functioned well through loose alliances to support demands such as equal representation for women does not lend itself easily to the kind of intensive and ongoing work required to formulate demands that can be translated into viable legislation and policy. Neither does it provide a way of dealing with differences in political perspectives or policy analysis. Last, but not least, the key areas in which feminists would like to see change occur represent some of the most intractable and complex areas of gender inequality, none of which permit of simple solutions, but in which as past experience suggests change is incremental and slow. This suggests the need for approaches which are both strategic and focused on short-term, medium-term and long-term objectives, and which recognize that there is no simple fix or one way of ensuring change such as gender mainstreaming or mandatory pay audits, for example.

Since the 1970s feminist organizations, broadly defined, have responded to changing state structures. In the post-devolution period, they have established a new relationship with the state, through the formal consultation mechanisms instituted by the Scottish government and through channels of access to the Scottish Parliament, such as the Equal Opportunities Committee and others, MSPs, and cross-party groups. There is some evidence of feminist impact on policy making, most notably in strategies to tackle violence against women, but also in some other areas. Feminist and other women's organizations have expressed frustration with the slow pace of change. Notable policy successes have not emerged as yet from a commitment to gender mainstreaming, but rather out of what might be described as 'traditional' lobbying strategies – a compelling argument for building capacity in this regard.

NOTES

1   See, for example, Shirley Henderson and Alison Mackay (eds) *Grit and Diamonds* (Edinburgh: Stramullion, 1990), Esther Breitenbach and Fiona Mackay (eds), *Women and Contemporary Scottish Politics* (Edinburgh: Polygon, 2001).

2   Scottish Women's Aid recently carried out an oral history project on the organization's early years and work, resulting in a DVD, *Women's Aid in Scotland: The Early Years, c. 1973–1980*. Rape Crisis Scotland has published an oral history: Eileen Maitland, *Woman to Woman: An Oral History of Rape Crisis Scotland, 1976–1991* (Glasgow: Rape Crisis Scotland, 2009). A history workshop on the WLM in Scotland took place in May 2009 as part of a Leverhulme funded project working to build up an archive of second wave feminism across the UK. As yet unpublished doctoral research by Sarah Browne, University of Dundee, has focused on the WLM in Scotland in the 1970s.

3   Doctoral research by Sarah Browne. I am grateful to Sarah for giving me access to her research.

4   As indicated in listings in publications such as *Scottish Women's Liberation Journal* and *Msprint*, produced in the late 1970s and early 1980s.

5   The seven demands of the UK women's movement, adopted at a series of conferences in the 1970s, were: equal pay for equal work; equal opportunities and equal education; free contraception and abortion on demand; free 24-hour childcare; legal and financial independence for women; an end to all discrimination against lesbians and the right of women to determine their own sexual orientation; freedom for all women from violence, or the threat of violence, and sexual coercion, regardless of marital status, and an end to all laws, assumptions and institutions that perpetuate male dominance and men's aggression towards women.

6   Personal communications from Judi Hodgkin and Fran Wasoff.

7   Jean Cuthbert and Lesley Irving, 'Women's Aid in Scotland: purity versus pragmatism?', in Breitenbach and Mackay, *Women and Contemporary Scottish Politics*, pp. 55–67.

8   See Ellen Galford and Ken Wilson, *Rainbow City: Stories from Lesbian, Gay, Bisexual and Transgender Edinburgh* (Edinburgh: Word Power Books, 2006); Bob Cant, *Footsteps and Witnesses: Lesbian and Gay Lifestories from Scotland* (Edinburgh: Word Power Books, 2008).

9   Section 2A of the Local Government (Scotland) Act (1986), was equivalent to Section 28 in England and Wales. It prohibited local authorities from the promotion of homosexuality or the promotion of 'the acceptability of homosexuality as a pretended family relationship'. Galford and Wilson, *Rainbow City*, p. 79.

10   These groups prepared a charter of demands, the *Scottish Women's Charter*, as a tool for lobbying a devolved assembly.

11   See the chapter by Esther Breitenbach in this volume.

12   Catriona Levy, 'A woman's place? the future Scottish Parliament', in Lindsay Paterson and David McCrone (eds), *The Scottish Government Yearbook* (Edinburgh: Unit for the Study of Government, University of Edinburgh, 1992), pp. 59–73.

13   Isobel Lindsay, 'Constitutional change and the gender deficit', in Woman's Claim of Right Group (eds), *A Woman's Claim of Right in Scotland* (Edinburgh: Polygon, 1991), pp. 7–13.

14   SCOW disbanded in 1992, with its members being urged to join the newly formed organizations Women's Forum Scotland and Engender. Kath Davies, 'The Scottish Convention of Women (SCOW)', paper presented to workshop on the Women's Movement and Contemporary Scottish Politics, University of Edinburgh, June, 2001.

15   See Henderson and Mackay, *Grit and Diamonds*.

16   Anita Shelton, 'Black women's agency in Scotland: a view on networking patterns', in Breitenbach and Mackay, *Women and Contemporary Scottish Politics*, pp. 47–53.

17   See, for example, Kate Phillips, letter to *Radical Scotland*, 38, April–May, (1989); Esther Breitenbach, '"Sisters are doing it for themselves": the women's movement in Scotland', in

Alice Brown and Richard Parry (eds), *The Scottish Government Yearbook* (Edinburgh: Unit for the Study of Government, University of Edinburgh, 1990); pp. 209–25; Alice Brown, 'Thatcher's legacy for women in Scotland', in *Radical Scotland*, April–May, (1991).

18   See Sue Lieberman, 'Women's committees in Scotland', in Alice Brown and Dave McCrone (eds), *The Scottish Government Yearbook* (Edinburgh: Unit for the Study of Government, University of Edinburgh, 1989), pp. 246–65.

19   Woman's Claim of Right Group (eds), *A Woman's Claim of Right in Scotland* (Edinburgh: Polygon, 1991).

20   Alice Brown, 'Women and politics in Scotland', *Parliamentary Affairs*, 49, (1), (1996), pp. 26–40.

21   See Esther Breitenbach, Alice Brown, Fiona Mackay and Jan Webb, *Equal Opportunities in Local Government in Scotland and Wales* (Edinburgh: Unit for the Study of Government, University of Edinburgh, 1999); and Esther Breitenbach and Fiona Mackay, 'Keeping gender on the agenda – the role of women's and equal opportunities initiatives in local government in Scotland', in Breitenbach and Mackay, *Women and Contemporary Scottish Politics*, pp. 147–162.

22   Fiona Mackay, 'The case of Zero Tolerance: women's politics in action?', in Breitenbach and Mackay, *Women and Contemporary Scottish Politics*, pp. 105–29 (p. 105).

23   Katie Cosgrove, 'No man has the right', in Breitenbach and Mackay, *Women and Contemporary Scottish Politics*, pp.131–46 (p. 144).

24   Mackay, 'The case of Zero Tolerance'; Fiona Mackay, 'The Zero Tolerance campaign: setting the agenda', *Parliamentary Affairs*, 49, (1), (1996), pp. 206–20.

25   Scottish Women's Convention, *Annual Report*, 2008.

26   See Strategic Group on Women, *Improving the Position of Women in Scotland: An Agenda for Action* (Edinburgh: Scottish Executive, 2003).

27   For an early assessment see Fiona Mackay, Meryl Kenny and Elena Pollot-Thompson, *Access, Voice . . . and Influence? Women's Organisations in Post-devolution Scotland* (GRADUS Case Study 2. Report for Engender/GRADUS Partnership, 2005).

28   Scottish Executive, *Equality Strategy: Working Together for Equality* (Edinburgh: Scottish Executive, 2000), p. 14.

29   See Fiona Mackay and Kate Bilton, *Learning from Experience: Lessons in Mainstreaming Equal Opportunities* (Edinburgh: University of Edinburgh Governance of Scotland Forum, 2000).

30   Ailsa Mckay, Rona Fitzgerald, Angela O'Hagan and Morag Gillespie, 'Scotland: using political change to advance gender issues', in Debbie Budlender and Guy Hewitt (eds), *Gender Budgets Make More Cents: Country Studies and Good Practice* (London: Commonwealth Secretariat, 2002).

31   See, for example, Mary Daly, 'Gender mainstreaming in theory and practice', *Social Politics*, 12, (3), (2005), pp. 433–50.

32   Scottish Executive, *Scottish Partnership on Domestic Abuse: National Strategy to Address Domestic Abuse in Scotland* (Edinburgh: Scottish Executive, 2000).

33   Fiona Mackay, 'Gendering constitutional change and policy outcomes: substantive representation and domestic violence policy in Scotland', *Policy and Politics*, (forthcoming).

34   Maddy Coy, Liz Kelly and Jo Foord, *Map of Gaps: The Postcode Lottery of Violence against Women Support Services* (London: End Violence Against Women and Equality and Human Rights Commission, 2007).

35   Strategic Group on Women, *Improving the Position of Women in Scotland*.

36   Scottish Government, *Gender Equality Scheme 2008–2011* (Edinburgh: Scottish Government, 2008).

37   Fiona Mackay, 'Devolution and the multi-level politics of gender in the UK: the case of Scotland', in Jill Vickers, Marian Sawer and Melissa Hausmann (eds), *Gender and Multilevel Governance* (Aldershot: Ashgate, forthcoming).

11

Women and political representation in post-devolution Scotland: high time or high tide?[1]

Fiona Mackay and Meryl Kenny

> *Actually to see a parliament with so many women is quietly thrilling, in a way that percentages are not [. . .] I expected the Scottish Parliament to look different, but it doesn't. It looks like the rest of life, where women and men are present in roughly equal numbers except when gender segregation is imposed – openly or otherwise – for a special reason.[2]*

The quiet thrill – expressed by the late feminist journalist, campaigner and writer Sue Innes, was shared by many Scottish women – trade unionists, feminists, community and party activists, and devolution campaigners – who were part of the broad coalition campaigning over the 1990s for equal political power in the new Scottish Parliament. Opportunities for 'women-friendly' change are created by reform processes. As noted by Breitenbach and Mackay in this volume, one of the most notable aspects of devolution – and visible achievements of this well-mobilized and strategic coalition – was the high level of women's political representation. The first elections to the Parliament in 1999 returned 37.2 per cent female MSPs, far outstripping Westminster, both in terms of proportions of women MPs overall and proportions of women returned to the House of Commons from Scottish constituencies. This chapter picks up the story of women's participation in formal politics in the post-devolution era (see the chapter by Burness in this volume for the period of 1918–90). Our particular focus is the new political arena of the Scottish Parliament. The primary aim is to report and analyse candidate trends and electoral trends 1999–2007 from the perspective of women's representation, as a foundation for future research.[3] We argue that historically high levels of women's representation are a key achievement of devolution in Scotland. However, prospects for sustaining performance are less certain. Underlying trends raise the question as to whether the first elections represent 'high time or high tide' for women's representation.

CAMPAIGNS TO IMPROVE WOMEN'S REPRESENTATION

The election of a substantial number of women MSPs in 1999 did not happen by accident, but was instead the result of sustained struggle by a diverse coalition of women's organizations, grassroots activists, female trade unionists, political party women, gender experts and their male allies.[4] The breakthrough of the 'electoral project' by party women and women's movement activists was enabled by the intersection of multiple paths of reform in the 1980s and 1990s, including party and political modernization at UK and Scottish levels, particularly reforms within the Labour party,[5] feminization of institutions,[6] and broader processes of devolution.[7] Over this period, international attention also became increasingly focused on the chronic minority status of women in politics and the UK became signatory to a number of international declarations and action plans, including the post-Beijing UN Women's Conference Platform for Action (1995), which committed states to: a) take measures to ensure women's equal access to and full participation in power structures and decision-making (Strategic Objective G1); and b) increase women's capacity to participate in decision-making and leadership (Strategic Objective 2). Meanwhile, developments in the UK were also influenced by debates and developments in Europe and beyond, including growing demands for party candidate quotas and constitutional equality guarantees.[8]

It was argued that women's equal political participation in decision-making was not only justified on the grounds of simple justice or democracy – although each of these arguments carried much force – but also that women needed to be present as a necessary condition for women's interests to be taken into account. The UN Platform for Action provides a typical claim of the time: 'Without the active participation of women and the incorporation of women's perspective at all levels of decision-making, the goals of equality, development and peace cannot be achieved.'[9] The arguments for gender parity in 'descriptive representation' were well rehearsed in the run-up to devolution and the belief that female politicians would 'make a difference' was instrumental in mobilizing women in the devolution campaign.[10]

Together, these contexts 'opened up new institutional, political and discursive opportunities for women activists to engender mainstream debates and to play a significant role in shaping new political institutions.'[11] Women activists working inside and outside the political parties, in particular Scottish Labour – as well as through generic reform groups and public arenas such as the Scottish Constitutional Convention (SCC)[12] and its Women's Issues Group – were able to frame their demands within these wider reform trajectories, successfully introducing a gendered perspective to the prospect of a 'new' and distinct Scottish politics.

Much of the debate within the SCC centred on plans for a more proportional electoral system and the need for mechanisms to increase the representation of women, concerns that were reflected in the convention's first report published in 1990 and that were ultimately integrated into the Labour government's White Paper on devolution. Following the 1992 general election, the Convention established a Scottish Constitutional Commission. The Commission delivered its report to the SCC in 1994, recommending that MSPs be elected by the Additional Member System (AMS) and also recommending a voluntary gender balance scheme in which parties would be asked to achieve a target of 40 per cent women in the Parliament within the first five years. The Commission's proposals were strongly criticized by 50:50 campaigners who had campaigned long and hard for a firm and statutory commitment to gender equality and who correspondingly saw the 40 per cent voluntary target as a 'weak substitute'.[13] Following the Commission's report, the Scottish Women's Co-ordination Group – a loose alliance of women activists – facilitated talks between women within the political parties included in the SCC in an attempt to find an alternative solution to ensuring gender-balanced representation. In the resulting cross-party Electoral Agreement of 1995, both the Scottish Labour Party and the Scottish Liberal Democrats recognized the importance of gender equality and committed to field equal numbers of male and female candidates, although the actual mechanisms for ensuring equal representation were left to the discretion of each individual party.

THE DEVIL'S IN THE DETAIL: PARTY MEASURES IN THE RUN-UP TO 1999

In terms of specific mechanisms to ensure gender balance, political parties can use a range of measures to increase women's political presence. These include reform to selection procedures to make them fairer and more transparent and to ensure that equal opportunities are taken into consideration: positive action measures such as balanced shortlists; and 'equality guarantees' – quota-type mechanisms such as All Women Shortlists (AWS), 'twinning' constituency seats or applying gender templates such as 'zipping' to party lists. Evidence suggests that strong equality guarantee measures are the most likely to result in substantial improvements in women's representation[14] and also that the adoption of quota-type measures by one political party may lead to a 'contagion' effect in which other political parties – or different levels of political system – respond by actively promoting women candidates as well, either through formal or informal measures.

In the run-up to the first elections to the Scottish Parliament in 1999, increased internal and external pressure was applied to all of the Scottish political parties with regards to women's representation. All of the parties stated their concern to see more women in politics and their intention to encourage women to come forward for selection. In addition, all of the parties improved their recruitment and selection procedures, for example, incorporating equal opportunities considerations in the process.[15] However, of the four main political parties – Scottish Labour, the Scottish National Party (SNP), Scottish Conservatives, and the Scottish Liberal Democrats – only Labour used strong equality guarantees prior to the 1999 elections. Recognizing that, under an AMS electoral system, most of its seats would be obtained through constituencies rather than regional lists, the party instituted a quota-type mechanism called 'twinning' in which constituencies are paired on the basis of 'winnability' and geography. Under this scheme, the female applicant with the highest number of party selectors' votes would be selected as candidate for one of the constituency seats, while the male applicant with the highest number of votes would be selected for the other seat.[16] The party also offered preparation courses for women, which included assertiveness training and public speaking, as well as financial support from the (UK) Emily's List.[17]

Labour's main electoral rival, the SNP, had also debated using strong equality measures in the 1999 elections. A statement of principle supporting gender balance was approved by party conference in 1995, and the party leadership had publicly pledged to deliver gender balance at a 50:50 campaign rally in 1996.[18] The gender-balance mechanism of 'zipping' – whereby women and men are alternated on party lists – was brought before a special conference in 1998, but was ultimately defeated, by a narrow margin of 257 votes for and 282 against.[19] Yet, despite its decision not to use any strong equality measures, the SNP did implement proactive unofficial measures encouraging women to stand for election, for example, holding a women's training day for prospective parliamentary candidates, and also placed women at the upper end of their regional party lists.[20] In addition, like Labour, the SNP used an approved panel of candidates and employed equal opportunities procedures.[21]

While the Scottish Liberal Democrats had signed the Electoral Agreement of 1995, they did not adopt strong equality measures in either constituency or list selections in the run-up to the 1999 elections. The party did adopt a 'softer' measure of gender-balanced shortlists, requiring that two men and two women be included on the shortlist in each constituency, which, unlike twinning, did not guarantee outcomes. Similar to the other parties, it also adopted a system that included a panel of approved candidates and the application of equal opportunities procedures. However, gender-balanced shortlists were not always achieved, due to the shortage of women applicants in several constituencies.[22] A proposal for gender-balanced mechanisms for list selections was put before the Scottish Liberal Democrat party conference in 1998, recommending that in regions where there was an imbalance among constituency candidates, a woman would be placed at the top of the regional list. However, the motion was eventually withdrawn in order to avoid a leadership defeat due to insufficient support.[23]

Meanwhile, the Scottish Conservative Party made few changes with regards to their selection process, and did not adopt any mechanisms, either formal or informal, to ensure gender balance. The party did implement panels of approved candidates, which it was already accustomed to doing for Westminster selections. However, the party remained firmly opposed to the use of positive action mechanisms, on the grounds that their selection process would award positions based on merit rather than special consideration for certain groups.[24] Although some female Conservatives were involved in 'round table talks' with other Scottish women activists, there is little evidence of 'any serious internal party debate or lobbying' on the issue of women's representation in the run-up to devolution.[25]

The first elections for the Scottish Parliament were held on 6 May 1999, and, as already highlighted, a record number of female MSPs were elected, 48 out of 129 total MSPs or 37.2 per cent. The election of the Scottish Parliament using a new, more proportional electoral system in part explains the relatively high levels.[26] However, for the most part, the results can be explained by Scottish Labour's implementation of strong equality guarantees in constituency seats as well as the SNP's use of unofficial measures to promote gender balance on its regional lists. As noted earlier, this was as a result of the party responses to internal and external pressure for action to tackle women's under-representation. Unlike established political institutions such as Westminster and local government, the creation of the Scottish Parliament presented parties with the prospects of a substantial increase in quantity of elected representatives and a blank slate in terms of incumbents. To put things in perspective, whereas only 21 women were elected as MPs for Scottish constituencies in the whole of the period 1918–1990 (see the chapter by Burness in this volume), more than double that number was elected in the first Scottish Parliament elections.

Since the first election, however, all of the main Scottish parties have been reluctant to promote gender equality in candidate selection in terms of 'strong' measures that guarantee equality of outcome. This is despite the introduction of permissive legislation by the UK government in 2002.[27] In addition, there appears to have been little informal targeting and promotion within the parties since 1999.[28]

CANDIDATE TRENDS AND PARTY PERFORMANCE 2003–7

The proportion of women rose again to 39.5 per cent in the second Scottish Parliament elections in 2003, seemingly heralding a new gender settlement in formal Scottish politics.[29] However, the underlying signs were that gains were fragile and liable to reversal. The number of women MSPs overall had been predicted to fall in the second election. This was, in large part, due to the SNP, who did not implement any official or unofficial measures leading up to the 2003 elections, nor did it proactively encourage female candidates to run, as it had in 1999. Only two political parties used specific equality measures in the 2003 elections, the Scottish Socialist Party (SSP) – which implemented a policy of gender balance on the regional lists – and the Scottish Labour Party. Scottish Labour had implemented twinning as a one-off measure and opted not to reuse it in the 2003 elections, relying instead on the effect of incumbency. However, the party intentionally selected women to fill the most winnable places on its candidate lists. Neither the Liberal Democrats nor the Conservatives took measures to promote women candidates, and while the Green Party had operated gender-balancing mechanisms in the past, it opted not to use any such measures before the 2003 elections. Green Party women headed only two out of the eight regional lists.

Had the 2003 results mirrored those of 1999 in terms of party share of the vote, there would have been an overall decrease in women MSPs. However, a number of factors led to a slight increase in women MSPs, from 37.2 per cent to 39.5 per cent. First, the main parties lost seats overall, with small parties and Independents gaining many of these seats. In particular, Labour's losses primarily affected male incumbents, meaning that the percentage of Labour women MSPs did not decrease overall. Second, the strong performance of small parties benefited women – particularly the SSP – resulting in four of the six SSP seats going to women. Finally, two of the three Independent MSPs elected were women. Rather than reflecting a systematic or system-wide improvement, then, the gains made in 2003 were achieved 'more by accident than design'.[30]

2007 ELECTION AND CANDIDATE TRENDS OVER TIME[31]

The 2007 Scottish Parliament elections were historic, with the SNP ending over 50 years of Labour dominance of Scottish politics. Yet, the elections also provided a cautionary tale, with the first drop in the number of elected female MSPs since the creation of the Parliament in 1999. Women candidates took 43 out of 129 seats in Holyrood (33.3 per cent, subsequently increasing to 45 out of 129 or 34.8 per cent),[32] compared with 39.5 per cent in the 2003 elections and 37.2 per cent in 1999. As Table 11.1 shows, 43 women and 86 men make up the 2007 Scottish Parliament. Women comprise 12 of 47 SNP MSPs (25.5 per cent), 23 of 46 Labour MSPs (50 per cent), five out of 17 Conservatives (29.4 per cent), and two out of 16 Liberal Democrats (12.5 per cent). The two Green MSPs elected are both male and the one Independent returned is a woman. For the first time, a minority ethnic MSP was elected, taking up his seat in the SNP parliamentary group.[33]

As in 1999 and 2003, a higher proportion of women MSPs was elected in constituency seats (26 women or 35.6 per cent) than on the regional lists (17 women or 30.5 per cent). This has now been a consistent trend across three elections[34] and stands in contrast to other country studies, where women are generally more likely to be elected under Proportional Representation (PR) systems rather than First-Past-the-Post (FPTP) systems.[35] This apparent anomaly can be explained by the fact that Labour was the most proactive party in terms of promoting gender balance in 1999 – implementing a 'twinning' policy for constituency seat selection contests – and is also the party which returns the greater proportion of MSPs via the constituency contests, rather than the regional lists. Over half of the total female MSPs elected in 2007 belong to Scottish Labour (23 of 43 women, or 53.5 per cent), the majority of whom were first elected in 1999 under the twinning scheme.

Figure 11.1 charts the performance of the four main political parties on women's representation over time. The high point in women's representation to date has been Scottish Labour at 56 per cent (in 2003), while the worst record on women's representation has consistently been the Liberal Democrats at 11.8 per cent (in 1999 and 2003, rising to just 12.5 per cent in 2007). When compared to its primary rival, the SNP, Scottish Labour Party performance on women's representation was closely matched by the SNP in 1999 (50 per cent to 42.9 per cent), but, since then, Labour has been at least 20 points ahead of its main competitor. The decline in SNP women MSPs over time is particularly striking,

Table 11.1 Scottish Parliament 2007 by party, gender and type of seat

Party	Constituency		Total seats constituency (% women)	List		Total Seats List (% women)	Total MSPs	Total women	Total men	% women (% women 2003)
	F	M		F	M					
Labour	20	17	37 (54.1%)	3	6	9 (33.3%)	46	23	23	**50% (56%)**
SNP	5	16	21 (31.3%)	7	19	26 (26.9%)	47	12	35	**25.5% (33.3%)**
Cons.	0	4	4 (0.0%)	5	8	13 (38.5%)	17	5	12	**29.4% (22.2%)**
Lib. Dems	1	10	11 (9.1%)	1	4	5 (20%)	16	2	14	**12.5% (11.8%)**
Greens	0	0	0 (0.0%)	0	2	2 (0.0%)	2	0	2	**0.0% (28.6%)**
Independent	0	0	0 (0.0%)	1	0	1 (100%)	1	1	0	**100% (66.7%)**
Total	**26**	**47**	**73 (35.6%)**	**17**	**39**	**56 (30.4%)**	**129**	**43**	**86**	**33.3% (39.5%)**

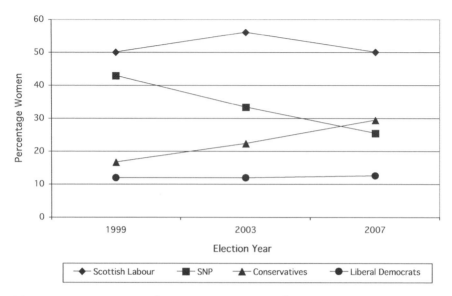

Figure 11.1 Proportion of women among MSPs, by party, 1999–2007

Source: Meryl Kenny

and establishes the SNP as the only major Scottish political party to experience an overall decrease in the percentage of women MSPs over two subsequent elections, dropping from 42.9 per cent women MSPs in 1999 to 33.3 per cent in 2003, and finally to 25.5 per cent in 2007. While the general trend among Scottish political parties seems to be one of stasis or decline in the number of women elected, both the Conservative Party and the Liberal Democrats have experienced small increases in the percentage of women overall. However, in numerical terms, the increase in Conservative women MSPs has been relatively small, moving from three women (in 1999), to four women (in 2003),[36] and finally to five women (in 2007). The Liberal Democrats have maintained the same number of women MSPs as in 1999 and 2003, but lost a seat overall in 2007.

CANDIDATE SELECTION: 1999–2007

The numbers of elected members provides part of the picture, but we need also to assess underlying trends in candidate selection: who gets to be selected to contest political positions. Figure 11.2 disaggregates figures by party, charting the performance of the four main Scottish political parties on numbers of women candidates over the three elections.

A wide range of performance among the different parties in the period 1999 to 2007 is highlighted in Figure 11.2. Scottish Labour has repeatedly selected a large proportion of female candidates, and at least 40 per cent of its candidate places in

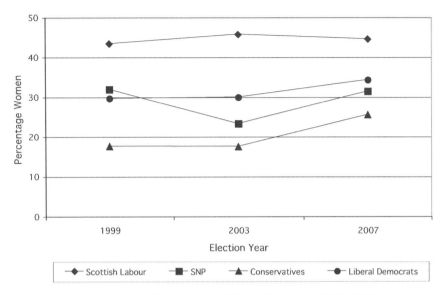

Figure 11.2 Proportion of women candidates, by party, 1999–2007

Source: Meryl Kenny

both constituency seats and on the regional list have consistently been filled by women. The Scottish Green Party has also maintained high numbers of women on the regional list, while the SSP overtook Scottish Labour on gender balance, nearly reaching parity on the lists (48.1 per cent in 2003). The SNP is the only party to see a major decrease in the number of women candidates in an election cycle, dropping from 21 women constituency candidates in 1999 to 16 in 2003 (from 28.8 per cent to 21.9 per cent) and dropping from 33 women list candidates to 19 women in 2003 (from 34.4 per cent to 24.7 per cent). In 2007, the SNP saw a substantial increase in the number of its women candidates overall – from 23.3 per cent women candidates in 2003 to 31.5 per cent in 2007 – which marks a return to its 1999 levels of women candidates. However, this has not translated into an increased number of seats for women candidates. Similarly, the Liberal Democrats continue to perform relatively well on numbers of women constituency and list candidates, ranging around 30 per cent, but have the worst record of any of the parties on women's representation with only two women MSPs overall, a number that they have consistently maintained over three elections. Finally, the Conservatives have seen a modest increase in 2007 in the number and percentage of women candidates, jumping from 13 women constituency candidates in 1999 and 2003 to 18 women in 2007 (from 17.8 per cent to 24.6 per cent), and from 12 women list candidates in 1999 to 16 in 2007 (from 17.4 per cent to 26.6 per cent).

While women were perhaps slightly less successful as candidates overall in the 2007 elections, the evidence, once this is disaggregated by party, suggests that this has less to do with women as candidates and more to do with the seats or positions on the list in which women candidates are placed. The success of prospective women candidates depends not just on being selected, but on being selected for 'winnable' seats – in the Scottish case, winnable positions either in constituencies or on the regional list. We return to the issue of winnability below.

PARTY STRATEGIES: KEEPING UP THE MOMENTUM?

In the run-up to the 2007 elections, apart from the Green Party, none of the political parties explicitly stated in their campaign material that women's representation was an issue that they were tackling in their candidate procedures.[37] This stands in stark contrast to 1999, when, as discussed above, women's representation formed a defining theme of the first elections to the Scottish Parliament. The issue does not appear to have retained high salience for any of the Scottish political parties, nor has it remained a matter on which parties have competed. Unlike the run-up to 1999, there was no vocal and visible mobilization of grassroots women to support party women and to put pressure on political élites. Although the 50:50 campaign (see earlier discussion, and the chapter by Breitenbach and Mackay in this volume) remained officially in existence, it lacked its earlier cohesion, leadership and leverage.

In terms of equality promotion and equality guarantees, most of the parties did little actively to promote women's representation, and none of the parties implemented strong equality guarantees. In constituency selections, both Scottish Labour and the Liberal Democrats had 'softer' mechanisms in place, in the form of official short-listing policies to promote gender balance. For the Liberal Democrats, shortlists should include at least one male and one female. For Scottish Labour, shortlists should include an equal number of men and women. These policies do not appear to have been strictly or uniformly enforced by either party in the 2007 elections, nor do these types of measure guarantee equality of outcome. Women candidates were also generally less likely to 'inherit' constituency seats – that is, to be selected to stand in constituency seats held by their own party in the previous election. Women were also less likely to be selected to fight 'winnable' constituency seats. In each of the four main Scottish parties – Labour, SNP, Conservatives, and the Liberal Democrats – only four of each party's top five most winnable ('target') seats were contested by women (four out of 20 seats overall, or 20 per cent).

In the selection of regional list candidates, women were again generally placed in poor positions. Only two parties applied gender-balance mechanisms to the lists, increasing the possibility that women would be placed in winnable positions. Scottish Labour implemented an official policy of 'zipping', alternating between men and women candidates. However, in 2007, only the South of Scotland regional list was topped by a woman. Labour men were ranked first in seven of the eight regional lists, with women ranked in second place in seven of the eight regional lists. It should also be noted that relatively few Labour members are returned by the list and, in most cases, the first placed candidate is the only one likely to be selected. Meanwhile, the Greens operated a 'gender template', allocating 40 per cent of list places to female candidates. The party stated that these places would be distributed so as to ensure that female candidates occupied 50 per cent of 'winnable' seats.[38] However, five of the eight regional lists were topped by men, and four of the regional lists had men in second place. After the collapse of the small party vote on the regional lists, only two Green MSPs were elected, both of them men.

The remaining parties implemented no gender equality measures on the lists in the run-up to the 2007 elections. Around a third of all places on the SNP regional list went to women, and women made up nearly a third of the top three places on the regional list. Again, however, it is the first and second places on each list that are most likely to be won. In the case of the SNP, six of the eight regional lists were topped by men, and seven of the eight regional lists also had men in second place. Only three of the top 16 (first and second) slots were allotted to women (18.7 per cent). The Liberal Democrats, as mentioned previously, generally placed women in poor positions: only two of their top 16 places were given to women (12.5 per cent). The Scottish Conservatives also took no positive action measures in the lead-up to the 2007 elections. It should be noted, however, that the party at the UK level under the leadership of David Cameron has strongly encouraged reform of party recruitment processes to increase the number of women and ethnic minority MPs.[39] Overall, the Conservatives fared slightly better, with six of the top 16 list places going to women (37.5 per cent). All five of the successful female Conservative candidates came from the lists.

SCOTTISH LABOUR: A CLASS APART?

This preliminary analysis of electoral and candidate trends points to a number of gendered puzzles in need of further exploration. The first puzzle concerns the Scottish Labour Party. On the one hand, Scottish Labour continues to perform as 'a class apart': over half of the female MSPs returned to the Scottish Parliament in 2007 belong to the Labour Party. The Labour Party has consistently maintained a strong gender balance in its parliamentary group – ranging from 50 per cent women in 1999 to 56 per cent women in 2003, and back to 50 per cent women in 2007.

How has Labour continued to perform so well? While Scottish Labour consistently has maintained a gender-balanced parliamentary group across three consecutive elections, it is incumbency – resulting from the one-off measures taken in the first elections – rather than the institutionalization of gender balance that accounts for this strong performance. Of the 23 Labour women returned to office in 2007, 20 are constituency MSPs. All of these 20 were first selected in 1999 under the since abandoned 'twinning' scheme. The underlying trend is one of decline in the number of female candidates. Analysis of the 2007 elections reveals clear gendered patterns of turnover: of the seven Labour MSPs elected to the Scottish Parliament for the first time in 2007 (two constituency MSPs and five regional list MSPs), only one was a woman. If we include these Labour MSPs returning to the Parliament after a term away, only two out of nine new MSPs were female.

Post-1999, Scottish Labour has been reluctant to implement or enforce strong equality guarantee measures such as twinning or AWS in Scottish parliamentary elections, although Scottish party officials continue formally to stress their commitment to gender-balanced representation. While the party does use 'softer' equality measures – such as gender-balanced shortlists – these policies do not appear to be strictly or uniformly enforced, nor do they guarantee outcomes. In part, the party's reluctance to make further equality guarantees post-1999 can be explained as an ongoing reaction to the controversies surrounding central (British and Scottish) party intervention in the run-up to the first Scottish Parliament elections. Those who 'lost out' in the 1999 selections frequently criticized the centralization of control in the process, accusing party officials of orchestrating an 'ideological cull' in an attempt to consolidate New Labour support within the party. These allegations of 'control-freakery' have become the dominant frame for interpreting candidate selection post-1999, reflected in both party discourse and the corresponding academic literature.[40] In response to these perceived controversies, the central Scottish party has increasingly withdrawn from the selection process, potentially signalling a return to the party's past tradition of decentralized constituency-based selection.[41]

THE PUZZLE OF THE SNP

Women have been present and prominent in the SNP since its inception. It has a long and impressive track record of recruiting and promoting women as candidates,[42] including Nordic levels of female MSPs in the first Scottish Parliament, and women have held high-profile leadership positions in both opposition and government. However, the transition from a minor 'protest party' at Westminster to a major party in the Scottish Parliament has, after the first elections, been accompanied by an overall decline in women's representation.[43] This begs the question as to why there appears to have been so little attempt to date to 'couple' the issue of women's equal representation with processes of party modernization and a more 'women-friendly' electoral strategy. This is especially puzzling in the context of the SNP's traditional problems in attracting women's votes[44] and deserves further scrutiny.

CONCLUSION

The high numbers of women in the Scottish Parliament is a significant achievement and is widely seen as a success story of devolution. However, the achievements cannot be regarded as secure. We argue that the Scottish case highlights the complexity and contingency of gains in women's formal representation and suggest that the elections of 1999 and 2003 may come to be seen as the 'high tide' of women's representation in post-devolution Scotland. While it is difficult to make claims on the basis of three elections, we argue that the one-off effects of positive action in 1999 – in particular, Scottish Labour's twinning policy – continue to have a significant impact on headline figures, masking underlying gendered patterns of erosion and decline in the recruitment and election of female candidates.

The Scottish experience raises the questions as to why reforms have not 'stuck', in the sense of becoming institutionalized in post-devolution party recruitment practices, and why reforms have not 'caught on', in the sense of being taken up by other parties and across other levels.[45] As demonstrated in the earlier discussion, after the first elections there has been little obvious 'contagion' in the sense of political parties adopting equality guarantees in order to compete with a leading party (in the Scottish case, Labour) on the issue of women's representation. The underlying candidate trends suggest that without the sustained use of such mechanisms and the institutionalization of party reforms, which promote a political culture in which women are viewed as credible candidates, progress will stall and drift.

Apart from the first elections, the issue of women's representation has not been a salient issue upon which parties compete. In part, this is due to complacency given the high levels of representation achieved in the first Parliament. The fragmentation of the 50:50 campaign post-devolution and the weakness of women's structures inside the main parties have also contributed to the difficulties in keeping the issue on the agenda.[46] Finally, there are signs of continued resistance and persistence of old norms and practices, whatever the changes to formal rules.[47]

Furthermore, as Table 11.2 highlights, gains made at the level of the Scottish Parliament have not 'caught on' in the sense of leading to improved performances at other levels of the political system. On the one hand, this can be explained by the fact that competition for candidacies has increased at Westminster, local government and the European Parliament over this period in the context of overall reduction in seats in each institution.[48] However, the stasis also suggests that party reforms of candidate procedures have not taken root or led to wider party discussions. We can also discern a process of 'contagion in reverse' as parties, including Labour, seek to avoid the apparent controversy of quota-type mechanisms. For example, a recent attempt by the Labour Party leadership to impose a women-only shortlist for the selection contest to replace a retiring Labour MP (in line with central party policy) was fiercely resisted as 'a Scottish Blaenau Gwent'.[49]

Why does the reduction in the number of women MSPs 'matter'? Increases in women's political presence often bring with them a set of expectations, namely that these women politicians will both 'stand for' and 'act for' women, resulting in institutional change and transformation.[50] Although by no means straightforward, studies of the first years of the Scottish Parliament have demonstrated that the high numbers of women MSPs have shaped both political priorities and

Table 11.2 Percentage of women elected by date of election and type of elected office

Year of election	1997	1998	1999	2001	2003	2004	2005	2007	2009
Scottish MPs	15.3	–	–	15.3	–	–	13.6[1]	–	–
MSPs	–	–	37.2	–	39.5[2]	–	–	33.3[4]	–
Scottish MEPs	–	–	25.0	–	–	28.6[3]	–	–	16.7[5]
Scottish Councillors	–	–	22.6	–	–	21.8	–	–	21.6

Notes:

1. The number of Scottish Westminster constituency seats was reduced from 72 to 59 before the 2005 UK general election as part of the Scottish Parliament (Constituencies) Act 2004.

2. Falling to 38.7 per cent by time of dissolution.

3. The number of Scottish MEPs was reduced from eight to seven prior to the 2004 European elections.

4. Standing at 34.9 per cent at time of writing (July 2009).

5. The number of Scottish MEPs was reduced from seven to six prior to the 2009 European elections.

Sources: House of Commons: http://www.parliament.uk/parliamentary_publications_and_archives/factsheets.cfm (accessed 5 May 2009); Scottish Parliament: http://www.scottish.parliament.uk/business/research/factsheets/ (accessed 5 June 2009); UK Office of the European Parliament: http://www.europarl.org.uk/section/european-elections/results-2009-european-elections-uk (accessed 15 June 2009); Electoral Reform Society: http://www.electoral-reform.org.uk (accessed 6 July 2009); Equal Opportunites Commission, *Sex and Power? Who Runs Scotland?* (Glasgow: EOC, 2007); Centre for Advancement of Women in Politics: http://www.qub.ac.uk/cawp (accessed 5 May 2009).

'ways of working', including the championing of family-friendly working hours. It is important not to overstate these developments – legacies from Westminster such as partisan politics and adversarial political styles continue to exert a substantial 'pull' on the Scottish Parliament. However, there is evidence that the increased and visible presence of women MSPs has contributed to a more 'feminized' politics, with some concrete policy outcomes. In particular, there has been substantial progress on action to tackle domestic violence, an agenda that was driven largely by women politicians and women's organizations.[51] Indeed, a recent UK-wide survey, jointly commissioned by the End Violence Against Women and the Equality and Human Rights Commission commended the strategic, gendered and integrated approach in Scotland as 'benchmark' against which developments elsewhere in the UK should be measured.[52]

The erosion in the gender balance of the Parliament has potentially far-reaching implications in terms of its symbolic importance, political culture and policy outcomes. The question, then, is whether this fall signals a temporary setback or whether it points to a return to 'politics as usual', signalling an 'inexorable drift back to the pre-devolution norm of male dominance and female marginalization in Scottish politics.'[53] What is clear is that there is little room for complacency as the Parliament enters its second decade.

NOTES

1   We borrow this question from Maria Eagle and Joni Lovenduski, *High Time or High Tide for Labour Women?* (London: Fabian Society, 1998).
2   Sue Innes, '"Quietly thrilling": women and the Scottish Parliament', in Esther Breitenbach and Fiona Mackay (eds), *Women and Contemporary Scottish Politics* (Edinburgh: Polygon, 2001) p. 249.
3   Space precludes a discussion of women as voters and women as party members, although both are areas that are relatively under-researched and in need of systematic examination.
4   See, for example, the articles by Alice Brown reproduced in Breitenbach and Mackay (eds), *Women and Contemporary Scottish Politics*: 'Women and politics in Scotland', pp. 197–212; 'Deepening democracy: women and the Scottish Parliament', pp. 213–29; 'Taking their place in the new house: women and the Scottish Parliament', pp. 241–7. See also Alice Brown, Tanyha B. Donaghy, Fiona Mackay and Elizabeth Meehan, 'Women and constitutional change in Scotland and Northern Ireland', *Parliamentary Affairs*, 55, (1), (2002), pp. 71–84; Esther Breitenbach and Fiona Mackay, 'Introduction: women and contemporary Scottish politics', in *Women and Contemporary Scottish Politics*, pp. 1–23; Fiona Mackay, Fiona Myers and Alice Brown, 'Towards a new politics? Women and the constitutional change in Scotland', in Alexandra Dobrowolsky and Vivien Hart (eds), *Women Making Constitutions: New Politics and Comparative Perspectives* (New York: Palgrave, 2003), pp. 84–98; Ronnie McDonald, Morag Alexander and Lesley Sutherland, 'Networking for equality and a Scottish Parliament: the Women's Co-ordination Group and organizational alliances', in *Women and Contemporary Scottish Politics*, pp. 231–40.
5   Meg Russell, *Building New Labour: The Politics of Party Organisation* (Basingstoke: Palgrave, 2005).
6   Joni Lovenduski, *Feminizing Politics* (Cambridge: Polity Press, 2005).

7   Fiona Mackay, 'Descriptive and substantive representation in new parliamentary spaces: the case of Scotland', in Marian Sawer, Manon Tremblay and Linda Trimble (eds), *Representing Women in Parliament: A Comparative Study* (London: Routledge, 2006), pp. 171–87; see also Meryl Kenny, 'Gendering institutions: the political recruitment of women in post-devolution Scotland' (Unpublished PhD thesis, University of Edinburgh, 2009).

8   Mona Lena Krook, *Quotas for Women in Politics: Gender and Candidate Selection Reform Worldwide* (Oxford University Press, 2009).

9   UN Global Platform for Action, 1995.

10 See Note 4 above.

11 Mackay *et al.*, 'Towards a new politics?', p. 84.

12 An unofficial but influential body established by key civil society organizations and actors together with some political parties which debated potential blueprints for a devolved parliament, including electoral systems (1989–95).

13 Brown, 'Deepening democracy', p. 220.

14 See, for example, Sarah Childs, Joni Lovenduski and Rosie Campbell, *Women at the Top 2005: Changing Numbers, Changing Politics?* (London: Hansard Society, 2005).

15 Brown, 'Deepening democracy'; Fiona Mackay, 'Women and the 2003 elections: keeping up the momentum', *Scottish Affairs*, 44, (2003) pp. 74–90; Meg Russell, Fiona Mackay and Laura McAllister, 'Women's representation in the Scottish Parliament and National Assembly for Wales: party dynamics for achieving critical mass', *Journal of Legislative Studies*, 8 (2), (2002), pp. 49–76.

16 See Brown, 'Taking their place'; Jonathan Bradbury, David Denver, James Mitchell and Lynn Bennie, 'Devolution and party change: candidate selection for the 1999 Scottish Parliament and Welsh Assembly elections', *Journal of Legislative Studies*, 6 (3), (2000), pp. 51–72; Jonathan Bradbury, James Mitchell, Lynn Bennie and David Denver, 'Candidate selection, devolution and modernization: the selection of Labour Party candidates for the 1999 Scottish Parliament and Welsh Assembly elections', *British Elections and Parties Review*, 10, (2000), pp. 151–72.; Russell *et al.*, 'Women's representation'.

17 Brown, 'Taking their place'.

18 McDonald *et al.*, 'Networking for equality'.

19 Russell *et al.*, 'Women's representation', p. 62.

20 Brown, 'Taking their place'.

21 See Note 16 above.

22 Bradbury, 'Devolution and party change'.

23 Russell *et al.*, 'Women's representation', p. 64.

24 Brown, 'Taking their place'.

25 Russell *et al.*, 'Women's representation', p. 65.

26 The comparative literature suggests that proportions of women are higher in proportional systems than in majoritarian systems, such as first-past-the-post. See, for example, Miki Caul, 'Women's representation in parliament: the role of political parties', *Party Politics*, 5, (1), (1999), pp. 79–98.

27 The Sex Discrimination (Election Candidates) Act, 2002, enables parties to adopt positive measures such as gender candidate quotas without falling foul of sex discrimination legislation.

28 Mackay, 'Women and the 2003 elections'; Fiona Mackay and Meryl Kenny, 'Women's representation in the 2007 Scottish Parliament: temporary setback or return to the norm?', *Scottish Affairs*, 60, (2007), pp. 25–38.

29 This section draws upon Mackay, 'Women and the 2003 elections'.

30   Mackay, 'Women and the 2003 elections', p. 75.
31   This analysis draws upon Mackay and Kenny, 'Women's representation in the 2007 Scottish Parliament'.
32   All figures in this chapter are based on initial election results.
33   Bashir Ahmad MSP (SNP) died in February 2009, and was replaced by Anne McLaughlin.
34   Although it should be noted that fewer women were returned to constituency seats in 2007 than in either 1999 or 2003.
35   Caul, 'Women's representation in parliament'.
36   This number fell to three women by the end of the 2003–7 Scottish Parliament.
37   See Mackay and Kenny, 'Women's representation in the 2007 Scottish Parliament', and Kenny, 'Gendering institutions'.
38   Scottish Green Party, 'Greens unveil top candidates for Holyrood election', Press Release, 4 September 2006.
39   There is some evidence that Cameron has informally promoted women's representation in Scotland. For example, Cameron attended a women's event at the Scottish Conservative Conference in March 2007, hosted by the women2win campaign, which was aimed at encouraging more Scottish women into Conservative politics.
40   See Kenny, 'Gendering institutions' for detailed analysis. Cutts *et al.* address similar dynamics at the UK level with regards to AWS. In the aftermath of the 2005 general election, media coverage overwhelmingly focused on the defeat of the AWS candidate, Maggie Jones, in the ultra-safe Labour seat of Blaenau Gwent, largely ignoring the successful election of 23 other AWS Labour women. The dominant frame, then, was one of 'AWS backlash', with the case of Blaenau Gwent offering 'proof' that AWS candidates lose votes. They critique this frame, arguing that there is no evidence of any significant 'AWS effect' in 2005. David Cutts, Sarah Childs and Ed Fieldhouse '"This is what happens when you don't listen": all-women shortlists at the 2005 general election', *Party Politics*, 14, (5), (2008), pp. 575–95.
41   Kenny, 'Gendering institutions'; see also Jonathan Hopkin and Jonathan Bradbury, 'British statewide parties and multilevel politics', *Publius: The Journal of Federalism*, 36, (1), (2006), pp. 135–52.
42   Catriona Burness, 'Drunk women don't look at thistles: women and the SNP 1934–94', in *Scotlands*, 1 (2), (1995), pp. 131–54.
43   Fiona Mackay and Meryl Kenny, 'Women's political representation and the SNP: gendered paradoxes and puzzles', in Gerry Hassan (ed), *The Modern SNP: From Protest to Power* (Edinburgh: Edinburgh University Press, 2009).
44   Lindsay Paterson, 'Sources of support for the SNP', in Catherine Bromley, John Curtice, David McCrone and Alison Park (eds), *Has Devolution Delivered?* (Edinburgh: Edinburgh University Press, 2006).
45   Comparative political science studies suggest that successful introduction of positive action and improved performance on women's representation by one party or one level of the political system sets in motion a dynamic of 'contagion' whereby other parties will respond in order to compete. See Richard E. Matland and Donley T. Studlar, 'The contagion of women candidates in single member district and proportional representation electoral systems: Canada and Norway', *Journal of Politics*, 58 (3), (1996), pp. 707–33.
46   Fiona Mackay, 'Women and the Labour Party in Scotland', in Gerry Hassan (ed.), *The Scottish Labour Party: History, Institutions, and Ideas* (Edinburgh: Edinburgh University Press, 2004), pp. 104–23; Mackay, 'Women and the 2003 elections'.
47   Kenny, 'Gendering institutions'.

48 Scottish Labour was exempt from Labour Party policy on AWS in 2001 and 2005 because of the anticipated reduction in Scottish MPs for Westminster. See Cutts *et al.*, '"This is what happens when you don't listen"'.

49 See Note 40 above.

50 See for example Sarah Childs, *New Labour's Women MPs: Women Representing Women* (London: Routledge, 2004); Lovenduski, *Feminizing Politics*; Fiona Mackay '"Thick" conceptions of substantive representation: women, gender and political institutions', *Representation*, 44, (2), (2008), pp. 125–39.

51 Mackay *et al.*, 'Towards a new politics?'; Mackay, 'Descriptive and substantive representation'; Fiona Mackay, 'Gendering constitutional change and policy outcomes: substantive representation and domestic violence policy in Scotland', *Policy and Politics* (forthcoming).

52 Maddy Coy, Liz Kelly and Jo Foord, *Map of Gaps: The Postcode Lottery of Violence against Women Support Services* (London: End Violence Against Women and Equality and Human Rights Commission, 2007).

53 Mackay and Kenny, 'Women's representation', p. 81.

12

Devolution, citizenship and women's political representation in Wales

Paul Chaney

INTRODUCTION

This chapter explores the impact of devolution on women's political representation – from the pro-devolution campaigns of the late 1980s and 1990s through to the present day.[1] It charts how constitutional reform and the creation of the National Assembly for Wales has overturned the country's dismal record of electing women candidates, for gender parity among Assembly Members (AMs) was achieved in elections to the second Assembly in 2003. While this progress is striking in both its nature and the speed with which it was accomplished, as the following discussion reveals, it has also been accompanied by failings and uncertainties: much remains to be achieved before devolution in Wales can be said to have secured the comprehensive mainstreaming of gender equality in representation, policy and law.

This account is organized in three sections. Initial attention is focused on how feminist campaigners responded to political opportunity structures presented by devolution. Their actions challenge some of the theoretical assumptions held by the literature on new social movements for, contrary to assertions that élite advocacy and insider strategies may be incompatible with a democratizing agenda, feminist activists in Wales were successful in lobbying for the inclusion of equalities mechanisms in the Assembly's founding statutes. Subsequent focus is placed upon women's representation in electoral politics. Initial attention centres on the way in which the main political parties have responded to issues of gender equality when putting forward candidates for election to the new legislature. This reveals a history of internal conflict within the parties, the adoption of positive action by those on the political left, and lingering concerns about the sustainability of the new gender balance in politics should existing affirmative action measures be withdrawn. The discussion also outlines a new dimension to gender equality following constitutional reform, namely the growth of electoral competition at an all-Wales level around gender and other modes of equalities in political parties' election manifestos. The third section of the chapter considers the impact of virtual gender parity on public policy. Discourse analysis reveals the effect female AMs have on women's substantive representation in political deliberation. Progress is then evaluated against the declaration made within days of the National Assembly opening its doors that mainstreaming equalities would be the official approach informing all subsequent policy-making. The discussion concludes by relating the changes in women's representation to the notion of a post-devolution mode of citizenship in Wales, one based on emerging rights, electoral politics, social policy, and welfare entitlement.

ENGENDERING DEMOCRACY

Prior to the creation of the National Assembly in 1999, Wales had a lamentable record in relation to women's political representation. Lipman offers the following description of the position in the early 1970s:

> In politics the situation is bathetic: Labour without a single woman Member of the House [of Commons] representing Wales, the Blaid [Plaid Cymru] feebly forming a woman's committee to try and repair huge gaping omissions . . . it seems to me that the feminist position in both parties has been steadily eroding.[2]

Indeed, throughout the period 1970–84 not a single woman represented a Welsh constituency at Westminster and, prior to 1997, an historical total of just four women had been elected to the British Parliament from Wales. Writing in 1990, one feminist activist summed up many women's dissatisfaction with the status quo and made the case for change:

> unless we want to reproduce the same inequalities and discriminations that exist in the present nation-state, we have now to work to ensure that when we have the first government in Wales, half of those serving on it will be women.[3]

During earlier decades, the marginalization of women in the formal political sphere was compounded by the underdeveloped nature of the women's movement. By the 1970s it was comprised of a fragmented collection of local groups and lacked the strategic movement-wide capacity, infrastructure and resources to mobilize as a collective force. This underdevelopment presented major challenges to feminist activists if they were to engage effectively with the growing campaign to create an elected Welsh legislature; a movement that began to (re-)gather momentum in the late 1980s. Their response was to employ the combined techniques of insider strategies and élite advocacy. In contrast to patterns of broad-based political activism and mass mobilization, these emphasize an individualized or small-group approach whereby 'social contracts or bargains between the individual and centers of political and economic power are negotiated, discussed and mediated'.[4] Yet Chandler summarizes the 'costs' of the insider/élite approach: 'rather than expand the horizon of democratic politics, this is a form of politics which is neither "democratic" nor "inclusive". It is focused around the "freedoms" of the individual advocate who engages in courtly politics and elite lobbying'.[5]

Approximately 25 influential women activists (gender experts, femocrats, politicians and trade union officials) worked within three main institutional settings to press their gender equality claims: the centre-left Welsh Labour Party; the multi-interest pro-devolution campaign (Campaign for a Welsh Assembly – renamed the Parliament for Wales Campaign in 1993); and, the Equal Opportunities Commission (EOC). Two reciprocal aspects characterize the relationship between these strategic women and the nascent women's movement: the former gave strategic direction and the appearance of a coherent movement which increased the salience of the notion of the 'women's movement' in dealings with the state; while, for the strategic women themselves, invoking the idea of the women's movement heightened their own democratic legitimacy in advancing gender equality claims. In the wake of a positive devolution referendum outcome in 1997, strategic women successfully advanced a claim for women in the process of establishing a new national legislature – most noticeably, during the drafting of the Government of Wales Act 1998 – as well as the National Assembly's Standing Orders. In the face of such campaigning the Secretary of State for Wales invited key figures in the EOC to draft equality of opportunity clauses that ultimately found their way into the devolution statute. The principal equality clause is an example of a 'fourth generation' equality duty and is unique among the devolution statutes for it requires government to take a proactive stance and promote equality for all persons and in respect of all Welsh Assembly Government functions.

Other institutional mechanisms that can be traced to feminist claims include: a statutory duty for the Assembly itself to have due regard to the principle of equality of opportunity in the conduct of its business and the creation of a cross-party Standing Committee on Equality of Opportunity. As Squires notes, embedding equalities mechanisms in constitutional law in this way 'has a series of significant benefits . . . it gives citizens legally enforceable rights in relation to elected representatives' actions thereby empowering citizens vis-à-vis the state'.[6] Subsequently, under the heading 'The Inclusive Exercise of Functions', the Government of Wales Act 2006 restructured and refined a number of the institutional mechanisms designed to promote gender and other modes of equality. Reflecting upon the initial process of engendering constitutional reform, one participant, the late Val Feld AM, said: 'I think that we have succeeded in putting in place every structural measure that we could reasonably expect to try to create a new framework and ethos that means equality has a good chance of flourishing.'[7]

POLITICS OF PRESENCE: ALL-WALES ELECTIONS

In preparation for the first elections to the National Assembly in 1999, three of the four main political parties heeded the call in the devolution White Paper: namely, that 'greater participation by women is essential to the health of our democracy'.[8] However, bitter infighting broke out when the Welsh Labour Party adopted positive action in its candidate selection procedures. Ultimately, this delivered a major advancement for it secured a 15:13 majority of women among the party's AMs.[9] Elsewhere, Plaid Cymru used 'zipping' to give women candidates preference in fighting regional seats (elected by proportional representation). This tactic resulted in six women being among Plaid's total of 17 AMs – yet, as with Labour's use of affirmative action, it too provoked internal party strife. The Welsh Liberal Democrats emphasized an informal route in order to encourage women – principally through training in candidacy procedures/skills. Overall, the combination of these measures led to substantial gains in respect of women's descriptive representation and, at a symbolic level at least, signalled a powerful discontinuity with the male-dominated politics of the past (see Table 12.1). In contrast to Westminster and Welsh local government where the proportion of women elected representatives still languished at 17.9 per cent and 20 per cent respectively, elections to the National Assembly saw 41.7 per cent elected.

In the second devolved elections Plaid Cymru, the principal opposition party, put women in the first two places on each regional seat list (no affirmative action measures were applied to constituency selections). Continuing strong opposition to gender equality within the Welsh Labour Party was evident as it discussed the use of powers under the Sex Discrimination (Election Candidates) Act (2002). Following a stormy debate, the use of All Women Shortlists (AWS) was narrowly passed by the party's annual conference. One woman candidate recalled the unsavoury nature of the internal divisions: 'it was very bitter and very nasty. . .. you would even hear [from men] "this isn't your place. We've been here a long time, we know what people want, we know how it works".'[10] Ultimately, Labour used such shortlists in six constituency seats, with women also selected to stand in four key marginal seats without resort to positive action measures. Nevertheless, women AMs and new candidates alike experienced antagonism, hostility – even intimidation – from sections of the local party membership. Elsewhere, the Welsh Liberal Democrats adopted a more proactive stance than in 1999 and required that all candidate shortlists contain at least one woman and one man. In addition, the party's Candidate Committee adopted *ad hoc* measures to ensure overall gender balance on constituency and regional lists (e.g. bringing in new candidates if gender disparities were evident). The result of the 2003 National Assembly elections proved to be a significant milestone, for gender parity was achieved (see Table 12.2).

Ahead of the 2007 Welsh elections some questioned whether the existing progress in women's representation would be sustained.[11] In the event there was a modest drop in the number of women elected. The new total was 28 out of 60 AMs (46.7 per cent) – with women making up a majority of constituency representatives (21 out of 40). However, men were significantly more likely to stand for election than women; of the total 197 constituency candidates, 141 (72 per cent) were male and 56 (28 per cent) female (see Table 12.3). Defying this trend, the Welsh Labour Party fielded more female than male candidates. Yet Labour's poor electoral performance saw female candidates take the brunt of

Table 12.1 Women candidates and elected AMs: 1999 elections to National Assembly for Wales

Political party	Women candidates	Women AMs elected	Women candidates	Women AMs elected	% of party's AMs
	Constituencies		Regional lists		
Welsh Labour	20	15	11	0	53.6
Plaid Cymru	8	2	14	4	35.3
Welsh Conservatives	12	0	18	0	0
Welsh Liberal Democrats	13	2	20	1	50
Independents/other parties	1	0	–	–	–
Total	**54**	**19**	**63**	**5**	**40**

Table 12.2 Women candidates and elected AMs: 2003 elections to National Assembly for Wales

Political party	Women candidates	Women AMs elected	Women candidates	Women AMs elected	% of party's AMs
	Constituencies		Regional lists		
Welsh Labour	23	19	24	0	66
Plaid Cymru	8	1	18	5	50
Welsh Conservatives	8	0	8	2	18
Welsh Liberal Democrats	13	2	11	1	50
Independents/other parties	9	0	45	0	0
Total	**61**	**22**	**106**	**8**	**50**

the party's losses and it experienced a net fall of three women AMs. However, a majority of Welsh Labour's current Assembly team are female, 16 out of 26 AMs (61.5 per cent – down from 66.5 per cent in 2003). Plaid Cymru gained three seats over its 2003 election total, and increased its total of women AMs by one to seven out of 15 (46.7 per cent compared to the pre-election figure of 50 per cent). The Welsh Liberal Democrats returned the same number of AMs as in 2003; three out of the six were women. In all three Assembly elections the Welsh Conservatives remained opposed to positive action measures. In the third Assembly elections

Table 12.3 Women candidates and elected AMs: 2007 elections to National Assembly for Wales

Political party	Women candidates	Women AMs elected	Women candidates	Women AMs elected	% of party's AMs
	Constituencies		Regional lists		
Welsh Labour	24	15	9	1	61.5
Plaid Cymru	9	2	10	5	46.7
Welsh Conservatives	10	1	4	0	8.3
Welsh Liberal Democrats	11	2	13	1	50
Independents/ other parties	2	1	43	0	100
Total	**56**	**21**	**79**	**7**	**47**

their total of women AMs fell from two in 2003 to just one in 2007, giving the party a rate of women's representation of just 8.3 per cent.

It is pertinent to question how the levels of women's representation in the National Assembly compare to those found elsewhere. Comparison between countries in terms of patterns and processes of political representation is problematic owing to variations in the number of different tiers of government, the scope of their respective responsibilities and degree of autonomy from national or other higher levels of authority. Nevertheless, the levels of women's representation achieved in Wales can be put into context by selective reference to international figures on the proportion of women in sub-national, regional/state assemblies. In the EU-15 Member States, the average proportion stands at 35.1 per cent;[12] in the United States it is 24.2 per cent,[13] and in Australia 33.5 per cent.[14] Thus, from an international perspective, the proportion of women elected to the devolved legislature in Wales since 1999 would appear exceptional. On one reading, the sustained nature of the gains made would seem to indicate that over the past decade, devolution in Wales has, 'normalized' virtual gender parity – with women variously comprising between 40 and 51.7 per cent of elected representatives; however, such a view risks overstating the permanency of these gains. As the literature on gender mainstreaming indicates,[15] positive action techniques such as zipping and AWS do not address the underlying structural and cultural causes of inequality and discrimination. Enduring opposition to gender equality measures in sections of the two main left-of-centre parties (and their outright rejection by the Welsh Conservative Party) mean that, without the continued use of affirmative measures, significant reversal of progress is a real prospect over future years.

Away from issues of sex equality among candidates, a further post-devolution development is inter-party electoral competition over the issue of gender and other modes of equality. Analysis of the political parties' election manifestos (see Table 12.4) reveals that constitutional reform has seen the main parties placing growing attention on gender equality as part of their potential programme of government. Allied to this, election study data relating to Wales reveal a further interesting development, the emergence of subtle differences in political behaviour (voting patterns and attitudes) between the sexes. This arises from gendered responses to political factors such as party ideology, policy programme and party leadership style. In turn, this is further nuanced by intra- and inter- gender differences based on ascriptive and non-ascriptive characteristics such as language, age, class, and national identity. This new phase of post-devolution electoral competition relating to the substantive representation of women can be located within a broader international trend as political parties attempt to extend their appeal beyond traditional supporters and maximize votes from targeted groups in increasingly heterogeneous societies. Analysis of party election manifestos and gender differences in political behaviour provide both a useful snapshot of future aspirations for equality between the sexes and a benchmark by which to check parties' delivery on earlier promises for gender equal politics.

The parties' manifestos for the first National Assembly elections in 1999 tended to acknowledge that the equality duty in the Government of Wales Act 1998 meant that they were now operating in a new political context (e.g. 'the Assembly has a crucial statutory responsibility to promote sustainable development and equal opportunities and both of these require action in all policy areas') – as well as set out specific gender equality proposals (e.g. to 'consider the diverse needs of men and women in providing public services').[16]

Not only did the 2003 and 2007 Welsh election manifestos devote more attention to equalities than those of 1999, they also broadened their scope, referring to a greater range of equality 'strands' – as well as intersectional issues. Moreover, they contained more detailed policy proposals. Notably, these later elections saw parties produce 'mini-manifestos' solely dedicated to equalities policies (e.g. Welsh Labour, 2003) or a series of themed mini-manifestos targeted at specific groups (e.g. Plaid Cymru, 2007 – younger people, older people, people with learning difficulties). Overall, the 2007 manifestos set out a variety of approaches to equalities. For example, policy proposals based upon: redistributive practices such as extending state aid (e.g. 'universal affordable childcare available from the end of maternity leave');[17] improving representation (e.g. 'promote the need to get more women and people from the BME community into public life');[18] and, strengthened legal rights (e.g. 'we will give a new impetus to the National Assembly's duty to promote equal opportunities and will seek devolution of statutory responsibility for equality and full legislative powers over the child protection system').[19] Some of the proposals went beyond the usual targeting of the public sector to include those in the private sector (e.g. to 'promote the role of managers, entrepreneurs and business leaders in promoting equality of opportunity and tackling discrimination in the workplace').[20] In contrast to the

Table 12.4 Gender equality: content analysis of party manifestos in the devolved elections, 1999–2007

Party	Incidence of 'equality'/'equal opportunities'			Incidence of 'women'/'gender'			Examples of gender equality policy commitments
	1999	2003	2007	1999	2003	2007	
Plaid Cymru (the Party of Wales†)	10	23	8	4	5	9	'encourage a greater range of members of society to be represented in local council chambers – particularly younger people and women' (1999, p. 12); 'We will also ensure that domestic violence is treated with the seriousness it deserves' (2003, p. 37); 'more sporting opportunities for women' (2007, p. 33); 'Universal affordable childcare available from the end of maternity leave will also help close the gender pay gap in Wales' (2007, p. 20).
Welsh Conservatives	0	2	10	1	1	1	'working for businessmen and women' (1999, p. 2); 'We would . . . further develop the Equal Pay Campaign' (2003, p. 34.); 'Welsh Conservatives believe that everyone has a right to live in dignity, seek employment and enjoy access to public services regardless of gender . . .' (2007, p. 25).
Welsh Labour†‡	6	24	23	6	19	21	'the Assembly will work to increase further the representation of women . . . within those public bodies to which it has power of appointment' (1999, p. 7); 'encouraging women to set up their own businesses' (2003, p. 2); 'Labour's Top Ten for Equalities . . . Equal Pay Campaign to encourage private sector employers to carry out pay reviews' (2003, p. 1); 'We will . . . support for cooperative enterprises which provide emergency childcare for women in work' (2007, p. 19).

Party	Incidence of 'equality'/'equal opportunities'			Incidence of 'women'/'gender'			Examples of gender equality policy commitments
	1999	2003	2007	1999	2003	2007	
Welsh Liberal Democrats†	7	11	14	0	5	13	'Consider the diverse needs of men and women in providing public services' (1999, p. 9); 'Encourage greater participation in sport by women by ensuring that Welsh leisure facilities have "women only" sessions staffed by female coaches' (2003, p. 6); 'We will assess the need to increase specific prison capacity in Wales, such as addressing the lack of a women's unit' (2007, p. 29); 'Promote the need to get more women and people from the BME community into public life' (2007, p. 41).

Key: † Manifesto has dedicated section on equality and/or women; or, ‡ separate, dedicated 'mini-manifesto' on equalities issued.

three main left-of-centre parties, the Welsh Conservative Party – traditionally less embracing of interventionist policies to promote equalities – devoted least attention to the matter in its election manifestos. Although, reflecting the growing salience of such issues in the devolved context, the party's leader signed an 'Equalities Declaration' during the 2007 election campaign noting that: the 'Welsh Conservatives believe that everyone has a right to live in dignity, find work, and access services regardless of gender, age, race, religion, disability, or sexual orientation'.[21]

GENDER AND PUBLIC POLICY

In the third section to this chapter we now broaden the focus on the substantive representation of women and explore the extent to which devolution has advanced gender equality concerns in public policy. Initial reference is made to political discourse analysis and an exploration of the impact of female AMs on the substantive representation of women. Attention is then focused on progress made against the devolved government's stated aim of mainstreaming equalities in public policy.

The literature on women's political representation highlights the importance of both the number of women parliamentarians and their diversity (e.g. in terms of age, political allegiance, career history, etc.) as key factors that shape the connection between the 'politics of presence' and women's substantive representation. Political discourse analysis is a suitable means to explore this relationship for having a diverse range of women elected representatives is important, not only to move away from one-dimensional, essentialist conceptions of gender and politics, but also because the 'experiential knowledge of descriptive representatives enhances their substantive representation of the group's interests by improving the quality of the deliberation'.[22] In other words, the presence of women means that they can draw upon 'situated knowledge' or first-hand experience to bring a gendered perspective to political deliberation in a way that cannot happen in male-dominated legislatures. Thus, the comparatively high proportion of women AMs elected to the National Assembly also allows for a more sophisticated analysis, one that looks beyond sheer numbers, and instead questions whether the benefits of descriptive representation are seen to operate regardless of who the women representatives are.

Earlier analysis[23] of the incidence in the Official Record of Assembly plenary debates (1999–2003) of key gender equality terms likely to reveal distinctive women's perspectives[24] identified a number of interesting aspects to the difference that women AMs were making to political deliberation. When reference to such key terms was disaggregated by the sex of the speaker there was a statistically significant difference[25] between male and female AMs. Women AMs had a greater propensity to engage in debate on 'women's issues' and made approximately two-thirds to three-quarters of all interventions using the key terms analysed (see Table 12.5).

Table 12.5 The incidence of key terms featuring in political debate recorded in the Official Record of the first term of the National Assembly for Wales, 1999–2003

Debating term	Female	Male
	% All references to topic	% All references to topic
Childcare	64.7	35.3
Domestic violence	70.2	29.8
Equal pay	68.0	32.0
'Women's issues'	77.8	22.2
Equality	52.2	47.8
All	59.8	40.2
N	532	358

Source: Paul Chaney, 'Critical mass, deliberation and the substantive representation of women: evidence from the UK's devolution programme, *Political Studies*, 54, (4), (2006), pp. 671–91.

Evidence from the Assembly's first term also revealed that women AMs had a significantly greater propensity[26] to introduce debate on gender equality topics than their male counterparts. Once again, such cases comprised approximately two-thirds to three-quarters of all instances when such terms featured in plenary debate.[27] A further notable feature of post-devolution politics is women AMs holding key positions of power in the executive and legislative branches of government; for example, as committee chairs, and members of the Assembly Government's Cabinet (where, during the Assembly's first term, women comprised a 5:4 majority). Discourse analysis of plenary debates reveals that women predominate in ministerial interjections on key equality topics,[28] again typically accounting for two-thirds to three-quarters of all such interventions. Moreover, when the plenary debates are analysed by sex, debate on women's issues was found to be more 'mainstreamed', in that it involved greater 'dispersion of influence' based on the participation of a greater proportion of the total number of elected women representatives when compared to men.[29] Overall, a mean of 67 per cent of women representatives engaged in debate on the equality terms analysed compared to 36.4 per cent of all male representatives. In total, when all references to equality and women's issues were combined, the gender difference was pronounced with 73.6 per cent of the female cohort engaging in debate compared to 47.4 per cent of the male AMs.

While the foregoing suggests that women AMs were more likely to engage in debate on equality issues – it is germane to ask about variations within the cohort of women AMs. Data on the total debating interventions made by the three most prolific debaters on each topic revealed that a key role is also played by individual women who intervene in debate much more frequently than other female colleagues; such 'equality champions' accounted for between, approximately, a third and a half of all women's interventions. The role of these individuals provides evidence that AMs' background and experience, not least a history of feminist activism, plays a key role in the link between the politics of presence and the substantive representation of women. It also underlines the importance of the election to the Assembly of key feminist activists from left-of-centre political parties and, civil and civic organizations.

Subsequent research[30] affirms that the impact of women AMs on the political discourse around equalities was not restricted to the Assembly's first term. Analysis of the total of 2,409 Oral Assembly Questions (OAQs) to Welsh ministers during the second Assembly (2003–7) also revealed marked gender differences (OAQs are tabled by opposition and backbench AMs for Welsh ministers to address on matters relating to their portfolio). Breakdown revealed that almost 4 per cent of the total OAQs (87 questions) contained the terms 'equality' or 'equal opportunities'. A significant gender difference was evident, with women AMs asking a majority of these questions (77 per cent).[31] This pattern was replicated when another procedural mechanism was examined. A total of 2,467 Written Assembly Questions (WAQs) to ministers were asked during the second Assembly. Almost 3 per cent of the total, some 72 questions, contained the key terms 'equality' or 'equal opportunities' and a further total of 155 (6 per cent) were concerned with the 'women's issues' of equal pay, domestic abuse, women's health and childcare. Again, women AMs had a markedly greater propensity than their male counterparts to ask such questions and accounted for 115 (or 74 per cent of the total).[32] Overall, the discourse analysis data 1997–2007 provide evidence of the difference that the presence of women AMs is making to post-devolution politics. It also underlines that, in the devolved context, the substantive representation of women depends not only on the overall proportion of women parliamentarians but also on who the women are.

We now turn to consider the government's strategy towards gender equality and public policy in the wake of devolution. An early indication of the political reprioritization of this issue became apparent at the first meeting of the Assembly's cross-party Equality Committee in July 1999, when a government minister set out the aim of *mainstreaming* equalities in public policy. This bold vision was subsequently defined as:

> equality issues should be included from the outset as an integral part of the policy-making and service delivery process and the achievement of equality should inform all aspects of the work of every individual within an organisation. *The success of mainstreaming should be measured by evaluating whether inequalities have been reduced.*[33]

The original government strategy paper on the topic acknowledged that there was a need to ensure that a 'proper framework [wa]s in place to support the delivery of the Assembly's duty on equal opportunities'.[34] Existing analysis reveals that it is this aspect, the creation of the institutional prerequisites rather than gender equality policy outcomes, which is most evident after a decade of devolved governance. Prominent examples of new institutional arrangements are, as noted: the Welsh government's statutory duty to promote equalities, and the dedicated Equality and Human Rights Division in the Assembly Government civil service.[35] Despite some initial success in developing institutional mechanisms for mainstreaming equality, four successive official reviews of the Welsh Assembly Government's approach to equalities and mainstreaming have highlighted a number of significant shortcomings and areas for improvement. Thus, the cross-party Equality Committee's Mainstreaming Review asserted that progress was being arrested because of leadership failings: 'there is a lot of positive activity going on but with little strategic direction . . . there [is] a high level of variation across the organisation.'[36]

The Review also made a series of recommendations to improve matters. For example, in order to address the variability between government departments it called on government ministers to ensure that equality is mainstreamed in all the policy areas for which they are responsible. In response, Cabinet approved the Welsh Assembly Government's new Mainstreaming Strategy in May 2006.[37] According to the government, the Strategy would: 'ensure equality and diversity considerations are integral to the development of all its policies and strategies enabling it to meet and exceed its statutory duties.'[38] Yet, seven years on from her initial strategy paper on mainstreaming equalities, Business Minister Jane Hutt AM conceded:

> when we consider how we change hearts and minds, it is about how we can enable the integration of the thinking, the planning and the policy making with mainstreaming equality, so that it is integrated into the everyday work of the civil service, and then, hopefully, the whole Welsh public service. That is beginning to emerge, *although it obviously has to be tested in terms of delivery*.[39]

Opposition AMs were quick to underline the shortcomings in the delivery aspects of the mainstreaming agenda. For example, Helen Mary Jones AM (Plaid Cymru) said: 'the Minister will understand if there is a slight sense of déjà vu for some of us present, because it has taken us a long time to get to this position.' She continued, 'to get this agenda sorted out, and I am sure that the Minister would agree, we really must have a political commitment to give it a priority.'[40]

What factors explain the comparatively limited progress made? One is the unworkable notion of the National Assembly as a corporate body – as set out in the Government of Wales Act 1998 – whereby all parties were notionally responsible for policy design and implementation – something that, in strict legal terms, characterized the Assembly's working prior to May 2007.[41] Moreover, the absence of primary legislative powers for the Assembly has been a further brake on progress for the present, complex and opaque division of powers between Wales and Westminster generally precludes a clear understanding of the devolved government's policy and law-making competencies. This is because the Assembly's founding statute was based upon an executive model of devolution. Rather than the traditional, internationally recognized parliamentary mode of operation (as, for example, set out in the Scotland Act 1998 whereby constitutional law defines the fields in which the legislature has law-making competency), under the executive model, prior to 2007, the National Assembly generally derived its powers from clauses in individual Acts of the UK Parliament. A precise knowledge of the Assembly's powers therefore required detailed understanding of all UK Acts that contain clauses devolving powers to Wales. While this system endures, following the Government of Wales Act 2006, the Assembly's powers have been significantly enhanced, and Legislative Competence Orders allow the passing of primary Welsh legislation (known as Measures of the National Assembly). However arcane these constitutional technicalities may appear, at times their effect has been to frustrate the work of policy-makers, blur the lines of responsibility for the promotion of equalities and, crucially, to blunt the level of scrutiny placed on the Assembly Government's adherence to its statutory equality duty. Thus, recent research revealed that approximately half of the Assembly's cross-party Equality Committee meetings featured examples of speakers' frustration and/or uncertainty stemming from limitations or lack of clarity in relation to Assembly's powers to promote equalities in different policy areas.[42] Examples of AMs' comments include: 'I would like some clarity on the implications of Acts of Parliament';[43] 'the trouble is that, as you quite rightly said, most of this is not devolved to us. The major issues are not devolved';[44] 'this is a cause for concern . . . I am not sure with whom the responsibility lies for this. Can you help us? What should we encourage the Assembly Government – or the Westminster Government if the Assembly does not have enough powers – to do about this?'[45]

In addition to the foregoing challenges, institutional resistance to mainstreaming within the government bureaucracy is a further factor that needs to be considered. This refers to overt – but mostly covert – ways in which organizational élites operate to subvert reforms that conflict with their traditional norms, interests and values. These are notoriously difficult to research, particularly in closed organizational contexts such as government bureaucracies.[46] Such problems were compounded by a lack of expertise and appropriate training. Weak lines of management responsibility for the mainstreaming agenda in government departments, ineffective monitoring, the lack of comprehensive equalities data, and inadequate resources were further factors adding to the malaise.

In the face of the acknowledged shortcomings, the Welsh Assembly Government's 2006 Mainstreaming Strategy outlined a revised approach, *inter alia*: 'we will develop, pilot and disseminate tools that take a generic approach to equality and diversity, standardised across [ministerial] portfolio areas. We will develop a tool kit which guides work cross-strand and thematically.'[47] The promised *Inclusive Policymaking Toolkit* emerged in 2008.[48] It is aimed at assisting in all areas of policy-making and sets out a fixed impact assessment procedure for officials to follow (although equality for the Welsh language is a worrying and glaring omission). The *Toolkit* advises officials: 'if the evidence suggests that there is actual or potential differential impact, or opportunities to promote equality, a Full Impact Assessment is required to identify all the implications of the policy on each of the equality groups.'[49]

A further aspect of the Strategy was the introduction of Single Equality Action Plans[50] to: 'provide clarity over [government] departments' equality priorities [and . . .] enable those developing policy to focus on the equality outcomes that are of the greatest significance to the respective department.'[51] The latter is a potentially significant development and one that is restated in the latest government Annual Equalities Report: 'in the Action Plans departments have been asked to identify key objectives within their Operational Plans *along with their outcomes across all equality strands*.'[52] On a face-value reading: declaration is out, delivery is in. If fully implemented, these appear to be significant remedial steps, for the provision of such equality indicators or benchmarks will be an important step towards the effective evaluation of government equalities policies and determining whether they have succeeded or failed.

The introduction of the new measures to address earlier failings coincided with the publication of an independent, externally commissioned equality audit of Assembly Government policies.[53] It highlighted a number of key weaknesses including that: 'delivering equality as a fundamental theme throughout policy implementation was not always articulated within policy documents.' Echoing earlier concerns over a 'declaratory' approach to equalities, the audit stated that policy documents: 'did not always directly refer to how they would – or direct others to – fulfil and go beyond their legislative obligations in order to eliminate discrimination, promoting equality of opportunity and good relations.' Moreover, it emphasized the fact that in government policies, 'direct reference to explicit measures for monitoring diversity strands was rarely evident'. Crucially, the audit found that, 'the understanding of the purpose and systematic processes of [equalities] impact assessment appeared to be limited'. A subsequent report commissioned by the Equality and Human Rights Commission noted that many of the problems identified by the earlier reviews had yet to be fully addressed.[54] It also highlighted key failings during the first years of devolution in the monitoring and scrutiny of government compliance with its statutory equality duty – as set out in the Government of Wales Act 2006.

In sum, a major gap between the rhetoric and realization of mainstreaming characterizes the first decade of devolution. As noted, progress has been made in relation to institutional structures and procedures to promote equalities – most recently with the introduction of new policy tools and impact assessment procedures. Yet, generally, there has been an emphasis on bureaucratic processes associated with government equalities initiatives rather than policy outcomes.

Against this background, there is emerging, albeit limited, evidence that the measures adopted in the wake of the government's 2006 Mainstreaming Strategy are beginning to shape the way that new policy documents address gender equality concerns. Indeed, more generally, where devolved government's policies incorporate gender equality considerations they raise an interesting prospect: in terms of welfare, gender and citizenship they often set out distinctive social policy frameworks and welfare entitlements that shape the relationship between women and the devolved state (see Table 12.6). Overall, much remains to be done before the mainstreaming agenda matches the progress seen in other aspects of women's political representation following the creation of the National Assembly.

Table 12.6 Social policy divergence: welfare support, funding and regulation in Wales

---

Equal pay in the public sector

The Equality Bill 2009 confers a legal power on the Welsh ministers to develop specific duties in Wales to help public authorities to fulfil the requirements of the new single equality duty, including equal pay.

State support relating to forced marriage and honour-based violence

The Welsh Assembly Government's *Forced Marriage and Honour Based Violence Action Plan* (2008) set out the aim of configuring state support and (devolved) welfare provision to address this issue. For example: 'Objective: To improve the capacity of education, social service and health professionals working in the community to handle forced marriage cases and the provision of victim centred services' (p. 7).

State grants for Higher Education students

Special Support Grants are available to both sexes via Student Finance Wales to provide funding for assistance with the costs of registered or accredited childcare during term time and short vacations, and the Parents' Learning Allowance contributes to the support of dependants in a learner's household. (In practice it is mainly women who benefit from this policy.)[1]

State support for carers

The Welsh Assembly Government's *Carers' Strategy for Wales Action Plan: A Paving Document* (2007) includes initiatives that will revise state support for carers. For example, 'consideration of developing a new grant scheme focused on contingency and emergency short term breaks for carers . . . Assess the availability and range of respite provision across Wales' (pp. 3–4). (Again, while open to both sexes, in practice it will be mainly women who will benefit from this policy.)

---

1 Student Finance Wales/ Welsh Assembly Government (WAG), *Guide to Funding – Making Learning Work For You* (Cardiff, Student Finance Wales/WAG, 2007).

Source: Paul Chaney, 'Critical mass, deliberation and the substantive representation of women: evidence from the UK's devolution programme, *Political Studies*, 54, (4), (2006), pp. 671–91.

DISCUSSION

The impact of devolution on women's representation in Wales is striking in a number of regards. It presents grounds for optimism as well as frustration and concern. The actions of feminist campaigners during the 1990s ensured that the new legislature was configured with institutional mechanisms that facilitate the promotion of gender equality. Following on from this, constitutional law can be said to have introduced a new mode of political citizenship, one that – via the equality duty and other clauses in the devolution statutes – offers new legal rights.

The right to vote in elections to a national legislature is a further dimension of post-devolution political citizenship. The evidence of party manifestos suggests that this has a clear gendered dimension. In a reciprocal process, political parties are increasingly attuning their manifesto programmes to incorporate gender equality commitments – while election study data indicate there are emerging gender differences in the electorate's attitudes to parties' policy programmes, performance, and style of leadership.

However, in terms of representation, it is the comparatively high proportions of women elected to the National Assembly that has drawn most attention. The figures for the first three Assemblies (41.7, 51.7 and 47 per cent respectively) place the devolved legislature in the upper echelons of the world rankings.[55] Yet, as the analysis in this chapter attests, it is too early to say whether this pattern is becoming 'normalized' in devolved politics. Significant threats to sustained progress remain. While affirmative action such as AWS may have delivered significant advances in relation to women's descriptive representation, it neither indicates that sex equality has been effectively mainstreamed within parties – nor guarantees future progress.

Reference to political discourse analysis reveals a probabilistic relationship between the number of female AMs and women's substantive representation. The evidence of political debates and questions to ministers during the first two Assemblies shows that women are significantly more likely than their male counterparts to raise gender equality issues in political debate. This has led to the reprioritization of gender equality in day-to-day politicking. However, as with descriptive representation, future progress in substantive representation is not guaranteed, for analysis reveals the disproportionate influence of individual 'equality champions' in advancing gender equality claims in political debate. Many of these individuals are feminist activists that were elected to the Assembly on its creation in 1999. Continued progress will depend upon their succession by like-minded individuals – or increased awareness of, and interest in, equality issues among their colleagues.

In terms of the post-devolution mainstreaming agenda there has been a major disconnect between political rhetoric and the reality of policy outcomes. While there has been some progress in putting in place institutional procedures to mainstream equalities, four successive official reports have highlighted government failure to deliver mainstreaming in public policy. In response, the devolved administration is currently implementing a revised strategy on mainstreaming with greater systematic use of impact assessments and policy tools. On the face of it, this augurs well, yet (given the hiatus in forming a coalition government after the 2007 elections) it is too early to judge whether it will fully address the earlier over-emphasis on process rather than delivery.

From a social policy perspective, the limited, yet growing number of policies that do address gender equality issues often provide different forms of state regulation, support and entitlements to those found in the UK's other polities – whether it be aid for female entrepreneurs, funding and provision of childcare, or a Wales-specific duty on equal pay. This growing policy divergence redefines the relationship between women and the state – and underlines the reality that devolution is introducing new forms of gender and citizenship in a quasi-federal UK.

NOTES

1 Unless stated otherwise, the term 'devolution' in this chapter refers to the creation of the National Assembly for Wales in 1999 – as opposed to the preceding era of 'administrative devolution'.

2 Beatrice Lipman, 'Diary of a Welsh liberationist', *Planet – The Welsh Internationalist*, 15, (2003), pp. 33–36 (p. 34).

3 Michelle Ryan, 'Women in the New Europe/Women and self-government', in *Plaid Cymru Summer School 1990: Self-Government in the Nineties* (Cardiff: Plaid Cymru, 1990), pp. 13–14.

4 Stephen Wood, 'Germany and the eastern enlargement of the EU: political elites, public opinion and democratic processes', *European Integration*, 24, (1), (2002), pp. 23–38.

5 David Chandler, 'Building global civil society 'from below'?, *Journal of International Studies*, 33, (2), (2004) pp. 313–39 (p. 335).

6 Judith Squires, 'The new equalities agenda: recognising diversity and securing equality in post-devolution Britain', in Alexandra Dobrowolsky and Vivien Hart (eds), *Women Making Constitutions: New Politics and Comparative Perspectives* (London: Palgrave, 2003), pp. 200–13 (p. 211).

7 Paul Chaney, 'Women and constitutional change in Wales', *Regional and Federal Studies*, 14, (2), (2004), pp. 1–23 (p. 22).

8 Welsh Office, *A Voice for Wales* (Cardiff, Welsh Office, 1997), p. 24.

9 Julia Edwards and Christine Chapman, 'Women's political representation in Wales: waving or drowning?', *Contemporary Politics*, 6, (4), (2000), pp. 367–81.

10 Paul Chaney, Fiona Mackay and Laura McAllister, *Women, Politics and Constitutional Change* (Cardiff: University of Wales Press, 2007), p. 197.

11 Equal Opportunities Commission Wales, *The Gender Agenda* (Cardiff: Equal Opportunities Commission Wales, 2006).

12 European Commission Directorate-General for Employment, Social Affairs and Equal Opportunities, *Women in European Politics – Time for Action* (Luxembourg: European Commission, 2009), p. 21.

13 The highest proportion of women in a state legislature in the US is in Colorado (39 per cent). Center for American Women and Politics, *Women in State Legislative Office 2009* (Rutgers, The State University of New Jersey: Center for American Women and Politics, 2009).

14 Circa 2009: New South Wales, 25/93, 27 per cent; Victoria, 40/128, 31.25 per cent;

Queensland 32/89, 36 per cent; South Australia, 47/69, 68 per cent; Tasmania, 8/17, 47 per cent; ACT, 7/17, 42 per cent; Western Australia, 24/91, 26.3 per cent; Northern Territory, 9/25, 36 per cent; Norfolk Island, 2/9, 22.2 per cent.

15   Shirin Rai, *Mainstreaming Gender, Democratizing the State? National Machineries for the Advancement of Women* (Manchester: Manchester University Press, 2003).

16   Welsh Liberal Democrats, *Liberal Democrat Manifesto for the National Assembly for Wales* (Cardiff: Welsh Liberal Democrats, 1999), p. 9.

17   Plaid Cymru, *Make a Difference* (Cardiff: Plaid Cymru, 2007), p. 20.

18   Welsh Liberal Democrats, *A Green, Fairer Future* (Cardiff: Welsh Liberal Democrats, 2007), p. 41.

19   Plaid Cymru, *Make a Difference*, p. 31.

20   Welsh Liberal Democrats, *A Green, Fairer Future*, p. 31.

21   Quoted in Anon., 'Parties backing anti-racism rally', 22 April 2007. http://news.bbc. co.uk/1/hi/uk_politics/wales/6579541.stm (accessed 3 February 2010).

22   Jane Mansbridge, 'Should blacks represent blacks and women represent women? A contingent "Yes"', *Journal of Politics*, 61, (3), (1999), pp. 628–57 (p. 636).

23   Paul Chaney, 'Delivery or déjà vu? gender mainstreaming and public policy', in Nickie Charles and Charlotte Davies (eds), *Gender and Social Justice in Wales* (Cardiff: University of Wales Press, forthcoming).

24   For example, domestic violence, childcare, equal pay for work of equal value between women and men, equality.

25   Chi Squared, P = 0.001.

26   Chi Squared, P = 0.001.

27   Chi Squared, df = 4, X^2 = 22.770.

28   Although not statistically significant (df = 4, X^2 = 5.881).

29   Not statistically significant.

30   Paul Chaney, 'Devolved governance and the substantive representation of women: the second term of the National Assembly for Wales, 2003–2007', *Parliamentary Affairs*, 61, (2), (2008), pp. 234–61.

31   Chi Squared, P = 0.001.

32   Chi Squared, P = 0.0001.

33   National Assembly for Wales, *Mainstreaming Review* (Cardiff: NAfW, Standing Committee on Equality of Opportunity, 2004), p. 6.

34   National Assembly for Wales, 'The approach to equal opportunities', paper presented to the Assembly Equality Committee (Cardiff: National Assembly for Wales, 1999).

35   Created to oversee policy work and compliance in relation to the equality and human rights clauses in the Government of Wales Act (1998), Sections 107 and 120 respectively.

36   National Assembly for Wales, *Mainstreaming Review*, 2004, p. 6.

37   Welsh Assembly Government, 'Mainstreaming equality in the work of the National Assembly', paper presented to the National Assembly Equality of Opportunity Committee, 27 September 2006 (Cardiff: NAfW, 2006).

38   Welsh Assembly Government, 'Mainstreaming equality'.

39   Welsh Assembly Government, 'Mainstreaming equality'.

40   The Record of Proceedings, Tuesday, 6 November 2007.

41   Although in reality attempts were made at operating along parliamentary lines after 2002.

42   Paul Chaney, *Equal Opportunities and Human Rights: The First Decade of Devolution* (Manchester: EHRC, 2009).

43   Transcript of Proceedings, 24 January 2007.

44   Transcript of Proceedings, 28 February 2007.
45   Transcript of Proceedings, 28 February 2007.
46   Gert Dierickx, 'Senior civil servants and bureaucratic change in Belgium', *Governance*, 16, (3), (2003), pp. 321–48.
47   Welsh Assembly Government, 'Mainstreaming equality'.
48   Welsh Assembly Government, *Inclusive Policymaking Toolkit* (Cardiff: Welsh Assembly Government, 2008).
49   Welsh Assembly Government, *Inclusive Policymaking Toolkit*, p. 4.
50   From April 2008.
51   Welsh Assembly Government, 'Mainstreaming equality', p. 3.
52   Ibid., p. 15.
53   Welsh Assembly Government, *Independent Equality Audit* (Cardiff: Welsh Assembly Government, 2007).
54   Paul Chaney, *Equal Opportunities and Human Rights* (Manchester: EHRC, 2009).
55   I.e. among international listings of sub-state 'regional' legislatures – and also when unitary state parliaments are included in the rankings.

13

The refuge movement and domestic violence policies in Wales

Nickie Charles

Since the emergence of the Women's Liberation Movement (WLM) in the late 1960s and early 1970s there have been significant changes in policies relating to women and gender equality in Britain at both local and national level. One of the seven demands raised by the movement was for 'freedom from intimidation by threat or use of violence or sexual coercion, regardless of marital status, and an end to all laws, assumptions and institutions which perpetuate male dominance and men's aggression towards women', and one of the ways in which women organized to ensure that this demand was realized involved the setting up of women's refuge groups and the securing of funding from local government under the 1977 homelessness legislation.[1] The first refuge group to be set up in Wales was Cardiff Women's Aid, which was established in 1975, with Welsh Women's Aid being set up in 1978. Prior to this there had been both a National Women's Aid Federation and a Scottish Women's Aid Federation, and subsequently the refuge movement took the form of separate federations in Wales, England, Scotland and Northern Ireland. Since the mid-1970s, the refuge movement has ensured that domestic violence remains on the political agenda and, as a result, it has become an important aspect of government policy in all parts of Britain. In this chapter I explore the influence of the refuge movement on domestic violence policy, focusing particularly on developments in Wales subsequent upon devolution. This necessarily involves a consideration of policy development in England because, as we shall see, the National Assembly has relatively little autonomy in relation to domestic violence policy. In order to do this I first explore how we can understand the relationship between social movements and policy development; I then outline the engagement of the refuge movement with the state at local and national level, focusing particularly on the changing policy context pre- and post-devolution. Finally I discuss some recent developments and the relationship between state feminism and the refuge movement as it has developed in Wales. Throughout I draw on findings from a recently completed research project investigating gender and political processes in the context of devolution.[2]

FEMINIST SOCIAL MOVEMENTS AND POLICY CHANGE

It is commonly argued that feminist social movements bring about policy change through engaging with the state and through developing new ways of understanding the world; that is, they have both political and cultural effects which are mutually reinforcing.[3] The state and the wider political environment of social movements, including political parties, have been conceptualized as the political opportunity structure, while the process of constructing meanings has been understood in terms of framing.[4] A consideration of framing also informs feminist explorations of the ways in which policy problems are constructed.[5] The idea of framing, and its application to the construction of policy problems, has been criticized for failing to take into account power relations[6] and, in order to overcome this problem, the idea of a discursive opportunity structure, which refers to dominant discourses or cultural meanings 'anchored in key political institutions', has been developed.[7] This makes explicit the power relations that structure and inhere in different definitions and ways of framing and under- standing domestic violence.[8] Furthermore, political opportunity structures are gendered (and also raced and classed) and this may be significant in whether or not they are open to feminist social movements. Similarly, the power rela- tions that underpin competing meanings and definitions are gendered, and struggles over definitions have very real repercussions both in terms of the distribution of resources and in terms of recognition.[9] The outcomes of such struggles therefore have implications for the effectiveness of policies in delivering social justice.

The political and discursive opportunity structures within Wales have been significantly altered with the advent of devolution; there is gender parity in the National Assembly and many of the women Assembly Members (AMs) see themselves (or are seen by others) as feminist. There is therefore a sense in which the National Assembly, which is a new institution where the descriptive representation of women has been achieved, provides an example of state feminism. Here we take that to mean bringing 'women's movement ideas and actors into the affairs of government and policy development to achieve feminist goals'.[10] Furthermore, the National Assembly was set up explicitly to be inclusive, not only of women and women's organizations but of other groups which had hitherto been marginalized from processes of government. And, as we have seen, an absolute duty to promote equality of opportunity is enshrined in the constitution of the National Assembly. Alongside this, the dominant political discourse within Wales emphasizes equality and social justice, something that marks it off from England.[11] However, it is not so much gender equality that is being referred to as class equality and social justice is understood in distributional terms.[12] This is reminiscent of the rhetoric of the immediate post-war years and resonates with the political culture of Wales where there is a long tradition of labourism and trade unionism. These changes in the gendering of the political opportunity structure, together with discourses of equality and social justice, have raised expectations about the possibilities of further change on the part of women's organizations in civil society and among women AMs.[13] In this sense they can be said to have contributed to a perception of the political opportunity structure as open to influence and created a 'policy window' which can be taken advantage of by the refuge movement.[14] The extent to which this happens will have implications for the translation of women's descriptive representation into substantive representation. In other words, real policy change in relation to domestic violence depends to a great extent on the ability of the refuge movement both to work closely with sympathetic AMs and to bring pressure to bear on them when necessary.

THE REFUGE MOVEMENT

The first WLM groups were established in Wales in the early 1970s – in Cardiff in 1970 and Swansea in 1972 – with the first all-Wales WLM conference being held in 1974.[15] The refuge movement in Wales emerged from the women's movement of the 1960s and 1970s and takes the form of Welsh Women's Aid and its member groups, of which there are currently 34.[16] Historically, refuge groups were organized as feminist collectives; they provided a form of feminist welfare and were campaigning groups as well as service providers.[17] In the early years refuge workers were usually women who had themselves been refuge residents, and the refuges were run collectively by all those who were in residence.[18] By the early 1990s, however, there was already a process of professionalization in train which eventually contributed to the abandonment of collective forms of organization by almost all Women's Aid groups in Wales. Prior to this, Welsh Women's Aid had been managed by delegates from local groups and employed a number of national workers who were based in Cardiff, Aberystwyth and Wrexham. By the end of the 1990s there was a feeling within the movement that this structure was no longer working, particularly in the context of increasingly complicated and accountable financial regimes which were being imposed on groups by local government and housing associations. In 2000 Welsh Women's Aid commissioned an evaluation which collected evidence from every member group as to their views on how the organization was working and how it could be improved.[19] As a result of this research and a subsequent management report, Welsh Women's Aid decided to abandon its collective form of organization and adopt a more hierarchical structure involving the appointment of a Director. The first Director was appointed in 2003; she was Sian James who was involved in the women's support groups during the Miners' Strike of 1984–5 and has subsequently gone on to become the Labour MP for Swansea East. Many, though not all, refuge groups have also adopted a hierarchical structure and abandoned their collective forms of organization. These changes have reduced groups' ability to engage in campaigning and other political work and resulted in what one refuge worker termed 'an organisation that runs a service'.[20] There is still, however, a strong sense among refuge groups of a commitment to feminist politics and feminist values.

The changes that the refuge movement has undergone since the 1970s can partly be seen as a result of the success of refuge groups and Welsh Women's Aid in establishing themselves as 'experts' on domestic violence and in attracting more substantial amounts of money from funders such as local government, housing associations and, in the case of Welsh Women's Aid, the Welsh Office (subsequently the National Assembly). But as well as putting Welsh Women's Aid and its member groups on a more secure financial footing and enabling them to provide services more effectively, the imposition of funding regimes can also restrict their autonomy, constraining the activities in which they are able to engage and affecting their ability to criticize policy development. This is particularly the case for local refuge groups, most of which now look to Welsh Women's Aid to engage politically, to instigate campaigns, and to respond to consultations that emerge from the National Assembly and from the Home Office.

As well as providing a feminist form of welfare and campaigning to influence government policy, the refuge movement and the feminist movement (of which the former was part) have engaged in a cultural politics which diffuses feminist meanings throughout society. One of the ways in which social movements influence cultural meanings and policy development is that women who have been involved in the movement move on to other areas of activity, whether this be joining political parties, working in educational institutions or moving into other social movement organizations such as trade unions. Between 1979 and 1997, the years when the Conservatives were in power, many feminist activists joined the Labour Party and were involved in developing policies which related to the demands of the women's movement. They were also active in local government, setting up women's committees and becoming local political representatives. Some of these women were later to be elected to the 1997 Labour government in Westminster and the 1999 Welsh Assembly Government.

Another way in which social movements engage in cultural politics is through struggles over meaning and the framing of issues. One of the major achievements of 'second wave' feminism was that domestic violence was redefined. It was no longer seen as a problem caused by deviant and possibly psychologically damaged men but as a profoundly gendered issue which arose from gendered relations of power and which was evident at all levels of society. Domestic violence was linked to systematically structured inequalities between women and men and the relative cultural valuing of masculinity and femininity (i.e. the mis/recognition of women as of lesser status than men). It was therefore profoundly gendered and it was overwhelmingly women who experienced domestic violence and men who were the perpetrators.[21] This definition emerged from the women's movement and linked domestic violence to the way in which society was structured, on the one hand, and the cultural devaluing of women, on the other. According to the analysis underpinning this understanding, the elimination of domestic violence would require a redistribution of resources between women and men and a cultural revaluing of women in relation to men; in other words the remedies would involve both redistribution and recognition and would pose a significant challenge to the gender order.[22] This definition has, however, become less influential as domestic violence has become part of the mainstream political agenda.

It has been argued that, in the process of influencing politics and policy development, the demands raised by social movements undergo a process of 'issue perversion'. This refers to the process whereby measures are taken which go some way towards meeting social movement demands and, although not meeting the original demands, they are sufficient to defuse the threat to the gender order that the original demands contained. It could be argued that this has happened in the case of domestic violence and that, in the process, the problem has been reframed such that it is no longer defined in gendered terms. In what follows I consider the way the framing of domestic violence has changed as it has become a central plank of criminal justice policy and how this process has marginalized more radical feminist voices and muted the challenge to the gender order implied in a feminist understanding of domestic violence.

REFRAMING DOMESTIC VIOLENCE

One of the major issues that the refuge movement faced in its early days was that the police were very reluctant to intervene in a 'domestic'. Male violence against women in the home was simply not taken seriously, and one of the first policy interventions of the refuge movement and feminists working closely with it was to try to change this attitude and the practices that flowed from it. One of the ways this was done was by refuge groups providing training for local police forces and working closely with them on domestic violence cases. Another was in trying to ensure that women had recourse to the law to protect them from violent men; this meant the criminalization of domestic violence. It was only by taking this route that domestic violence would be seen as serious by the police and women would receive some degree of protection. By the same token, feminists also undertook to establish a business case for the elimination of domestic violence, something that was already being done by feminists in the US. In order to persuade politicians and employers to take domestic violence seriously, it was necessary to convince them not only that it was a crime, but that its costs to industry were too high to be ignored; it was not enough that it was a violation of women's human rights and something that should simply not be tolerated. These arguments have been extremely successful, so much so that domestic violence, having been defined in legislation in the 1970s as a housing and homelessness issue, is now primarily defined as a criminal justice issue, and the Women and Equality Unit, under Jacqui Smith, commissioned and published research showing its financial costs to employers and to the state.[23] In this process, however, the gendered nature of domestic violence has receded from view – it has been redefined and reframed in gender-neutral terms. Defining it in this way has implications in terms of resources and, in particular, affects the way in which Women's Aid groups are able to operate and who controls both domestic abuse fora and the development of local domestic violence strategies.[24]

In the course of developing policies which take domestic violence seriously, therefore, feminists have contributed to its redefinition as a criminal justice issue. Domestic violence has been reframed as a problem of individual/family violence rather than involving gendered power relations and being mainly violence committed by men against women. The policies that do this were largely developed by the Labour Party while it was out of power and have been enacted in various pieces of legislation since it returned to power in 1997. As criminal justice is outwith the remit of the National Assembly, the overarching policy framework is the same as in England. It is therefore important to detail the policy framework that governs development of domestic violence policy in England and Wales before exploring how the refuge movement has influenced policy development in Wales.

THE POLICY CONTEXT

Since the 1997 general election the Labour government in Westminster has given domestic violence a higher political profile. In 1999 it published a policy document, *Living Without Fear* [25] and, in 2003, it produced a consultation paper, *Safety and Justice: The Government's Proposals on Domestic Violence.*[26] In both these documents domestic violence is placed firmly within the context of crime reduction and defined as a criminal justice issue.[27] Various pieces of legislation have been passed since 1997, including the 1997 Protection and Harassment Act, the Sexual Offences and Female Genital Mutilation Act, which became law in 2003, and the Domestic Violence, Crime and Victims Act 2004, which applies in England and Wales. The 1998 Crime and Disorder Act requires that police and local authorities form partnerships with the aim of reducing crime, including domestic violence, in their local area; in Wales these partnerships are known as Community Safety Partnerships and are one of the main planks of the domestic abuse strategy.

It is within this policy framework that domestic violence policy in Wales has developed, although, in comparison with Scotland, a 'made-in-Wales' policy was slow to emerge; indeed it was not until 2002 that the Working Group on Domestic Violence and Violence against Women was set up by the Welsh Assembly Government. This slow start has been attributed, *inter alia*, to the lack of pressure from women's organizations, which, in turn, relates to the weakness of civil society in Wales more generally.[28] Thus, 'In comparison with Scotland, Welsh devolution got off to a faltering start'.[29] There were various reasons for this, including a lack of support for devolution in the population at large, the limited powers of the Assembly, and unpropitious political circumstances that included 'the loss of a secretary of state, and three of the four Assembly party leaders within the first year of its inception'.[30] These circumstances meant that the birth of the Assembly was neither accompanied nor preceded by a groundswell of support in civil society and pressure from civil society organizations for strategic policy developments. Thus, although in Wales feminist activists had been involved in drawing up the constitutional blueprint for the National Assembly and in ensuring, through the 'absolute duty', that equality of opportunity was promoted in all its activities, feminist pressure in relation to domestic violence was not so evident. Indeed there was a feeling among refuge groups that the presence within the Welsh Assembly Government in key positions of women who had been involved in the refuge movement would be enough to secure their future. This contrasts markedly with Scotland and may help to explain the different trajectory of domestic violence policy in the two jurisdictions.[31]

NATIONAL LEVEL

Despite the weakness of civil society within Wales, the influence of the refuge movement on policy development is apparent from its connections with key women within the Welsh Assembly Government and the incorporation of feminist social movement organizations into processes of policy formation. It was Jane Hutt, in her capacity as Minister for Health and Social Services, who set up the Working Group on Domestic Violence and Violence against Women in Wales in 2002. In the 1970s she had been one of the founder members of Welsh Women's Aid and still retains connections with the refuge movement. The establishment of the working group ensured that consultation with feminist organizations was built into the development of the Welsh Assembly Government's strategy on domestic violence in two ways: through their membership of the working group and their participation in the consultation process which preceded the final drafting and publication of the strategy. In this way, Welsh Women's Aid and other domestic violence organizations are able to participate in the policy-making process. Furthermore, they are regularly called on to give evidence to Assembly committees; their presence is therefore institutionalized at several levels within the National Assembly.

Not only did Jane Hutt set up the working group, she was also instrumental in raising the profile of domestic violence within and without the Assembly through her support for initiatives such as International Women's Day and Days of Action against Violence against Women. Interviews with senior civil servants suggest that it is largely ministers who drive policy development, and the development of the domestic violence strategy can certainly be seen as a result of the commitment first of the Minister for Health and Social Services, Jane Hutt, and then the Minister for Social Justice and Regeneration, Edwina Hart. Both these women have made domestic violence a priority and have consistently lent public support to domestic violence initiatives, such as the helpline, which was set up in 2004, and the strategy itself, which was published in 2005. This lends credence to the argument that key strategic women are critical in ensuring that descriptive representation is translated into substantive representation and that so-called women's issues are attended to. It is also the case that a number of women AMs have come into politics through working in the refuge movement and that they retain links with local Women's Aid groups. This experience is drawn on by women in debate and in their contribution to the development of policy. Thus women AMs have been the ones to take the lead in debating domestic violence and, within the National Assembly, women ministers and AMs have been pressing the domestic violence agenda and have had some success in ensuring that it maintains a relatively high profile.[32]

At national level, therefore, the differently gendered and new political opportunity structure not only provides openings for social movements to press their demands but also enables them to engage in political processes within this new political institution. Furthermore, the significant number of women AMs who have connections with refuge groups ensures that the question of domestic violence remains relatively high on the political agenda. Their engagement with the issue also demonstrates one of the ways that feminist social movements bring about cultural change although, as we shall see, such diffusion also brings with it the likelihood of issue perversion.

LOCAL LEVEL

At local level, the involvement of the refuge movement in the development of local domestic abuse strategies varies and is at the discretion of the Community Safety Partnerships. These are identified by the Home Office and in the all-Wales strategy as the 'key local partnership' for delivering the domestic abuse strategy. The strategy recommends that domestic abuse fora be invited to contribute to the development of local domestic abuse strategies in order that the voices of 'victims' be heard, and it suggests that domestic violence agencies may be invited to participate in Community Safety Partnerships.[33] As in England, domestic abuse co-ordinators have been appointed at local level; indeed one of the recommendations of the strategy was that the development of an all-Wales network of domestic abuse co-ordinators would be encouraged. In the event it was in 2005, at the same time as the launch of the strategy, that a network of domestic abuse co-ordinators was established and, in 2006, the Welsh Assembly Government guaranteed recurring funding to all Community Safety Partnerships for domestic abuse co-ordinators. It is domestic abuse co-ordinators who are charged with developing local domestic abuse strategies.

There is considerable variation in the way in which local government and local authorities engage with the issue of domestic violence and domestic violence agencies. Thus in one of our areas the activities of local refuge groups was very constrained due to the funding regime that was in operation; groups were no longer able to provide training for other agencies and they were confined to service provision only. In another, the local domestic violence agency was centrally involved in the development of the strategy and in its monitoring. This variation in participation, together with the control of the domestic violence agenda by statutory agencies, suggests that at local level the political opportunity structure may not be as open to the refuge movement as it is at the level of the National Assembly. This may in part be affected by the gendering of political representatives – at the time of our research the proportion of women councillors in Welsh local government ranged from 3 per cent to 33 per cent and averaged 22 per cent – and a lack of key strategic women or other sympathetic actors within local government. In addition, there are far fewer self-identified feminists to be found among local councillors than among AMs and there is a difference between the Welsh Assembly Government and local government in the priority that they give to domestic violence. There are also contrasts between the Assembly and local government in terms of priority given to equality policies, with equal opportunities at local government level being less well developed than at the level of the Assembly and lagging behind their counterparts in Scotland.[34] Local authority responses to the introduction of the gender equality duty exemplify these differences.

THE GENDER EQUALITY DUTY

The gender equality duty was introduced in April 2007 by the UK government and required public sector organizations actively to promote gender equality. In the wake of its introduction we found that several refuge groups had experienced pressure from their local authorities to provide services to men as well as to women. Such pressure was justified on grounds of equality and local authorities appeared to be interpreting the gender equality duty as meaning that women and men should receive the same treatment regardless of differences in need. There are no grounds for this interpretation in the gender equality duty itself. Indeed the Code of Practice stipulates that:

> Women make up the substantial majority of victims of domestic violence and rape. It would not be appropriate, therefore, for a local council to seek to fund refuge services on a numerically equal basis for men and for women. The promotion of equal opportunities between men and women requires public authorities to recognise that the two groups are not starting from an equal footing and identical treatment would not be appropriate.
>
> The Gender Equality Duty requires public authorities proactively to address the individual needs of women and men in all their functions . . . This might mean providing services to one sex only . . . The most common examples of this in practice are rape crisis centres or refuges for women who are victims of domestic violence.[35]

This response to the gender equality duty on the part of some local authorities has been taken up by the Equality and Human Rights Commission (EHRC) in Wales in two ways: it has provided funding for Welsh Women's Aid to investigate the extent of the problems faced by local refuge groups and it has written to all local authorities reminding them that 'domestic abuse is one of the most serious forms of gender inequality'.[36] Problems arising from the implementation of the gender equality duty are not peculiar to Wales; Southall Black Sisters were threatened with the withdrawal of their funding because the local authority argued that there was no longer any need for specialist provision for minority ethnic women. Southall Black Sisters took Ealing Council to court but before the case was heard, the council settled out of court. And the Government Equalities Office commissioned urgent research at the beginning of 2009 to investigate 'whether recent changes in national and local policies and funding arrangements, such as the gender equality duty, have disproportionately affected the violence against women voluntary sector'.[37] It is of note that in Wales the Welsh Assembly Government has not taken a lead on this question; this has been left to the EHRC (Wales), although they have stepped in to compel at least one local authority to reinstate funding to a Women's Aid group that they had cut.

A GENDER-NEUTRAL DEFINITION

The other issue which is of concern to the refuge movement and other organizations in the domestic violence sector is the gender-neutral definition of domestic abuse that informs domestic abuse strategies at local and national level. We suggest that the way this is being taken up by the domestic violence sector is indicative of an ongoing frame dispute,[38] the outcome of which will have significant implications in terms of social justice for women.

The principles underlying the all-Wales domestic abuse strategy are equality, which, because of the absolute duty, threads through all Welsh Assembly Government policy development, 'protection and support for victims, perpetrator accountability' and 'prevention'.[39] The link between domestic violence and gender-based inequalities is not, however, drawn out in the strategy document and the definition of domestic abuse is, like its English counterpart, gender-neutral. It is defined as:

> the use of physical and/or emotional abuse or violence, including undermining of self confidence, sexual violence or the threat of violence, by a person who is or has been in a close relationship.[40]

The fact that a gendered definition has been abandoned within Wales and at Westminster represents a change in the way domestic abuse is understood and framed. Instead of being an aspect of a patriarchal society which is in need of transformation in order that gender equality may be achieved and women may live free of the fear of violence – whether physical, sexual or psychological – it includes a very wide range of abusive behaviour that needs to be eradicated. The only thing that distinguishes domestic violence from any other form of assault or abuse is that it takes place in and around the domestic sphere, not that it is a manifestation and abuse of male power over women. And, as with the gender equality duty, the gender-neutral definition of domestic violence has been challenged neither by the National Assembly nor by women AMs or ministers.

The Welsh Assembly Government has accepted and worked with this framing, ensuring that the Home Office's gender-neutral definition of domestic violence is the one that prevails in Wales as well as England. This contrasts with Scotland, where a gendered definition of domestic violence has been retained and its feminist framing, although challenged, has not (yet) been displaced. It has been left up to the refuge movement and other women's equality and human rights organizations to contest the gender-neutral definition.

These two issues, the way in which the gender equality duty is being interpreted by some local authorities and the gender-neutral definition of domestic abuse prevailing at local and national level, were raised as a matter of concern by several of the local domestic violence organizations and domestic abuse co-ordinators whom we interviewed. They did not wish to deny that some men experience domestic abuse and require provision, but what they were concerned about was that resources may be diverted from women-only organizations leading to a decline in the provision of services to women. Their fears seem to be justified, given the pressure that some women's refuges are experiencing from local authorities to open their doors to men in the name of equality.

ENDING VIOLENCE AGAINST WOMEN

There is evidence that these concerns are now being channelled into a co-ordinated campaign to challenge the non-gendered framing of domestic violence and violence against women more generally, with a range of organizations coming together around a violence against women agenda. Welsh Women's Aid, in their submission to the 2008 investigation into domestic violence services in Wales carried out by the Communities and Culture Committee, re-emphasized that

> Domestic abuse is a crime committed predominantly against women, with 77% of victims of domestic violence being women, and the government's definition should recognise this. Almost half of women in England and Wales experience domestic violence, sexual assault or stalking during their lifetime.[41]

They also pointed to the UN Declaration on the Elimination of Violence against Women, which defines domestic violence as

> Any act of gender-based violence that results in, or is likely to result in, physical, sexual or psychological harm or suffering to women . . . This definition incorporates the fact that domestic abuse concerns the misuse of power and it highlights that it enhances the inequality against women.[42]

There is now pressure being brought to bear on government in England and Wales to adopt this definition and recent events in Wales have added new impetus to this campaign.

In 2007 the third Assembly elections were held and, for the first time, the Welsh Assembly Government was formed by a coalition between Plaid Cymru and Labour. This resulted in a change in ministerial portfolios and the Social Justice and Local Government portfolio was taken by Brian Gibbons (Labour). This meant that, for the first time since the National Assembly came into being, equalities and domestic violence were not being overseen by women who were identified by many as feminist. Some of those we talked to in the violence against women sector voiced concern about this as, in their view, the minister's predecessors had been very committed to ensuring that domestic violence remained in the public eye and on the political agenda and they were not sure that this would continue to be the case. In March 2009 the Home Office, under the then Home Secretary, Jacqui Smith, launched a consultation exercise with the aim of developing a strategy to end violence against women and girls. No such consultation was launched in Wales and this omission was met with dismay by the refuge movement and other organizations that had taken up the issue of domestic violence and violence against women. In response to this a campaign was launched specifically targeting the minister and demanding that the Welsh Assembly Government develop an integrated strategy to tackle violence against women. Welsh Women's Aid and Women's Voice (Wales Women's National Coalition) circulated the Home Office's questionnaire with the following introduction:

> The Welsh Assembly Government has decided not to follow the Violence Against Women and Girls Strategy that will emerge and the Home Office, as it stands, will not be coming to Wales to hear the views of the people in Wales. Welsh Women's Aid and Women's Voice believe that the views of the people in Wales are crucial to such an important debate. We have produced this questionnaire to ensure that the Home Office has an understanding of the issues that are specific to Wales, especially in areas that are non devolved to the Welsh Assembly Government.[43]

In response the Welsh Assembly Government published a statement which included the following:

> I hope it is clear from this that Wales is not in any way 'opting out' of the UK government consultation on examining the need for a violence against women strategy.[44]

And it has now committed itself to developing a strategic violence against women plan.

These developments indicate that the Welsh Assembly Government is responsive to pressure from social movements. In this case the launch of the Home Office consultation led directly to the formation of the Wales Violence Against Women Action Group which brings together several women's organizations which are involved in the End Violence Against Women (EVAW) campaign and which is co-ordinated by Women's Voice. The campaign draws together disparate feminist voices which have been unhappy with the gender-neutral definition of the all-Wales strategy and with what they see as the misuse of statistics. They explicitly link domestic violence to gender inequality and women's human rights and, in the process, are engaged in a struggle over meaning.[45] They point to Scotland, which has retained a gendered definition of domestic violence and which already has a strategy to end violence against women. It is noteworthy that the impetus for the development of such a strategy has not come from within the National Assembly but from social movement organizations which retain a gendered analysis of both domestic violence and violence against women. Their voices have been silenced since the adoption of a gender-neutral domestic abuse strategy, indeed we were told by one of the domestic abuse co-ordinators that it has been difficult to argue against this gender neutrality, particularly as it has been seen as important to ensure that services are available for children. However, now they are challenging the framing of domestic violence which underpins the gender-neutral definition and are reasserting the links between violence against women and unequal, gendered power relations.

What is emerging in Wales, and in England, can be seen as a frame dispute which is likely to have implications in terms of resource distribution. There are two aspects to this. The gender-neutrality of the definition of domestic violence and the way in which official statistics are being used in Wales legitimate an argument for resources to be deployed to support male victims of domestic violence. This, together with the way in which some local authorities are interpreting the gender equality duty as implying gender neutrality and a requirement to treat women and men the same, has implications for the recognition of the nature of domestic violence which can in turn be linked to distributional issues, specifically the availability of resources for women's refuges. This could result in services for those women least able to make provision for themselves being jeopardized.[46]

FRAME DISPUTES

This chapter has explored the influence of the refuge movement on the development of domestic violence policy in Wales, focusing particularly on the period since devolution in 1999. As we have seen, the development of domestic violence policy in Wales is very closely related to its development in England because of its location within the crime reduction programme and the retention of central control over this by the Home Office. This means that there is limited possibility of developing domestic violence policies which are distinctively Welsh, something that has been achieved in Scotland and something that the Welsh Assembly Government has been able to do in other areas, such as education. This is also a concern of those involved in the violence against women coalition who are currently trying to 'Welshify' the English EVAW campaign materials. Given this framework, however, and the recognized weakness of civil society organizations at the time of devolution, the input of the refuge movement to the development of domestic violence policy by the Welsh Assembly Government has been significant. This has been achieved by the incorporation of refuge movement organizations into policy-making processes within the Welsh Assembly Government and through the connections of women political representatives with the refuge movement and their commitment to furthering the domestic violence agenda within government.

In this way, women's movement ideas and values have been brought into the processes of government and can be seen as an example of state feminism. Whether or not the incorporation of social movement actors and ideas into government has achieved feminist goals, however, is a moot point, particularly in light of the ongoing frame dispute over the way in which domestic violence and violence against women are defined. It could be argued that acceptance of the gender-neutral definition represents a form of liberal feminism which is based on an understanding of equality as implying sameness, and that it is this form of feminism which predominates within the National Assembly. In contra-distinction to this, the refuge movement, and the violence against women sector as a whole, represent a more radical feminist framing of violence against women. Their voices have, until now, been silenced by the acceptance of the gender-neutral definition by the Welsh Assembly Government and by the domestic violence champions within it. The fact that it is only now that opposition to this framing of domestic violence has emerged suggests that it may be more difficult for a feminist challenge to be mounted if feminist organizations have been incorporated into policy development, and when women who are identified as feminist are driving policy within government. Such incorporation is one of the mechanisms which contributes to issue perversion.

The dominance of the gender-neutral definition is related to the control of the domestic violence agenda by statutory agencies and the incorporation of domestic violence into the crime reduction programme. In other words, this discursive framing of domestic violence in gender-neutral terms is located in institutionally based and gendered power relations. And although the polit-ical opportunity structure is differently gendered at the level of the National Assembly, within local government and statutory agencies, such as the police, men still predominate. This has implications not only for the way domestic viol-ence is defined, but also for the way in which domestic violence strategies are developed and implemented at local level.

Finally, the way in which domestic violence is framed has important policy and resource implications. Defining it in gender-neutral terms has, together with the gender equality duty, created pressure on refuge groups to open their doors to men and end specialist provision for women with the result that scarce resources are being 'shared' between provision for women and men. There is also a failure to recognize that domestic violence is rooted in structural inequalities based on gender; these inequalities are therefore not challenged, neither is the cul-tural devaluing of women in relation to men which legitimates violence against women. Framing domestic violence and violence against women as gendered, which is what is done in Scotland and by the UN, has very different implications in terms of resources and recognition and, if it were adopted, would make poss-ible the development of policies which challenge the gender-based inequalities and cultural values which underpin domestic violence. The outcome of this frame dispute, however, does not depend solely on the strength of the refuge movement or the wider violence against women movement. Many organizations are now engaged with the violence against women agenda; there has been a diffusion of feminist values throughout society and there are now far more actors engaged in contestations over meaning. This is an indication of the success of the refuge movement in bringing about cultural change, but paradoxically it also makes it more difficult for radical feminist voices to be heard and for policies to be developed which not only provide support for women and children who have experienced domestic violence, but also aim to eliminate domestic violence and violence against women by recognizing and tackling its basis in gendered inequalities and relations of power.

NOTES

1   Nickie Charles, *Feminism, the State and Social Policy* (Basingstoke: Palgrave Macmillan, 2000).

2   ESRC grant number RES-000-23-1185 awarded to Nickie Charles (Principal Investigator, University of Warwick), Charlotte Davies and Stephanie Jones (Swansea University). As part of the research we conducted interviews with 31 Assembly Members, 27 councillors and senior officials, 30 representatives of civil society organizations at local and national level, four senior civil servants and one statutory equalities body.

3   Charles, *Feminism, the State and Social Policy*; Sasha Roseneil, *Disarming Patriarchy* (Milton Keynes: Open University Press, 1995).

4   Robert D. Benford and David A. Snow, 'Framing processes and social movements: an overview', in *Annual Review of Sociology*, 26, (2000), pp. 611–39; Wendy Ball and Nickie Charles, 'Feminist social movements and policy change: devolution, childcare and domestic violence policies in Wales', in *Women's Studies International Forum*, 29, (2006), pp. 172–83; Nickie Charles, 'Feminist politics and devolution', in *Social Politics*, 11, (2), (2004), pp. 297–311.

5   Carol Lee Bacchi, *Women, Policy and Politics: The Construction of Policy Problems* (London: Sage, 1999).

6   Nancy Naples, 'Materialist feminist discourse analysis and social movement research: mapping the changing context for "community control"', in David Meyer, Nancy Whittier and Belinda Robnett (eds), *Social Movements: Identity, Culture, and the State* (Oxford University Press, 2002), pp. 226–46.

7   Myra Marx Ferree, 'Resonance and radicalism: feminist framing of abortion in the United States and Germany', in *American Journal of Sociology*, 109, (2), (2003), pp. 304–44 (p. 308).

8   Jeff Hearn and Linda McKie, 'Gendered policy and policy on gender: the case of "domestic violence"', in *Policy and Politics*, 36, (1), (2008), pp. 75–91.

9   Hearn and McKie, 'Gendered policy and policy on gender'; Nickie Charles, 'Setting the scene: devolution, gender politics and social justice', in Nickie Charles and Charlotte Davies (eds), *Gender and Social Justice in Wales* (Cardiff: University of Wales Press, forthcoming).

10   Amy Mazur and Dorothy McBride Stetson, 'State feminism', in Gary Goertz and Amy Mazur (eds), *Politics, Gender and Concepts: Theory and Methodology* (Cambridge University Press, 2008), pp. 244–69. See also Joni Lovenduski, *Feminizing Politics* (Cambridge: Policy Press, 2005).

11   Mark Drakeford, 'Social justice in a devolved Wales', *Benefits*, 15, (2), (2007), pp. 171–8.

12   Charles, 'Setting the scene'.

13   Sandra Betts, John Borland and Paul Chaney, 'Inclusive government for excluded groups: women and disabled people', in Paul Chaney, Tom Hall and Andrew Pithouse (eds), *New Governance – New Democracy?* (Cardiff: University of Wales Press, 2001), pp. 48–77.

14   Catherine Marshall, 'Policy discourse analysis: negotiating gender equity', in *Journal of Educational Policy*, 15, (2), (2000), pp. 125–56.

15   Paul Chaney, Fiona Mackay and Laura McAllister (eds), *Women, Politics and Constitutional Change: The First Years of the National Assembly for Wales* (Cardiff: University of Wales Press, 2007).

16   Welsh Women's Aid, *Communities and Culture Committee, Scrutiny Enquiry: Domestic Abuse, Response from Welsh Women's Aid* (2008). Available online at: http://www.assem-blywales.org (accessed 12 October 2008).

17   Nickie Charles 'Feminist politics, domestic violence and the state', in *Sociological Review*, 43, (4), (1995), pp. 617–40; Charles, *Feminism, the State and Social Policy*.

18   Nickie Charles, 'The refuge movement and domestic violence', in Jane Aaron, Teresa Rees, Sandra Betts and Moira Vincentelli (eds), *Our Sisters' Land* (Cardiff: University of Wales Press, 1994), pp. 48–60.

19   Nickie Charles, Madi Gilkes and Anthea Symonds, *Evaluation of the Organisational Structure of Welsh Women's Aid* (Swansea: University of Wales Swansea, 2001).

20   Charles, 'Feminist politics and devolution'.

21   Hearn and McKie, 'Gendered policy and policy on gender'.

22   Nancy Fraser, 'Social justice in the age of identity politics: redistribution, recognition, and participation', in Nancy Fraser and Axel Honneth, *Redistribution or Recognition? A Political-Philosophical Exchange* (London: Verso, 2003), pp. 7–109.

23   Sylvia Walby, *The Cost of Domestic Violence* (London: Women and Equality Unit, Department of Trade and Industry, 2004).

24   P. Harvie, 'The local domestic violence multi-agency forum as a policy and practice option: a case study' (Unpublished PhD thesis, Birkbeck College, University of London, 2007).

25   Women's Unit, *Living without Fear: An Integrated Approach to Tackling Violence against Women* (London: Women's Unit, Cabinet Office, 1999).

26   Home Office, *Safety and Justice: The Government's Proposals on Domestic Violence* (London: Home Office, 2003).

27   Charles, 'Feminist politics and devolution'.

28   Lindsay Paterson and Richard Wyn Jones, 'Does civil society drive constitutional change?', in Bridget Taylor and Katarina Thomson (eds), *Scotland and Wales: Nations Again?* (Cardiff: University of Wales Press, 1999).

29   Drakeford, 'Social justice in a devolved Wales', p. 172.

30   Ibid., p. 172.

31   Nickie Charles and Fiona Mackay, 'Engendering devolution: comparing domestic violence politics and policy in Scotland and Wales', paper presented to the Engendering Policy and Devolution conference, University of Warwick, November 2008.

32   Chaney *et al.*, *Women, Politics and Constitutional Change*.

33   Welsh Assembly Government, *Tackling Domestic Abuse: The All-Wales National Strategy* (Cardiff, 2005).

34   Esther Breitenbach, Alice Brown, Fiona Mackay and Jan Webb, *Equal Opportunities in Local Government in Scotland and Wales* (Edinburgh: Unit for the Study of Government in Scotland, University of Edinburgh, 1999).

35   End Violence Against Women (EVAW), *Making the Grade? 2007: The Third Annual Independent Analysis of UK Government Initiatives on Violence against Women* (London:

EVAW: 2007), p. 9. Available online at: http://www.endviolenceagainstwomen.org.uk (accessed 12 October 2008).

36   Equality and Human Rights Commission, letter to local authorities in Wales (2008).

37   Government Equalities Office (2009).

38   R. D. Benford, 'Frame disputes within the nuclear disarmament movement', in *Social Forces*, 71, (1993), pp. 677–701.

39   Welsh Assembly Government, *Tackling Domestic Abuse*, p. 3.

40   Ibid., p. 6.

41   Welsh Women's Aid, *Domestic Abuse, Response*.

42   Ibid.

43   Welsh Women's Aid and Women's Voice, 'Together we can end violence against women and girls', questionnaire (n.d.). Available online at: http://www.welshwomensaid.org/news/24332.html (accessed 23 June 2009).

44   Brian Gibbons, Minister for Social Justice and Local Government, 'Ongoing work in Wales to prevent violence against women', written statement by the Welsh Assembly Government, 27 February 2009.

45   L. N. Predelli, 'Women's organisations and claims-making in the United Kingdom, with a focus on policies addressing violence against women', paper presented to the First European Conference on Politics and Gender, Belfast, January 2009.

46   Charles, 'Feminist politics and devolution'.

Selected bibliography

Women and political participation in England, 1918–1970

Andrews, Maggie, *The Acceptable Face of Feminism: The Women's Institute as a Social Movement* (London: Lawrence and Wishart, 1997).
Beaumont, Catriona, 'The women's movement, politics and citizenship, 1918–1950s', in Ina Zweiniger-Bargielowska (ed.), *Women in Twentieth Century Britain* (London: Longman, 2001), pp. 262–77.
Caine, Barbara, *English Feminism, 1780–1980* (Oxford University Press, 1997).
Francis, Martin and Ina Zweiniger-Bargielowska (eds), *The Conservatives and British Society* (Cardiff: University of Wales Press, 1996), pp. 194–223.
Graves, Pamela, *Labour Women in British Working Class Politics, 1918–1939* (Cambridge University Press, 1994).
Hollis, Patricia, *Ladies Elect: Women in English Local Government, 1865–1914* (Oxford University Press, 1987).
Law, Cheryl, *Suffrage and Power: The Women's Movement, 1918–1928* (London: I.B. Tauris, 1997).
Pat Thane, 'Visions of gender in the British welfare state', in Gisela Bock and Pat Thane (eds), *Maternity and Gender Policies: Women and the Rise of the European Welfare States, 1880s–1950s* (London: Routledge, 1991), pp. 93–118.
Pugh, Martin, *Women and the Women's Movement in Britain*, 2nd edn (London: Macmillan, 2000).
Smith, Harold L. (ed), *British Feminism in the Twentieth Century* (Aldershot: Edward Elgar, 1990).
Vickery, Amanda (ed.), *Women, Privilege and Power: British Politics, 1750 to the Present* (Stanford: Stanford University Press, 2001).

'Providing an opportunity to exercise their energies': the role of the Labour Women's Sections in shaping political identities, South Wales, 1918–1939

Andrews, Elizabeth, *A Woman's Work Is Never Done* (Ystrad Rhondda: Cymric Democrat Publishing Society, 1951).
Beddoe, Deirdre, *Out of the Shadows: A History of Women in Twentieth-Century Wales* (Cardiff: University of Wales Press, 2000).
Cowman, Krista, '"Giving them something to do": how the early ILP appealed to women', in Margaret Walsh (ed.), *Working Out Gender: Perspectives from Labour History* (Aldershot: Ashgate, 1999), pp. 119–34.
Evans, Neil and Dot Jones, '"To help forward the great work of humanity": women in the

Labour Party in Wales', in Duncan Tanner, Chris Williams and Deian Hopkin (eds), *The Labour Party in Wales 1900–2000* (Cardiff: University of Wales Press, 2000), pp. 215–40.

Graves, Pamela, *Labour Women: Women in British Working-Class Politics, 1918–1939* (Cambridge University Press, 1994).

Hannam, June and Karen Hunt, *Socialist Women Britain, 1880s to 1920s* (London: Routledge, 2002).

Marriott, John, *The Culture of Labourism: The East End between the Wars* (Edinburgh: Edinburgh University Press, 1991).

Masson, Ursula, 'Florence Rose Davies, ILP, County Councillor, c. 1875–1959', in Keith Gildart, David Howell and Neville Kirk (eds), *Dictionary of Labour Biography Volume XI* (Basingstoke: Palgrave Macmillan 2003).

Masson, Ursula and Lowri Newman, 'Elizabeth Andrews', in Keith Gildart, David Howell and Neville Kirk (eds), *Dictionary of Labour Biography: Volume XI* (Basingstoke: Palgrave MacMillan, 2003), pp. 1–11.

Newman, Lowri, 'A distinctive brand of politics: women in the South Wales Labour Party, 1918–1939' (Unpublished MPhil. thesis, University of Glamorgan, 2003).

Pugh, Martin, *Women and the Women's Movement in Britain 1914–1959* (London: Macmillan, 1992).

Williams, Chris, *Capitalism, Community and Conflict: The South Wales Coalfield, 1898–1947* (Cardiff: University of Wales Press, 1998).

Count up to twenty-one: Scottish women in formal politics, 1918–1990

Woman's Claim of Right Group (eds), *A Woman's Claim of Right in Scotland: Women, Representation and Politics* (Edinburgh: Polygon, 1991).

Burness, Catriona, 'Drunk women don't look at thistles: women and the SNP, 1934–94', in *Scotlands*, 1, (2), (1995), pp.131–54.

Burness, Catriona, 'The long slow march: Scottish women MPs', in Esther Breitenbach and Eleanor Gordon (eds), *Out of Bounds: Women in Scottish Society, 1800–1945* (Edinburgh: Edinburgh University Press, 1992), pp. 151–73.

Hetherington, Sheila, *Katharine Atholl, 1874–1960: Against the Tide* (Aberdeen: Aberdeen University Press, 1989).

Lee, Jennie, *My Life with Nye* (Harmondsworth: Penguin, 1981).

Mann, Jean, *Woman in Parliament* (London: Odham, 1962).

Simpson, Emma, '"Mainly manly": the Scottish Constitutional Convention and the implications for women's representation' (Edinburgh University Politics Honours dissertation 1990).

Scottish Constitutional Convention, *Towards Scotland's Parliament, Consultation Document and Report to the Scottish People, Oct 1989* (Edinburgh: Scottish Constitutional Convention, 1989).

Scottish women's organizations and the exercise of citizenship c. 1900–c. 1970

Arnot, Julie, 'Women workers and trade union participation in Scotland 1919–1939' (Unpublished PhD thesis, University of Glasgow, 1999).

Baxter, Kenneth, 'Estimable and gifted'?: women in party politics in Scotland c. 1918–1955' (Unpublished PhD thesis, University of Dundee, 2008).

Ewan, Elizabeth, Sue Innes, Sian Reynolds and Rose Pipes (eds), *The Biographical Dictionary of Scottish Women* (Edinburgh: Edinburgh University Press, 2006).

Gordon, Eleanor, *Women and the Labour Movement in Scotland 1850–1914* (Oxford: Clarendon, 1991).

Hughes, Annmarie, 'Fragmented feminists? The influence of class and political identity in relations between the Glasgow and West of Scotland Suffrage Society and the Independent Labour Party in the west of Scotland, c. 1919–1932', in *Women's History Review*, 14, (1), (2005), pp. 7–31.

Innes, Sue, 'Constructing women's citizenship in the inter-war period: the Edinburgh Women Citizens' Association', in *Women's History Review*, 13, (4), (2004), pp. 621–47.

Innes, Sue and Jane Rendall, 'Women, gender and politics', in Lynn Abrams, Eleanor Gordon, Deborah Simonton and Eileen Janes Yeo (eds), *Gender in Scottish History since 1700* (Edinburgh: Edinburgh University Press, 2006), pp. 43–83.

King, Elspeth, 'The Scottish Women's Suffrage Movement', in Esther Breitenbach and Eleanor Gordon (eds), *Out of Bounds: Women in Scottish Society 1800–1945* (Edinburgh: Edinburgh University Press, 1992), pp. 121–50.

Leneman, Leah, *A Guid Cause: The Women's Suffrage Movement in Scotland* (Aberdeen: Aberdeen University Press, 1991).

Macdonald, Lesley Orr, *A Unique and Glorious Mission: Women and Presbyterianism in Scotland 1830–1930* (Edinburgh: John Donald, 2000).

McDermid, Jane, 'School board women and active citizenship in Scotland, 1873–1919', in *History of Education*, 38, (3), (2009), pp. 333–48.

Rafeek, Neil, *Communist Women in Scotland* (London: Tauris, 2008).

Smitley, Megan, '"Woman's mission": the temperance and women's suffrage movements in Scotland, c. 1870–1914' (Unpublished PhD thesis, University of Glasgow, 2005).

Smyth, J. J., *Labour in Glasgow 1896–1936: Socialism, Suffrage and Sectarianism* (East Linton: Tuckwell, 2000).

Smyth, James J., 'Rents, peace, votes: working-class women and political activity in the First World War', in Esther Breitenbach and Eleanor Gordon (eds), *Out of Bounds: Women in Scottish Society 1800–1945* (Edinburgh: Edinburgh University Press, 1992), pp. 174–96.

Wright, Valerie, 'Education for active citizenship: women's Organisations in interwar Scotland', in *History of Education*, 38, (3), (2009), pp. 419–36.

The 'women element in politics': Irish women and the vote, 1918–2008

Bourke, Angela, Siobhan Kilfeather, Maria Luddy, Margaret MacCurtain, Gerardine Meaney, Mairin Ni Dhonnchadha, Mary O'Dowd and Clair Wills (eds), *The Field Day Anthology of Irish Writing, Vol. 5: Irish Women's Writing and Traditions* (Cork: Cork University Press, 2002).

Claffey, Una, *The Women Who Won* (Dublin: Attic Press, 1993).

Commission on the Status of Women (Dublin, 1972), Prl. 2760.

Connolly, Linda, *The Irish Women's Liberation Movement: From Revolution to Devolution* (Cork: Cork University Press, 2002).

Cullen, Mary and Maria Luddy (eds), *Female Activists. Irish Women and Change 1900–1960* (Dublin: Woodfield, 2001).

Cullen Owens, Rosemary, *A Social History of Women in Ireland 1870–1970* (Dublin: Gill & Macmillan, 2005).

Galligan, Yvonne, Eilis Ward and Rick Wilford (eds), *Contesting Politics* (Boulder, CO/Oxford: Westview/Political Studies Association of Ireland, 1999).

Hill, Myrtle, *Women in Ireland: A Century of Change* (Belfast: Blackstaff, 2003).

Knirck, Jason, *Women of the Dáil: Gender, Republicanism and the Anglo-Irish Treaty* (Dublin; Portland: Irish Academic Press, 2006).

MacCurtain, Margaret and Donncha Ó Corráin (eds), *Women in Irish Society: The Historical Dimension* (Dublin: Arlen House, 1979).

McNamara, Maedbh and Paschal Mooney, *Women in Parliament: Ireland: 1918–2000* (Dublin: Wolfhound, 2000).

Murphy, Cliona, *The Women's Suffrage Movement and Irish Society in the Early Twentieth Century* (London and New York: Harvester Wheatsheaf, 1989).

National Women's Council of Ireland, *Irish Politics: Jobs for the Boys* (Dublin 2002).

Second Commission on the Status of Women (Dublin, 1991), PL 9557.

Ward, Margaret, *Unmanageable Revolutionaries: Women and Irish Nationalism* (London: Pluto Press, 1983).

'Aphrodite rising from the Waves'? Women's voluntary activism and the women's movement in twentieth-century Ireland

Beaumont, Catriona, 'Women and the politics of equality: the Irish women's movement, 1930–1943', in Mary O'Dowd and Maryann Valiulis (eds), *Women in Irish History* (Dublin: Wolfhound, 1997), pp. 185–205.

Bourke, Angela, Siobhan Kilfeather, Maria Luddy, Margaret MacCurtain, Gerardine Meaney, Mairin Ni Dhonnchadha, Mary O'Dowd and Clair Wills (eds), *The Field Day Anthology of Irish Writing, Vol. 5: Irish Women Writing and Traditions* (Cork: Cork University Press, 2002).

Clear, Caitriona, *Nuns in Nineteenth-Century Ireland* (Dublin: Gill and Macmillan, 1987).

Connolly, Linda, *The Irish Women's Movement: From Revolution to Devolution* (Dublin: Lilliput, 2003).

Coulter, Carol, *The Hidden Tradition: Feminism, Women and Nationalism in Ireland* (Cork: Mercier Press, 1993).

Cullen Owens, Rosemary, *Smashing Times: A History of the Irish Women's Suffrage Movement 1889–1922* (Dublin: Attic Press, 1995).

Daly, Mary E., 'Women in the Irish Free State, 1922–1939: the interaction between economics and ideology', in Joan Hoff and Maureen Coulter (eds), *Irish Women's Voices Past and Present* (Indiana: Indiana University Press, 1995), pp. 99–116.

Earner-Byrne, Lindsey, 'Reinforcing the family: the role of gender, morality, and sexuality in Irish welfare policy, 1922–1944', *The History of the Family*, 13, (4), (2008), pp. 360–9.

Ferriter, Diarmaid, *Mothers, Maidens and Myths: A History of the Irish Countrywomen's Association* (Dublin: ICA, 1994).

Kennedy, Finola, *Cottage to Crèche: Family Change in Ireland* (Dublin: Institute of Public Administration, 2001).

Murphy, Cliona, *The Women's Suffrage Movement and Irish Society in the Early Twentieth Century* (Philadelphia: Temple University Press, 1989).

Smyth, Ailbhe, 'The contemporary women's movement', in *Women's Studies International Forum*, Special Issue on Feminism in Ireland, 11, (4), pp. 331–41.

Stopper, Anne, *Mondays at Gaj's: The Story of the Irish Women's Liberation Movement* (Dublin: The Liffey Press, 2006).

Tweedy, Hilda, *A Link in the Chain: The Story of the Irish Housewives Association 1942–1992* (Dublin: Attic Press, 1992).

Ward, Margaret, *Unmanageable Revolutionaries: Women and Irish Nationalism* (London: Pluto Press, 1983).

Conflicting rights: the struggle for female citizenship in Northern Ireland

Brown, Alice, Tahnya Barnett Donaghy, Fiona Mackay and Elizabeth Meehan, 'Women and constitutional change in Scotland and Northern Ireland', *Parliamentary Affairs*, 55, (2002), pp. 71–84.

Callaghan, Marie Hammond, 'Surveying politics of peace, gender, conflict and identity in Northern Ireland: the case of the Derry Peace Women in 1972', *Women's Studies International Forum*, 25, (2002), pp. 33–49.

Connolly, Linda, *The Irish Women's Movement from Revolution to Devolution* (Hampshire and New York: Palgrave, 2002).

Edgerton, Lynda, 'Public protest, domestic acquiescence: women in Northern Ireland', in Rosemary Ridd and Helen Calloway (eds), *Caught up in Conflict: Women's Responses to Political Strife* (London: Palgrave MacMillan, 1986), pp. 61–79.

Evason, Eileen, *Against the Grain: The Contemporary Women's Movement in Northern Ireland* (Dublin: Attic Press, 1991).

Fearon, Kate, *Women's Work: The Story of the Northern Ireland Women's Coalition* (Belfast: Blackstaff Press, 1999).

Galligan, Yvonne, Eilis Ward and Rick Wilford (eds), *Contesting Politics: Women in Ireland, North and South* (Colorado and Oxford: Westview Press, 1999).

Hill, Myrtle, 'Ulster: debates, demands and divisions: the battle for (and against) the vote', in Louise Ryan and Margaret Ward (eds), *Irish Women and the Vote: Becoming Citizens* (Dublin: Irish Academic Press, 2007), pp. 209–30.

Hill, Myrtle, 'Lessons and legacies': feminist activism in the North c. 1970–2000', *Women's Studies Review*, 9, (2004), pp. 135–50.

Hill, Myrtle, *Women in Ireland: A Century of Change* (Belfast: Blackstaff Press, 2003).

Hinds, Bronagh and Anne Marie Gray, *Women and the Review of Public Administration* (Belfast: The Review of Public Administration in Northern Ireland, 2005).

Kinghan, Nancy, *United We Stood: The Official History of the Ulster Women's Unionist Council 1911–1974* (Belfast: Appletree Press, 1975).

McAliskey, Bernadette (Devlin), 'A peasant in the halls of the great', in Michael Farrell (ed.), *Twenty Years On* (Dingle: Brandon, 1988), pp. 75–88.

McNamara, Maedbh and Paschal Mooney, *Women in Parliament: Ireland 1918–2000* (Dublin: Wolfhound Press, 2000).

McWilliams, Monica, 'Struggling for peace and justice: reflections on women's activism in Northern Ireland', *Journal of Women's History*, 6, (4), (1995), pp. 13–39.

McWilliams, Monica, 'Women and political activism in Northern Ireland 1960–93', in Bourke *et al.* (eds), *The Field Day Anthology of Irish Writing, Volume 5: Irish Women's Writing and Traditions* (Cork: Cork University Press, 2002), pp. 374–77.

McWilliams, Monica and Avila Kilmurray, 'Athene on the loose: the origins of the Northern Ireland Women's Coalition', *Irish Journal of Feminist Studies*, 2, (1), (1997), pp. 1–21.

Miller, Robert Lee, Rick Wilford and Freda Donoghue, *Women and Political Participation in Northern Ireland* (Aldershot, Brookfield, USA, Hong Kong, Singapore, Sydney: Avebury, 1996).

Morgan, Valerie and Grace Fraser, 'Women and the Northern Ireland conflict: experiences and responses', in Seamus Dunn (ed.), *Facets of the Conflict in Northern Ireland* (London: MacMillan Press, 1995), pp. 81–96.

Roulston, Carmel, 'Gender, nation, class: the politics of difference in Northern Ireland', *Scottish Affairs*, 18, (1997), pp. 54–67.

Shannon, Catherine, 'Women in Northern Ireland', in Mary O'Dowd and Sabine Wichert (eds), *Chattel, Servant or Citizen: Women's Status in Church, State and Society* (Belfast: Institute of Irish Studies, 1995), pp. 238–53.

Shepard, Christopher, 'Women activists and women's associations in Ireland, 1945–68' (Unpublished PhD thesis, Queens University Belfast, 2007).

Urquhart, Diane, *Women in Ulster Politics 1890–1940* (Dublin: Irish Academic Press, 2000).

Ward, Margaret, '"Ulster was different?" Women, feminism and nationalism in the North of Ireland', in Galligan *et al.* (eds), *Contesting Politics*, pp. 219–39.

Ward, Margaret, 'Gender, citizenship and the future of the Northern Ireland Peace Process', *Eire/Ireland*, 40, (3&4), (2005), pp. 262–83.

Ward, Rachel, *Women, Unionism and Loyalism in Northern Ireland: From 'Tea-Makers' to Political Actors* (Dublin: Irish Academic Press, 2006).

Wilford, Rick, Robert Miller, Yolanda Bell and Freda Donoghue, 'In their own voices: women councillors in Northern Ireland', *Public Administration*, 71, (1993), pp. 341–55.

'*Apathetic, parochial, conservative*'? Women, élite and mass politics from 1979 to 2009

Campbell, Beatrix, *The Iron Ladies: Why Do Women Vote Tory?* (London: Virago Press, 1987).

Campbell, Rosie, *Gender and the Vote in Britain* (Colchester: ECPR Press, 2006).

Campbell, Rosie, Sarah Childs and Joni Lovenduski, 'Do women need women MPs', *British Journal of Political Science* (forthcoming).

Campbell, Rosie, 'Women's equality guarantees and the Conservative Party', *Political Quarterly*, 77, (1), (2006), pp. 18–27.

Childs, Sarah, *Women and British Party Politics: Descriptive, Substantive and Symbolic Representation* (London: Routledge, 2008).

Childs, Sarah, Joni Lovenduski and Rosie Campbell, *Women at the Top* (London: Hansard, 2005).

Evans, Elizabeth, *Women's Representation and the Liberal Democrats* (London: University of London, 2009).

Hayes, Bernadette, 'Gender, feminism and electoral behaviour in Britain', *Electoral Studies*, 16, (2), (1997), pp. 203–16.

Inglehart, Ronald and Pippa Norris, 'The developmental theory of the gender gap: women and men's voting behaviour in global perspective', *International Political Science Review*, 21, (4), (2000), pp. 441–62.

Lovenduski, Joni, *Feminizing Politics* (Cambridge: Polity Press, 2005).

Maguire, G. E., *Conservative Women: A History of Women and the Conservative Party, 1874–1997* (London: Palgrave Macmillan, 1998).

Norris, Pippa, 'Gender: a gender-generation gap?', in Geoffrey Evans and Pippa Norris (eds), *Critical Elections: British Parties and Voters in Long-Term Perspective* (London: Sage, 1999), pp.146–63.

Norris, Pippa, Joni Lovenduski and Rosie Campbell, *Gender and Political Participation* (The Electoral Commission, 2004).

Phillips, Anne, *The Politics of Presence* (Oxford University Press, 1995).

Pugh, Martin, *Women and the Women's Movement in Britain*, 2nd edn (London: Macmillan, 2002).

Shepherd-Robinson, Laura and Joni Lovenduski, *Women and Candidate Selection in British Political Parties* (London: Fawcett, 2002).

Feminist politics in Scotland from the 1970s to 2000s: engaging with the changing state

Breitenbach, Esther, '"Sisters are doing it for themselves": the women's movement in Scotland', in Alice Brown and Richard Parry (eds), *The Scottish Government Yearbook* (Edinburgh: Unit for the Study of Government, University of Edinburgh, 1990), pp. 209–25.

Breitenbach, Esther and Fiona Mackay (eds), *Women and Contemporary Scottish Politics: An Anthology* (Edinburgh: Polygon, 2001).

Henderson, Shirley and Alison Mackay (eds), *Grit and Diamonds* (Edinburgh: Stramullion, 1990).

Lieberman, Sue, 'Women's committees in Scotland', in Alice Brown and Dave McCrone (eds), *The Scottish Government Yearbook* (Edinburgh: Unit for the Study of Government, University of Edinburgh, 1989), pp. 246–65.

Mackay, Fiona, 'Gendering constitutional change and policy outcomes: substantive representation and domestic violence policy in Scotland', *Policy and Politics* (forthcoming).

Mackay, Fiona, Meryl Kenny and Elena Pollot-Thompson, *Access, Voice . . . and Influence? Women's Organisations in Post-devolution Scotland* (GRADUS Case Study 2. Report for Engender/GRADUS Partnership, 2005).

Women and political representation in post-devolution Scotland: high time or high tide?

Bradbury, Jonathan, David Denver, James Mitchell and Lynn Bennie, 'Devolution and party change: candidate selection for the 1999 Scottish Parliament and Welsh Assembly elections', *Journal of Legislative Studies*, 6 (3), (2000), pp. 51–72.

Breitenbach, Esther and Fiona Mackay (eds), *Women and Contemporary Scottish Politics: An Anthology* (Edinburgh: Polygon, 2001).

Mackay, Fiona, 'Women and the 2003 elections: keeping up the momentum', *Scottish Affairs*, 44, (2003), pp. 74–90.

Mackay, Fiona and Meryl Kenny, 'Women's representation in the 2007 Scottish Parliament: temporary setback or return to the norm?', *Scottish Affairs*, 60, (2007), pp. 25–38.

Russell, Meg, Fiona Mackay and Laura McAllister (2002), 'Women's representation in the Scottish Parliament and National Assembly for Wales: party dynamics for achieving critical mass', *Journal of Legislative Studies*, 8 (2), (2002), pp. 49–76.

Devolution, citizenship and women's political representation in Wales

Chaney, Paul, 'Devolved governance and the substantive representation of women: the second term of the National Assembly for Wales, 2003–07', *Parliamentary Affairs*, 61, (2), (2008), pp. 234–61.

Chaney, Paul, 'Women and constitutional change in Wales', *Regional and Federal Studies*, 14, (2), (2004), pp. 1–23.

Chaney, Paul, Fiona Mackay and Laura McAllister, *Women, Politics and Constitutional Change* (Cardiff: University of Wales Press, 2007).

Edwards, Julia and Christine Chapman, 'Women's political representation in Wales: waving or drowning?', *Contemporary Politics*, 6, (4), (2000), pp. 367–81.

Equal Opportunities Commission, *The Gender Agenda* (Cardiff: Equal Opportunities Commission Wales, 2006).

Rai, Shirin, *Mainstreaming Gender, Democratizing the State? National Machineries for the Advancement of Women* (Manchester: Manchester University Press, 2003).

Squires, Judith, 'The new equalities agenda: recognising diversity and securing equality in post-devolution Britain', in Alexandra Dobrowolsky and Vivien Hart (eds), *Women Making Constitutions: New Politics and Comparative Perspectives* (London: Palgrave, 2003), pp. 200–13.

The refuge movement and domestic violence policies in Wales

Aaron, Jane, Teresa Rees, Sandra Betts and Moira Vincentelli (eds), *Our Sisters' Land* (Cardiff: University of Wales Press, 1994).

Ball, Wendy and Nickie Charles, 'Feminist social movements and policy change: devolution, childcare and domestic violence policies in Wales', in *Women's Studies International Forum*, 29, (2006), pp. 172–83.

Chaney, Paul, Fiona Mackay and Larua McAllister (eds), *Women, Politics and Constitutional Change: The First Years of the National Assembly for Wales* (Cardiff: University of Wales Press, 2007).

Charles, Nickie, *Feminism, the State and Social Policy* (Basingstoke: Palgrave Macmillan, 2000).

Charles, Nickie 'Feminist politics and devolution', in *Social Politics*, 11, (2), (2004), pp. 297–311.

Charles, Nickie and Charlotte Davies (eds), *Gender and Social Justice in Wales* (Cardiff: University of Wales Press, forthcoming).

Hearn, Jeff and Linda McKie, 'Gendered policy and policy on gender: the case of "domestic violence"', in *Policy and Politics*, 36, (1), (2008), pp. 75–91.

Lovenduski, Joni, *Feminizing Politics* (Cambridge: Policy Press, 2005).

Mazur, Amy and Dorothy McBride Stetson, 'State feminism', in Gary Goertz and Amy Mazur (eds), *Politics, Gender and Concepts: Theory and Methodology* (Cambridge University Press, 2008), pp. 244–69.

Walby, Sylvia, *The Cost of Domestic Violence* (London: Women and Equality Unit, Department of Trade and Industry, 2004).

Index

Aaron, Jane 29, 41
Abercorn, Duchess of 114
Aberdeen 154
    women on council 66
Abertillery, Labour Party Women's
    Section 31
Aberystwyth 211
abortion 5, 6, 7, 24, 102
Abortion Act 1967 8, 124, 155
Abortion Law Reform Association
    24
Action, Information, Motivation
    (AIM) 106
Ad Hoc Committee on the Status
    of Women in Ireland 104
Additional Member System
    (AMS) 172, 173
Adoption Act 1926 21
age of consent 20
    in Ireland 98, 109n. 38
Ahmad, Bashir 187n. 33
Alderton, Mrs 48
Alexander, Mrs 103
all women shortlists 4, 58, 139,
    140, 141, 143, 145, 148, 149, 173,
    182, 192, 194, 205
Alliance Party 127, 129
Anderson, Elizabeth 70
Andrews, Elizabeth 30, 31, 32, 33,
    35, 36, 38, 40
Anglo-Irish Treaty 81
Anglo-Irish War 81
anti-slavery movement 12
Antrim 117
Arbroath Women Citizens'
    Association 68
Armagh 117
    county 124
    women's prison 121, 122
Arnot, Julie 72
Asquith, H.H. Prime Minister 80
Astor, Nancy 51
Atholl, Katharine, Duchess of 51,
    53, 59, 65

Bain, Margaret 45, 53, 56
    see also Ewing
Balfour, Frances 69
Band of Hope 69
Barnes, Monica 88

Basque children 38
Bastardy Act 1923 21
Battle of the Bogside 122
Baxter, Kenneth 65, 67
Baxter, Lady 49
Beijing, UN Women's Conference
    127
    see also United Nations
Belfast 118, 124
    University Constituency 116
    City Council 115
    Corporation 117
Belfast Women's Advisory Council
    118
Belfast Women's Citizens'
    Association 5
Belfast Women's Citizens' Union
    118
Belfast Women's Collective 123
Bevan, Aneurin (Nye) 53
Bingham, Adrian 16
Bill of Rights for Northern Ireland
    133
Billington-Greig, Theresa 64
Birrell, Derek 126
birth control 24, 71
    see also contraception
black and minority ethnic
    women's groups in Scotland
    157, 163
Blaenau Gwent 183, 187n. 40
Blair, Catherine 68
Blaney, Niall 86
Blood, May 129
Bloody Sunday, 1972 4, 122
Bondfield, Margaret 51
British army 120
British Federation of Business and
    Professional Women 24, 68
British Federation of University
    Women 24
British Women's Temperance
    Association Scottish Christian
    Union (SCU) 69, 72
Brown, Alice et al. 133
Browne, Noel 85
Browne, Sarah 68
Brun, Bairbre de 131, 132
Buckland, Patrick 122
Burgess, Isabella 66

Business and Professional
    Women's Association, Dundee
    74

Cambridge City Council 17
Caernarvonshire 30
Callen, K. M. 73
Calvert, Lilian 116
Cameron, Catriona 49
Cameron, David 142, 143, 144,
    181, 187n. 39
Campaign for a Scottish Assembly
    57, 58
Campaign for a Welsh Assembly
    191
    see also Parliament for Wales
    Campaign
Campaign on Social Justice (CSJ)
    119
Campbell, Elma 49
Cardiff 30, 211
Cardiff Women's Aid 209
Catholic
    Church 53
    communities (in Northern
        Ireland) 3
    Emancipation 8
    hierarchy and Irish
        Countrywomen's
        Association (ICA) 101
    ideology 3, 6
    women and social activism
        99
Catholic Social Service
    Conference 100
Catholic Women's Suffrage Society
    20
Catholicism in Ireland 79
Catholics, discrimination against
    119
Cazalet-Keir, Thelma 23
Central Distress Committee,
    Wales 1926 34
cervical screening 74
Chandler, David 190
Chamberlain, Neville 21
charabanc outings 39, 40
Chichester, Dehra 115
    see also Parker, Dehra
Children's Allowance, Ireland 98

Church of Scotland
  admission of women to
  eldership 70
  ordination of first woman
  minister 70
Church of Scotland Deaconess
  Hospital 70
Church of Scotland Woman's Guild
  63, 70, 73, 163
Churchill, Winston 23, 52
Civic Forum 160
civil rights movement (Northern
  Ireland) 119
Citizens Action Committee 120
Citizens Defence Association 120
Claim of Right for Scotland 57
Clann na Poblachta 84, 85
Clar na mBan (Women's Agenda)
  127, 128
Clarke, Kathleen 82, 84
Clear, Catriona 99
Clinton, Hillary 128
Clydebank 66
  rent strike 71
Coatbridge 50, 54
Collins, Michael 82
Commission on the Status of
  Women, Ireland 4, 85–6, 87,
  102, 104
    Second Commission on Status
    of Women 90, 91
Committee on Sexual Offences
  against Children and Young
  Persons in Scotland, 1924–5 69
Communist Party 3, 71, 73, 119
Community Safety Partnerships
  214, 215
Concannnon, Helen 84
Conditions of Employment Act
  1935 84, 98, 108n. 25
Connolly, Linda 87, 97, 102
Conservatism and women 2
Conservative and Unionist
  Women's Franchise Association
  12
Conservative government 11, 156
Conservative Party, 16, 25, 47, 57,
  65, 139, 140, 143, 144, 148, 150,
  159, 212
  see also Unionists
  Scottish Conservatives, 173, 174,
  175, 176, 178, 179, 180, 181
  values 13
  Welsh Conservatives 193,
  194, 198
  women members 15
  women MPs from Scotland 45
  Women's Advisory Committee
  15

Women's Sections 142
Women's National Advisory
  Committee (WNAC) 142
Conservative Women's
  Organisation (CWO) 142, 143
Conservative Women's Reform
  Association 20
constitution
  of Ireland, 1922 81
  of Ireland, 1937 6, 84, 98
Constitutional Convention,
  Northern Ireland 126
Constitutional Convention,
  Scottish 57, 58
  see also Scottish Constitutional
  Convention
contraception 5, 6, 7, 98, 102, 104
  prohibition of in Ireland 98
Contraceptive Action Campaign
  106
Contraceptive Train 105
Cook, Robin 156
Co-operative Women's Guild 5, 63
Corish, Brendan 85
Costello, Eileen 82
Coughlan, Mary 92n. 2
Council for the Status of Women,
  Ireland 86, 88, 102, 128
Council of Women Civil Servants
  18
councillors, local
  see also local government
  women as percentage of in
  England 141
County Tyrone 119
'Coupon Election' 1918, 29
Cowan, Minna 65
Cowman, Krista 37
Crime and Disorder Act 1998 214
Criminal Justice (Sexual Offences)
  Act 1993 88
Criminal Law Amendment Act
  1922 20
  see also age of consent
Cumann na nGaedheal 82
Cumann na mBan 81, 96, 115, 121
Cumann na Saoirse (the League of
  Freedom) 82, 93n. 22
Curran, Margaret 163

Dáil (Éireann) 3, 4, 7, 79, 81, 82,
  84, 85, 87, 88, 89, 90, 92, 98
Daily Mail 16
Davies, Rose 34, 35, 36, 37
Davis, Margaret 32
Davison, Mary (Molly) 85
Delap, Kathleen 101, 109n. 53
DemocraShe 127
'democratic deficit' 159

Democratic Dialogue 125
Democratic Party, US 80
Democratic Unionist Party (DUP)
  126, 129, 132
Denton, Baroness Jean 128
Derry 117, 120
Derry Women's Aid 121
Devlin, Bernadette 4, 116, 120,
  121–2,135n. 42
  see also McAliskey, Bernadette
Devlin, Joseph 115
Dickson, Anne Letitia 116, 136n.
  63
Direct Rule (of Northern Ireland
  from Westminster) 116, 122,
  125, 126
divorce 6, 21, 23, 98, 102
  law reform 4, 7, 8, 19, 22, 24
Dodds, Diane 132
Dollar 66
domestic violence policy 164, 185,
  209, 212, 213, 214
Domestic Violence, Crimes and
  Victims Act 2004 214
Dominion status (for Ireland) 81
Down 117
Dublin Trades Union Council 84
Dublin Women's Suffrage
  Association (DWSA) 80, 97
Dunbarton East 45, 56
Dundee 154
  election of Prohibition Party
  MP 69
  women on council 66
Dundee Women Citizens'
  Association (DWCA) 68
Dungannon 119

Eagle, Maria 185n. 1
Edinburgh 154, 155
  National Vigilance Association
  Edinburgh and East of
  Scotland Branch 69
  South constituency 48
  to London march 64
  women on council 66
Edinburgh Association for
  Promoting Lady Candidates
  at School Board and Parochial
  Elections 65
Edinburgh District Council 154
  see also Zero Tolerance
  Campaign
Edinburgh National Society for
  Women's Suffrage 63
Edinburgh Parish Council 66
Edinburgh School Board 65
Edinburgh Women Citizens'
  Association (EWCA) 67, 68, 69

Education Act 1944 23
education authorities
    Scotland 65, 67
    Perthshire 65
education boards 11
education committees, Scotland 65
Education (Scotland) Act 1872 65
Electoral Agreement 173, 174
Electoral Commission report on
    gender and political participation
    147, 148
emigration, female 103
Emily's List 174
End Violence Against Women
    (EVAW) 85, 220, 221
enfranchisement of women 1, 2, 12
    full, Ireland 1922, 8
    full, UK 1928 8
    partial 1918 5
Engender 159, 162, 163
Equal Opportunities Commission
    (EOC) 24, 142, 145, 151 fn 26,
    162, 163, 191
        Northern Ireland 123, 128
equal pay 5, 19, 22, 23, 24, 51,72,
    73, 85
Equal Pay Act 1970 24
equal rights of guardianship of
    children 19, 21
Equalities Declaration 198
Equality and Human Rights
    Commission (EHRC) 185, 203,
    217, 218
Equality Bill 145
Equality Commission for Northern
    Ireland 131
equality duty, Wales 191, 195, 200
    see also 'absolute duty', 215.
equality guarantees 4, 172, 180
equality mainstreaming 190, 198,
    200, 201, 205
        review by Welsh Assembly
            Equality Committee 201
Ervine, David 132
European Social Survey, 2002 147
European Women's Lobby (EWL)
    128
Evans, Elizabeth 141
Evans, Neil and Dot Jones 30,
    33, 39
Ewing, Winnie 53, 55, 56
Ewing, Margaret 53, 55
    see also Bain, Margaret

Fabian Society, Women's Group
    20, 24
Falls Road Women's Centre 124
family allowances 21
Fawcett, Millicent Garrett 19, 20

Fawcett Society 7, 23, 24, 59
Fearon, Kate 125
Feld, Val 191
female circumcision in Kenya 51
Fennell, Nuala 88
Ferriter, Donald 101, 104
Fianna Fáil 82, 85, 87, 88, 89
Fine Gael 82, 83, 85, 87, 88
Fitzgerald, Eithne 91
Fitzgerald, Garrett 87, 88
Foreign and Commonwealth
    Office 133
Ford, Patricia 116
Forrest, Miss 80
Forum for Peace and
    Reconciliation 128
Forum for Political Dialogue 128
Fox, Mildred 90
'frame disputes' 221–3
franchise, campaigns for extension
    of in 1920s 22
Fraser, Helen 48
Fraser, Jean S. 49
Free Trade Movement 12
Freeman, Peter 38
Fyfe, Maria 55, 58

Gaelic Athletic Association 90
Galligan and Wilford 79
Gardiner, Frances 89
gender equality duty legislation
    163, 217, 218, 219
gender equality
    analysis of party manifestos,
        Wales (table) 197–7
    mainstreaming 163, 164
gender generation gap in voting 149
General and Municipal Workers'
    Union 72
Geoghegan-Quinn, Maire 88
Gibbons, Brian 219
Glasgow 47, 48, 49, 154, 155
    Govan 56
    Maryhill 57
    National Vigilance Association
        Branch 69
    rent strike 1915 71
    St Rollox 50
    Springburn 53, 54
    women on council 66
Glasgow and West of Scotland
    Association for Women's Suffrage
    64, 65
Glasgow Association for
    Promoting Lady Candidates
    at School Board and Parochial
    Elections 65
Glasgow Society for Equal
    Citizenship (GSEC) 68, 69

Glasgow Trades Council 72
Glasgow Women's Housing
    Association 71
Glen-Coats, Lady 48
Good Friday Agreement 1998 4, 6,
    129, 130, 131, 132
Goschen formula 59n. 1
Government Equalities Office 218
Government of Ireland Act 1920
    114
Government of Wales Act 1998
    191, 195, 201
Government of Wales Act 2006
    191, 203
Grant of Monymusk, Lady 53
    see also Tweedsmuir
Gray, Anne Marie 132
Greater London Council 158
Green, Beatrice 31
Green Party 57, 159, 175, 176, 179,
    180, 181
Greene, Sheila 85
Greenock 66
Gregory, Sir William 80
Griffiths, Jim 30
Guardianship of Infants Act 1925
    98

Hague, William 151n. 19
    reforms in Conservative party
    143
Hamilton Advertiser 55
Hamilton by-election 55
Hanham, Harry 55
Hardie, Agnes 50, 53, 54
Harkin, Cathy 121
Harkin, Marion 92
Harman, Harriet 146
Harney, Mary 87, 88
Harrison, Brian 52
Hart, Edwina 215
Hart, Judith 53, 57, 58
Hart, Maidie 70
Hart, Mrs 34
Haughey, Charles 86
Hayes, Bernadette 149
Heath, Edward 142
Hemat Gryffe Women's Aid 157
Henry, Mary 130
Herbison, Peggy 53, 59
Hetherington, Sheila 51
Hewitt, Patricia 146
Hinds, Bronagh 132
Hockin, Margaret 103
Hollis, Patricia 16
Home Office 212, 218, 220, 221
Home Rule party, 1880s 80
    question 80, 81, 96
    struggle against 114

Homeless Citizens League 119
homosexuality, law on 8
    legalization of male
        homosexual relationships,
        England and Wales 24
    decriminalization of in Ireland
        88
    liberalization of law in Scotland
        156
Hoppen, K. Theodore 80
Horsbrugh, Florence 59
House of Commons,
    women's representation in 140,
        145–6
    MPs elected to, by sex and
        party (table) 140
Housewives League 23
housing issues 24, 67, 70, 71
housing reform 34, 36–7
    housing and homelessness
        legislation and domestic
        violence 213
Human Rights Bill 116
Husband, Agnes 66
Hussey, Gemma 88
Hutt, Jane 201, 215

Inclusive Policymaking Toolkit
    202, 203
Independent Labour Party
    Scottish 49, 50, 53
India Bill, 1935 52
India Home Rule 51
Industrial Courts Act 1919 20
Infanticide Act 1922 21
Inglis, Elsie 64, 69
Innes, Sue 171
International Alliance of Women
    104
International Council of Women
    68
Inter-Parliamentary Union, league
    table of women's representation
    140
Ireland
    civil war 82
    independence 8, 83
    partition 8
    ranking for proportion of
        women parliamentarians 79
    under-representation of
        women in politics 89
    votes for women in 114
    women's suffrage movement
        in 80–1
Irish Citizen 97
Irish Countrywomen's Association
    (ICA) 6, 98, 100, 101, 102, 103,
    104, 118

Irish Free State 3, 97, 98, 100
Irish Housewives' Association
    (IHA) 5, 6, 84, 97, 102, 104, 118
Irish Local Government Act 1898
    80
Irish Local Government and
    Women's Suffrage Association 80
Irish National Teachers'
    Organisation 84
Irish People 85
Irish Republican Army (IRA) 8, 121
    organizations 90
Irish Times 101
Irish Volunteers (later IRA) 81
Irish Women's Citizen's
    Associations (IWCA) 97, 98
Irish Women's Federation League
    96
Irish Women's Franchise League 80
Irish Women's Social and
    Progressive League 6, 98
Irish Women's Liberation
    Movement 88
Irish Women's Suffrage and Local
    Government Association 5, 96, 97

James, Sian 211
Joint Committee of Women's
    Societies and Social Workers 98
Jones, Dot
    see Evans, Neil
Jones, Helen Mary 201
Juries Act 1927, Ireland 98, 108n.
    24
juries, women on 20
Justices of the Peace 34

Kilmarnock 65
Kilmurray, Avila 128
King, Elspeth 65
Kingston, Lucy 95, 98, 107n. 3
Kinning Park Co-operative Society
    71

Labour Party 3, 12, 16, 20, 24, 29,
    35, 47, 50, 58, 65, 66, 70, 71, 73,
    139, 141, 143, 144–5, 148, 149,
    150, 154, 158, 172, 183, 212, 214
    activities, involvement of
        children in 38, 39
    constitution and opening of
        membership to women 30
    culture 37
    educating women 31–33
    empowering mothers 31
    in Ireland 82, 85, 89
    relationship of SCWG to 71
    Scottish Labour Party Women's
        Conference 50

Scottish Labour 172, 173, 175,
    176, 178, 179, 180, 181, 182,
    183
Swansea rally and mass
    demonstration 37
Welsh Labour 190, 191, 192,
    193, 195, 219
West Wales Advisory
    Committee 32
women MPs from Scotland 45
Women's Advisory Councils
    32, 33, 35
Women's Conference 14, 35
    women's day and weekend
        schools 32–33
Women's National Executive
    Committee 145
Women's Sections 14, 30
    in Scotland, 50
    in Wales 29, 31, 32, 34, 37,
        38, 40
Labour Woman 32, 34, 37
Ladies' Auxiliary of the Ancient
    Order of Hibernians 115
Ladies Land League 80
Late Late Show, The 105
Laverty, Maura 84
Law of Property Act 1922 21
League of Nations 20
Lee, Jennie 51, 52, 53, 54
Legal and Financial Independence
    Campaign 155
    Edinburgh and Glasgow
        groups 156
legal profession, opening of to
    women 19
Legion of Mary 100, 118
Leith Town Council 66
lesbian feminism 156
Lesbian and Gay Pride marches
    156
Lesbian Line 156
Liberal government, refusal to
    implement women's suffrage 12
Liberal Democrats 57, 139, 140,
    141, 143
    Scottish Liberal Democrats
        173, 174, 175, 176, 178, 179,
        180, 181
    Welsh Liberal Democrats 192,
        193
    Women MPs from Scotland 45
Liberal Federation 48
Liberal Party 14, 16, 29, 30, 47, 64,
    66, 68, 141
    election victories 47
    women's sections 48
    Women's Educational and
        Social Council 48

Liberal Unionism 47
Lindsay, Isobel 59
Lipman, Beatrice 190
Liverpool 14, 17
Living Without Fear 214
Local government 2
  and domestic violence in Wales 216–17
  and women in Scotland 65–7
  curtailment of powers in Northern Ireland 4
  municipal councils: representation of women, 1920–70 (table) 16
  municipal vote 11
  reforms and reorganizations 8
  reorganization, Scotland, 1929 65
  women councillors in Ulster 117
  women councillors in Wales 34
  women's and equal opportunities committees 160
  women's representation 3
Lockhart, Lady 49
Lower Prices Council 84
Lovenduski, Joni 146, 185n. 1
Loyalist Prisoners Committee 121
Luddy, Maria 99, 100, 117
Lynch, Jack 87, 88

McAleese, Mary 89, 92
McAliskey, Bernadette 119
  see also Devlin, Bernadette
Macardle, Dorothy 82
McCafferty, Nell 104, 105, 120
McCluskey, Patricia 119
McConnachie, Catherine 70
McCrystal, Angela 119
McCurley, Anna 53
MacDonald, Mamo 104
MacDonald, Margo 53, 56
Macdonald, Mrs Coll 52
McDowell, Kathleen 84
McGuiness, Catherine 85
McLaughlin, Anne 187n. 33
McLaughlin, Florence 116
McLean, Agnes 72–3, 77n. 76
McLeish, Henry 162
Macmillan, Harold 25
McMordie, Julia 115, 117
McNab, Clarice 66
  see also Clarice McNab Shaw
McNabb, Dinah 116
Maconachie, Elizabeth 116
MacSwiney, Mary 81, 83
MacSwiney, Terence 81
McWilliams, Monica 123, 128, 129, 130, 131

maintenance allowance 20
Magdalene institutions 69
Malcolm, Lavinia 66
Mann, Jean 50, 53, 54
Manning, Maurice 84
Markievicz, Constance, 3, 81, 82, 88, 97
marriage bar 5, 18, 22
married women's rights to property 5
Married Women (Maintenance) Act 1922 98
Marriot, John 37, 38
Masson, Ursula 29, 41
maternal and child welfare 5, 34, 35, 67, 68, 70
Matrimonial Causes Act 1923 21, 98
Matrimonial Proceedings and Property Act 1970 24
May, Theresa 142
Mayhew, Lady Jean,128
Members of the Legislative Assembly (MLAs), Northern Ireland 130
Merioneth 30
Michie, Ray 48
Midwives Act 1902 19
Mill, John Stuart 15
Millar, Ella Morison 66
Miller, Lily 66
Miller, Robert Lee *et al.* 126
Miners' Strike, 1984–5 211
miners, reaction to rejection of nationalization 29
Ministry of Health Welsh Consultative Council 36
missionaries 63
Moloney, Helena 84
Montrose Burghs by-election 49
Moray and Nairn 55
Morrice, Jane 131
Mother Ireland 120
Mothers' Union 100
Mowlam, Mo 130
multi-level governance 166
municipal feminism 154, 157–9
Murnaghan, Sheila 116
Murphy, Irene 132

National Assembly for Wales, 189, 190, 192, 209, 212, 214, 216, 218, 219, 221, 222
  and domestic violence policy 209
  Assembly Government Cabinet 199
  election manifestos 195
  elections, 2003 192

incidence of terms featuring in political debate (table) 199
  Official Record of Assembly plenary debates 198
  Oral Assembly Questions 200
  powers 202
  Standing Committee on Equality of Opportunity 191, 200, 203
  Standing Orders 191
  women candidates and elected AMs: 1999 elections (table) 193
  women candidates and elected AMs: 2003 elections (table) 193
  women candidates and elected AMs: 2007 elections (table) 194
  women's representation in 194, 205
  Written Assembly Questions 200
National Council for the Unmarried Mother and her Child 21
National Council of Women 17, 20
National Council of Women in Ireland 89, 91
National Government 52–3
National Federation of Women Workers (NFWW) 71, 72
National Party of Scotland 49–50
National Strategy on Domestic Abuse 164
National Union of Mineworkers 50
National Union of Societies for Equal Citizenship (NUSEC) 17, 18, 19, 20, 21, 67
National Union of Women Teachers 18
National Union of Women's Suffrage Societies (NUWSS) 17, 64
National Union of Women Workers 17
National Vigilance Association 8, 69
National Women's Aid Federation 209
National Women Citizen's Association 24, 53
National Women's Council (Ireland) 5, 98
National Women's Council of Ireland 128
New English Law of Property 1926 21
Newport 30

Newport Citizen 38
Newport Searchlight 39
Norris, Pippa 148, 149
North Lanark 53
    by-election 52
Northern Ireland
    attitudes to gender roles 7
    elections 1921 114
    elections to Northern Ireland
        Assembly (table) 131
Northern Ireland Assembly 4, 126,
    130, 131, 132, 133
Northern Ireland Civil Rights
    Association (NICRA) 119, 120
Northern Ireland Civil Service,
    marriage bar 120
Northern Ireland Committee
    of the Irish Congress of Trade
    Unions 131
Northern Ireland Federation of
    Women's Institutes 118
Northern Ireland Forum 129
Northern Ireland Office 122
Northern Ireland Voluntary Trust
    128
Northern Ireland Women's
    Coalition (NIWC) 128–30, 131
Northern Ireland Women's
    European Platform (NIWEP)
    127, 128
Northern Ireland Women's Rights
    Movement (NIWRM) 123, 124
Northern Men's Federation for
    Women's Suffrage 6
nuns 99

O'Callaghan, Kathleen 81
O'Callaghan, Margaret 99
O'Carroll, Maureen 84
O'Connell, Daniel 80
O'Driscoll, Margaret Collins 82
Observer 122
OMOV (One Member One Vote)
    145, 151n. 24
Opsahl Commission 125
Orange Lodges 114

Paisley 48
Paisley, Rhonda 126
Pankhurst, Christabel 47
Pankhursts (WSPU) 64
parish councils 67
Parker, Dehra 115
    see also Chichester, Dehra
Parliament for Wales Campaign
    191
    see also Campaign for a Welsh
        Assembly
peace process (Northern Ireland) 6

peace organizations and
    demonstrations 64
Pearse, Margaret 81
Pearse, Patrick 81
pension rights 19, 24
People's Democracy 121
Perth 66
Phillips, Anne 146
Plaid Cymru 190, 192, 193, 195,
    201, 219
policewomen, employment of 22
    attempt to secure introduction
        of in Ireland, 98, 109n. 37
Poor Law Boards 11
    Ireland 80, 83
    Ulster 117
Poor Law Guardians 2
Porter, Elisabeth 128
Preston, Lancashire 14
Primrose League 3, 12, 141
Progressive Unionist Party (PUP)
    132
Prohibition Party 69
prostitution 19, 64, 69, 70
Protection and Harassment Act
    1997 214
Protestant parties, Edinburgh and
    Glasgow 66
Protestant Action 66
Public Safety Act 1927, Ireland 82
Pugh, Martin 98
Purvis, Dawn 132

Queen's University, Belfast 121, 123

Radical Scotland 158
Rafeek, Neil 73
Rape Crisis Centre 106
Rape Crisis Scotland 163
Rathbone, Eleanor 17, 21
Referendums in Ireland, right to
    life of foetus, divorce 89
Reform Act 1884 11
Reform Act 1918 19
refuge movement 209, 211–13,
    215, 216, 218, 219, 222, 223
Relatives Action Committee (RAC)
    121, 127
religion in Irish society 100
religious belief and public life 8
Rent Restriction Act 1915 71
rent strike 71
Representation of the People Act
    1918 64, 95, 97
Representation of the People Act
    1928 115–6
reproductive rights 5, 6
Rhondda, Ton Pentre 30
Rice, Bridget 84

Rice, Margery Spring 68
rising, Ireland 1916 81
Robinson, Mary 85, 86, 89, 92,
    128
Roche, Adi 92
Rogers, Brid 131
Romford, Essex 30
Rosemary-Scallon, Dana 92
Rothermere, Lord 16
rural life for women in Ireland
    103

St Andrews 154
St Joan's Social and Political Union
    18, 20
Sacks, Paul 90
*Safety and Justice: The
    Government's Proposals on
    Domestic Violence* 214
Sagar, Pearl 129, 130
school board membership 2
    see also education boards
school boards
    England and Wales 11
    Scotland 65
Scotland
    Calvinist heritage 7, 156
    percentage of women elected
        by date of election and type
        of elected office (table) 184
Scots Independent 49
Scotsman 47, 52
Scottish Abortion Campaign 155
Scottish Assembly 57, 58, 157
    referendum for 156
Scottish Churches League for
    Women's Suffrage 64
Scottish Constitutional
    Commission 172, 173
Scottish Constitutional Convention
    157, 159, 172
Scottish Convention of Women
    (SCOW) 70, 157, 167n. 14
Scottish Co-operative Women's
    Guild 68, 70–1, 73
Scottish Council for Women's
    Trades (SCWT) 71
Scottish Council of Women
    Citizens' Associations 68
Scottish Executive 164
    see also Scottish Government
        Equality Unit 162, 163
    Equality Strategy 163
Scottish Government
    Gender Equality Scheme 165
Scottish Liberal Federation 48
Scottish Minorities Group 156
Scottish National Anti-Suffrage
    League 65

Scottish National Party 2, 45, 49, 55–6, 173, 174, 176, 178, 179, 180, 181, 182
Scottish National Society for the Prevention of Cruelty to Children 69
Scottish Parliament 3, 58, 59, 72, 154, 156, 159, 160, 162, 166, 171, 175, 183, 185
  campaign for equal representation in, 58, 159, 160, 161, 180, 183
  by party, gender and type of seat, 2007 (table) 177
  committee structures 160
  elections 1999 173, 174
  equal opportunities as founding principle 162
  proportion of women candidates by party, 1999–2007 (figure) 179
  proportion of women MSPs, by party 1999–2007 (figure) 178
  Standing Equal Opportunities Committee 160, 162, 166
  women's representation in 171, 176, 182
Scottish Protestant League 67
Scottish Socialist Party 175, 176
Scottish Trades Union Congress (STUC) 71, 73, 159
  Women's Committee 58, 72
  Women's Conference 72
Scottish Unionist Association 65
Scottish Women's Aid Federation (SWAF) 155, 209
Scottish Women's Aid 163, 164
Scottish Women's Budget Group 163
Scottish Women's Charter 167n. 10
Scottish Women's Claim of Right 57
  see also Woman's Claim of Right
Scottish Women's Convention (SWC) 162, 163
Scottish Women's Co-ordination Group 159, 173
Scottish Women's Hospitals 64
Scottish Women's Liberation Conference 1972 154
Scottish Women's Liberation Journal 155
Scottish Women's Rural Institute 5, 68–9, 73
Scrymgeour, Edwin 68, 69
Searchlight on Spain 52
'Second wave' feminism 1, 63, 212
  in Scotland 153

Second World War
  abolition of marriage bar 22
  co-options to local councils in Scotland 66
  decline in women's campaigning 23
Section 2A (Local Government Scotland Act) 156, 167n. 9
separation, changes in grounds for 20
sex and turnout at general elections (figure) 147
Sex Discrimination Act 1975 4, 8, 24, 145
  extension of to Northern Ireland 123
Sex Discrimination (Election Candidates) Act 2002 145, 192
sexual abuse 5
  child sexual abuse 69
Sexual Offences and Female Genital Mutilation Act 2003 214
sexual orientation 156
Shakti Women's Aid 157
Shankill Road 129
Shannon, Catherine 119, 120
Shaw, Clarice McNab 54, 65
  see also McNab, Clarice
Shaw, George Bernard and 'coupled vote' 53
Sheehy-Skeffington, Eoin 85
Sheehy-Skeffington, Hanna 82, 83, 96, 98
Shepard, Christopher 118
Shetland 154
Side, Katherine 133
Sieff, Rebecca 54
Sinn Féin 3, 81, 82, 97, 108n. 16 and 17, 115, 127, 129, 131, 132
Sinnott, Kathy 92
Skinnider, Margaret 84
Smethwick 47
Smith, Jacqui 213, 220
Smith, John 145, 148
Smyth, Ailbhe 98, 105
Social Democratic and Labour Party (SDLP) 127, 129, 130, 131, 132
Social Democratic Party 57, 141
social policy divergence: welfare support, funding and regulation in Wales (table) 204
Socialist Women's Group 123
Societies for Equal Citizenship 5
Southall Black Sisters 217
Soroptimists 157
Speaker's Conference of House of Commons 150
Special Powers Act 119

Squires, Judith 191
Standing Conference of Dundee Women's Associations 68
Standing Joint Committee of Industrial Women's Organizations 21
Stephens, Kathleen 130
Stirling 154, 158
Stormont 3, 4, 115, 116
  Stormont Rule, 1922–72 114–8
Strategic Group on Women 162, 163, 164
Summerskill, Edith 23
Swann, Annie S. 48
Swansea 211
Swinson, Jo 53

Tanaiste (Deputy Prime Minister) 79, 88
Tanner, Duncan 39
tax allowances 24
Teachta Dála (TD), deputy to the Dáil 81
temperance movement 8, 12
  Scottish 63, 69
Temperance Poll Act 1920 69
Temperance (Scotland) Act 1913 69
Thane, Pat 141
Thatcher, Margaret 45, 57, 142, 151n. 12, 156
Thatcherism 154, 158
Times 15
Townswomen's Guilds 18, 24, 68, 157
trade unions 24, 154, 158
women in trade unions, Scotland 71–3
Trinity College Dublin 102
'Troubles' (Northern Ireland) 120
  victims of 133
Tweedsmuir, Lady 53, 54, 59
Tweedy, Hilda 104
twinning of seats 4, 173, 175, 176, 181, 182, 183

United Kingdom (UK)
  general election, 1997 79
  legislative frameworks within 8
  Women's Liberation Conference, Birmingham 156
Ulster Covenant Campaign 81, 92n. 15
Ulster Defence Association (UDA) 121
Ulster Unionism 81
Ulster Unionist Council 114
Ulster Unionist Party (UUP) 126, 129, 132

Ulster Volunteer Force 132
Ulster Women's Unionist
  Association (UWUA) 114, 115,
  116, 117
Union of Jewish Women 18, 21
Unionists 47, 48, 49, 50, 52, 55
  Party 66, 68
  Women's Unionist Association
    49
Unionism
  in Northern Ireland 113, 114
United Irishwomen (UI) 100
United Nations (UN) 128
  Platform for Action 172
  UN Declaration on
    the Elimination of
    Violence against Women
    219
UN Security Council Resolution
  (UNSCR) 1325 132–3
University College Dublin 102
University of Ulster 128
Urquhart, Diane 114, 115, 117

venereal disease 70
voting behaviour and gender 2
  in Wales 195
voting preferences in 1950s 25
  women as voters 15, 146–150

Wales
  women's representation in
    190, 205
Wales Violence Against Women
  Action Group 220
Walker, Mary Lily 66
Ward, Rachel 130
Waring, Margaret 116
Waters, Mrs B. Berthon 84, 85
Waugh, Margaret 86
Webb, Keith 55, 56
Welsh Assembly 3, 59
  see also National Assembly for
    Wales
Welsh Assembly Government 212,
  215, 217, 218, 219, 220, 221, 222
  Annual Equalities Report 203
  Equality and Human Rights
    Division 201, 207n. 35
  Mainstreaming Strategy 201,
    202, 203
  Working Group on Domestic
    Violence and Violence
    Against Women 214, 215
Welsh language 203

Welsh Women's Aid 209, 211, 212,
  215, 219, 220
West Perthshire by-election 48
Westminster 3, 4, 7, 122, 123, 171
  boosting women's
    representation at 58
  representation of women from
    Northern Ireland 116
  representation of women from
    Scotland 45, 46, 171
  representation of women from
    Wales 40
  women's representation 4,
    53, 139
Widows and Orphans Pensions,
  introduction of 21
Williams, Eliza 34
Winchester, Noreen, 135n. 48
Withers, Mrs 34
woman provost, first in Scotland 66
Woman's Claim of Right 159
  see also Scottish Women's
    Claim of Right
Woman's Party 47
Women2win 144
Women's Advice Centre 124
Women's Advisory Group 162
Women Against Imperialism
  (WAI) 123, 127
Women's Aid 6, 124, 213, 218
  in Scotland 161
Women and Equality Unit 213
women candidates and MPs, UK
  and Northern Ireland (table) 13
Women Citizens' Associations 5,
  17, 21, 64, 67, 73
Women's Coalition, Northern
  Ireland 4
Women's Co-operative Guild 14,
  18, 21, 34, 74
Women's Emancipation Bill 20
women's entry to professions 20
  to higher education, 64
Women for Westminster 53, 54
Women's Freedom League 21, 64,
  67, 74
women's health enquiry 68
Women's Housing Sub-
  Committee to the Ministry of
  Reconstruction 36–7
Women in Scotland Consultative
  Forum 160, 162
Women's Institutes
  England 5, 17–18, 24, 103
  Wales 32

Women into Politics 127
Women's Issues Group, Scotland
  58, 159, 172
Women's Labour League 12, 30,
  34, 50, 144
Women's Liberal Federation 11,
  141
Women's Liberation Movement
  1, 3, 5, 6, 7, 24, 63, 74, 144, 154,
  165, 209
  see also 'second wave' feminism
  demands, 155, 167n. 5
  in Ireland 87, 88, 89, 91, 96,
    102, 105
  in Northern Ireland 123
  in Scotland 156, 157
  in Wales 190, 211
Women's Ministry 148
Women's Missionary Association
  of the Presbyterian Church in
  Ireland 118
Women's National Commission 70
Women's National Liberal
  Federation 15
women's parties 2
Women's Peace Crusade 67
Women's Voice (Wales Women's
  National Coalition) 220
women police officers 5, 69
women prisoners campaign 124
Women's Progressive Association,
  Ireland (later Women's Political
  Association) 86, 87, 88
Women's Protective and Provident
  League (WPPL) 71
women's right to sit on juries 5
Women's Sanitary Improvement
  and Health Visitors' Union 18
Women's Talent Bank, Ireland 87
Women's Social and Political
  Union (WSPU) 64
Working Class Wives 68
World Union of Catholic Societies
  101
Wrexham 211
Wright, Valerie 68
Wyse-Power, Jenny 82, 84

Young, Lady 142
YWCA 20, 69, 72

Zero Tolerance campaign 154, 161
'Zipping' in party lists 173, 174,
  180, 194
Zweiniger-Bargielowska, Ina 25

Printed in Great Britain
by Amazon.co.uk, Ltd.,
Marston Gate.